KU-239-595

Black Diamonds

Black Diamonds

The Rise and Fall of an English Dynasty

CATHERINE BAILEY

VIKING
an imprint of
PENGUIN BOOKS

VIKING

Published by the Penguin Group
Penguin Books Ltd, 80 Strand, London WC2R 0RL, England
Penguin Group (USA) Inc., 375 Hudson Street, New York, New York 10014, USA
Penguin Group (Canada), 90 Eglinton Avenue East, Suite 700, Toronto, Ontario, Canada M4P 2Y3
(a division of Pearson Penguin Canada Inc.)
Penguin Ireland, 25 St Stephen's Green, Dublin 2, Ireland
(a division of Penguin Books Ltd)
Penguin Group (Australia), 250 Camberwell Road, Camberwell, Victoria 3124, Australia
(a division of Pearson Australia Group Pty Ltd)
Penguin Books India Pvt Ltd, 11 Community Centre, Panchsheel Park, New Delhi – 110 017, India
Penguin Group (NZ), 67 Apollo Drive, Rosedale, North Shore 0632, New Zealand
(a division of Pearson New Zealand Ltd)
Penguin Books (South Africa) (Pty) Ltd, 24 Sturdee Avenue, Rosebank, Johannesburg 2196, South Africa

Penguin Books Ltd, Registered Offices: 80 Strand, London WC2R 0RL, England

www.penguin.com

First published 2007
3

Set in 12/14.5pt Monotype Bembo
Typeset by Rowland Phototypesetting Ltd, Bury St Edmunds, Suffolk
Printed in Great Britain by Clays Ltd, St Ives plc

A CIP catalogue record for this book is available from the British Library

ISBN: 978-0-670-91542-2

In memory of my grandmother Eve, with love

List of Illustrations

The author and publishers are grateful to the following for permission to reproduce photographs: Roy Young for 1–2, 5–6, 13–16, 18–19, 27–8, 32–3, 52–3; Michael Bond, *Way Out West: The Story of an Errant Ancestor* for 7–10; Thunder Bay Historical Museum Society for 11–12; V & A Images/Victoria and Albert Museum for 17; Brian Elliott for 20–22, 24, 29, 31, 47; British Coal/Eastwood Collection for 23, 26; Yorkshire Mining Museum for 25; Hulton Archive/Getty Images for 30; Martyn Johnson for 34, 38; Griffith Philipps for 35–7, 39, 41–3, 51; Peter Diggle for 40; Dorothy Wilding/J.F. Kennedy Library for 44; J.F. Kennedy Library for 45; Portman Press Bureau/J.F. Kennedy Library for 46; BEA/France for 48; Elma Casson for 49; Geoffrey Howse for 50

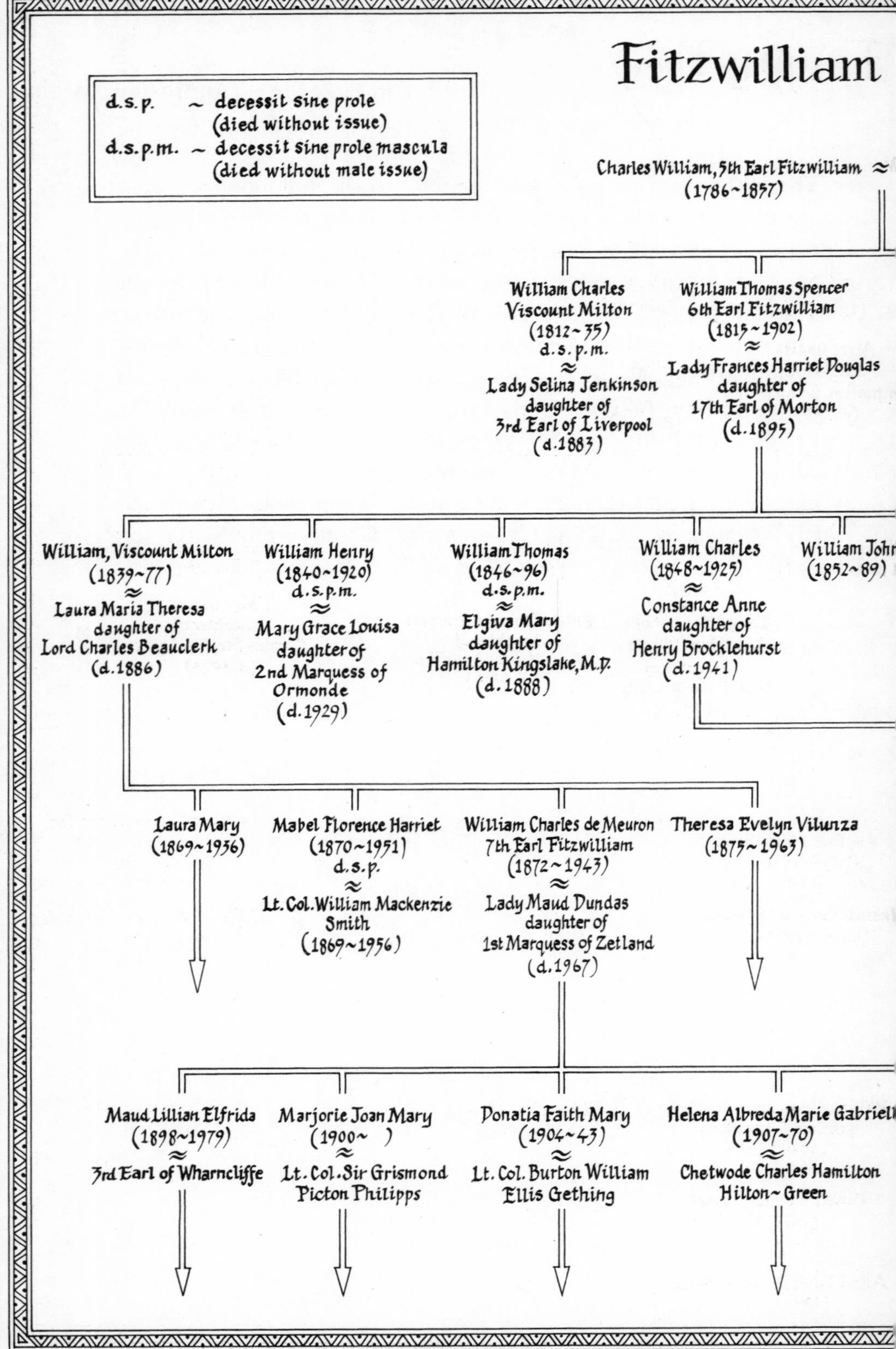
Fitzwilliam
d.s.p. ~ decessit sine prole
(died without issue)
d.s.p.m. ~ decessit sine prole mascula
(died without male issue)
Charles William, 5th Earl Fitzwilliam ≈
(1786~1857)
William Charles
Viscount Milton
(1812~35)
d.s.p.m.
≈
Lady Selina Jenkinson
daughter of
3rd Earl of Liverpool
(d.1883)
William Thomas Spencer
6th Earl Fitzwilliam
(1815~1902)
≈
Lady Frances Harriet Douglas
daughter of
17th Earl of Morton
(d.1895)
William, Viscount Milton
(1839~77)
≈
Laura Maria Theresa
daughter of
Lord Charles Beauclerk
(d.1886)
William Henry
(1840~1920)
d.s.p.m.
≈
Mary Grace Louisa
daughter of
2nd Marquess of
Ormonde
(d.1929)
William Thomas
(1846~96)
d.s.p.m.
≈
Elgiva Mary
daughter of
Hamilton Kingslake, M.D.
(d.1888)
William Charles
(1848~1925)
≈
Constance Anne
daughter of
Henry Brocklehurst
(d.1941)
William John
(1852~89)
Laura Mary
(1869~1936)
Mabel Florence Harriet
(1870~1951)
d.s.p.
≈
Lt. Col. William Mackenzie
Smith
(1869~1956)
William Charles de Meuron
7th Earl Fitzwilliam
(1872~1943)
≈
Lady Maud Dundas
daughter of
1st Marquess of Zetland
(d.1967)
Theresa Evelyn Vilunza
(1875~1963)
Maud Lillian Elfrida
(1898~1979)
≈
3rd Earl of Wharncliffe
Marjorie Joan Mary
(1900~)
≈
Lt. Col. Sir Grismond
Picton Philipps
Donatia Faith Mary
(1904~43)
≈
Lt. Col. Burton William
Ellis Gething
Helena Albreda Marie Gabriell
(1907~70)
≈
Chetwode Charles Hamilton
Hilton~Green

Family Tree

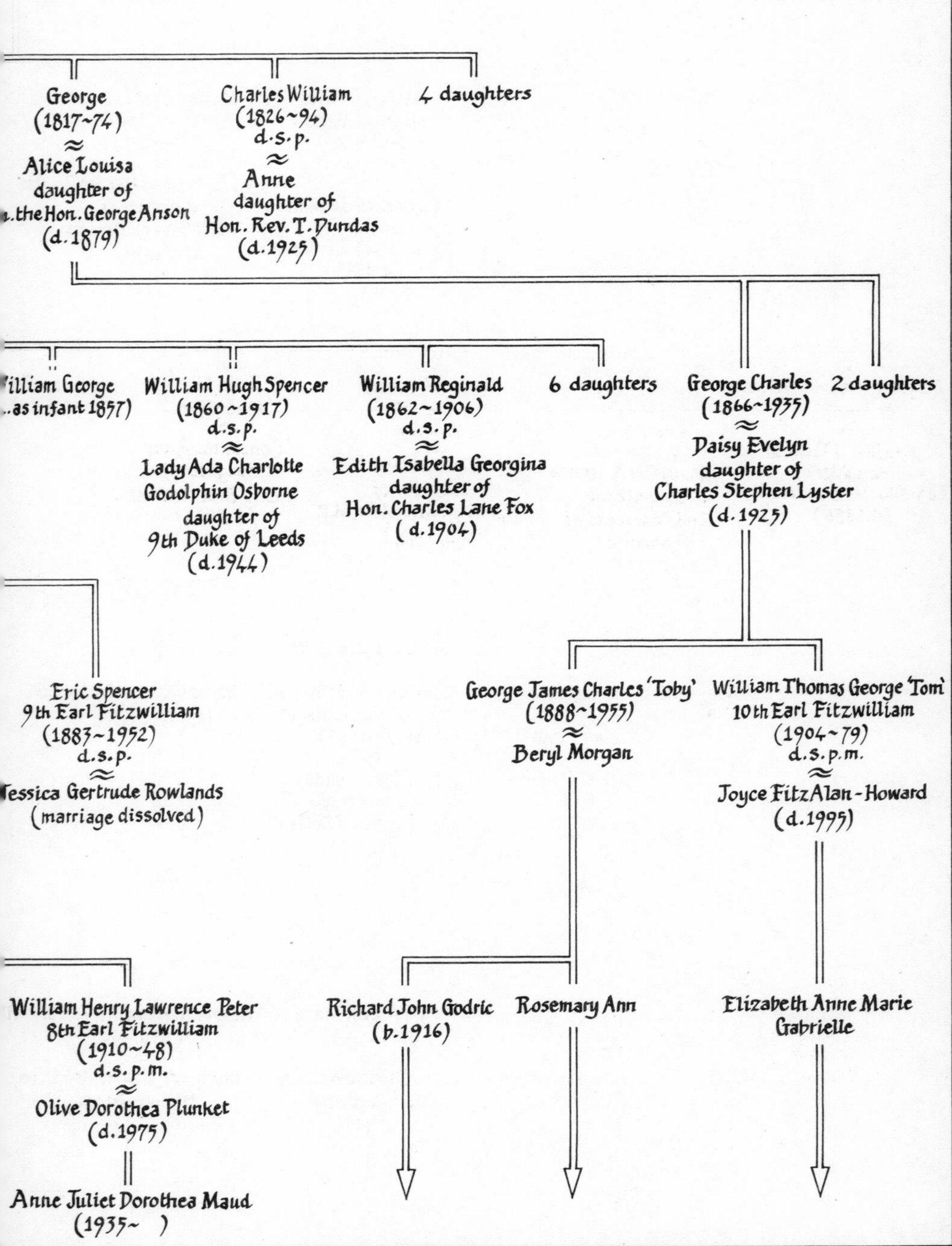

Mary, daughter of 1st Baron Dundas
(d.1830)
George
(1817~74)
≈
Alice Louisa
daughter of
the Hon. George Anson
(d. 1879)
Charles William
(1826~94)
d.s.p.
≈
Anne
daughter of
Hon. Rev. T. Dundas
(d.1925)
4 daughters
illiam George
as infant 1857)
William Hugh Spencer
(1860~1917)
d.s.p.
≈
Lady Ada Charlotte
Godolphin Osborne
daughter of
9th Duke of Leeds
(d.1944)
William Reginald
(1862~1906)
d.s.p.
≈
Edith Isabella Georgina
daughter of
Hon. Charles Lane Fox
(d.1904)
6 daughters
George Charles
(1866~1935)
≈
Daisy Evelyn
daughter of
Charles Stephen Lyster
(d.1925)
2 daughters
Eric Spencer
9th Earl Fitzwilliam
(1883~1952)
d.s.p.
≈
essica Gertrude Rowlands
(marriage dissolved)
George James Charles 'Toby'
(1888~1955)
≈
Beryl Morgan
William Thomas George 'Tom'
10th Earl Fitzwilliam
(1904~79)
d.s.p.m.
≈
Joyce FitzAlan-Howard
(d.1995)
William Henry Lawrence Peter
8th Earl Fitzwilliam
(1910~48)
d.s.p.m.
≈
Olive Dorothea Plunket
(d.1975)
Anne Juliet Dorothea Maud
(1935~)
Richard John Godric
(b.1916)
Rosemary Ann
Elizabeth Anne Marie
Gabrielle

Acknowledgements

I owe a debt of gratitude to the former household and Estate staff employed at Wentworth – and their descendants – who shared their memories of life at the house, and in the villages owned by the Fitzwilliam family in the inter-war years, especially to May Bailey, the late Godfrey Broadhead, Peter Diggle, the late Bert May, Geoffrey Steer and Joyce Smith. Similarly, I am indebted to all those former miners employed at Elsecar and New Stubbin collieries – the mines owned by the Fitzwilliams prior to the nationalization of the coal industry – who spoke to me about their experiences and who, in many instances, related stories their fathers and grandfathers had told them. In particular, I would like to thank Charles Booth, the late Ralph Boreham, Jim McGuinness and Walt Hammond. I am grateful also to Roy Young, whose meticulous research into the history of Wentworth House and its community has been an invaluable source of material.

I would like to thank Lady Juliet Tadgell, Sir Philip Naylor-Leyland, Griffith Philipps, Philip Doyne and the late Charles Doyne – descendants of the Earls Fitzwilliam – for their help and for the opportunity to research their collections of family archive. Further, I am indebted to Lady Barbara Ricardo, the granddaughter of the 7th Earl Fitzwilliam, for her memories of Wentworth in the mid-twentieth century, and to Michael Shaw Bond, the great-grandson of William, Viscount Milton, for his discoveries, published in his book *Way Out West: On the Trail of an Errant Ancestor.*

I am grateful to the staff of the following libraries and archives for their assistance: the British Library, the Borthwick Institute for Historical Research at the University of York, the London Library, the Department of Manuscripts and Special Collections at Nottingham University Library, the Wellcome Library of Medical History, the Newspaper Library at Colindale, Lambeth Palace Library, the

Royal Archives at Windsor Castle, Elsecar Heritage Centre, the National Coal Mining Museum for England, the Bodleian Library at the University of Oxford, the Imperial War Museum, the Bureau d'Enquêtes et d'Analyses pour la Sécurité de l'Aviation Civile in Paris, the Council for the Protection of Rural England, the National Trust, the John F. Kennedy Library, the Public Record Office, the Sheffield Archives, the Doncaster Archives, the Northamptonshire Record Office, the Doncaster Local Studies Library, the West Yorkshire Archive Service, and the Archives and Local Studies section at Rotherham Library.

I have drawn on the research and writings of many authors and, although their contribution is evident in the Notes, I should like to thank several individually for permission to quote from their work. They include Lynne McTaggart for *Kathleen Kennedy, Her Life and Times*, Garden City, NY, Dial Press, 1983; Laurence Leamer for *The Kennedy Women: The Saga of an American Family*, New York, Villard Books, 1994, and Georges Borchardt Inc. on behalf of the authors Peter Collier and David Horowitz for permission to quote extracts from their work *The Kennedys: An American Drama*, New York, Summit Books, 1984. I am grateful also to A. M. Heath Ltd for permission to quote from George Orwell's *The Road to Wigan Pier*.

Additionally, I would like to thank Dr Quentin Outram at Leeds University Business School for showing me the records of the Mineral Owners Association of Great Britain; Brian Elliott, Geoffrey Howse and Mel and Joan Jones for their knowledge of the former mining communities of South Yorkshire; the pupils of the Lady Mabel College of Physical Education for their recollections of their time at Wentworth; Marilyn Farnell for her research at the John F. Kennedy Library; Amanda Smith for her formidable research among the papers of Joseph P. Kennedy, published in her collection of his letters, *Hostage to Fortune: The Letters of Joseph P. Kennedy*, Viking/Penguin, 2001; Jill Dempsey for permission to quote from Matilda Kingdon's diary; Eddie Pearcy for his assistance in tracking down the motor gunboat crew members of Operation Bridford; William Sieghart, Hugh Dehn and the late Anthony

Sampson for their help in overcoming hurdles; Theo Caveman for his inspiration; and the miners of the Lady Windsor Colliery at Ynysybwl, who, many years before this book was conceived, allowed me the unforgettable experience of spending a day underground with them.

Throughout, I have been buoyed by the encouragement of my literary agent, David Godwin, and my editor at Viking, Eleo Gordon. I am tremendously indebted to both of them. I would also like to thank Susan Cole, Rowan Cope, Joanna Waller, Christopher Kemp, Jasper McMahon and Hywel Williams for their comments on the manuscript, and Helen Campbell for her painstaking copy-editing.

Lastly, I would like to thank those without whom the completion of the book would not have seemed possible: my mother, Carol Bailey, and the rest of my family, Dorothy Cory-Wright, Sara Tibbetts, Martyn and Christine Johnson, and Jody Tresidder.

A note on Wentworth House. Its full name is Wentworth Woodhouse. However, it has always been known locally – and by members of the Fitzwilliam family, who lived in it – as Wentworth House, and is referred to thus throughout the book.

A note on prices. Contemporary values for the figures quoted have been calculated on the basis of a comparison of the Retail Price Index for a given year, unless otherwise stated. The figures have been sourced from economichistory.net, compiled by Professor Lawrence Officer at the University of Illinois.

Preface

A crowd of thousands shifted nervously on the great lawn in front of Wentworth House, waiting for the coffin to be brought out. It was the winter of 1902: 'February,' as one observer remarked, 'in her worst mood.' Two hundred servants, dressed in black, stood stiffly along the length of the façade facing the crush of mourners. Shrouds of fog enveloped the statues and pediments crowning the house; an acrid smell clung to the mist, catching in the nostrils, effluent from the pits, foundries and blast furnaces in the valley below. The fog drained everything of colour. Now and then it lifted to reveal a portion of the house: on a clear day the crowd could have counted a thousand windows, but that morning most of it was obscured.

The hearse, a glass coach, swathed in sable and crêpe, was ready outside the Pillared Hall. It was drawn by four black horses: plumes of black ostrich feathers adorned their bridles and black-tasselled cloths were draped across their backs. Mutes, the customary Victorian funeral attendants, stood by them; macabre figures, veils of black crêpe trailed from their tall silk hats. Bells tolled in the distance. In the nearby villages the shops were closed and the curtains in the houses drawn fast.

At the stroke of midday, three hours after the crowd had first begun to gather, the coffin, mounted on a silver bier, was carried out of the house. It was followed by a procession of housemaids and footmen bearing hundreds of wreaths of flowers. A brilliant splash of colour in the bleak scene, they drew a murmur from the crowd.

The oak coffin contained the body of William, the 6th Earl Fitzwilliam, one of the richest men in Britain. He had left a legacy of £2.8 million pounds – more than £3 billion at today's values. In the century to come, only one Englishman, Sir John Ellerman, the shipping magnate, would leave a larger fortune. The dead Earl was among the very wealthiest of Britain's twentieth-century aristocrats.

His money had come from land and a spectacular stroke of luck. In the late eighteenth century, the Fitzwilliams' Yorkshire estates – over 20,000 acres in total – were found to straddle the Barnsley seam, the main artery of the South Yorkshire coalfield. Wentworth House, situated nine miles north-east of Sheffield, lay at its heart.

The Earl was born in 1815, the year of Waterloo. Over the course of his lifetime his wealth had increased a thousandfold. Rapid technological advances, spurred by the huge demand for coal, had made it possible to sink mines deeper and deeper along the lucrative Barnsley seam. The Earl's collieries, as one contemporary noted, were 'within rifle shot of his ancestral seat': by the close of the century, mines and pit villages crowded the hills and valleys around the house.

In the early 1900s, Arthur Eaglestone, a miner from Rotherham, writing under the pseudonym of Roger Dataller, described a dawn journey through the Earl's country:

> The train bored its way through the grim litter of steel manufactories, the serried heaping of coal and ironstone stocks, the multiplicity of railway metals, the drifting steam of locomotives . . . As we gobble up one hamlet after another, cottages and farmhouses loom up mere outlines, islands in the mist; but as the light becomes clearer certain chimneys and headstocks appear upon the horizon, a reminder of the vast subterranean activity with which we are connected. As one headstock falls in the distance, another rises to meet us – the inescapable, the endless chain of winding. We shall not escape the headstocks. We may vary the route as we please, but the gaunt pulley-wheels, and the by-product plant, a column of smoke by day, a pillar of fire by night, will still be in attendance.

The Earl's death at the age of eighty-six – after he caught a sudden chill – had stunned the district. His life had been spent overseeing his vast estates and enjoying his wealth. For a man of few other achievements, the local newspaper's coverage of his demise was extraordinary:

A feeling of awe crept over the people of this neighbourhood when it was whispered vaguely from behind the veil that he had entered the Valley of the Shadow, and was sleeping by the side of the shore of that silent sea which lies between the world and 'that undiscovered country from whose bourne no traveller returns'. But great and mighty is all-conquering Death, it is beyond even his sublime strength to convert the waters of the tideless sea. He was a noble lord, and moreover, a man who had the respect of all who knew him and the affection of those who knew him best. He now sleeps the sleep that knows no waking. Death the Conqueror has laid his icy hands upon him.

In 1902, tens of thousands of people across the South Yorkshire coalfield were wholly dependent on the Earl for a living. On the morning of his funeral, they were drawn to Wentworth House.

'The workmen on the various estates were in strong force,' the *Sheffield Daily Telegraph* reported,

A remarkable feature of the proceedings was the great muster of miners. Genuine sorrow cannot be bought with gold or wrung from the hearts of an unwilling community. It must spring from love or admiration. Wentworth is by no means easy of access and curiosity nor a perfunctory sense of duty could never have brought together thousands of mourners under such dispiriting conditions. Through the slush and the searching rain the mourners came to the funeral. Old men who had worked for the Earl for 50 years risked serious illness for love of their noble master and trudged sorrowfully from station or neighbouring village to swell the mournful gathering.

The size and grandeur of Wentworth House were but faintly suggested through the haze of mist and fog. It was built for the Earl's ancestor Thomas Wentworth, later Marquess of Rockingham, in the 1720s. Designed by Henry Flitcroft, it had taken more than fifteen years to complete and its façade was the longest in Europe.

The house had a room for every day of the year and five miles of passageways. One guest, a Baron von Liebig, resorted to crumbling wafers along the route from his bedroom to the dining room so that he could find his way back after dinner. Thereafter, guests were presented with a crested silver casket containing different-coloured confetti.

The house lay in parkland encompassed by a nine-mile-long stone wall. Humphrey Repton, the famous eighteenth-century landscape designer, had sculpted the Park; twelve follies – towers, columns and a mausoleum built in the classical style – marked its highest points. Millions of tons of coal lay under the land but so rich was the Earl, he had no need to mine it. Yet even he could not inure Wentworth from the grime that trespassed inside the boundaries of the Park. Coal dust carried from the nearby collieries settled in the sheaves of corn grown in the fields. The streams running through them were orange: 'ochre water', as the locals called it, polluted by the mines that honeycombed the district.

Shortly after one o'clock, a bugler sounded the Last Post. It was the signal for the 5,000-strong cortège to begin the mile-long walk to the village church. As if on cue, the fog lifted as the mourners moved off. A thousand miners from the Earl's pits led the procession, flanked by an escort of fifty soldiers from the Yorkshire Dragoons.

The family's downfall was unthinkable. William, Earl Fitzwilliam, had left a great fortune. Four sons – each named William after him – survived him. The coal industry was booming: the family's wealth and power seemed as solid and unshakeable as the foundations of their vast house.

Yet the Fitzwilliams and the thousands who worked for them were about to become the central figures in an approaching catastrophe.

What was unthinkable on that day in February 1902 happened.

Introduction

In 1902, Wentworth was the largest privately owned house in Britain. It still is today.

Its size is truly extraordinary, almost impossible to visualize. Imagine Buckingham Palace: the glorious, sweeping East Front at Wentworth is almost twice as long. Marcus Binney, the architectural historian, sees it as 'unquestionably the finest Georgian house in England'. Sir Nikolaus Pevsner wrote glowingly of its 'interiors of quite exceptional interest'. But unlike the much cherished Chatsworth or Blenheim, few have heard its name and fewer still have actually seen it. It is England's forgotten palace.

Today, the house looms blank and shuttered. The home of a reclusive figure, it is closed to the public. 'I've never seen him,' remarked a former postmistress in the nearby village. 'And no one I know ever has.'

The baroque West Front of the house is hidden behind a screen of tall cedars, but the 600-foot-long Palladian East Front can be glimpsed from the Trans-Pennine Way, the public footpath that runs through Wentworth Park. The first impression is a familiar one: the pediments, pillars and domed pavilions the hallmarks – be they on a breathtaking scale – of a grand stately home. But look a little longer and something jars. Longer still and the image is unnerving – even chilling. It is like looking at a picture one knows intimately from which something is missing, though it is impossible to say what.

The clues can be found in the fields that sweep away from the house. Time is not written on the land as it is on the adjacent façade; there are no hedgerows, ditches or centuries-old oaks. The fields are bare and desolate, as if denuded by some unseen hand. The traces of the past have been kicked over.

An obsession with secrecy corrupts the twentieth-century history of the house. The *Wentworth Woodhouse Muniments* – the family and estate papers of the Earls Fitzwilliam and their ancestors, the Marquesses of Rockingham and the Earls of Strafford – form one of the most important historical archives in Britain today. Rich in correspondence, there are thousands of letters and papers dating back to medieval times. But in 1900 the transparency of centuries comes to a halt: few family papers exist in this impressive historical collection after this date.

Their absence is no accident. In July 1972 the 10th and last Earl Fitzwilliam ordered his employees to destroy the bulk of Wentworth's twentieth-century records. Sixteen tons of documents were hauled by tractor from where they were stored in the Georgian Stable Block to Trawles Wood, a beech copse in the valley below Wentworth that was used in the eighteenth century as a dumping ground for the household's refuse and rubbish. There, the documents were burnt in a bonfire that blazed, night and day, for three weeks. Other smaller fires had preceded it: in a deliberate attempt to hide from history, the private papers of the 7th, 8th and 9th Earls – the tenants of Wentworth in the first half of the twentieth century – were destroyed after their deaths. The cull even extended to the personal papers of their employees. Peter Diggle, the son of Colonel Heathcote Diggle, a Fitzwilliam family trustee and the manager of their estates, watched his father burn documents that chronicled three decades of working as an adviser to the 7th Earl: 'The Fitzwilliams had a secret life and if you have a secret life then there are things that must be destroyed.'

The twentieth-century Fitzwilliams were obsessive in guarding their secrets, both in the systematic destruction of the family papers and in vows of silence. 'My grandmother made me promise that I would not tell anybody about these private things that went on at Wentworth,' Ann, Lady Bowlby, the granddaughter of Maud, Countess Fitzwilliam, who lived at Wentworth from 1902 until 1948, recalled. 'She didn't want it all broadcast. It was to do with the Communistic trait of the world then.' 'That generation of the family were very proud, very private and very destructive. It was in their blood,' Ian Bond, another of the Fitzwilliam descendants, remembered. 'They wanted to destroy things as they themselves had been destroyed. They lived through the downfall of the family. They had experienced a huge sea change. They saw so many sadnesses. They did not want to remember. The world had passed them by.'

The world has also passed Wentworth House by. Although it is the largest and one of the most beautiful of England's stately homes, the story of what happened there during the twentieth century is a deep mystery because of the loss of the Fitzwilliam family's archives. Fragments remain: a few scattered but precious collections of family papers have survived. These – and the memories of those who lived and worked at the house and in the pit villages around it – were the beginnings of this book.

The story starts at the edge of the void; at the moment when the official history of Wentworth House stops.

PART I

I

In the crush of mourners, one man walked alone behind the glass hearse.

William Charles de Meuron Wentworth-Fitzwilliam – 'Billy Fitzbilly', as the miners called him, or Lord Milton, as his courtesy title styled him – was William, Earl Fitzwilliam's grandson and heir. In addition to the main family seat and estate at Wentworth, his £2.8 million inheritance included a 100-room mansion and 90,000 acres at Coollattin in Ireland; a fifty-room house in the heart of London's Mayfair; eighty racehorses; a further 5,000 acres of land dotted around Yorkshire; a priceless collection of paintings and books and a massive portfolio of shares. The income from his coal holdings alone would bring in more than £87,700 a year.*

'Milton looked very tall and good-looking,' Lord Halifax, a neighbour of the Fitzwilliams who went to the Earl's funeral, told his sister enviously. Aged thirty in 1902, wearing the dress uniform of an officer in the Ox and Bucks Light Infantry, Billy cut a dashing figure. He was classically good-looking, according to the benchmarks of the Edwardian era. Even-featured, with warm, smiling eyes, he had thick dark brown hair and a sprucely clipped moustache. His face still bore the colour of the African sun: he had recently returned from the Transvaal where he had won a DSO fighting in the Boer War.

A brilliant huntsman and polo player, Billy, the heir to one of the richest aristocrats of the twentieth century, was educated at Eton and Trinity College, Cambridge. From 1895 – when he was twenty-three – until he became the 7th Earl Fitzwilliam, he sat as MP for Wakefield. Prior to that, in his late teens, he had served as ADC to the Viceroy of India. These are matters of record: the scant details

*Over £6 million at today's values.

that can be firmly established about him at this stage of his life. Little else is known. 'He had a perfect horror of publicity of any sort or kind,' his sister, Lady Mabel Smith, recalled. 'It ran all through his life from when he was quite a boy. It was one of his chief characteristics.'

In a vaulted cellar beneath a large house in Southern England there are sixteen trunks containing Billy's personal effects: the things he regarded as precious. There is a pair of black and tan hunting boots that still bear the worn creases of the chase; a set of tiger's teeth; a miner's lamp and helmet and a battered leather cigar case: inside it, the disintegrated flakes of a Monte Cristo that he never smoked. There are boxes of wax seals and rolls of parchment bearing grants of title. The things Billy was proud of are also there: the DSO awarded during the Boer War; the plumed hat and ceremonial robes he wore for his inauguration as Mayor of Sheffield in 1909, and a handwritten letter from King George V, dated July 1912. At the bottom of one trunk there are hundreds of silver buttons stamped with the Fitzwilliam crest – a winged griffin and two coronets. Some are as small as a 5-pence piece, others the size of an old half crown: the spare buttons for Billy's shooting and hunting jackets, they were also the tokens of livery, worn by his servants on the breasts and sleeves of their tailcoats.

Things, not words, are all that remain. The trunks contain few papers. There are no letters written by Billy, or copies of letters that he received, although, tantalizingly, the paraphernalia of writing has been kept. One trunk, stamped with a coronet and Billy's initials, contains monogrammed letter folders and notepaper holders, and the large blotting pad that once lay on his desk. Framed in dark green leather, it is stained with use. The imprint of hundreds of back-to-front words, hieroglyphs impossible to decipher, are scattered across it.

The true identity of Billy Fitzwilliam is the first of the Wentworth mysteries. If his spiteful, meddlesome aunts are to be believed, we cannot be absolutely sure who he *really* was.

On the eve of his grandfather's funeral, the scandal and controversy that were to dog his succession had ignited behind the walls of Wentworth House.

2

It had been raining for days; torrents of water, blackened by coal dust, cascaded from the roof gutters. Squalls of wind, blowing straight off the moors, whipped across the Park, driving the rain horizontally against the thousand windows, as if tiny fragments from the gravel drive around the house were being hurled from outside. The clock in the North Tower at the furthest end of the East Front struck three, the signal on a dark winter afternoon for the lampmen to begin their evening round.

Upstairs, in the 'Duchess of Kent', the state bedroom reserved for royalty and other important guests, the body of the dead Earl lay in a four-poster bed that was crowned by a cornice of gold. A pistachio-coloured silk valance ran beneath it, trailing luxurious hangings and thick braided tassels. Gold and green were the primary colours of the state bedroom; the principal items of furniture – the intricately carved mahogany Louis Quinze bed and a pair of Sheraton cabinets, eight feet tall – were formal and austere. The hand-painted wallpaper, a heavy yew-green, embossed with tiny clusters of silk flowers, added to the room's sombre tone.

The body had been there for five days. Even in death, the retinues of staff at Wentworth continued to serve the Earl. His servants had washed and dressed his corpse, and a plain oak coffin, made by the Estate carpenters from one of the oaks in the Park, chosen by the Earl some years before he died, stood ready for the following morning's burial.

The temperature in the room was as cold as the dead Earl; deliberately so, the chill necessary to slow the process of decomposition. A ring of white and gold oval-backed chairs formed a crescent around the bed, carefully positioned by footmen for the succession of visitors – members of the family, senior servants and the local nobility – who had come to pay their last respects.

It was a world away from the pit villages nearby, where the Earl's miners stood up their family corpses in the corner of their front parlour rooms to make way for the crush of mourners, and where, in the overcrowded cottages, dead relatives frequently shared the family's beds. As late as the 1920s, a boy from Greaseborough, one of the Fitzwilliams' villages, told his teacher, 'Please, Miss, they're goin' ter bury our Ernest tomorrow, he's in t' big bed in t'room now. Our Jimmy wouldn't sleep wi' him last night – 'e wor frightened – but I worn't, 'e carn't hurt ya, 'e's dead and wrapped in a sheet, so I sleep next 'im and our Alice next to me, an' our Joe at t' bottom.'

The Fitzwilliam household accounts for February 1902 show that eighty-five servants were on duty to serve the twenty house guests staying at Wentworth for the funeral.

Aside from the senior servants – the house steward, the butler, the groom of chambers, the chef, the housekeeper, and Lord Fitzwilliam's personal valet – there were four kitchenmaids, four still-room maids, eight charwomen, one steward's room boy, two confectioners, six under-chefs, two brewers, six housemen, two lampmen, seven footmen, three scullery maids, nine housemaids, two under-butlers and one clockman.

Almost all the house guests were members of the Fitzwilliam family; the Earl's children and grandchildren, and his cousins, nephews and nieces. They brought their own valets and ladies' maids, adding a further twenty-two servants to the total.

By comparison to the outdoor staff at Wentworth, the number of indoor servants was small. More than 300 workers were required for the upkeep of the grounds, stables and Home Farm. There were gardeners and groundsmen, park keepers, gamekeepers, deer keepers, a bear keeper, forestry workers, mole catchers, millers, grooms, coachmen, stable lads, farm hands, huntsmen, kennel men, carpenters, slaughtermen and mechanics. The Fitzwilliams' annual wage bill for the Estate and household staff at Wentworth came to more than £1 million in today's money. It did not include the wages of the thousands who worked at their collieries and chemical factory, and on the family's other estates in Yorkshire and Ireland.

Yet living conditions at Wentworth were medieval. The 6th Earl had made few concessions to the modern world; the servants of the great feudal overlords would have slotted easily into its daily routine.

The house had five miles of corridors: coal, wood, water, food and light all had to be carried great distances by hand.

Elfrida, Countess of Wharncliffe, Billy's eldest daughter, who was five when the 6th Earl, her great-grandfather, died, described the house as it was at the time of his death. 'There was no electric light, no gas, no central heating. In our living rooms we had glorious raging fires, so the bedrooms and day nurseries were warm, but otherwise the entire mansion was like an icehouse. In the hard winters that we used to have then, going downstairs to be with my mother after tea was a very chilly affair, we could never go along the passages without heavy shawls and spencers.'

'Spencers', short, close-fitting woollen jackets, woven in the Fitzwilliam tweed, were also issued to servants and guests to wear when moving from room to room.

There was no hot or cold running water at Wentworth. One water pump – hand-pumped and cold water only – served each of the four floors. Hot water was heated in vast cauldrons on the stoves in the kitchen in the basement. There were no toilets or bathrooms. 'Baths – carried into the bedrooms by footmen – were tin baths,' recalled Lady Elfrida. 'The hot water was brought up from the kitchen two floors below. Depending on the location of the bedroom it was sometimes over a furlong away. The servants carried the water in large brown metal cans. The baths were filled by the footmen and emptied by the housemaids. A cotton cover hung over the side of the bath. You only used the cloth if you wanted a soak. The footman would come in and pour fresh hot water under the edge of it before inquiring, "Is there anything more, Sir?", regardless of the sex of the bather.'

Even human waste had to be carried by hand. The 6th Earl had installed one flushing toilet for his personal use; aside from this, there were no other toilets, flushing or otherwise, in the guest and family apartments at Wentworth. Close-stools were used; a detachable porcelain bowl mounted in a wooden box. To empty the bowls, the servants covered them with a cloth and carried them through the corridors down to the basement where they were washed out before being returned to the rooms.

The lighting at Wentworth in 1902 was equally arcane. Two men, Moses and his assistant – known as Aaron by the family – were employed seven days a week to light the house. Their day began before dawn. Oil lamps, with large glass funnels, and candles were the only source of artificial light. Every morning, Moses and Aaron walked the length of the house blowing out and replacing the candles they had lit in the chandeliers and wall sconces, and collecting the oil lamps they had put out the evening before. The lamps required a great deal of maintenance; Moses and Aaron had their own room, the lamproom, located in the basement. The wicks had to be trimmed and the lamps filled, cleaned and polished, before being put back in place around the house. 'They did nothing else except lamps,' recalled Lady Elfrida, 'never had a day off, never wanted one. When my father succeeded, he insisted that Moses and Aaron should each have a Sunday off and a day off in the week. Moses couldn't understand this and went in tears to the head steward and said, "What have I done wrong, I've always worked on a Sunday, now I've got to do nothing, what have I done?"'

On the afternoon of the 6th Earl's funeral, Moses and Aaron began their round earlier than usual. With twenty members of the Fitzwilliam family staying, together with their personal valets and ladies' maids, the two men had further to travel – to the bedrooms in the outer reaches of the East and West fronts.

Beginning shortly after lunch, it took the lampmen as long to light the house as it did for the sky outside to turn from day to night. Although at Wentworth the night was never black, it was red; a reflection of the glow from the after-burn from the hundreds of chimneys that ringed the Park.

Moving slowly through the house, on reaching the Duchess of Kent room, Moses and Aaron were required to place a lamp on the ebony and gilt pedestal by the dead Earl's bed, and to light the candle branches of the cheval mirror on the wall next to it – in preparation, so they assumed, for the family's last farewell.

Yet, contrary to late Victorian custom, there was to be no final gathering of the clan at the Earl's bedside that night. The House Steward's Book for 24 February 1902 records that most of the family took supper on trays in their rooms; the few letters that survive in the Fitzwilliam archives reveal that they were not only avoiding one another, they were barely speaking. When they did communicate, it was in the heat of blazing rows, or via hurriedly scrawled and acrimonious notes.

The tension at Wentworth, as reported by friends and neighbours of the Fitzwilliams who visited the house in the days before and after the 6th Earl's funeral, was unbearable. The Halifax family, who lived a few miles away at Hickelton Hall, were frequent callers. 'Agnes and I were over at Wentworth again yesterday where we saw most of them,' wrote Lord Halifax to his sister Emily. 'They one and all looked greater wrecks than you can conceive. I feel sure Lady Mary has really been odious to poor Lady Alice, really tormenting her and making herself, and stirring up others to be, thoroughly disagreeable.' Lady Mary Sutton, Lord Halifax's daughter, writing to her brother, said, 'Affairs at Wentworth seem in a most wretched state – none of the aunts speak to Billy – one of the trustees, Mr Doyne, is ill with scarlet fever, and the other, Lord Zetland, being Maud's father won't act alone so nothing can be done – and it is said that Lady Alice is trying to appropriate everything she can.' Ten days after the funeral, Lord Halifax, who was due to meet his sister in London, and reluctant to commit the latest news to paper, sent her a cryptic note, 'Agnes tells me the rows at Wentworth are portentous and of this more on the day.'

The rows were between Billy Fitzwilliam and his uncles and aunts. Billy was the only son of Viscount Milton, the late Earl's eldest son, who had died twenty-five years earlier in 1877. The Earl had produced fourteen children: eight boys and six girls. Five had died in his lifetime: those who survived him, gathered at Wentworth for the funeral, were in their late fifties and sixties.

With the exception of two of them, there was little love lost between the aunts and uncles and their nephew. Billy had been estranged from them for many years, leaving them to hold sway over the elderly and fragile Earl, and to dictate the running of the house and the Estate. Billy had been at Coollattin, the family's seat in Ireland, when he heard the news of his grandfather's death. Some indication of the deep divisions within the family can be found in a letter written by his favourite cousin, Kathleen Doyne, to another family member. 'I think in my yesterday's note I told you we had just had a wire from Billy to say that poor old Grandpapa had passed away. It seems that the dear old man had bronchitis and had been ill for a week or more but no one until just the last let Billy know.' The 'reptiles', as Kathleen refers to the aunts and uncles, had deliberately denied Billy the chance to see his grandfather before he died. 'As to the funeral,' she wrote, 'Billy was dreading the ordeal more than he could say, and no wonder.'

A clue to the tensions at Wentworth lay within the fabric of the house itself.

There was one wing that Moses and Aaron did not visit on their lamp round: the nursery wing, an important part of any great country house. Staffed by posses of nursery maids and governesses, this was where the blood line was raised; the sons who would carry on the title, the daughters who might bring wealth and prestige to the family by marrying well.

In 1896, when he was twenty-four years old, Billy had married Maud Dundas, the eldest daughter of the Marquess of Zetland. They had three young daughters and were hoping for a son and heir. Yet, as Elfrida, Countess of Wharncliffe, remembered, the nursery wing at Wentworth in 1902 was all but derelict. No instructions had been given by the 6th Earl to renovate it; the wing had not been touched for nearly fifty years. 'They'd done nothing for Billy Fitzwilliam's family to come into – nothing! You wouldn't believe it, the nurseries that we were put into with the peacock paper – it was falling down on to the floor. Damp! It was in the most desperate state. The windows were falling out of the frames, there was glass out of the window frames themselves. They'd done nothing to it, nothing, not a bit.'

It was as if Billy and his family did not exist.

Early that evening, the tense atmosphere in the house escalated with the arrival of Lady Alice. She had travelled by train from London, where she had been ill for some days with an attack of flu, carried on a day bed, accompanied by a doctor and two nurses.

Of all the Earl's children, Alice had been closest to her father. A dominant character, she had run her father's affairs for more than three decades. She was a shrewish-looking spinster in her late fifties, with mouse-brown hair and a pale pinched face. Wentworth had been her home since birth. In the last ten years of the Earl's life, aside from a few old family retainers, ancient wet nurses and governesses, Alice, her unmarried sister, Charlotte, and their elderly father were the only occupants of the house.

Billy loathed his Aunt Alice – as his daughter, Elfrida, remembered, 'She made the milk go sour just by looking at it' – and he loathed her for good reason. Lady Alice was the chief conspirator in a plot hatched by Billy's uncles and aunts to oust him. They believed their nephew was an impostor, a fraudulent claimant to their father's fortune and to the Fitzwilliam title.

Elfrida put it bluntly: 'They wanted to kick him out.'

A century on, much of what lay behind the impostor allegation is obscure; perhaps deliberately obscured. The trail is almost cold: the fire that burnt for three weeks at Wentworth in 1972, consuming sixteen tons of the Fitzwilliams' correspondence, had been preceded by others. The private papers of all but two of the conspirators have been destroyed; a systematic destruction that extended across collateral branches of the family, as well as along the main line.

Earl Fitzwilliam's letters, Billy's and Maud's, and the correspondence of eight out of ten of the aunts and uncles who conspired against Billy, or who were privy to the conspiracy, have not survived.

Only two of the protagonists' papers have been preserved: those of William Henry Wentworth-Fitzwilliam and Lady Frances

Doyne, who in 1902 were the eldest son and daughter of the dead Earl. Conceivably, their letters could focus the things that have been blurred: the personalities and motives of the conspirators, the evidence they had to support their charge against Billy. Potentially, they could transform into words the powerful currents of emotional static that we know, from the household records and the reports of neighbours, crackled along the corridors on the eve of the Earl's funeral.

Frances Doyne was born at Wentworth, and grew up there during the 1850s and 1860s, before marrying Robert Doyne in 1867 and moving to Ireland. Her letters are stored in a large black chest in a garage in Yorkshire.

The chest, the type of patrician travelling trunk that would have taken two footmen to carry, dates from the mid-nineteenth century and contains over a thousand letters, densely packed in tight bundles. Covering the years 1840–1910, the letters have been kept inside their original envelopes. Each bears a stamp, a postmark, and the embossed crests of countless aristocratic families, fashioned in a myriad of colours, or the stencilled name of a famous or forgotten stately home.

The letters are revealing in what they do not reveal. For the years spanning the impostor affair, there are no letters at all. But chillingly, there are scores of empty envelopes. The dates, the postmarks, the family crests, the houses from which they were sent, show that the letters, written by members of the Fitzwilliam family to Lady Frances and her children, could have told the story of this controversial episode in the family's history. But someone, at some point, has removed them.

Only one letter from the period – a tantalizing handwritten note delivered by a servant at Wentworth on the eve of the late Earl's funeral – survives in William Henry Fitzwilliam's otherwise extensive collection. If there was a dark secret behind Billy's identity, it is one that his generation of the family seemed determined to take to their graves.

Hundreds of millions of pounds rested on the truth about who Billy really was. If, in 1902, when he succeeded his grandfather, it had been proved that he was an impostor, the Fitzwilliam title and fortune, the great estates, the industrial interests and the priceless art treasures would have passed down a different line. As long as a paper trail existed, if Billy really was the Earl who never should have been, as his aunt, Lady Alice, the chief conspirator, believed, his – and his descendants' – phenomenal wealth would remain vulnerable to other family contenders who could prove that he was not the man he claimed to be.

Here, perhaps, lies the answer to the gaping void in the family papers – the systematic destruction in bonfire after bonfire of the Fitzwilliams' twentieth-century history.

To find the truth about who Billy really was, or at least his version of it, it is necessary to look at a small bundle of papers – among the very few to have survived – that Billy kept securely in a safe at his house at Coollattin until the day he died.

Tied with a pink silk ribbon, marked with a handwritten label, 'Controversial correspondence regarding the 7th Earl Fitzwilliam's Inheritance', the documents originate from Johnson and Long, the firm of solicitors Billy appointed to defend him against Lady Alice's attack. The collection, numbering about ten documents, represents only a fraction of what must have been an extensive correspondence. Strict criteria appear to have governed which documents were deemed important enough to be kept. They shed no light on the evidence against Billy; they tell only his side of the story: they are the crucial testimonies of proof he needed to demonstrate that he really was who he claimed to be.

Their interest lies in what they say about the impostor allegation and in what kind of truth they tell.

3

According to Lady Alice, Billy Fitzwilliam was 'a spurious child' that had been substituted at birth.

It was an old ruse, one that had been around for centuries. There was even a word for such babies: changelings. In aristocratic and royal circles, precautions to guard against the danger of a substitution had long been in place. The Home Secretary was required to attend all royal births – a practice that continued until 1930, when the late Princess Margaret was born. Aristocrats were equally cautious; at births where the devolution of prestigious titles, great fortunes and vast tracts of land were at stake, interested parties from tangential branches of the family, or their representatives, were in attendance to ensure that a changeling was not introduced.

Convention was broken at Billy's birth. He was born thousands of miles from Wentworth in the wilds of Canada; there were no other members of the Fitzwilliam family present. Tucked among the bundle of documents Billy kept in his safe is a tattered fragment of newspaper, torn from the pages of *The Times*, dated 5 September 1872, some six weeks after the event. The circumstances of his birth, as the report reveals, were bizarre:

> . . . near Fort William and on the borders of civilization – but it may well be confessed, of an uncouth and uncomfortable civilization, it may be mentioned that a son and heir to the noble house of Fitzwilliam has been born on the banks of the Kaministiquia River, on the north shores of Lake Superior.

The report continued:

> An Ontario paper, in mentioning the birth of the infant, remarks that 'the cries of the young stranger will be echoed by those of Indian

papooses, and the tender sympathy of the tawny squaws in their wigwams with the coroneted mother in her tent, will show a touch of nature which makes the whole world kin. Unless the waves of the democratic revolution surge over England, or this last shoot of an ancient tree be untimely cut off, a native Canadian will succeed to one of the noblest titles, most princely estates, most honourable and honoured names in England and England's history.'

A 'stranger' indeed – a cuckoo in their nest, so Lady Alice and her brothers and sisters believed. Lord Milton, their elder brother, they alleged, had been guilty of a fraudulent and criminal act. Moments after giving birth, and on his instructions, Lady Milton, the 'coroneted mother', had been knocked unconscious by chloroform, so that Billy, the son of a white settler, could be substituted for the couple's newborn baby girl.

Billy's documents reveal the substance of the conspirators' allegation, but in the process of selecting which were kept, any letters or legal briefs containing details of the evidence his accusers held to corroborate their charge were deliberately destroyed. It is clear, however, that in 1896, the year the aunts and uncles first alleged that he was an impostor, Billy had no means of refuting it. It seems he himself did not know who he really was; all traces of his entry into the world appeared to have been lost.

His parents had been dead for many years; Laura, Viscountess Milton, had died in 1886, and Lord Milton almost ten years before her. Billy's birth certificate, a key piece of evidence in his defence, had disappeared. If he was to prove that he was not the changeling his aunts and uncles believed him to be, witnesses to his birth, and his birth certificate, had to be found.

Billy knew he would receive no help from the Fitzwilliam family. From the outset, they had refused to credit his existence. Traditionally, the Fitzwilliams had celebrated the arrival of a new heir with lavish parties for tens of thousands of their tenants and employees. When Billy was born, there was silence from Wentworth: no announcement, no acknowledgement even. The British Press limited itself to carrying extracts from Canadian and

American newspapers. Clearly the Fitzwilliams' response had been 'no comment'; it was as if Billy was being wiped from the family history even as his life began.

In 1896, at the age of twenty-four, Billy, Viscount Milton, was compelled to search for the proof he needed behind his family's back. He hired a solicitor who also practised as a special investigator – the early-twentieth-century equivalent of a private detective. His name was Thomas Bayliss.

Some years later, Bayliss described his brief. 'Certain members of the family said the Viscount was not the son of the late Viscount and Viscountess Milton, suggesting that he was a spurious child introduced into the bed of the Viscountess . . . My work as a specialist extended over a period of several years – from 1896 to 1900 inclusive. I was not allowed to make inquiries from members of Viscount Milton's family, and inquiries had to be made in Canada, the United States and abroad. I wrote many hundreds of letters and consulted very many documents in various parts of the country, with the object of tracing the pedigree of Viscount Milton, and of procuring evidence of his legitimacy.'

Five people, as Bayliss discovered, had been present at Billy's birth: his parents, Lord and Lady Milton; a midwife called Hannah Boyce; Dr Thomas Millar; and a nursemaid named Tilly Kingdon. In 1900, Bayliss, after a four-year investigation, finally succeeded in tracking down two of them: the doctor and the midwife. Both were asked by Johnson and Long, Billy's solicitors, to make a statement about the circumstances surrounding his birth.

'Gentlemen,' wrote Dr Millar in response to the lawyers, 'the *indisputable* facts connected with the birth of Viscount Milton are as follows':

Sometime in July 1872 – I forget the exact date and have no means of verifying it – the late Viscountess Milton was delivered of a son (the present Viscount Milton), about 9 o'clock or 10 o'clock in the evening at Pointe de Meuron the head of navigation of the Kaministiquia River in a little wooden shanty, 12 miles from Fort William, a Hudson Bay post situated at the mouth of the above-named river in the province or department of Alghany, Canada.

The late Lord Milton, the nurse brought out especially for the purpose of attending her ladyship, and myself as medical attendant, were the only persons present, and no other person except the children's nurse attended and then only occasionally during the convalescence of her ladyship. As mentioned by you, chloroform was administered, but not to the point of producing complete unconsciousness, only for the mitigation of pain (I add this detail, for I know nothing of the purport or import of your inquiries on this point, so have thought it better to be quite explicit).

The child's name, date of birth, parentage and other particulars etc were recorded by the Governor of the Fort in the district court, and the birth was also made the subject of an article in the *Toronto Globe.* My intercourse with Lord and Lady Milton extended over a course of 4 or 5 years during which time, with few intermissions they were under my daily observation. Excepting a Catholic priest and the household of the fort, there were no white people for many miles around, consequently no white women or children ever visited us, our only visitors were Indians – for the most part patients of mine – black flies and mosquitoes and plenty of them.

Hannah Boyce's statement, sworn before a Commissioner of Oaths in London, concurs with Dr Millar's:

While we were at Pointe de Meuron Lady Milton on the 25th [*sic*] of July 1872 gave birth to a son. I delivered her. Just at the last pains Dr Millar came into the room and gave her a little chloroform. I was the first who saw and handled the child and there is absolutely no doubt it was a male child. While we were at Pointe de Meuron there were no other white people there, only Indians.

Both Boyce and Millar categorically refute each of Lady Alice's allegations: Viscountess Milton had given birth to a boy, not a girl; she had not been chloroformed to the point of unconsciousness at any point during, or after, labour; a 'changeling' could never have been substituted because, in an area populated by Indians, there were no other white babies for miles around.

The two testimonies leave no room for doubt. Billy was clearly who he claimed to be: the legitimate heir to the 6th Earl's title and fortune. His case seems cut and dried.

But was it?

There are some strange anomalies in Billy's documents.

In January 1901, after Hannah Boyce had made her statement in London, she sent Mr Barker, Billy's solicitor, a 'small cutting' from, as she claimed, 'an old diary written on the day of Lord Milton's birth'. The entry, just one sentence, read:

> 1872 July 26 – the first cry from a lovely boy gave joy to each of our little party in the lonely forest where no other white persons ever live.

How fortuitous that a line written thirty years previously should so succinctly inform the reader of two of the points Billy's lawyers were so anxious to hear. The handwriting is shaky and spidery, more obviously that of a sixty-eight-year-old than that of the thirty-eight-year-old Boyce would have been in 1872. The diary entry is dated 26 July, yet oddly, and evidently written with the same pen and at the same time, '1872' is scrawled above it. It is curious that the year was recorded six months into the diary: on the original document, someone has put a large cross in pencil beside '1872', as if they too found it odd. Was Hannah Boyce telling the truth or was she perhaps a little too eager to please?

Among Billy's documents there is a letter from Hannah Boyce to Billy's solicitor, Mr Barker, which shows that she was paid £5 for her testimony; not personally by Billy, but through Barker. It was a lot of money to a village midwife, as she then was – the equivalent of a year's wages.

Twelve years later – in 1913 – Billy would pay her again. More than a decade after he had become the 7th Earl Fitzwilliam, Hannah, who had fallen on hard times after a street hawker had swindled her of her life savings, sent his wife, Maud, a letter, begging for her help:

Dear Lady Countess Fitzwilliam will you please excuse me being the old nurse of Lady Milton I trust you will pardon the liberty I am taking writing. It is now very many years I well remember being sent to 4 Grosvenor Square to see the Countess Fitzwilliam, she that engaged me to travel to Canada with Lady Milton as her nurse and midwife. Neither shall I ever forget the joy of Lord and Lady Milton at the birth of a son. As you do not know who I am I will remind you of my calling on you at the Castle Ryde. I gave you an advertisement I had cut from a Canadian paper of the birth of the present Lord Fitzwilliam. Mr Raymond Barker seen me several times as I went to London and signed an affidavit for which he gave me five pounds at that time. I never thought I should ever require help I am now over 80 years old I have been ill for several months I am getting better but cannot get strength. I have worked very hard helping the poor mothers in the village over their confinement. Four years ago I lost all our life savings leaving us with only the old age pension to depend on. I can only appeal to your sympathy if you could help me a little just now I should be most grateful. Again apologizing for writing to you it is the first time I ever wrote a letter asking any one to give me help I am very sorry to do so now. I remain your humbl [*sic*] servant, Hannah Boyce.

Maud showed the letter to Billy; wary of sending money directly to Hannah, he wrote a short note to Mr Barker: 'Lady Fitzwilliam has received the enclosed from Mrs Boyce, I have not allowed her to send anything as I thought it safe to leave that matter in your hands. Will you send £5 or £10 on my behalf.'

Quite why Billy 'thought it safe' to leave the transaction to Mr Barker is unclear. Perhaps it was because he doubted the credibility of her original statement, and did not want to be seen to be paying her, as if she were a bought witness.

One further inference remains to be drawn from Billy's documents.

On 10 March 1902, Thomas Bayliss, the solicitor and special investigator hired by Billy between 1896 and 1900, appeared before the Lord Chief Justice at the Royal Courts of Justice in London, charged with professional misconduct. Billy, who three weeks earlier had succeeded to his grandfather's title and fortune, had instigated proceedings to have Bayliss struck off the rolls.

There had been a serious falling-out between the peer and his private detective. On the face of it, the dispute appears to have been about money. Billy accused Bayliss of embezzling £1,500, claiming he had submitted 'fictitious' invoices to account for the stolen money. Bayliss argued that the invoices, far from being fabricated, represented his charges for the special investigation into Billy's legitimacy, conducted over a period of four years.

The judge ruled that Bayliss had submitted a 'fictitious claim' for his work. Bayliss lost the case; he was found guilty of serious professional misconduct and struck off the rolls. The assumption, from the published court report, and the verdict in the case, is that Bayliss was corrupt; more crucially, the implication in the judge's ruling was that the 'strange allegations as to Earl Fitzwilliam's identity', as one newspaper referred to the case, were a figment of Bayliss's imagination.

Bayliss may have been guilty of some form of embezzlement, but Billy's documents show that what he said in court was true. He had investigated Billy's legitimacy, and he had played an important part in procuring the evidence necessary to rebut the impostor charge: moreover, a letter from Johnson and Long shows that in 1900, Bayliss was the lawyer responsible for coordinating Billy's defence in anticipation of a legal challenge by the Fitzwilliam family. Bayliss had, as he claimed in court, submitted a detailed brief to Billy's barrister, Mr Butcher. Writing in November 1900, Billy's solicitor attached a note to the brief: 'In lieu of the questions submitted by Mr Bayliss's case, Counsel is requested to advise Lord Milton what steps he should take in order to guard against any attack such as is suggested on the part of certain members of his family.' Intriguingly, neither Bayliss's brief nor Mr Butcher's response has survived among Billy's collection of documents; they have been pruned. The supposition has to be that both documents contained negative information, possibly details of the evidence on which Lady Alice's allegation was based.

Oddly, the £1,500 pounds at issue (the equivalent of around

£105,000 today) was money that Billy had already made available to Bayliss. It is unlikely that he would have advanced such a large sum had he not been anticipating a costly and difficult investigation, involving inquiries abroad. Though a sizeable figure, it was not a huge amount to a man who had recently inherited £2.8 million, or £3.3 billion at today's values; so why would Billy want to quibble, and so publicly, over what for him was a relatively small sum?

It seems that Bayliss possessed information that Billy wanted to suppress; a breach of confidence, or the fear of it, was what drove him to bring the case.

The two men had parted company at the end of 1900. Shortly after, Billy served a Writ of Attachment on the solicitor to recover the £1,500 he claimed he owed him. Bayliss responded angrily; an extract from the letter he sent to Billy was read out during his trial:

> You cannot be surprised that I intend to hit out hard. By your underhand shuffling I consider you have forfeited all claims to the confidence about your affairs that I scrupulously observed. I have been interviewed by a representative of the Press to whom I have given information of your dealings with me.

The precise nature of Billy's 'underhand shuffling' was not specified in court. Nor did anything ever appear in the Press. What is clear, though, is that Billy, after receiving the solicitor's threatening letter, wanted to silence him – and for good. If it had been simply a matter of money, he could have pursued the debt recovery action via the Writ of Attachment. Instead, he chose to lodge a complaint with the Law Society, the solicitors' governing body. To seek to have Bayliss struck off the solicitors' rolls was a more vitriolic way to proceed; if successful, it ensured censure and humiliation, and an end to Bayliss's legal career.

Yet Bayliss was nearing seventy: in 1902, his career was almost over. It seems that Billy's true aim in discrediting his professional integrity was to destroy the credibility of the information his solicitor had threatened to reveal.

Billy's documents cannot be regarded as conclusive. In offering a resolution to the mystery of his identity, they raise more questions than they answer. That the heir to one of Victorian England's greatest industrial fortunes was born in a wooden shack in an Indian camp, miles from anywhere, in a region plagued by mosquitoes and black flies is in itself mysterious.

As vouched for by his sister, Lady Mabel Smith, Billy had a 'perfect horror of publicity': an obsession with secrecy, as she remembered, had been one of his chief characteristics from childhood. But why, from such an early age, had he been so secretive? Was it because he knew he was not his father's son? Or was there something else he wanted to hide?

Billy's documents point to his father, William, Viscount Milton. He, if Lady Alice is to be believed, was the guilty party; a man so desperate to produce a son and heir that he was prepared to abandon his newborn baby daughter and replace her with Billy.

4

William, Viscount Milton, the eldest son of William, the 6th Earl Fitzwilliam, was born in July 1839. He died just thirty-eight years later. It was beginning to look as if the family was cursed: he was the second of three successive heirs to die before reaching the age of forty.

In William's case, the Fitzwilliams were doubly cursed. His death, in 1877, came as a relief.

'One of the hard lessons one has to learn, one which I fear I have been rebellious about, is to trust one's children cheerfully to God when they suffer,' wrote his mother, Harriet, Countess Fitzwilliam, on the afternoon he died. 'I have been a long time learning it – but I hope I know it now. I call to mind so often now the time when my dear William seemed to stand very near to death as a little boy – how I prayed for his life to be spared! And could not say "Thy Will Be Done" and now I remember how much sooner he might perhaps have been with his God had I been more submissive, how much suffering he and others might have been spared and now I do most earnestly hope that his sufferings may not have been in vain and that we may all learn all that God in His mercy designed us to learn from it.'

To the British public, in the course of his short life, William Milton became a hero – one of the most famous and fêted of the nineteenth-century explorers. At the age of twenty-four, after an epic and hazardous journey across the Rocky Mountains, he discovered a land route that linked the Atlantic to the Pacific. On his return to England in 1864 he received a rapturous response from the Press. 'Lord Milton is something better than a Lord; he has proved himself to be a fine, heroic young man, of true English pluck and daring,' wrote *The Ilustrated Times*. 'Lord Milton,' the panegyric continued, 'is no shiftless Lord Dundreary, neither is he a mere pleasure-hunter, but a genuine Englishman – a splinter off the old Hartz rock – brave, tough, wise, energetic.' Milton's book, *The North-West Passage by Land*, an account of his journey published in 1865, ran into five editions in eight months and was still in print at the end of the century.

Yet he was no hero to the family. After his death, his name was taboo.

'My grandfather never spoke about his father,' recalls Billy's granddaughter, Lady Barbara Ricardo. 'We never knew anything about him. Were never told anything. Never knew about the book he wrote of his great adventures in Canada. There wasn't even a copy of it in the library at Wentworth. There were tens of thousands of books there – not one single copy!'

More than a century after Milton's death, his great-grandson, Michael Bond, set out to retrace his journey across North America and Canada. 'I couldn't believe there was so little to go on. It was like trying to build an ancient invertebrate from its trace fossils. He has all but been blanked from the family records. Remarkably for the heir to an Earldom, even his will has disappeared.'

Bond had touched the edge of the void in the family archives; it is from the mid-nineteenth century, around the time of Milton's birth, that the destruction of the Fitzwilliam papers begins. 'I imagined that the family would have been proud of its explorer son,' Bond wrote. 'So where were the biographies, the photograph albums, the archived letters, the gilt-framed portraits and the relics of the Wild West?'

Was he an embarrassment, Bond wondered. Had he done something inexcusable? Searching through the family archives, at the bottom of one meagre file containing rough drafts of Milton's speeches, a few scraps of letters, and some notes from his secretary, Bond made a significant discovery, one that accounts for the mystery surrounding Milton's life and explains why his name was taboo. 'I found a small bundle of papers that would transform the way I looked at Milton,' he wrote. 'At first they resembled unpaid bills: lists of products and a signature, some numbers, his name at the top. But they turned out to be prescriptions for medicines, and not for the common cold: opium, lavender oil, belladonna, orange rind, chloral hydrate, strychnine, potassium bromide. Such sedatives and stimulants were common remedies at that time for epilepsy.'

The bad blood of a man who appeared to be among the most blessed in mid-Victorian England gives the impostor affair a fresh twist.

'Fits are treated as madness and madness constitutes a right as it were to treat people as vermin,' Lord Shaftesbury, whose son, Maurice, was an epileptic, remarked in 1851.

In the mid-nineteenth century, epilepsy was tragically misunderstood. Doctors diagnosed it as a form of madness: there was no cure for it, and no understanding of what caused it. Deriving from the Greek word *epilepsis*, meaning 'a taking hold of', a state of being seized by some power of a mysterious nature, even its name supported the belief that it had some supernatural cause.

A terrifying and stigmatizing mythology had formed around the disease, still lodged in the popular consciousness centuries after it had been created. Islamic lore attributed epileptic fits to the blow of a ghost; in the Ottoman Empire, they were said to betray an illicit sexual love affair, brought on by a jealous spirit's attempt to choke the guilty party. But in mid-Victorian England, to devout Christians like Earl Fitzwilliam, it was the verdict of the Bible that was the most damning. When Christ healed a child suffering convulsions, the episode was represented as the casting out of a demon: 'a spirit taketh him and he suddenly crieth out; and it teareth him that he foameth again' (Luke 9:39).

Over the centuries, the treatment for epilepsy had been as barbarous as the views attributed to its cause. In the first century, at the Colosseum in Rome, epileptics waited to drink the blood of mutilated gladiators: 'They think it most valuable to sip the blood, still warm, still flowing, from the wounded themselves and thus to imbibe the breath of life immediately from the fresh opening,' Pliny recorded. In later centuries, various body parts were prescribed to treat the disease: the sixteenth-century Parisian physician Jean Fernel recommended a mixture of mistletoe, powdered human skull and peony seeds gathered when the moon was waning. When Milton was growing up, miners in the pit villages around Wentworth used an old folk remedy to treat epileptic fits: a dried calf's tongue was tied with a piece of string and placed around the afflicted person's neck.

The ingredients of Milton's prescriptions and the few letters that survive from his doctors indicate that he was sent to the top medical specialists of the day. From the onset of his illness, his parents spared no expense in the search for a cure for their eldest son and heir. Milton was treated by Sir Alexander Morrison, a prominent Edinburgh physician, and a disciple of a group of French doctors, based at the notorious Paris lunatic asylum, Salpêtrière. Though widely regarded as the leading experts of their day, their views were almost as malevolent as the Ancients', serving only to heighten the stigma and shame attached to the illness. Dr Beau, who conducted a study of sixty-seven epileptics at the Salpêtrière asylum in 1833, concluded that his patients' epilepsy had been caused by sorrow, morbid terror and masturbation. Dr Beau's findings were replicated in further experiments conducted by other experts during the 1830s and 1840s. Even as late as the 1880s, the British neurologist Sir William Gowers was still attributing epilepsy to excessive masturbation.

Demons, self-abuse, fear; it was hardly surprising the Fitzwilliams themselves took fright.

During much of Milton's childhood, their solution, which was typical of their class, was to keep him out of sight. Like other wealthy 'lunatics', he was exiled from his family from an early age, funnelled into the shadowy network of 'madhouses' that offered a cloak of secrecy: the private asylums and single-lodging establishments, both at home and abroad, that had proliferated in the first half of the nineteenth century.

His fits began before he was eleven years old. In 1850, Milton's father sent a letter to his father, the 5th Earl, from the Fitzwilliams' estate in Ireland.

William may have to remain here longer than I had anticipated, as his health is not very settled, and he has had many but only slight attacks of unconsciousness. The Edinburgh doctors recommend quiet, and no amusement of an exciting tendency.

Shortly after, Milton was sent to Avignon in France. Writing home to his mother at Wentworth, his anxiety about the long, enforced periods of separation from his family is painfully clear:

Please do let me know as soon as possible when you want me to come home for certain, and when and where we shall all be the next coming and midsummer holidays, if you knew how I long for an answer I am sure you would send one directly. On 15th April I shall have been here 3 months which was the greatest time you said I should stay and as I abominate being away here most thoroughly I really must come home then, and not go away again anywhere for an awfull long time except to Eton.

In their search for a cure, to the consternation of the round of specialists they consulted, the Fitzwilliams tried everything. An undated letter from one doctor mysteriously contains a lock of Milton's hair: 'I see no prospect of all this business finishing,' he wrote. 'Dr Willis saying that he can cure the thing appears to me very extraordinary.'

Dr Willis was the notorious proprietor of an asylum called Shillingthorpe. In 1847, the *Medical Practitioner* ran the following advertisement:

This Asylum for the Insane was established by the celebrated Dr Francis Willis, who had the happiness of restoring his Majesty George the Third from the serious malady with which he was afflicted in 1788. It is now conducted by his grandson, Dr Francis Willis, Fellow of the Royal College of Physicians, in the style of a country gentleman's residence. It is exclusively adapted for persons moving in the upper ranks of society. The Invalids are separately provided for in their own private apartments, and do not associate with each other, unless they are capable of joining Dr Willis's family. The numbers are very limited.

Shillingthorpe was one of several 'aristocratic' asylums that flourished in the mid-nineteenth century. Modelled on grand country houses, they boasted aviaries and bowling greens, cricket pavilions and pagodas. One establishment, Ticehurst, even had its own hunting pack. Catering exclusively for the sons and daughters of the well-born, the intention was to mimic 'Society': dances, billiards, Latin and Greek lessons, cards and concerts were among the many forms of activity on the curriculum.

When Milton was at Shillingthorpe, Dr Willis was known as a strong disciplinarian. His excessive fondness for the use of mechanical restraints – strait-waistcoats, handcuffs, hobbles, leg-locks and the 'coercion chair' – was criticized by the Lunacy Commissioner in 1854: 'It is painful to know that such views are entertained by a few physicians, who are men of education, but apparently proud of adhering to ancient severities.'

Despite Dr Willis's severity, Shillingthorpe's royal imprimatur lent it an extra cachet. Yet the luxurious comforts on offer at the aristocrats' asylums rendered them the more grotesque. They were desperate places. Many of the patients were not insane; like Milton, some were epileptics, others had been incarcerated by their families simply for falling in love beneath their class. At Ticehurst, in April 1847, one patient, Augustus Gawen, was admitted for proposing marriage to a fisherwoman, and another, Henrietta Golding, was confined after 'she had shewn strong inclinations to form an improper connection with a Person of very inferior grade.' The psychological scars inflicted on patients like these must have been considerable. The availability of private apartments meant that the patients did not live cheek by jowl, as they did in the paupers' asylums, but Milton, and men and women like Augustus Gawen and Henrietta Golding, would have had some exposure to the other inmates – patients who were clinically mad. In 1857, lifting the veil of secrecy that shrouded the asylums tailored for 'persons moving in the upper ranks of society', William Browne, the Superintendent of Crichton Royal, was keen to stress that high birth did not diminish the ravages of madness. The 'manic glorying in obscenity and filth' was by no means confined to the working classes: 'They are encountered in victims from the refined and polished portions of society, of the purest life, the most exquisite sensibility . . . Females of birth drink their urine . . . outlines of high artistic pretensions have been painted in excrement; poetry has been written in blood, or more revolting media . . . Patients are met with who daub and drench the walls as hideously as their disturbed fancy suggests; who wash or plaster their bodies, fill every crevice in the room, their ears, noses, hair, with ordure; who conceal these precious pigments in their mattresses, gloves, shoes, and will wage battle to defend their property.'

This, then, was the hinterland of Milton's childhood.

During his teenage years there were times when he appeared to be better; he was well enough to go to Eton and from there to Trinity College, Cambridge, although his attendance was often interrupted by his illness. When he was sixteen his father, writing to his grandfather, told him, 'I am sorry to say that William has had another attack like those he has had, but it was very much slighter, and there was only one, whereas he has had two on the previous occasions.' And in another letter, when Milton was eighteen: 'William, I am happy to say, is much better than when I left here 3 weeks ago, and I believe has had very little tendency towards a reversal of his old attacks and although he had tendencies when he first came here from London still those tendencies appear to be diminishing. He is evidently much stronger, and his face is fatter, and he does with far less medicine.'

Milton's grandfather replied: 'I hope the ups tendency to illness in William will go on – in medicine I have no great faith but I have great faith in diet which I hope will be enforced upon him systematically and perseveringly.'

But the 'ups tendency' the family longed for did not continue. Milton's illness, and the profound feelings of guilt and shame that accompanied it, dogged every step of his life. In a letter to his parents, written when he was thirty-two, he begged to be forgiven. 'Dear Father and Mother will you forgive me for all the pain and trouble I have caused you. When you know what I have suffered I know you will. Pray for me dear Father and Mother. Your loving and repentant son.'

His father was unforgiving. Pride and ignorance led him to treat his son, to use Lord Shaftesbury's words, 'like vermin'. William, 6th Earl Fitzwilliam, moulded in the cast of the Victorian patriarch, was a figure who inspired fear and awe among his family and his employees. After his death, one society writer said, 'It is almost impossible to make a stranger realize the tone and style of the late Earl Fitzwilliam's method of life at his Yorkshire seat, Wentworth. It must have been the nearest approach to the baronial splendour of the Middle Ages which the modern aristocracy can furnish.' When his yellow coach, 'horsed by four prancing chestnuts', flanked by outriders and running-men dressed in the Fitzwilliam livery, travelled through the pit villages and the streets of Rotherham and Sheffield, women curtseyed, and the men removed their caps and bowed.

The 6th Earl was a man of few words. Evelyn Dundas, who sat next to him at a dinner at Wentworth in the 1890s, described him as the most difficult and 'silent of hosts'. Throughout the meal she struggled to find conversation. When it reached a standstill, at a loss as to what to say though determined to elicit some response, she asked him 'which reflection of himself in his spoon he preferred – the convex or concave'. Privately, his reticence translated into relationships with his children and grandchildren that were formal and cold. 'A good many of them were frightened of him,' said his granddaughter Lady Mabel Smith. He used his wealth as a weapon of control; letters that survive in the Fitzwilliam archives show that he advanced or withheld money depending on his children's behaviour and continuously altered the amounts he planned to leave them in his will. Family to the 6th Earl meant duty, power, prestige and position; where these precepts were challenged, love and loyalty did not count.

Increasingly, as the Earl's hopes for a cure for his son faded, he realized that his illness placed the family in jeopardy. The stigma of lunacy threatened the Fitzwilliams' fortune and position – their potential for alliances through marriage with other great noble houses. It also threatened their social omnipotence. Endemic to epilepsy was the risk of public humiliation – an eventuality of which members of the aristocracy were particularly fearful. Even Lord Shaftesbury, the great Whig reformer and philanthropist, expressed horror at the thought of being humiliated in front of his tenants and employees when his son suffered a fit in public: 'Maurice fell yesterday in the Park. I trembled lest a vast crowd should be gathered. Sent away the children and sat by his side as though we were lying on the grass, and by degrees he recovered and walked home.'

In the early 1860s, new research determined that what had previously been a minority view among doctors had become medical fact: mental illness, including epilepsy, was hereditary, sending shivers through the aristocracy for whom pedigree was everything. Milton's illness had corrupted the Fitzwilliams' blood.

That the Earl had reached this view became evident on 27 July 1860, Milton's twenty-first birthday.

At Wentworth, the coming of age of the eldest son had traditionally been celebrated on a lavish scale. In 1807, when Milton's grandfather, the 5th Earl Fitzwilliam, came of age, the family gave a party for 10,000 guests. *The Iris*, a Sheffield newspaper, carried a report:

May 5th 1807
Yesterday being the 21st anniversary of the birthday of Lord Milton, the only son and heir of Earl Fitzwilliam, the day was most munificently celebrated at Wentworth House. Two oxen weighing together 240 stone were roasted whole on the lawn, in sheds erected for the purpose; these had been feeding for upwards of three years past, and are supposed to have been the finest and fattest beasts ever grazed in this county. Twenty sheep had also been previously roasted in quarters, which with the beef, bread, etc and more than 10,000 gallons of strong ale, principally brewed

several years ago for this festival, were distributed among the multitudes who assembled in the park, and whose numbers, notwithstanding the wetness of the day, have been estimated at 10,000.

During the forenoon and in the evening the roads on every side of Wentworth were darkened with crowds of people on foot, on horseback, in gigs, in chaises, coaches, carts and wagons. Yet rainy and unfavourable as the day was, none who travelled to Wentworth had occasion to complain of the fare – except those who by their gluttonous and drunken indiscretion made beasts of themselves and converted the bounty of Lord Fitzwilliam and his son at once in the means and the punishment of sinning. About a thousand of the tenants and others were entertained most sumptuously in the House itself.

The household accounts show precisely what the crowds consumed:

3 roasted oxen, 336 stone in weight
2 Scotch bullocks, 130 stone
26 roasted sheep, 177 stone 6 pounds
3 lambs
3 calves
10 hams
54 fowls
240 bushels of wheat
555 eggs
75 hogsheads of ale
6 hogsheads of small beer
473 bottles of good wine
23 gallons of rum
18 gallons of brandy
13 gallons of rum shrub [*sic*]

Viscount Milton's party, half a century later, was a very different affair. He was not even there. Nor was his family. Instead, it was quietly celebrated by 180 tenants, who drank toasts to the young

Lord with specially brewed ale, while the house masons and carpenters played cricket on the lawn.

It was a crushing snub to Milton, proof that his father refused to recognize him for who he was – the heir to his title and fortune. Yet again, it seems he had been sent away. Only one member of his family appears to have given the occasion any thought: his younger brother, William Henry, the Earl's second son. 'I have been thinking as William is just 21 that we ought to give him a birthday present; there is plenty of time to think of it before he comes home', Henry, as he was known in the family, wrote to his older sister, Frances. 'I should like to give him something really worth having, and if all of us brothers and sisters were to subscribe together we might get something very good, and if you can not spare much now, I am quite sure Mama will forward you some money. I know he often thinks that we do not care for him and he would very much like to have something from us all. I will give five pound but I do not mean that I want you to give the same, for I know you have more things to buy than I have. If we could get up between us £10 or £15 it would be very nice. He will never be 21 again you know.'

William Henry was Milton's favourite brother; he was also his father's favourite son. De facto, the Earl regarded Henry as his heir. Yet problematically, primogeniture dictated that Milton would succeed to the title and estates. Disinheriting an eldest son was a complex and all too public procedure; in light of the low life expectancy of epileptics in mid-nineteenth century England, the Earl decided to ride the matter out. As long as Milton died before he did, Henry, his second son, would succeed.

Some months after his twenty-first birthday, in April 1861, Milton blew his father's strategy apart; without consulting him, he announced his engagement to Miss Dorcas Chichester, the daughter of Lord Chichester, and the niece of the Marquess of Donegal. On hearing the news the Earl took to his bed, unable to cope with the strain of the whole affair. What horrified him above all else was the thought that his eldest son might now produce an heir. If he were to do so, Milton's bad blood would feed into the direct Fitzwilliam line.

In the days after the announcement, letters flew back and forth from Wentworth, as Lord and Lady Fitzwilliam connived with close family members to stop the marriage from going ahead. 'There appears some reason to fear an immediate marriage,' Milton's mother wrote to his Uncle George. 'My head is so weary I cannot judge of anything or write clearly either I fear.'

The situation came to a head when the Earl received a threatening letter from Lord Chichester, Dorcas's father. Sharply reminding the Earl that both his daughter and Milton were of age and therefore did not need the Earl's permission to marry, Chichester accused him of slighting his family by objecting to the marriage.

Behind Milton's back, the Earl replied to Lord Chichester's letter, knowing that what he had to tell him would bring the engagement to an end:

> My son's conduct has been so unsteady and his health so bad that I do not feel justified in consenting to his taking upon himself the serious responsibility of a married life. I feel sure you will think with me that I should not be doing right in withholding from you these facts, a knowledge of which will probably drastically alter your judgement as to your daughter's prospects of happiness. My son suffers from fits which cause at times great mental excitement sometimes followed by considerable depression of spirits.

Three days later the engagement was called off.

The Earl had not consulted his son before sending the letter; nor was he prepared to discuss it after it had been sent. Lady Fitzwilliam, writing on behalf of her husband, sent Milton's Uncle George a copy of the letter to Lord Chichester, with the following instructions. 'He wishes you to read the enclosed letter and consider when it should be given to William or if it should be withheld.'

No letters survive to reveal Milton's feelings for Dorcas

Chichester, or what he felt about the way his father had behaved. Within a few months, relations between them were destined to get worse. In the spring of 1862, the Earl's patience finally snapped.

5

On the morning of 26 May 1862, Milton stood in the dock at the Police Courts in Bow Street in London, as the magistrate delivered his verdict. He had been charged with fraudulently obtaining a pair of diamond earrings from a pawnbroker:

With respect to the charge before me, I can assure you, Lord Milton, if I had come to the conclusion that Your Lordship had any guilty intention with reference to the possession of the earrings, I should have sent you at once for trial, but my belief is there was no guilty intention. You are young and inexperienced, and evidently require good guidance, and I wish to remind you that considering your station, you are pre-eminently bound to obey the law, as your station will not protect you from the consequences of violating the law. The earrings will of course be given up to the pawnbroker. The act was the act of a foolish person, and therefore you, Lord Milton, are discharged.

In the weeks following his broken engagement, Milton, in deliberate defiance of his father, had been mixing with bad company in gaming houses and brothels in London's West End. The diamond earrings had been deposited at a pawnbroker's in Bond Street by Madame Rachel, a second-rate courtesan, who, according to police reports, traded as an 'enameller of women's faces'. She had won the earrings, which belonged to a 'ladyfriend' of Milton's, at a game of cards. Milton, wanting to please his 'ladyfriend' by returning the earrings to her, went to the pawnbroker's shop to redeem them. He offered the broker a cheque for £200, which he declined, saying 'it was too much; the earrings were only worth £65'. At which point, Milton put them into his pocket and walked out of the shop.

In his defence, Milton argued that he had simply intended to take care of the earrings until their legal title was established. His lawyers, pleading that he suffered from 'ill health', said that he had been acting under the influence of a 'woman much older than himself'.

His acquittal did not assuage his father. Angered by the negative publicity and the embarrassment to the family, the Earl ordered Milton out of England. Rather than send his frail son to a spa resort in Europe, he chose to banish him to the wilds of Canada. Making only the smallest of concessions to Milton's fragile health, he paid for a young doctor, twenty-nine-year-old William Cheadle, to accompany him into exile.

Cheadle recorded their departure on 19 June 1862 from Liverpool Docks on the steamship *Anglo-Saxon*, bound for Quebec.

Sailed at 5, only 25 Cabin passengers as yet. Weather very drizzling on leaving in the tender but soon became fine though cloudy. Had the temerity to smoke two pipes immediately on the ship's getting under way. About 6 o'clock 3 little devils found stowed away amongst the coals, hauled out, ship brought to, and the boat from a pilot vessel signalled to come alongside, when they were quickly sent over the side with a bag of biscuits from the Captain. They did not appear at all disconcerted at being discovered, but went away grinning, one waving a biscuit in farewell.

As Milton watched the vanishing wake of the pilot vessel returning the stowaways to shore, he must have longed to go with them. Yet again, as he had experienced throughout his childhood, he was being sent away against his will. Only one member of his family – his brother Henry – had waved him off from the quayside. 'I am sorry I did not look up at the last moment I saw you,' wrote Milton later that evening, 'but I could not manage it I felt so unhappy at going away. Please give my love to all the little ones and remember me to all other people at home, with best love your affectionate brother, Milton.'

The weather, during what became a horrendous crossing, can only have heightened Milton's despair. Two days off the coast of

Ireland the ship ran into a violent storm. 'Weather blowing stormy very,' Cheadle noted in his journal.

A gale of wind and sea during the night and still continuing. Turned out to breakfast. Lord Milton wisely taking his repast in his berth. I got through a little breakfast but had to bolt downstairs, was sick and expected to have to endure frightful tortures, but recovered in a few minutes. Hardly anyone at table. Felt seedy and spent most of the day in my berth.

The following day, the storm continued, a day Cheadle describes as 'certainly one of the longest days I ever passed'. And the next day:

Turned out towards 11, and shortly after Lord Milton put in his first appearance for two days. Both felt very uncertain. No catastrophe however occurred. Still very rough wind dead ahead, the vessel pitching tremendously, being very lightly laden – cargo tea. Everyone appears to have suffered and several passengers who have crossed the Atlantic several times agree that they never suffered so much before. Take the precaution however of having our meals in the passage, or on deck.

At night, phosphorescence made the heavy seas look angrier still; the crest of each wave 'breaking in light' and the wake of the ship 'a path of brilliant scintillation'. And on the fifth day when the storm began to subside, eerily, at intervals through the morning, they saw joists of timber swirling past the boat. Later in the day, the source of the wreckage became evident.

About 1 o'clock, the Captain whilst talking with us on deck suddenly exclaimed: 'By Jove, there's the wreck of a vessel.' After some little time we discovered a small object on the horizon, which by the help of glasses we made out to be the hull of a ship, dismasted and no one on board and almost directly in our course. We altered our course a little N. so as to pass under her stern which was towards us, and at about 2 yards distance read her name 'Ruby'. She was completely waterlogged, the waves which were not very high washing over her. The masts (2, a schooner) had evidently been cut away, and her sides down to the level of the deck were broken up so that only the skeleton beams were left. The bowsprit was carried away, and the boats had either been the refuge of the crew, or washed away and the men drowned. They had evidently made a good struggle for life, but from the dreadfully battered state of the hull it would seem doubtful whether the boats could live in such a sea as there must have been.

On the eighth day, a thick fog descended. The ship slowed to half speed, its whistle blowing in short bursts.

Very cold and raw. Now in the region of ice about 100 miles from Cape Race. Great caution used. 2 lookouts in the bows, two officers on the bridge. The Captain had the 'Canadian' when she was lost, struck on a piece of ice which was under water and not seen. Shock so light that he standing on the bridge did not perceive it. Keel torn out so that she filled rapidly about 40 lost. Stop the engines every few hours to sound.

As the steamship crept through the dense fog, it was a grim foreshadowing of Milton and Cheadle's next journey into the unknown. Determined to prove himself to his father, Milton refused to allow his health to encumber their plans. The two men had mapped an ambitious expedition across Canada: to find the most direct route through British territory to the gold regions of Cariboo and from there to explore the little-known country on the western flank of the Rocky Mountains.

It was wild and dangerous country, populated largely by tribes of Indians. Writing in the 1850s, Robert Ballantyne, a Hudson Bay Trader, had warned,

When starving, the Indians will not hesitate to appease the cravings of hunger by resorting to cannibalism; and there were some old dames with whom I was myself acquainted, who had at different periods eaten several of their children. Indeed, some of them, it was said, had also eaten their husbands.

Prejudice led many Europeans to exaggerate, but in the 1860s, in the remote fur-trading regions north of the Great Lakes, cannibalism was still prevalent among the tribes, and Indians were continuing to claim the scalps of white settlers.

While Cheadle, a Cambridge graduate and an accomplished oarsman, was stockily built and physically strong, Milton was weak and of slight physique, and frequently debilitated by epileptic attacks. His health posed a considerable handicap over the terrain they planned to cross. Yet, over distances of hundreds of miles, much of it on foot or on horseback, sleeping in tents in the open at night, Milton would endure some of the most hostile country in the world.

Their journey took them along precipitous mountain trails, often in driving blizzards of snow; across barely navigable rivers that had claimed many lives; through dense, unmapped forests, where paths had to be hacked with axes and many a traveller had been lost. And always, in these remote and wild regions, there was the danger of starvation, the travellers' only source of food coming from whatever they could shoot or carry. There were other dangers too: from diseases such as smallpox, which had ripped through some of the small communities along their route, from wild bears and wolves, and from the hostile indigenous tribes.

It would be nearly two years before Milton saw his family again; for nine months of that time, he had no contact at all with them. Yet despite his unhappiness at the outset, the expedition to Canada was the making of him. In the rugged and inhospitable landscape he found peace and tranquillity, a ballast against, and refuge from, the pressures and prejudice at home. He was fascinated by the people he met, developing a particular affinity with the Indians and becoming fluent in Cree. His empathy with the tribesmen is apparent in his book, *The North-West Passage by Land*, where he describes his first sighting of an Indian:

He was leaning against a tree, smoking his pipe with great dignity, not deigning to move or betray the slightest interest as the train went past him . . . We could well imagine the disgust of these sons of silence and stealth at the noisy trains which rush through the forests, and the steamers which dart along lakes and rivers, once the favourite haunt of game, now driven far away. How bitterly in their hearts they must curse that steady, unfaltering, inevitable advance of the great army of whites, recruited from every corner of the earth, spreading over the land like locusts – too strong to resist, too cruel and unscrupulous to mingle with them in peace and friendship.

Milton and Cheadle's expedition achieved its goal; they succeeded in mapping a route across Canada from the Atlantic to the Pacific. On 7 March 1864, Milton returned to England; he was received like a conquering hero, fêted by everyone from the Royal Geographical Society to Fleet Street. 'So long as in the cause of science the nobility showed such skill, enterprise and perseverance, as that of Viscount Milton,' claimed Sir John Richardson, the famous Arctic explorer, 'England might be proud of her aristocracy.'

6

'Poor squinny dwarfish little Lord Milton is desperately in love with Lady Mary, daughter of Lady Ormonde, who won't have him,' Lady Frederick Cavendish noted in her diary shortly before Christmas 1866.

Lady Frederick was staying with the Duke of Devonshire at Chatsworth. Twenty miles from Wentworth, Chatsworth was within visiting distance, a three-hour journey by horse and carriage, or a little over an hour's gallop across the lowlands of the Pennines. The Fitzwilliams and the Devonshires were part of the same social milieu: the Dukes of Dorset and Omnium as they really existed – two of twenty-nine prodigiously wealthy families, with incomes ranging from £75,000 to £290,000 a year.* With the exception of Barons Leconfield and Overstone and Viscounts Boyne and Portman, the twenty-nine super-rich were Dukes, Marquesses or Earls. They hunted together, shot together, danced together; most important of all, they married one another.

This was the world to which Milton returned from the wilds of North America.

Life during the winter months in the grand country houses, particularly for women, as Lady Frederick records in her diary, followed a strict, if at times dull, routine. In the course of her four-week stay at Chatsworth, while the 'gentlemen went shooting', the women stayed at home, occasionally playing 'furious games of tennis-battledore in the banqueting room'. Between the endless round of meals, there was little else to do except gossip. Problems with servants was one of the favourite topics. 'I am worried by my new maid turning out huffy with the Duke's household, and unmanageable when I tell her to show my gowns to other people,'

*Approximately £4.5 million to £17 million at today's values.

grumbled Lady Frederick in her diary. 'This is the 4th I have had that has behaved ill in her rapports with some fellow-servant or other, and they have not a notion that they can be in the least to blame, though by their own showing (certainly in this one's case) all grows out of the pettiest jealousy and pride.' Hierarchy and precedence were preoccupations of the servants as much as they were of those they served.

Marriage was another constant theme in the daily round of gossip. Hours were spent discussing potential candidates and possible matches. In the mid-nineteenth century, the sons and daughters of the aristocracy were obliged to marry well. A 'good' match was never a romantic one; social rank and fortune were the priorities – love came last.

Milton's new celebrity status clearly cut no ice with Lady Frederick; the inference in her diary entry is that 'poor squinny dwarfish little Lord Milton' was the runt of the Fitzwilliam litter. But as Lady Frederick well knew, many were the congenitally defective – but immensely rich – Earls that had made good marriages. What intrigued her, and the reason for the gossip being worthy of note, was that Mary Butler had turned Milton down. Dark-haired and rather simple-looking, with a weak chin, Mary was no beauty. She was unlikely to receive an offer that would come close to matching his.

'It is no light thing to refuse such love and gives such pain,' Mary wrote to Milton's elder sister Fanny in the spring of 1867. 'I really think I was doing what I believe to be right and it won't let him hope anymore. Why should I be the disappointment of his life? Don't write to me dearest Fanny till you quite like to do so. I do not expect an answer to this – what is there to say?'

Since the summer of 1866, Milton had pursued Mary relentlessly, hoping to win her over. She was twenty years old – seven years younger than him – when they first met. The eldest daughter of the Marquess of Ormonde, she had grown up at the family's seat, the beautiful Kilkenny Castle in Tipperary in Ireland, where her father owned great tracts of land. Socially, she was as good a match for him as he was for her. His parents ought to have been thrilled. But despite Milton's love for Mary, for the second time in his life, Lord and Lady Fitzwilliam intervened in an attempt to wreck his chance of marriage.

Mary was warned off in the same way as Dorcas Chichester had been: she was told that Milton was mentally ill. Her initial reaction was not as his parents had intended: to begin with, it almost had the opposite effect. 'When I knew he was ill I so often thought whether I had any possible right to make a fellow creature so miserable,' Mary confided to Milton's sister Fanny, 'and it was very hard to see my way. Thank God that I believe that as it is, it is best, and if we wait He will show us how. I know that it has been good for me, you don't know the good it has done me, painful as it has been. I would not now even wish it had not been, as far that is as I myself am concerned by it. For him I would have given anything it might have been spared him.'

It is evident from Mary's letters to Fanny that she did not love Milton as he loved her. But in the 1860s, the absence of love was not a bar to marriage. On the contrary, daughters of the aristocracy who refused a good offer on romantic grounds risked incurring the wrath of their parents and the extreme displeasure of the family of the man they had spurned. In such cases it was usual for social relations to be broken off. Yet, after Milton had been jilted by Mary, the Ormondes and the Fitzwilliams remained on the best of terms.

Mary appears to have been ignorant of the Fitzwilliams' motives – and of the fact the family were secretly delighted by her refusal to marry Milton. 'It was very kind of you writing to me again,' she told Fanny. 'It was so very kind – you always seem to think of my trouble in this matter, instead of the arrogance and pain I have caused you and yours and I am so grateful to you.' The impression from reading Mary's letters is that she could not quite believe her luck at having escaped censure and social exile. 'Will you thank dear Lady Fitzwilliam for her more than kind letter to me, it was the greatest comfort to me,' and in a letter sent several weeks later, she looked forward to the prospect of seeing Fanny, and her sister Mary. 'You may be certain that if we are in London I shall not miss such a great pleasure as seeing you and dear Mary, as you say you will come! Please give her my very best love and to Lady Fitzwilliam and if it is not impertinent will you thank her from me for the kind way she spoke of me in her letter to Mama.'

Mary spent eighteen months agonizing over whether she should marry Milton; she finally turned him down in the spring of 1867. No words of his survive to demonstrate the heartbreak he must have suffered at being rejected by the woman he loved. But his anger at the way his family had behaved, and his determination to marry regardless of his parents, became clear in the events that transpired within weeks of the end of the affair.

In early July, Lady Fitzwilliam sent her eldest daughter a peevish note. 'Dearest Fanny, I have written to William [Milton] and to Laura – in short I have written till I am stupid – I hope your father will come back here tomorrow and that we may return to London on Monday Please God. Is the Guards Hall put off – find out and let me know.'

Without telling his parents, a month earlier, Milton had secretly proposed to Laura Beauclerk, the eighteen-year-old niece of the Duke of St Albans. Though Lady Fitzwilliam knew her son was about to get married, she had no idea where, or more crucially when. She had not met her future daughter-in-law; when she first heard the rumour of an engagement, she was not even sure of her name.

Little is known of Laura, beyond a photograph that survives, and the testimony of her granddaughter, Lady Elfrida. 'I never knew her,' she said, 'but they say she could charm the birds off the trees.' Both Laura's parents were dead. Her father had been tragically drowned six years earlier trying to rescue a lifeboat crew off the coast of Scarborough, and her mother had died when she was ten years old. Lord and Lady Fitzwilliam had no one with whom to connive, or on whom to put pressure to abandon the wedding.

The couple were married on 10 August 1867 in London at St George's, Hanover Square. Laura's ring was crafted from a piece of gold Milton had sieved from the Fraser River at Cariboo in British Columbia.

Admitting defeat, Lady Fitzwilliam confided in Fanny: 'May God grant that she poor little darling find a haven in our family,' she wrote to her daughter after the wedding.

Laura Beauclerk did not find a haven in the Fitzwilliam family; instead, for much of her married life, she and Milton sought refuge thousands of miles away in an isolated forest on the eastern slopes of the Allegheny Mountains in Virginia. Here, at Milton Hall, the house they built together, they could lead their own lives, free from the stigma the family attached to Milton's illness and free from the guilt – on both sides – that came with it.

Implicit in Milton's self-imposed exile was a condemnation of his family and the rigid conventions of his class. In April 1872 he left England for good. Laura was six months pregnant. En route to their new home in America, he arranged for the birth of their third child to take place in Pointe de Meuron, a dangerous and isolated spot in the heart of the Indian territories, north-west of Fort William in Canada.

The child was Billy.

Of all the episodes in Milton's life, this premeditated and inexplicable detour into the wilderness for the birth of his son and heir is the most mysterious.

In February 1872, Hannah Boyce, the midwife who delivered Billy, had been invited to attend an interview at 4 Grosvenor Square, the Fitzwilliams' house in London. 'The late Lady Milton asked me if I would go with her to Canada to attend her in her confinement which she expected in the following July,' Boyce said in her statement sworn before a Commissioner of Oaths in 1901. 'I agreed to go and we sailed from Liverpool on the 20th April 1872 in the steamship *Scotia*. It was quite evident that Lady Milton was then in the family way.'

The couple were barely in a fit state to travel. In the five years since their marriage Milton's health had deteriorated rapidly. His fits were occurring with greater frequency. Previously, as William Cheadle had noted in his diary during their travels through Canada, warning symptoms had appeared before an attack, enabling Milton to remove himself from prying eyes. But towards the end of the 1860s, they began to come without warning, forcing him to withdraw for longer periods from public life. Soon after returning from Canada, he had been elected MP for a constituency in the West Riding of Yorkshire. With increasing regularity, the newspapers carried announcements apologizing for the state of his health. His epilepsy was never mentioned, an elaborate excuse was invented instead. 'Lord Milton, MP,' reported *The Times* in 1869, 'has been obliged to withdraw temporarily from Parliamentary life in consequence of a severe attack of inflammation in the eyes, which required him to confine himself to a darkened room.' His illness prevented him from spending his last Christmas at Wentworth, where his position as the eldest son and heir required him to attend traditional events, such as the Boxing Day hunt. 'On Tuesday there was a really excellent hunt,' Lady Fitzwilliam wrote to her daughter in Ireland. 'Thousands out – 17 of the family on horseback, some more in a carriage – a grand day. Had a nice run round and killed in Cortworth on the side of the hill in view of a multitude, everybody seeming very happy. Your brothers were very grand – helping Father in every way to give pleasure to the poor people and seeming to enjoy their tasks. They certainly were rewarded by the enjoyment of a vast number of people. Dear William [Milton] is better but we dare not rely too much on his improvement yet . . .'

Laura's health was little better than Milton's. In the five years since their marriage, though she had borne Milton two daughters, she suffered from arthritis and a chronic kidney disease, and seems to have been ill as regularly as her husband. Frequently, according to announcements in the papers, they were unable to keep appointments because Lady Milton was 'not in a sufficiently strong state to travel'.

Yet, extraordinarily, given how fragile Laura was, Milton insisted on risking his wife's health on a transatlantic crossing when she was six months pregnant. After his own experiences on the SS *Anglo-Saxon* nine years earlier, he knew exactly how punishing, if not perilous, the crossing could be.

As it proved, Milton's health was hardly up to the journey

either. Writing to his parents midway across the Atlantic, he told them,

> The voyage so far has been pleasant and prosperous. Laura is pretty well, and so are the children, especially Daisy. Mabel has not been well but is better. As for myself I hardly know what to say – I feel very ill, and utterly unable to manage anything for myself and can only trust in God and leave everything to Dr Millar and to Laura to decide and most thankful I am to have such a man as Millar to go with us.

As a safeguard against poor health and the dangers of childbirth – and to help look after their two young daughters, aged two and three – Milton had asked the family physician, Dr Millar, to accompany them. Hannah Boyce, the midwife, and a nursemaid called Matilda (Tilly) Kingdon were also travelling in the party.

Laura's baby was due in July. After crossing the Atlantic, the Miltons had plenty of time to get to Callaghan, a small town on the eastern slope of the Allegheny Mountains, where they planned to settle. But rather than heading directly to Virginia, after arriving in New York on 30 April, they made their way to Fort William at Thunder Bay, on the Canadian side of Lake Superior. In the course of a journey spread over twenty-three days, they changed trains four times and caught six boats. Their final destination, Pointe de Meuron, nine miles upstream from Fort William on the Kaministiquia River, was so remote that the last leg of their journey was by canoe.

In her diary Tilly Kingdon recorded their arrival at the small Indian settlement:

> 25th May went to our woodland home. We were rowed up this delightful river by some half-breeds, and whilst on this delightful river the shades of night gathered around us and we were truly rowing on the river on a moonlight night. I saw (but happily not felt) for the first time in my life a mosquito, but by no means the last, as they were much too familiar during our stay here, we arrived at 10 p.m., and were received by one man, a half-breed, who only spoke very broken English. Babtiste

by name, he was busy outside the front-door making a fire on the ground, in the centre of three projecting pieces of wood, on which hung suspended by string a large iron pot, with water in. Our domicile was void of furniture, we made the dear children some beds on the floor, with their waterproofs and other wraps, and they were soon asleep. We had brought eggs with us, so that we had boiled eggs and tea, we did not undress, but made ourselves as comfortable as possible, and slept pretty well, the half-breeds laid on the kitchen floor.

Milton had chosen a small farmhouse for the birth of his child. Built of slatted timber, it was situated on its own, on a sharp bend in the river, surrounded by dense forests and steep cliffs. Aside from the large families of Indians that lived in wigwams clustered around an old Hudson Bay fur-trading post a mile or so downriver, there were no other people for miles around.

It was surely not the sort of place to bring a heavily pregnant wife and two small children. Certainly, Pointe de Meuron frightened Laura. Tilly Kingdon's journal shows that after a fight among the half-breeds, she was so upset that she became ill:

. . . the half-breeds came from the Fort very intoxicated, and fought, and used very abusive language to each other in their own tongue, which frightened her Ladyship very much. She was very ill indeed for 2 days and nights, but gradually recovered, as she gained her strength, she found her left leg was quite stiff, and she was unable to use it. Lord Milton got her two rude sticks from out of the woods to help her along a little . . .

The lengths to which Milton went in order to get his family to Pointe de Meuron, and the primitive conditions he exposed them to, indicate that he had a strong reason to be there. He wanted his child to be born in British territory, but why choose such a remote and hostile spot? Why not Toronto, or some other relatively civilized place instead? There is nothing to indicate that Milton had been to Pointe de Meuron before; in both his and Cheadle's account of their 1863 expedition, their route took them nowhere near it.

Could it have been because the small Indian settlement offered

Milton the seclusion to execute his plan to swap his wife's newborn child for Billy, if the baby was a girl? Re-reading Dr Millar's statement, he said, 'Excepting a Catholic priest and the household of the fort, there were no white people for many miles around, consequently no white women or children ever visited us, our only visitors were Indians – for the most part patients of mine – black flies and mosquitoes and plenty of them.' But in the town of Fort William, nine miles downriver from Pointe de Meuron, there were plenty of white women. Dr Millar was Milton's trusted physician: 'My intercourse with Lord and Lady Milton extended over a course of four or five years during which time, with few intermissions they were under my daily observation,' he told Billy's lawyers. Had Dr Millar conspired with Milton to introduce a substitute baby? Might he have had the connections in Fort William to obtain one?

Implausible, but not impossible. Back home in England, at Wentworth, Milton's family were suspicious from the outset. Flouting tradition, they refused to acknowledge Billy's birth, let alone celebrate it.

Yet there is a danger of reading too much into their silence. The Earl had done all he could to prevent his eldest son producing an heir; it may simply have been an expression of a fervently held wish – that his grandson Billy, the product in his mind of a corrupted bloodline, had never been born.

It is impossible to know whether, in 1902, Lady Alice had a genuine case against her nephew; whether she could have proved that he had been swapped at birth. The loss and destruction of Billy's opponents' papers, documents that could have told the other side of the story, that might have revealed the evidence against him – if it ever existed – means that it is not possible to say.

Ultimately, the conspiracy against Billy failed. Ironically, its failure had nothing to do with documents – the minutiae of sworn witness statements, the supporting evidence of either side. It turned instead, like so many of the dramatic moments in the Fitzwilliams' twentieth-century history, on sentiment.

Thirty years after Billy's birth, the bitterness and acrimony had not subsided. So powerful, so raw were these feelings, that at Wentworth, hours before the 6th Earl was buried, Lady Alice and her siblings could not bear the thought of their nephew being in the same room as their dead father's body.

A servant's errand gives the mystery of the impostor affair a final twist.

7

On the eve of the 6th Earl's funeral, a footman walked briskly through the Picture Gallery on the principal floor of Wentworth House. He was dressed in the Fitzwilliam livery. His hair was pomaded, he wore a stiff winged collar, a black tailcoat, knee breeches and buckled shoes. Rows of tiny silver buttons, embossed with a winged griffin and two coronets, ran up the sleeve of his jacket to just below the elbow. Instead of the usual white tie, he was wearing black tie and a black waistcoat, in mourning for the dead Earl.

He had been summoned by a bell to Cliffords Lodgings, a suite of bedrooms along the West Front. The Picture Gallery was the quickest route..A long red and white room, stretching fifty yards, bisected by impressive stone columns, it was one of the few connecting passages between the Palladian and baroque façades of the house. The intricate carving on the magnificent ceiling was picked out in gilt; the wooden friezes above the great oak bookshelves were also painted gold; so were the picture frames around the many old masters lining the walls. There was a portrait of Shakespeare that had once belonged to Dryden, a cupid by Guido, a Raphael, and a painting of Mary Magdalene by Titian. Though splendid, the gallery was cosily furnished and used as a sitting room by the family. A range of smells wafted through it: the heady scent from vases of hothouse flowers grown in Wentworth's greenhouses, the bitter smell of coal smoke from the grates that burnt along its length; the sweet tang of lime leaves, scattered discreetly along the skirting boards, the housekeeper's remedy for 'keeping mice away'.

Treading softly, his feet making little sound on the parquet floor as he hurried through the gallery, the footman knew from the gossip in the servants' hall, the flurry of hand-delivered notes and the tense, highly charged atmosphere in the house, that many of the assembled family members were not on speaking terms. Through rival camps of trusted servants, they were watching one another's every move. The upset had been caused by a rumour. It was said that earlier that day Henry Fitzwilliam had taken his nephew, Billy, to the Duchess of Kent room to pay his last respects to the dead Earl.

Turning right at the end of the Picture Gallery, the footman entered Cliffords Lodgings. Though modest in comparison to the state guest rooms, the bedrooms here commanded fine views over the oak trees in the Park, planted in the pattern of the troop formations at the Battle of Blenheim. His journey from the servant's cubicle at the bottom of Pantry Stairs, behind the Pillared Hall, had taken almost four minutes.

Quietly, precisely, he knocked on the door, the way he had been taught to. Henry Fitzwilliam, the Earl's oldest surviving son and the man at the centre of the rumours, handed him a note, instructing him to deliver it to his sister, Lady Alice, who was staying in another room in the house.

The note has survived. Everything else must be pieced together.

Written hurriedly, with a quill pen, on the distinctive duck-egg-blue Wentworth House notepaper, it was the final signal to Lady Alice that Henry would have nothing to do with the conspiracy to kick Billy out.

'Yes,' it read. 'Billy asked me to go with him to see dear Father. He said I would rather go with you than with anyone else. Father looked so calm, so peaceful – one could not wish anything else for him.

'As to Billy I am very fond of him. I think he is of me. I want to be a good friend to him for his own and for his father's sake.'

This last sentence, gently expressed, was dramatic in its implications. Henry had switched sides. Without his collaboration, Lady Alice was thwarted in her move to expose Billy as an impostor. Henry was the sole executor of the 6th Earl's will: if Lady Alice challenged Billy's identity in court, she would have to bring her case against her elder brother. After Billy, Henry was the next in line to the Fitzwilliam title and fortune. His opposition made a nonsense of any potential legal challenge. Lady Alice could hardly commence proceedings against her brother when he was not only adamant that those proceedings were inappropriate, but would ironically be the one person who stood to benefit were her claim to succeed.

Had Henry sided with Lady Alice and the other conspirators, everything might have been his: the Earldom, the coalfields, Wentworth, the fifty-room house in Grosvenor Square, the estate in Ireland, the portfolio of shares. But he turned his back on the chance to become one of the richest men in Britain.

To begin with, Henry had been part of the plot.

In the mid-1890s, when the impostor allegation was first made, he was nearly sixty years old; the lures of an Earldom and a huge fortune were tempting.

His entire life had been lived as heir 'de facto'. He was his father's favourite son, the one the 6th Earl had wanted to succeed him. He was the person on whom the Earl had depended in a crisis, and on whom he leant in times of grief, most notably when his brother, John, was killed on the lawn in front of Wentworth after the horse he was riding tripped and crushed him.

Henry had received a £200,000* bequest from his father – substantially more than his younger brothers, who were given £50,000 each. In appointing Henry the executor of his will, it seems the Earl had left it up to Henry to decide whether to contest Billy's succession or not.

It is possible that Henry came to doubt the validity of the evidence Lady Alice relied on to support her charge and was himself convinced by the documentation Billy had assembled to show that he was his father's son. Conceivably, he decided to place his family's interest above his own, electing to avoid the scandal that a high-profile legitimacy case would bring. Perhaps, if he had had a son of his own, his decision might have been different. Yet regardless of the reasoning that may have run through Henry's

* £14,468,000 at today's values.

mind, had he not been the man of principle that he was, if he had chosen to press the case against Billy, there is every chance he might have succeeded. In the days before DNA testing, the strange circumstances of Billy's birth might have made it difficult for his lawyers to prove his legitimacy in a court of law. Crucially, the documents Billy kept in his safe reveal that in certain respects his solicitors believed his case to be weak. In 1900, they were short of proof that the Earl regarded Billy as his heir. The one letter they held had been written eleven years earlier. They had nothing more up to date.

Twenty-five years after Milton's death, Henry's loyalty to his brother held strong. The message he sent to his siblings on the eve of the Earl's funeral was clear: he wanted to be a 'friend' to Billy 'for his own and for his father's sake'.

The relationship between the two brothers had been a primary one in both their lives. Henry was the one member of the Fitzwilliam family to have loved Milton unconditionally. From a young age he had been sensitive to his difficulties, and to his feelings. 'I know he often thinks that we do not care for him,' he wrote to his brothers and sisters, when he had urged them to club together to buy Milton a twenty-first birthday present. After Earl Fitzwilliam sent Milton into exile, Henry was the only one to see him off from Liverpool Docks. In later years, when Milton was living in self-imposed isolation in the wilds of North America, Henry continued to look after his brother. 'Only those who have been in great trouble far away from friends and help can guess how grateful we are to dear good Henry,' Laura wrote in 1874, after the family was quarantined by scarlet fever. 'His case arrived a few days ago and as we unpacked it the tears ran down William's face. He said "this is just like Henry". He, William [Milton] is now wearing the things Henry sent out. The baby is in one of Reggie's shirts which is just the thing to keep him warm after his scarlet fever. William gave an exclamation of delight when he saw the razors and Daisy said "Oh good old Uncle Henry to send razors to cut off Father's prickly beard, I shan't mind now when father kisses me."'

In a sanctimonious letter to Henry, his mother also thanked him for sending the things out to the young family. 'So you see dearest Henry,' she wrote, 'your kind help was well bestowed and it has given great pleasure to our dear William and anything that lightens and cheers his sorrowful existence is indeed a cause for gratitude to our Heavenly Father who does not willingly afflict the children of men.'

But perhaps the truest indication of Henry's sensitivity to his brother's feelings is to be found in his refusal to marry Mary Butler while Milton was still alive. Mary was the woman Milton had loved so passionately before his marriage to Laura. Henry and Mary married within five months of Milton's death, when Henry was thirty-six, and Mary thirty.

To the last, Henry stood by his brother; it was he who rallied the family to Milton's bedside when he died.

On Sunday 14 January 1877 a telegram arrived at Wentworth. It was from Laura: Milton was in Rouen, desperately ill. Henry left for France immediately. From Victoria station in London, as he waited to catch the train to Dover, he wrote to warn his sister Fanny, who was living in Ireland and who had also been close to Milton.

> I fear that dear William is very seriously ill and that any improvement must be very slow while a turn for the worse which might come on any time would make his condition very dangerous. Darling Fan I can't disguise from myself and must not hide from you that the time may not be long; I can not pray to have such a life of sickness and misery prolonged when if God takes him he will be so happy. As he has had sorrow here so may he have happiness in heaven.

Three days later, Milton died. He was thirty-seven years old. What he died of, and why he was in northern France, we do not know. As with so much of his life, there is no official record.

Milton was buried at Wentworth in a quiet, private ceremony. 'There was little to indicate the exalted position of him to whose memory the last tribute was being paid,' reported the local newspaper. 'The funeral route was the shortest and most private which could be chosen, more than half of it being through the gardens at the back of Wentworth House, and the work of the bearers was consequently much lighter than it would have been had the road through the Park and the village been selected.'

Milton's funeral was in stark contrast to the lavish send-off usually accorded to an eldest son. As Michael Bond, Milton's great-grandson, remarked, 'They tried to sneak him out the back way.'

It was Henry who chose the words inscribed on Milton's tomb.

> Fear not for I have redeemed thee,
> I have called thee by thy name,
> Thou art mine
>
> (Isaiah 43)

In siding against Alice and his other brothers and sisters, Henry headed off a scandalous court case that would have damaged the Fitzwilliams' reputation. Yet days after the old Earl was buried, he was caught up in the fallout from the family dispute that he had done his best to ensure would remain private. Incredibly, for a man who had just inherited the early-twentieth-century equivalent of more than £3 billion pounds, so great was Billy's hatred of his Aunt Alice that he would spend the next two years disputing the ownership of a handful of worthless trinkets and a few ordinary tables and chairs.

On 15 March 1902, less than three weeks after his grandfather's funeral, word reached Billy that his aunt had been 'thieving'.

Alice had hedged her bets. She knew that if she failed in her bid to oust her nephew, when Billy succeeded to her father's title and fortune, she would be turned out of Wentworth House. Furtively, in collusion with a number of her sisters and behind the rest of the family's back, she had been preparing for that day for years. From early in 1896, Alice had systematically removed large quantities of furniture and other household goods from Wentworth and from Coollattin, the Fitzwilliams' Estate in Ireland. The last wagonload of booty had been smuggled out under Billy's nose: it had left Wentworth a few days after the old Earl died.

Billy was incensed when he was tipped off about the thefts. Not knowing what had been stolen, or where the 'spoil', as he called it, had been hidden, he instructed his solicitor, Mr Barker, to confront his Aunt Alice. Reporting back to Billy, Barker wrote:

I asked her to furnish me with a statement, showing all the articles which have been removed from Wentworth and Coollattin since the 5th April 1896 with the date of removal and showing the various articles which are claimed by her and her sisters specifying in each case upon what circumstances such claim is founded. I spoke about the things which had been removed from Wentworth since the late Earl's death and told her they should be returned and she has promised to ascertain what they were and where they are.

Alice refused to return the things. Nor would she reveal what had been removed. As Billy's solicitor discovered, she had hidden her 'spoil' well. Scattered around London, it had been stored at numerous furniture warehouses, or deposited at 'places of safekeeping', as Alice termed them. These included the London and Westminster Bank, the department store Barkers of Kensington, Mr Muntz's antique shop in Bond Street, and her sister Mary's house in South Street.

Under pressure from Billy and his solicitors, Alice finally produced an inventory. It ran to twenty-three pages – a list of more than 1,000 items. In spite of their number, their total value amounted to no more than a few hundred pounds. An extract from the inventory shows that most of the articles taken from Wentworth were pieces of day-to-day household furniture:

Pink bedroom: Easel, dressing stool, bath and footstools, looking glass, cupboard, bed and bedding, small square zither table.

Sitting-room: 3 round tables, small square table, 3 common easels, carved wood bracket shelves, blue backed music stand, small easy chair, 3 small occasional chairs, rough drawing table, small round table with a centre leg, small book cupboard and a rush bottom stool; 2 silver gilt tea spoons in case, silver gilt inkstand, small brass standard lamp, a pair of velvet frames.

Billy carefully went through every page of the inventory, determined to challenge anything he could. Placing a tick beside the items he believed to be his, he insisted they should be returned. Claim followed counter-claim, as aunt and nephew fought each other for particular items. Alice was adamant that she had only removed things that had belonged to her, claiming that she had bought them, or that they had been given to her by her parents or by other members of the family. She had stored a sizeable number of items at 4 Grosvenor Square, the Fitzwilliams' palatial London residence. Under the terms of the old Earl's will, Alice and her sisters were bequeathed the right to live there for twelve months after his death. Billy did not have access to the house. Fearing that in the course of their remaining tenure his aunts would steal yet more of his inheritance, he asked his trustees to instruct Messrs Robinson, a firm of probate valuers, to take an inventory. Not only did they list the heirlooms – the usual practice when settling a large estate after a death – they itemized the entire contents of the house. Their inventory shows that even in the servants' rooms they were meticulous to the last:

4th and 5th housemaid bedroom: coal scuttle and scoop, shovel, kettle, linen basket, poker, wire fireguard, paper basket, two brass beds, a hammer and a broom.

The argument between Billy and his aunt tore through the family, causing further bitterness and anger. Henry, as the executor of the old Earl's will, was compelled to act as mediator: his integrity, his sense of fair play and his exasperation at the behaviour of his brothers and sisters – and theirs at his – emerge in his reply to a letter from his younger brother, Charles, who had asked him to go to London to mollify Alice.

Dear Charley
I am very sorry Alice is seedy. I don't agree with you about my going up to London.

I want everything to be on a business footing, so far as my business is concerned. I am not inclined to go and talk soft meaningless nothings with people who think nothing of doing their best behind my back to blacken me in any way they can. What is necessary is that everything taken from Wentworth after Father's death, without my knowledge, shall be returned, and that satisfactory evidence shall be shown as to the ownership of all the items in that enormous list of things claimed. No one wants Alice or anyone else not to have what belongs to them, but surely, in a case of this kind, common sense will say that the claims must be satisfactorily substantiated.

I write in plain terms to you; if I write a business letter to my sisters I am supposed to be a devil and a wretch.

After a year of wrangling, an impasse had been reached: at the expense of huge legal bills, many times more than the articles under dispute were worth, Billy instructed Mr Barker to obtain further details from Lady Alice as to precisely why she claimed certain items were hers. In a letter, the deadpan tone of which was as absurd – given Billy's vast wealth – as the solicitor's instructions, he duly reported back to the Earl's secretary:

The inkstand and his reading glasses are said to have been given to Lady Alice by Mr Thomas Fitzwilliam. The brass standard lamp is said to have been given to Lady Alice by her sisters and others. The two silver open work Sardinieres (small oval), one silver basket, and the silver mounted claret jug are all stated to have been purchased by Lady Alice. As regards the six china handled knives, the handles are said to have been given to Lady Alice by the late Lady FW and she had the blades put in. The silver sugar basin (blue lining) and sugar sifter – this it is said was a Christmas present to Lady Alice from the late Lord Fitzwilliam given in the presence of Mr Charles Fitzwilliam and it is said that it is a copy of an original at Wentworth which Lord Fitzwilliam wished to give to Lady Alice, but which she refused. Silver cruet said to have been bought by Lady Alice.

After a year of passing endless marked-up lists to and fro, Billy's solicitor's patience had been tested to the limit. Barker closed his letter with the suggestion that the matter should be brought to a close:

> The case set up by Lady Alice seems to me to depend upon allegations of hers that such and such things were given to her by the late Lord and Lady FW and others.
>
> How far these allegations are warranted I do not know, but my experience is that in cases of this kind such allegations are always far more easily made than refuted, and I suppose (as for instance in the case of the Christmas present said to have been made in the presence of Mr Charles Fitzwilliam) Lady Alice would, if the matter were ever adjudicated in Court, produce some evidence in support of her contention. Moreover the onus of disproving the allegations made would, I think, rest on Lord Fitzwilliam.
>
> I know the intrinsic value of the articles in question is not the prevailing element in the matter as far as Lord Fitzwilliam is concerned, but it seems to me he must now decide whether he will acquiesce in the matter now put forward on the part of Lady Alice Fitzwilliam, or have the whole matter dealt with in a Court of law.

But as Mr Barker knew, the dispute had nothing to do with inkstands or sugar basins: it was about revenge, and the pursuit of a personal vendetta.

Ultimately, Billy decided not to pursue the matter in the courts. Nervous of the publicity a high-profile court case would attract, he had already exacted his revenge. Alice left Wentworth, her home since childhood, the day after her father's funeral. She never went back. One of the first things Billy did on becoming the 7th Earl Fitzwilliam was to turf her out of the house. Approaching her mid-sixties, after decades of living in the grand style, Alice was compelled to eke out her days on a small estate in Berkshire. Such was Billy's loathing for her that he did not even allow her to return to Wentworth to collect her things.

With 365 rooms at his disposal, Billy would spend tens of

thousands of pounds refurbishing Wentworth over the course of the next seven years. In transforming his grandfather's house, he was stamping his mark on it: after the rows and bitterness that had overshadowed his succession, at last it was truly his.

PART II

8

I don't know who my forebears were, for storied urns and animated busts are not in our family keeping. Our names are not preserved in ornate brass, and long stone effigies stiffly recumbent are not of us and our house.

We have no ancient banneroles: no antiquity of rags on poles; no ancient heraldry; no splendid armour of Castile.

No mediaeval parchment has our name, no cunning fingers traced our lineaments, or gave us awkward life upon the old-time screed. And yet we are not upstart here. Our roots are deeply driven in the earth; and all we are and all we have is of the soil – how intimately you who do not know the mine can never guess. Three hundred years and more my horny-handed forebears were wrestling with the coal.

Roger Dataller: *From a Pitman's Notebook*, 1925

In the 1920s, 'Roger Dataller' – or Arthur Eaglestone, as his real name was – worked at New Stubbin colliery, one of the Fitzwilliams' pits. Writing under a pseudonym for fear of losing his job, he was one of a number of miners to record the working conditions underground.

Coal, one of the most emotive subjects in twentieth-century British politics, lies at the heart of the story of the Fitzwilliam family. In the first decades of the century, within a thirty-mile radius of Wentworth House, there were more than 120 collieries, employing some 115,000 men.

In photographs from the period the miners are of similar stature, short, with broad shoulders, and chests out of kilter with the rest of their frame. Coalmining was in their blood. It had shaped their bones. They were the children and grandchildren of men and women who had started work in the mines as young as five years old.

For generations of miners, the pit had a magnetic, almost

mystical draw. Writing of his childhood in the years before the First World War, Jim Bullock, a miner at Bowers Row, a colliery village near Castleford, remarked,

As kids we used to dodge the watchman and sneak up to the shaft mouth, and sometimes we used to climb over the guard fence and look down into the inky blackness of the pit shaft. Then we would throw a stone over and listen to its descent into the very bowels of the earth. We used to come away from this daring adventure very subdued, awed by the fearsome depth and blackness and sheer size of it all. But these shafts still drew us back, time after time, with a sort of hypnotic compulsion. Practically every kid in the village had a relative mauled, broken, or killed by this pit, and yet we still played round it and we all knew as we grew up, no matter what we did, that some day it would claim us.

'"Well, aye, aye", as we broad Yorkshire people say – but the Pit will claim its own. Seventy-five per cent? Perhaps it may be more,' another miner said.

In the pit villages of the West Riding, previous generations of miners, their experiences, and the conditions they had had to endure, were not forgotten: remembering was an integral part of life.

'The times I liked best of all, were when the twelve of us were all sitting round the fire with my father talking, particularly about his boyhood and the things that happened when his father was a lad,' Jim Bullock recalled. 'He used to talk about the flooding of a mine in which there were forty-four children. Only eighteen escaped, twenty-six drowned. He used to tell us then about his father and mother – that was my grandfather and grandmother – how they were carried on the back of their parents to work in the pit.'

On street corners, groups of old men held court, young boys clustered around them, listening, fascinated, in the words of one, to the tales of 'accidents, explosions, good bosses and bad bosses' they had to tell.

In the mid-nineteenth century the Government published a

report in which men, women and children recorded, in their own words, the conditions underground. Their experiences were the Yorkshire miners' heritage; their fathers and grandfathers had been boys like seven-year-old John Saville, who, in 1842, worked as a 'trapper' at a Sheffield pit.

I've worked in the pit about two weeks. I stand and open and shut the door all day. I'm generally in the dark and sit me down against the door. I like it very well. It doesn't tire me. I stop 12 hours in the pit. I never see daylight now except on Sundays. They don't ill use or beat me. I fell asleep one day and a corve ran over my leg and made it smart. When I go home I wash myself and get my drinking [supper] and sit me down on the house floor. I've tea and bread and butter to my drinking. I've sometimes dry bread, sometimes bread and cheese and sometimes red herring and potatoes to my dinner [lunch] in the pit. I know my letters. I've never been to school at all. I go to Park Sunday School and they teach me writing. I go to chapel every Sunday. I don't know who made the world. I've never heard of God.

Thomas Moorhouse, ten years old, an orphan, was also interviewed by Samuel Scriven, one of the Sub-Commissioners of the Report. When Thomas's body was examined, it was covered in wounds from his master's belt.

I ran away from him because he used me so bad. He stuck a pick twice into my bottom. He used to hit me with the belt and fling coals at me. When I left him, I used to sleep in the cabins upon the pit bank and in the old workings, where I laid upon the shale. I used to get what I could to eat and for a long time ate the candles that the colliers had left behind. I had nothing else to eat.

Boys of Thomas's age were employed as 'hurriers' to haul corves of coal weighing up to 6 cwt through the tunnels.

David Swallow, a miner in his fifties, described the conditions in which the boys worked.

The roads are very wet in some of the pits. The boys are continually wet at their feet, sometimes plastered up to their knees in dirt and sludge as bad as any coach horse can possibly be. With being continually wet on their feet and legs they have inflammations in those parts, on their legs and knees. Boils and rheumatism in all parts of the body, particularly in their lower parts, in all their different stages and degrees. A loaded corve is about 6cwt. Where the road rises very fast, it is very heavy work indeed, so that they have to have large pads fixed to their heads and then the hair is very often worn off, bald and so swollen as that sometimes it is like a bulb filled with spongy matter, so very bad after they have done their day's work, that they cannot bear it touching.

In the 1840s, women, as well as young children, were employed underground. Samuel Scriven saw women and girls 'chained, belted, harnessed like dogs in a go-cart, black, saturated with wet and more than half-naked, crawling upon their hands and knees and dragging heavy loads behind them'.

In 1900, sixty years after the Royal Commission reported, Britain's status as the richest and most powerful nation in the world depended on coal. It was her biggest export: it powered the factories and the vast network of railways spawned by the Industrial Revolution; it fuelled the steamships that carried her trade around the world, and the Imperial Fleet that protected them.

But the human cost of its extraction was high. Although women, and children under the age of thirteen, had been banned from working underground, more than a million miners worked in conditions that had barely improved since the Commissioners reported in 1842. Thousands were killed or seriously injured every year. In pit villages across the country, the miners and their dependants – estimated to embrace over 10 per cent of Britain's population – lived in appalling conditions, oppressed and exploited by the coal owners and forced to endure grinding poverty during periods of slowdown. For the majority, there was no safety net: no unemployment, sickness or injury benefit.

In the first decades of the twentieth century, 88 per cent of the British population owned nothing. As defined by the statisticians, it meant they were worth less than £100. One per cent of the population owned two-thirds of the nation's wealth. Over the years that followed, in the battle to redress the flagrant social injustices inherent in these statistics, coal would become the driving force behind social, political and economic reform: the quest by those who owned nothing to have something.

The South Yorkshire coalfield was one of the key battlefields on which this class war was fought out. On a bitterly cold morning in the winter of January 1903, some of the first salvos were fired in a village eight miles from Wentworth House.

9

They called it 'a hell upon earth'. The worst village in England.

Standing at the head of the Don Valley in the shadow of a chain of rocky north-facing limestone slopes known as the Crags, Denaby was a pit village of 8,000 inhabitants. Writing in a state of 'numb despair', one visitor said that what he had to describe was 'so repulsive that many who have never been near it will probably refuse to credit the story'.

Denaby was not a village that any visitor would be pleased to see. Most days, it was very hard to see at all, shrouded by a pall of smog that rose at 4.30 every morning, as if a switch had been thrown, a blue-grey blanket of smoke lifting from a thousand waking homes. Four thousand miners were employed at Denaby's two pits, each receiving a monthly allowance of a ton of coal. Fires, used for heating, hot water and cooking, were lit every day. Summer or winter, an hour before the start of the morning shift, coals were mended in grates that had smouldered overnight, sending plumes of smoke furling from the village chimneys. Seeping upwards, high above the village, the thick smog blotted the view of the Don Valley from the Crags.

On the morning of 6 January 1903, there were no home fires burning at Denaby. For the first time in living memory, as the sun rose over the Crags, the valley could be seen stretching to the west. In the mid-distance were slag heaps, railway tracks and clouds of drifting steam: crowding the near horizon were the smokestacks, headstocks and foundries of Sheffield, Rotherham and Barnsley: beyond, in the far distance, lay the thin green line of the Derbyshire hills. The familiar sounds of heavy industry that, in the words of one miner, 'filled the air, twangling and discordant, like Prospero's magic island', floated in from far away.

Looking down from the Crags on to the grids of terraced

housing, months of trauma were evident in the scene below. The two collieries, Denaby and Cadeby Main, towered over the village, their headstocks immobile. Nothing moved: empty wagons, packed close together or randomly abandoned, clogged the thick lines of railway metals that tangled and twisted through the village, the arteries that moved the coal around and out of the pits. The winding machines on the slag had stopped. The village was as still as the Don, the river that slugged between the two collieries. Putrid and stagnant, it had long lost its silver of legend; even the village children were warned from its banks.

A few hours after dawn, a column of 200 policemen, drafted in from around the county, snaked through the centre of the village, the iron on their heavy toe-capped boots sparking on the cobbles. They had come to evict 3,000 families from their homes.

The authorities were expecting trouble: unconfirmed reports indicated that miners in the neighbouring pits would declare a 'play' day and flock in their thousands to the village to demonstrate against the evictions. Four companies of troops were on standby at Sheffield and York, and a force of more than 100 policemen stood in reserve, ready to be moved in by train at the first sign of trouble.

A large number of Denaby's 8,000 residents lined the square and the streets leading into it, watching the police march past. 'Suffering was etched on the faces in the crowd,' wrote the Reverend Jesse Wilson, the Minister of the Methodist Chapel.

We had the women between the 30s and 50s, whose mouths were many, but whose crusts were few. The troublous times had put 20 years upon many of them, and they looked old and haggard long before their age warranted it. Hardships were saddening and making the distance between themselves and the grave perceptible. The cry of the children was breaking their hearts. We had the boys and girls with corduroy suits falling to pieces and muslin frocks hanging together by threads, shoes out at the toes, while the stocking feet were gone altogether. Their pinched faces indicated pinched stomachs. They were hungry and you could see it.

The children crackled and rustled when they moved; sheets of newspaper were layered under their clothes to provide extra warmth.

The Denaby miners had been on strike for twenty-seven weeks. Their houses belonged to the 'Masters', the Denaby and Cadeby Main Collieries Company, one of the most oppressive and ruthless companies in the South Yorkshire coalfield. It had issued the eviction orders to coerce the men back to work.

Miners in villages nearby, working at family-run pits like the Fitzwilliams', called Denaby a 'rough 'oyl', 'a reet plecque', meaning a very bad place. 'You hadn't much trouble at the family pits, Fitzbillies [Earl Fitzwilliam's], etc. There weren't much trouble, you know, at little pits. You see, there was a stronger set of owners at Denaby, they could rule the roost,' recalled Fred Bramley, a miner at Denaby Main. 'I heard it quoted that the owner, Mr Buckingham Pope, said that he had a square yard of gold and he'd sink it before the miners would win.'

Six months earlier, the strike had begun with an argument over a layer of dirt.

'Bag muck', an uneven seam of soft dusty rock that ran between the beds of coal, was one of the banes of a collier's life. Up to eight inches thick, it had to be removed before the coal could be mined. Faceworkers were paid according to the amount of coal they extracted, rather than the number of hours they worked. Time spent bagging the muck cost the miners money. Most collieries in the South Yorkshire coalfield paid their men a separate rate for bringing it out of the pit. But not at Denaby. In the months before the strike, the faceworkers were coming across seams of dust that were as much as forty inches thick. When they refused to remove the dirt, the company drafted in extra labour to bag it, deducting the cost from the miners' wages. On 29 June 1902, they downed tools and walked out of the pit. The bag muck dispute involved just 180 men at Denaby Main, yet the entire workforce of both village collieries – 3,500 men – came out with them.

Twenty-seven weeks later, the strike had long ceased to be

about dirt. On the miners' part, after months of hardship, it was a stand against the sway of the coal owners.

The company was typical of a new set of owners that emerged in England's coalfields in the second half of the nineteenth century: the corporate coal owner.

At Denaby, there were no family or territorial ties, no shared memories and experiences stretching back through centuries to lend a semblance of binding between the masters and men. Duty, loyalty, responsibility, concern – even affection – all seams in the complex layer that characterized the Fitzwilliams' relationship with their colliers, were absent at the company's two pits.

Both masters and men were outsiders, drawn by the lure of large profits and wages.

The company, formed by a syndicate of West Midlands prospectors, had come to Denaby in the early 1860s – frontiersmen in the coal rush that swept along the eastern edge of the Barnsley seam in the last decades of the nineteenth century.

Before the two pits were sunk, Denaby was a small rural hamlet with a population of 204. It lay in open country on fertile agricultural land. In summer, lavender and corn grew in the fields that were broken by copses of dark elms. In 1863, the syndicate leased the land from the local gentry in return for mineral royalties on any coal it found. Four years later, coal was struck beneath the limestone, a quarter of a mile underground. By 1900, the two pits, Denaby and Cadeby Main, employed 4,000 miners and were among the most productive in South Yorkshire, producing one and a half million tons of coal a year, all of it hewn and shovelled by hand.

To accommodate the miners, the company had constructed some of the worst slum housing in the north of England.

One key opened the front door of all but three of the houses in the village, every one of them built from the same mud-yellow, coal-blackened brick. There were rows and rows of them, over 1,000 in total. Two-storeyed, two-up, two-down, terraced houses, hastily and cheaply constructed. Laid out in grids, they straddled the pit. Forty-nine houses were crammed to an acre: there was not a patch of green or a tree in sight. A local miner described them:

> The oldest houses have been built in the backyard of the colliery itself: rows of grim boxes identical in size, and conceived, one feels, in the mind of some satanic toymaker. The bare yards are unpaved – a pother of dust in the dry weather, a quagmire in wet. I find it impossible to think of Denaby without an inordinate impulse to seize upon the architect of this monstrosity and haul him by the nose through the horror of his own creation.

Winter or summer, sweeping a six-square-yard area in front of the houses yielded two barrowloads full of dust or muck.

Phyllis Holcroft, a mother of ten, lived in one of the houses. For a family of twelve, it consisted of a living room, kitchen, scullery and two bedrooms upstairs. It had no water, gas or electricity. She wrote an account of what it was like to live there.

> It's a dirty hole, dust getting everywhere. It blows in from the backs and under the door at the front. You can never open the windows, what with the dust and the stink from the middens. There's no garden for the children to play, only the area round the dustbins and W.C.s. There's damp walls, damp floors, walls and floors leaving each other. It's a wonder I don't go off my head with worry keeping the place. There's ten of us in here it's a mercy the middle lads are on nights at the pit. Where would the young uns sleep besides? There's four of them in the back room at the top. The two lads take the bed when they come off the shift. The girls – our Sheila and our May – sleep with us. We're always ill what with sleeping altogether all crowded in.

'People from the other places roundabout looked down on you,' remembered Robert Shepherd, a miner from Denaby. 'The houses were lacking in many amenities, the streets were very close together and the sanitation was poor.'

The houses cost 5 shillings a week to rent, the company

deducting the money from the miners' wages to ensure they never got behind with the rent. They had no running water: there were no lavatories or sinks. One tap served each street. All household rubbish, including human waste, went into 'middens' – open-sewer trenches.

The middens were in the 'backs', the name given to the narrow lane that ran behind the terraces – the area where the children played and the women hung out their washing. The back door of each house opened directly on to the lane. Opposite, at a distance of less than five yards, was a long low building, where there was a lavatory for every house. The midden trenches ran underneath it.

'Each midden served a WC on either side so that with the cinders from the fires continually piled into this and a convenient shovel, any person using the WC on either side, could straight away be able to cover their tracks, (so to speak) by shovelling down sufficient cinders on to the disgusting trench below,' remembered Tom Hibbard, a miner living in Denaby. 'We always had to make sure that our "midden" had plenty of cinders available. We had our own doors with just a board with a central hole inside. I know I was always glad to get out away from the flies that were everywhere.'

The middens were emptied by hand. Once a week, the 'night-soil' men, armed with shovels, would pile the muck from the trenches into a sewage cart, releasing a noxious smell that lingered for days. Epidemics of typhoid, enteric fever, diphtheria and other faeces-borne diseases were common in the village; unsurprisingly, infant mortality rates in 1899 were 250 in every 1,000.

Visiting Denaby at the turn of the century, a Church minister wrote:

The ruin of the children is especially sad. The first thing that impressed me when walking down the main street at Denaby was the large number of children with sore eyes. I saw more ophthalmic girls in the street in twenty minutes than I see in the slums of London in twenty days. 'We've had an epidemic of it about for some months,' people in the village told me, as though that explains everything. Yes, but why do epidemics of ophthalmia come? Because the home life is defective and because children are not properly and individually cared for. 'It's the dirt as does it,' one man frankly told me.

The minister was appalled by the company's 'despotic powers', which he believed caused the miners to drown their sorrows in drink. The entire village was owned and run by the company: the houses, the shops, the church, the pub. It knew how much its miners drank, whether they were religious, which of their children were causing trouble on the streets, how much individual families spent on food and whether their credit status was good or bad at the local shop. It even had its own police force to round up children playing truant from school, and drunken miners after closing time at the pub. Owning the only public house in the village gave the company a profitable monopoly over drinking. As one miner commented ruefully to a colliery policeman who had taken charge of him for being drunk and disorderly, 'This is a funny place, first we go to the pit office to get the money, then the Company gives us a place where we can pay the money back to it, and then, when the money's gone, it provides you to take care of us.'

'Care' did not feature in the company's equation. It did not need to. In 1903, a coal owner had few statutory obligations. Pensions, health benefits, compensation for deaths and injuries in the workplace were optional. Wages, too, were optional; coal owners were not legally bound to pay a minimum, or even a weekly, wage. Miners across the country were paid piecemeal for the amount of coal they extracted. When trade was bad, the Denaby and Cadeby Main Collieries Company, like many other coal owners, closed the mines, or put its miners on short-time, meaning the colliers earned less, or nothing. Even the weather had a bearing on take-home pay. The main market for Denaby's coal was Eastern Europe and Russia. If the Baltic Sea froze, the pits would stop; no wages were paid until the sea thawed.

At the turn of the twentieth century, the Welfare State was not there to catch a man when he fell. The miner's financial security, the quality of his life, his very existence, was entirely dependent on the character of the owner of the pit.

Death, more than anything else, was the hallmark of a coal owner. In the years leading up to the First World War, over 1,000 men were killed annually in Britain's coalmines. In the majority of cases, so violent was the way of dying that there was little left of the miner. His body was scraped off the walls of a tunnel, or swept from the floor, and put in pieces into a sack.

Arthur Eaglestone, the miner at the Fitzwilliams' New Stubbin colliery, described the first time he witnessed a death underground:

He was quite dead when we found him – squashed by a fall of stone. The smell of blood was everywhere, a slaughterhouse reek, and sickening. His body seemed to be almost completely covered by the tremendous boulder that had fallen. Only one hand was visible and the upper portion of his forehead – nothing else. His mate wept openly, speaking sometimes with a strangled incoherence, a clucking babble of words, but no one took much notice, for the man was dead enough, and the only help we wanted was in rolling the stone away. If trembling went for anything we were all goosey. I didn't want to stay. I didn't want to look on IT! My heart sickened at the thought of all that mangled flesh. So craven of spirit I slid my lamp around my thigh, seeking comfort in the shadow that my body threw upon the rock.

'If the jack's not coming,' said Morgan, 'we'll try again. All together . . . now then . . . heave ho!' We gathered in, crowding against the protuberance like Rugby players in a football scrum. Our fingers touched the hard rock gingerly at first, as though it held some sacred quality, but Morgan's harsh controlling voice with 'Now then, no playing! put to it . . . put to it! . . . all ready? . . . heave!' inspired us to lofty physical effort . . . and so we pushed . . . the stone lifted. 'Shove the block in,' hissed Morgan, 'quick! . . . now . . . heave! . . . ah!'

Oh! he was there all right. The first thing that I saw was the sloppy pool of dirt that was his body. And then his face all coal and wax in the midst of which two eyes wide open, staring, shone strangely golden in the swinging lamplight, with the same illumination that a cat's have, in firelight, or sunlight.

And then again in thick and cloying waves, the stench of blood . . . the indrawn sighing of the rescuers . . . the thin insistent hissing of the face itself . . . S-S-S-S-S.

The hiss, from the coalface, came from gas, a serial killer underground.

Mortality rates depended on conditions at the pit. No pit was the same. There were hot pits, wet pits, cold pits. The miners likened them to a woman: each had its own particular bad and fickle moods, the 'she-devil' waiting to take her revenge in human lives.

Denaby, 422 yards deep, and Cadeby, 118 yards deeper, were hot pits. It was estimated that the mean rate of increase in temperature was 1 degree Fahrenheit for every forty-six feet in depth. On a warm summer's day, the temperature in the tunnels rose to well over 100 degrees.

The 'she-devil' at Denaby was gas. The deeper the pit, the greater the danger from firedamp, chokedamp or blackdamp, the names the miners gave to the natural gases that lurked between the strata of rock and coal.

Firedamp could blow a man to pieces or bury him under a fall of stone. Chokedamp, released into the atmosphere following an explosion, could suffocate him. If the rescue party failed to arrive, death by chokedamp was slow. Michael Smith, trapped with forty miners on the wrong side of a roof fall in the Seaham explosion of 1880 – a disaster that claimed 164 lives – had hours to scratch a message to his wife on his tin water bottle before he died. His death was a double tragedy: the couple had recently lost their youngest child:

Dear Margaret there were 40 all together at 7 am. Some were singing Hymns, but my thoughts were on my little Michael that him and I would meet in heaven at the same time. Oh Dear Wife, God save you and the children and pray for me Dear Wife. Farewell, my last thoughts are about you and the children, be shure and learn the children to pray for me. Oh what an awfull position we are in.

In 1903, Denaby and Cadeby were among the deepest and most dangerous pits in the country; in the previous decade, thirty-nine miners had been killed, compared to five, for example, at the Fitzwilliams' two collieries.

The man Arthur Eaglestone pulled from under a stone was lucky to work for the Fitzwilliams. The family paid compensation to the widows of miners killed at their pits; they were also given a pension and subsidized housing. At Denaby, it was company policy to evict the dead miner's family from their house within weeks of bereavement. 'Those days, the only form of compensation a miner had was a club-round by the other workmen,' George Cheshire, a miner at Denaby, recalled, 'and if they didn't lose a day's work the company put in the same amount as that collected.'

This meagre gesture was brutal in its deliberate flouting of a long-cherished tradition. Historically, after a fatal accident, as a mark of respect to the dead man and his family, the miners had stopped work and come out of the pits. In the early 1900s, when the average wage at Denaby was 28 shillings a week,* the widows' collections rarely amounted to more than £10 or £12. The company lost thousands of pounds when the miners stopped the pit, yet still it refused to pay out compensation for a death; it knew that its offer to match the 'club-round' would force the men to continue their shift.

By default, the miners had their own barbaric practices. Such was the imperative of compensation, however small, that at Denaby and Cadeby Main, and at other collieries in the South Yorkshire coalfields, a dead man sometimes died twice. No coal owner paid out compensation, however small, to the widow of a man who died a natural death underground. For the sake of their wives and children, the miners mutilated the bodies of heart attack victims, or men who had died from some other natural cause. 'Well, he was dead now and there was to be no compensation,' wrote Jim Bullock, from Bowers Row colliery, 'so three or four of such a man's mates would pull him under an old prop which supported

* £101 at today's values.

a bad piece of stone. They would lay him there, knock the prop away and let the muck bury him. He was then taken out killed. A compensation would have to be paid.'

In the absence of a benevolent coal owner, jeopardy and uncertainty were the keynotes of a collier's existence. The dangerous conditions in the workplace, the poor sanitation at home, the lack of available medical expertise, hovered over his family life. He lived on a roller-coaster, never knowing what he would be earning the following week. He could be injured, or ill. Rheumatism or nystagmus, or any one of a number of illnesses miners were prone to, might stop him from working. The pit might close, or lay him off, or put him on short time. In coal-mining villages across England at the turn of the twentieth century, so frequent was short-time working, that it was customary for a flag to be run up, or a bellman sent round every evening, to announce whether or not the pit would be operating the following morning.

At Denaby, for 3,500 miners and their families, the roller-coaster was about to dip.

At 9.30 on the morning of 6 January 1903, the column of 200 policemen marched out of the main square in the village, heading for Firbeck Street, the first of ten rows of terraced housing they were under orders to clear that day.

A grim procession rumbled edgily through the narrow streets. The roads into the village, wet from the previous day's rain, had been churned to a bog by scores of carts and drays, sent in sympathy by tradesmen from the neighbouring towns of Mexborough, Conisbrough and Doncaster, to help the miners move the contents of their homes. The wagons now formed up in single file behind the columns of policemen, followed by thousands of villagers.

The police cordoned off Firbeck Street at both ends. A guard of mounted officers and a dozen men on foot formed a barrier against the crowds. The side streets and the entrances to the 'backs' were also guarded. At the edge of the cordon, a lone organ-grinder played 'I Hear Thee Speak of a Better Land'.

A number of houses were already empty; their owners had 'flit' to avoid the shame of eviction. Sprigs of Christmas holly still hung in some of the windows, and in others the occupants had left painted signs: 'Not Lost, But Gone Before' and 'Happy New Year'; some simply read 'Gone For Ever'.

Starting at the top of Firbeck Street, the police worked their way down. At every house the procedure was the same: the miners and their families were asked to stand to one side while their possessions were removed from their homes. The heavier items were lowered down ladders from the upper windows by chains of policemen. Linoleum was torn from the floors, pictures taken from the walls, beds unfastened, the babies' cots and dolls bundled out. By midday, the streets resembled an impromptu open-air market; household effects were strewn along the length of them: mattresses, beds, chairs, tables, sofas, fenders, clocks, sewing and wringing machines, piled in heaps.

Reporters from local and national newspapers stood with the miners and their families, watching the evictions. 'There goes my beautiful Turkey carpet,' one man was overheard to say as a policeman deposited a tattered old hearthrug, woven from bits of old rags, on the road in front of him. On Annersley Street, one of the miners took on the role of auctioneer, ringing a handbell, shouting out inflated prices for the meagre possessions littering the streets. But despite the black humour, the distress – particularly among the women – as one reporter observed, was acute:

> Their eyes were strangely big and their white faces wore a look like that of the hunted hare when the dogs are on it. 'It isn't the police fault,' they said, 'they're only servants who've got to do as they're bid. It's him,' and their eyes went in the direction of the handsome colliery offices where the all-powerful managing director worked. One would break down and, with a sudden turn, would seek a corner alone in a still open house. In a minute or two she would come out again, her eyes red and swollen, but walking proudly as though to defy those who accused her of crying, and the men stood quietly whispering to one another.

On the first day of the evictions, the police cleared eighty-two families out of their homes. The expected trouble did not materialize; as one miner was heard to say, 'We have been quiet so far, and it will be better to be quiet now.' That night, the temperature in Denaby dropped 10 degrees. Hard frosts and snow were forecast. A further 650 families were to be turned out on to the streets over the next three days.

The evicted families had to find somewhere to go. For many it was difficult. Few had relatives in the area. Most of Denaby's inhabitants were immigrants who had come to the village in the last decades of the nineteenth century from Ireland, and from worn-out pits in the North Staffordshire and Shropshire coalfields. Many of the families – like Ernest Godber's – were large: 'My father moved to Denaby from Derbyshire. "There were fourteen of us altogether, mother, father and fourteen children. They didn't all come to Denaby though, one got run over with a steam-roller, and one got shot, doing summat he shouldn't a done I expect – that were afore I were one year old, but we heard about it anyways.' The Godbers were lucky to find accommodation at a shopkeeper's house in Mexborough. Others too crowded into small cottages belonging to friends in the neighbourhood. One woman, the mother of seven children, moved into a house where there were nine children already.

But of the 3,500 evicted, there were 267 men, women and children who had nowhere to go. They were looked after by the Reverend Jesse Wilson, Denaby's Methodist minister. A hundred and forty of them were housed at his chapel and at the school he ran; the remainder were put up in local authority tents erected in fields on the edge of the village.

Jesse Wilson was a miner's son who had grown up in the Yorkshire pit village of Castleford, south of Leeds. Before going to Denaby, he had preached for seventeen years in the Welsh valleys. There was a strong Methodist tradition in the pit villages in south Yorkshire, as there was throughout England's coalfields. The Church of England clergy owed their livings to the landowners and coal owners who were careful about the political outlook of the person they appointed to look after the souls and spiritual wellbeing of their miners. To be a Methodist was a mark of independence: as well as spiritual solace, it offered the miners a means of unguarded self-expression and conferred a sense of self-respect. Wilson's strong sympathy for the families sprang from his own experiences as a child. On the Sunday following the evictions, speaking from the pulpit, he told his depleted congregation why he wanted to help them:

When I was a boy a bitter struggle rose between Capital and Labour and my Father was thrown out of work through no fault of his own and I learnt to know what scarcity of food meant. During the strike, my mother was taken dangerously ill and I accompanied my father on foot to Leeds, a distance of about nine miles, to fetch medicine. Returning to the village, when we entered it, we were accosted by a neighbour who told us my mother had died. I'll never forget my father at that moment – a strong man bowed down by grief. Shortly after, two of my brothers also died. A kind friend came to our relief, and I now feel duty bound to do likewise.

Besides housing as many of the homeless as he could squeeze into his school and chapel, Wilson distributed food parcels and blankets and clothing to the families living in the fields outside Denaby. 'There were two classes of tent,' he recorded in his journal, 'the marquee and the bell-tents. In the former a large stove was fixed up for heating and cooking purposes: the latter being too small for a stove, it was fixed outside with pieces of wood nailed together to prevent the wind blowing out the fire. Beds were placed on wooden floors a few inches from the ground in the marquee, while in the bell-tents straw was spread over the wooden floor, and the mattresses placed on top.'

The tents had been erected at the bottom of a slope. Someone had hoisted a Union Jack on a pole, prominently displayed, at the entrance to the field. Water from the sleet, snow and rain that fell in the days after the evictions poured down the hill and saturated the grass, transforming it into a carpet of mud. Two children were born in the tents that January, both christened Jesse, a mark of gratitude to the Reverend. Two also died – one from blood poisoning after grazing his knee.

Sightseers in their thousands came by train to Denaby to look at the marquees. 'Many seemed to think it was a kind of peepshow minus the usual fee for admission,' wrote the Reverend Jesse angrily. In caring for the families, he saw at close hand the reality of their lives:

I was returning from an appointment in Conisbrough and determined to see how the people were faring. The air was dry, the wind intensely bitter and the ground crisp. I was muffled up to the mouth and yet shivered with cold; I failed to keep warm even when walking briskly. I reached the field and entered. I went into the marquee first and saw a sight which saddened and sickened me. A few feet from the stove were a man and a boy lying on a mattress with a thin covering over them. The boy was lying with his face to the man's back and with his arms over the man, pulling himself as closely to the man as possible to create warmth, and yet he shivered with cold. His teeth rattled in his mouth. I went to the bell-tents, and in one were five lovely children fast asleep, forgetful of the hard lot they were passing through. They lay on a mattress with a thin sheet thrown over them, while a few inches above their little heads was the tent canvas, blowing in and out at the pleasure of the wind.

10

It was first light, the Monday after the evictions at Denaby.

Along the road to the colliery, a sharp east wind shook the overhead gas mantles in and out of incandescence. Out of the gloom, shadowy figures converged. The stark mathematical outline of the colliery rose ahead of them, the spokes on the still pulley wheels grimly distinct.

That morning – 12 January 1903 – 3,000 miners had made an early start to attend a union meeting in a field adjoining the pit. Walking from their temporary lodgings in the neighbouring towns and villages, some had covered distances of seven or eight miles.

Two hundred yards behind the colliery, a few solitary policemen banged the last nails into the boarded-up windows in the houses. It had taken three days to turn 750 families out on to the streets, now deserted. 'Thank God it's over,' one policeman said, 'such pitiful work has never before been my lot.'

Fred Croft, the Chairman of the Denaby and Cadeby Main Strike Committee, addressed the men from a dray that had been wheeled into the field and now served as a makeshift platform. 'If we are beaten we are ruined,' he told them. 'If the struggle lasts another two years I hope you'll stand like braves to the foe. We have shown the world what we mean to do. We intend to fight on. We have put up with things thousands would not have stood. It is time the men of this country arose and said what should be done. If we do not take this step, conditions will become worse and worse. It is the men with the money who make the weak suffer.'

Croft's words – and the loud applause – carried over the empty streets behind.

'Dust thou art, and unto dust shalt thou return.' The colliery company, in what it believed to be a 'wicked and causeless strike', was equally determined not to give ground. It had taken the roof from over the miners' heads. To crush them into submission, its next step, in effect, was to threaten them with death.

Starvation was the company's chosen weapon of execution; the law courts, the executioner.

On 14 January, four days after the last families had been evicted, a judge in London ordered the miners' strike pay to be stopped.

From the outset, the company had claimed the payments were illegal. When the men walked out of the pits, they had been in breach of the Yorkshire Miners' Association's rules. It was a spontaneous action: no ballot was taken, nor did the men serve notice on the company. The union's rules stipulated that before strike action could be endorsed, any stoppage had to have a two-thirds majority by ballot, and that the men had to serve notice on their employers. Unless these rules were observed, the strike was unofficial and no strike pay could be disbursed. On 17 July, three weeks after the miners at the Denaby and Cadeby pits had gone on strike, to circumvent its rules for the purpose of issuing strike pay, the Yorkshire Miners' Association ordered the men to return to the collieries to serve notice on the company.

Days later, William Howden, a miner at Cadeby and one of the few opposed to the strike, took out an injunction against the union to prevent it distributing strike pay, claiming the stoppage was both illegal and unofficial. Howden was a company stooge. Lord Beveridge later remarked: 'The colliery company, wishing to make the strike impossible, were almost openly financing the nominal plaintiff and were really at the bottom of the action. Why they don't get sued for maintenance of another's suit I can't say.'

The company paid Howden's legal expenses and gave him a subsistence allowance while he pursued his case. It dragged through the courts for months. When it finally came to appeal in January 1903, the judge was clearly biased against the striking miners. At one point during the hearing, as Beveridge noted, he made his prejudice quite obvious, openly stating that he wanted the strike pay stopped in order to bring the strike to an end. He directed the jury to uphold the injunction on the grounds that the men had illegally broken their contracts on 29 June, and that they could hardly return to work on 17 July for the purpose of handing in their notices to terminate contracts that had been terminated three weeks earlier.

Strike pay was all the miners had to survive on. The weekly allowance of 9 shillings per man,* 1 shilling for every child under the age of thirteen, and 4 shillings and sixpence to lads – boys between the ages of fourteen and eighteen who worked at the pit – meant that, while many of the families in Denaby went hungry, they were not starving. But without strike pay, they would.

'It was a terrifying time for our people,' recalled Robert Shepherd, who was nine in January 1903, when the payments were stopped.

In the absence of the Welfare State, short of uprooting and seeking work elsewhere, whether the miners starved or not depended largely on the kindness of others. In Edwardian England, the poor and the needy were looked after by their communities. Charity was part of the weave of society, the threads running through it from the bottom to the very top.

As Consuelo Vanderbilt Balsan, Duchess of Marlborough, recalled, the poor ate the scraps of food from 'Society's' plates:

> It was the custom at Blenheim to place a basket of tins on the side table in the dining room and here the butler left the remains of our luncheon. It was my duty to cram this food into the tins, which we then carried down to the poorest in the various villages where Marlborough owned property. With a complete lack of fastidiousness, it had been the habit to mix meat and vegetables and sweets in horrible jumble in the same tin. In spite of being considered impertinent for not conforming to precedent, I sorted the various viands into different tins, to the surprise and delight of the recipients.

At Wentworth, once a week, the slaughterman from the Home Farm drove round the Fitzwilliams' villages in a cart, piled high

* £33 at today's values.

with the carcasses of animals the house had not managed to consume. They were cut up into joints of meat and distributed among the poor. At Christmas, every tenant on the estate was given a ham and a side of beef.

The culture of giving was also dominant among the working classes. In mining communities, when the pits were working, people helped those who had fallen on hard times. The miners were clannish: their common bond was their knowledge of one another. Often, they lived in the same village from birth to death, and many never travelled far from it. At Denaby, there were no gardens to separate the houses, or hedges or high walls; the partition walls were so thin in the terraced cottages that you could join in the conversation next door. Coal and food were shared; from an early age children were brought up to run errands for the elderly in the village, or for families who had been brought down by injury or illness.

Communities were tightly bound; you looked after your own. It was both a strength and a weakness. The problem for the Denaby miners during the hard strike months in the winter of 1903 was that if they belonged to anyone, it was to the coal owners who were bent on crushing them into submission. The village was surrounded by land owned by Britain's wealthiest aristocratic families – the Duke of Norfolk, Earl Fitzwilliam, the Earl of Scarbrough, Viscount Halifax – but their charity was feudal, based on centuries-old ties of sentiment and mutual self-interest. There was no binding at Denaby, the miners were outsiders; in times of conflict and strife they were left to fend for themselves.

Initially, their plight had moved the country. Throughout the week of the evictions, it was front-page news. Donations of food and money poured in from all over Britain. A Grimsby merchant sent two tons of fish and a Sheffield businessman promised twenty stone of flour each week until the strike was over. Some offered homes to the miners, or to take their children in for a month or two. One woman, writing from Chesterfield, said, 'I have myself a little boy aged ten so they won't be lonely.' Collections were held at football matches at Sheffield, Manchester and Nottingham, and miners at pits as far afield as South Wales donated money from their wages.

After the evictions, Denaby dropped out of the headlines; the village was forgotten and the donations from around the country slowed to a trickle. The soup kitchens and bread queues run by the churches and the chapels, and by armies of local women volunteers, were not able to feed the proverbial five thousand. Groups of miners toured the district, begging what they could. The Reverend Jesse Wilson spoke to a woman in the tents waiting for her husband to return:

> The poor mother was seated outside in front of the tent stove, half blinded with the smoke, which seemed to hesitate as to which way it would go; then suddenly would take a whirl as if determined to fly all ways at the same time. She was anxiously waiting the return of her husband who had been away nearly all the day in the hope of picking up a few pennies for the hungry ones at home. I could see that a dread of failure arising from his long absence was in her face. Had he succeeded he would have been back long since, for she said, 'He cannot stand the youngsters starving.'

In the weeks following the evictions, the magistrates' courts at Doncaster, Rotherham and Barnsley were clogged with poaching cases. Traditionally, poaching had been a means of supplementing the family diet. After strike pay was stopped, it became a necessity.

The pit villages in the South Yorkshire coalfield were set amidst rich sporting estates. Away from the western edge of the Don Valley, coal, iron and steel, while scarring the land above, had not claimed it. In the summer, the hedgerows along the small country lanes connecting one village to another were crowded with cow parsley and wild flowers, and in spring, with hawthorn blossom. Fields of crops encircled the collieries. 'The corn stands rank on rank,' wrote Arthur Eaglestone, 'a million ears, silent and bristling, or flowing like the tide when the wind sweeps along its liquid surface. The twin steel chimneys of the pit rise up beyond, and the dead straight cinder track is hidden in the depths.' In a strange ritual, enacted whenever the pits were working, hundreds of coal-black men ran directly from the pithead into these fields at the end of their shifts, to recover stores of matches and tobacco they had buried at the base of the stalks of corn, or hidden in cracks in the stone walls that enclosed them.

The miners were countrymen, skilled in the art of poaching. They looked upon it as their right to take something from someone who had much more than they had. It was just another fight with the coal owner: 'He robs us all day, we'll rob him all night.' A good poacher could call the hares on the back of his hand, with a peculiar sort of sound, walking round and round in decreasing circles, while the hare watched hypnotized.

Men, and young boys, walked miles through moonless nights across the great estates of South Yorkshire, and the lucrative poaching grounds in the Dukeries, an area to the south of Rotherham where the Dukes of Portland, Leeds, Norfolk, and Earl Manvers, some of the wealthiest coal owners in England, had their stately homes.

Fred Smith, a miner from Kiveton Park colliery, born in 1891, looking back on his childhood, wrote, 'I could go on for years about food. It seems to have been one long struggle for food. Thousands of experiences crowd into my mind, and the idea of food runs through them like a thread.' Among the most memorable was the night Fred went poaching with his father on the Duke of Portland's land at Welbeck Abbey:

> Six miles or more we travelled, mostly across fields, only using the road to cross. Outside a small wood near Whitwell Common, we stood and listened for a long time, an hour I should think, and the romance of the night sounds sent cold shivers down my spine. The far-off bark of a farm dog, the crow of a pheasant in the wood, the staccato yelp of a fox and the stir of life in the undergrowth. The laws of nature were being enacted in the night and their long arm stretched into the heart of a nine-year-old little poacher. I was part of that nature and was going into the night to kill, to kill so that I might eat.

Crossing the Worksop Road into Welbeck Park, they came to a wood where there were 'hundreds of pheasants as tame as fowls'. Half a mile away, Fred could see Welbeck Abbey, the Duke of Portland's home, 'its windows alive with lights and its turrets gleaming'. Three fires blazed on the other side of the wood. 'On the air came the faint scent of cigar. The old man sniffed and said he thought that the yogs [gamekeepers] were on the watch and had given themselves away by smoking.'

Fred's father knew the estate well. He also knew what lay beneath it. As a boy, he had worked as a carter for the 5th Duke of Portland, wheeling stone from the local quarry, used to construct a vast network of underground rooms that extended for twelve miles under the Welbeck estate. There was a ballroom that could accommodate 2,000 people and a riding school with a gallop a quarter of a mile long, lit by 8,000 jets of gas. One tunnel led to a suite of rooms covering four acres, and another to stables, cow-houses and dairies, where more than sixty people were employed.

The Duke of Portland was one of the richest coal owners in England. In the 1860s, when construction first began, a miner working at one of his collieries earned around £50 a year. The Duke's annual income was in the region of £108,000. Whimsy, not wages, drove him to burrow underground; an eccentric and a recluse, he could not bear to be seen.

The Duke spent his life wandering his estate at Welbeck. Tenants, labourers and servants were forbidden to speak to him, or even to acknowledge his presence. If they chanced upon the Duke, their instructions were to pass him by 'as they would a tree'. The man who dared touch his hat would be instantly dismissed. The temptation to stare must have been strong. Winter or summer, the Duke dressed in the same peculiar fashion. His trousers were tied inches above the ankle with a piece of string; he wore a heavy sable coat that touched the ground, and an old-fashioned wig. On top of the long wig, he wore a hat two feet high. Rain or sunshine, he carried an umbrella to hide beneath if anyone passed. He never mingled in society and was never seen at court. When he drove out on his estate, it was alone, in a black carriage, drawn by black horses, with the blinds down.

The same carriage transported him to London. Directly underneath Welbeck Abbey there was a circular courtyard, where eight underground roads and passageways converged. It was the hub of the tunnel network. Two hundred yards in radius, built from red brick, it had a vaulted roof and a platform made from stone. Lit by gas lamps, it was where the Duke would wait for his carriage to collect him, the noise of the horses' hooves and the clatter of wheels against the brick echoing along the tunnels, announcing its imminent arrival minutes before it thundered into the courtyard, sweeping in a majestic half-circle up to the platform where the Duke stood. From here, the carriage proceeded down the longest tunnel, almost one and a quarter miles, to Worksop station, where it was loaded, with the Duke inside it, on to a specially built railway wagon. Four black horses, harnessed in the Duke's livery, waited at Euston station, enabling him to continue his journey, uninterrupted, and unseen, to his house in Cavendish Square.

'My father knew every inch of these tunnels,' wrote Fred Smith. Above ground, dotted across their poaching grounds, were scores of circular glass windows. They had been installed, at intervals of twenty feet, to light and ventilate the tunnels. Thirty years after Fred's father had worked on their construction, the skylights offered him and his son a line of escape in the event of discovery.

'My father took the gun parts from his pocket, fastened them together, and we silently crept into the plantation. "I'm going to have two shots," he said. "Look, them's the two," and looking up into a tree I saw two objects not unlike footballs, apparently hanging twenty feet high amongst the branches. "Get ready to pick up the first one. I'll pick up the other," and up went the gun to his shoulder. I began to shiver. My heart seemed to stop when – Bang! and then Bang! and all the silences of the night were racked as by the crack of doom. "They'll hear us at the Abbey," I exclaimed. "Never mind the Abbey, get after that bird," he whispered, and I scrambled after the pheasant. I picked it up. It was warm and wet and sticky with blood and feathers. "Got it?" I heard him whisper. "Well, come on then," he urged. "Can't you hear them coming?" Yes, I could hear them coming. Men shouting, dogs barking, and to this accompanying hullabaloo, we flew to the tunnel window. I went down first, he following and pulling the window down behind him. We scuttled along the dark tunnel until we came down to a part where it was open. There we climbed out and walked across the Park to another cover where we shot two more pheasants.'

A blinding snowstorm swept full in the teeth of crowds of men and women, pressed up against the squads of policemen, mounted and on foot, guarding the entrance to the platform at Conisbrough railway station, a mile from Denaby. There were two or three thousand miners and their families; some held banners bearing the slogan 'Till Death or Victory' and the Denaby and Cadeby Main colliery colours; others waved sheep's heads, pierced through by long spikes. As the crowds waited for the trains to pull into the station, they sang 'Rule Britannia', accompanied by bandsmen from the collieries' brass bands.

It was a Monday, six weeks after the evictions. The trains were coming in from Doncaster every twenty-five minutes. Steam from the locomotives drifted across the tracks, blurring the swirling snow. The crowd surged and roared as each train disgorged its passengers: scores of men – 'blacksheeps' – protected by the cordons of police, who had come from across the north of England to take the miners' jobs.

The Denaby and Cadeby Main Collieries Company had paid for their tickets. In a final bid to bludgeon the miners back to work, the company had opened the pits, and advertised for 5,000 new workers. The crowds cajoled then bullied the men, imploring them to go home, hissing and threatening those who walked on through the police lines up the road from the station to the collieries, a mounted escort accompanying them through the empty streets to the pit gates.

The striking miners were fighting from the last ditch. The law courts had banned their strike pay; the colliery company was drafting in men to take their jobs and their former homes. In the preceding days, they had even lost the support of their own union, which had ruled that they should return to work. Though 1,500 of them continued to hold out, for some 2,000 men and boys the intimidation and hardship proved too much. In dribs and drabs, through February and early March, they returned to work. The strike was officially declared over in the third week of March. The miners went back on the same terms under which they had left the pits nine months earlier. Defeat was resounding: the strike had been for nothing.

The company was not benevolent in victory. It saw in it a means to get rid of the troublemakers from its pits. Five hundred of Denaby and Cadeby's miners were not taken back on.

Ironically, for years after it ended, the Denaby Bag Muck Strike, which at the outset had seemed a parochial affair, assumed centre stage in the national battle between capital and labour, one that between 1900 and 1906 was being fought out in the Inns of Court.

In this unhappy period, it seemed that capital, through its natural alliance with the judges, had an unfair advantage. From 1871, when trades unions were first made legal, it had not been possible for companies to issue criminal proceedings following industrial action. Subsequently, in the last decades of the nineteenth century, they had looked for, and come up with, ingenious methods of restraining organized labour in the civil courts.

The most controversial of these was the 1902 Taff Vale Judgement, when the Law Lords ruled that a union could be sued for damages resulting from industrial disputes. At a single stroke, it appeared that the House of Lords had disabled labour's most effective weapon: implicitly, the ruling threatened a workman's right to strike.

The judgement caused a deep sense of grievance. Workers across a range of industries throughout the country felt victimized, and ostracized from the political process. Industrial action was the one lever they possessed to raise wages and working conditions. There was little point in having a nominal right to strike if, when exercising this right, the trades unions became liable for damages.

Ramsay MacDonald, the Secretary of the burgeoning Labour Party and a future Prime Minister, responding to the Taff Vale decision, urged the unions to support their own parliamentary candidates. 'Trades Unionism is being assailed,' he said, 'not by what the law says of it, but by what judges think the law ought to say of it. That being so, it becomes necessary for the unions to place men in the House of Commons, to challenge the decisions which I have no doubt will follow this.'

The Bag Muck Strike became the first test of the Taff Vale decision. During its last months, the Denaby and Cadeby Main Collieries Company, jumping on the Taff Vale bandwagon, initiated legal proceedings against the Yorkshire Miners' Association claiming damages of more than £160,000 for the loss of coal production from the day the miners downed tools. If successful, the proceedings would bankrupt the union, enabling the company to achieve its ultimate goal – a non-unionized workforce, 'a labour-free pit'.

The case would take four years to work its way through the courts. As the historian George Dangerfield wrote in his book *The Strange Death of Liberal England*, 'At the heart of that legal web which their law lordships had spun, with such intricate cunning, to entrap the Unions, there lurked the greedy spider of organized capital. The combination was formidable and sinister. When Wealth and Law go hand in hand, where shall a man turn?'

11

On the evening of 30 July 1909, the royal yacht, the *Victoria and Albert*, dropped anchor off the south railway jetty at Portsmouth harbour. It carried a crew of 300 officers and ratings, and a staff of thirty personal servants. It was a floating palace: the state rooms and bedrooms had fluted ceilings and carved ornamental fireplaces; the corridors on the ship were as wide as the passages in any grand country house. The King, Edward VII, was on board. He travelled comfortably, as always, with his fox terrier, Caesar, and a cherished crocodile dressing-case which contained his diary, personal jewellery, a few photographs and a miniature of the Queen. He liked his favourite servants to travel with him: an Austrian first valet, Meidinger, who woke his master with a glass of warm milk and a biscuit at seven o'clock, and an English second valet, Hawkins, who made the King's bed and was forbidden to turn the mattress on Fridays.

30 July was a Friday. Out at sea, a few miles off Portsmouth, the entire Northern Fleet of the British Navy was assembled. There were 150 ships in total: 24 battleships, 16 armoured cruisers, 8 other cruisers, 4 scouts, 48 destroyers, 42 submarines and 8 auxiliaries: eighteen nautical miles of boats, massed in parallel lines, led by the flagships *Dreadnought*, *Indomitable*, *Inflexible* and *Invincible*.

The King had come to Portsmouth for the Spithead Review, the 'Sovereign's Pageant', as the London *Times* called it, a spectacular display of Britain's sea power, and a symbol of her power across the globe.

Gathered in the dark in readiness for the 'final scene', the battleships glowed, lineaments of gold stretching to the far horizon. Countless electric lamps illuminated the contours of gun turrets, bridges and decks. A strong wind ruffled the surface of the sea. There was no danger of the Fleet being blown off course. Coal-fired engines powered through the night holding each ship rigidly to its station in the eighteen-mile line.

The Fleet had dominated the headlines in recent months. Germany had inched ahead in the race to build faster and bigger battleships, raising fears that Britain's Navy was vulnerable to attack. As the King settled in on the royal yacht for a quiet night, eighty miles away, at Limehouse docks in the East End of London, the Chancellor of the Exchequer, David Lloyd George, rose to his feet to deliver a speech at a missionary hall. By the following morning, the eyes of the King and Britain's aristocracy, far from being focused on the threat to the Empire from an external aggressor, had turned anxiously, uncomprehendingly, to the enemy within.

It was a stiflingly hot night in London. There were no gentle sea breezes to cool the air. At the Edinburgh Castle, the missionary hall in Limehouse, the atmosphere was charged from the outset. Four thousand people had come to hear Lloyd George speak. All the windows in the hall were open. Outside, groups of suffragettes, who had packed the houses overlooking the hall, jeered and shouted abuse. At moments, the noise drowned the Chancellor's words. But they were intended to carry far beyond his immediate audience:

I went down a coalmine the other day. We sank into a pit half a mile deep. We then walked underneath the mountain, and we did about three quarters of a mile with rock and shale above us. The earth seemed to be straining – around us and above us – to crush us in. You could see the pit props bent and twisted and sundered until you saw their fibres split in resisting the pressure. Sometimes they give way and then there is mutilation and death. Often a spark ignites, the whole pit is deluged in fire, and the breath of life is scorched out of hundreds of breasts by the consuming flame. And yet when the Prime Minister and I knock at the door of these great landlords and say to them – 'Here, you know these poor fellows who have been digging up royalties at the risk of their lives, some of them are old, they have survived the perils of their trade, they are broken, they can earn no more. Won't you give them something towards keeping them out of the workhouse?' – they scowl at us and we say – 'Only a ha'penny, just a copper.' They say, 'You thieves!' And they turn their dogs on to us, and you can hear their bark every morning.

The Chancellor brought his speech to a close with a threat. 'If this is an indication of the view taken by these great landlords of their responsibility to the people who, at the risk of life, create their wealth, then I say their day of reckoning is at hand.'

It was one of the most explosive, most radical speeches in British political history, a vicious and unprecedented attack by a Minister of the Crown on the aristocratic oligarchy that in Edwardian Britain still governed the country, and whose quasi-feudal estates still stretched across the shires. Driving the speech were the inflammatory notions of unfairness and social injustice, of the unequal distribution of wealth and power, of a parasitical class which held the reins of the country in its hands and which alone could dictate whether the social welfare of the masses advanced.

For more than an hour Lloyd George held his audience in thrall, moving them to howls of rage and laughter. 'A fully equipped Duke costs as much to keep up as two dreadnoughts, and Dukes are just as great a terror, and they last longer,' he quipped. He attacked three Dukes – Westminster, Norfolk and Northumberland – by name. Speaking to an overflow meeting in an adjacent hall immediately afterwards, he issued a challenge: 'I say to you, without you we can do nothing; with your help we can brush the Lords like chaff before us.'

At 11.30 on the morning after the Chancellor's speech, the *Victoria and Albert* sailed out of Portsmouth harbour in hazy sunshine. As she entered the Solent, a flotilla of thousands of boats spread before her as far as the eye could see. Bobbing between the formidable massed lines of the Northern Fleet, yachts, sloops, barges, 'hurrah boats' and 'steam pinnaces', brilliant with bunting, crowded the water, waiting to greet the King. Martial music from the brass bands on the destroyers and the cheers of tens of thousands of officers and ratings that ringed the ships' decks, forming necklaces of crisp white and navy blue, carried on the wind. A gun salute signalled the start of the set piece of the review. The King watched as the battleships and destroyers broke their lines, sweeping round, torpedoes blazing, to mount a simulated attack on HMS *Dreadnought*, the flagship of the Fleet.

The awesome display of firepower did nothing to lift his mood. It was a black day for the King: news of Lloyd George's speech at Limehouse had reached him earlier that morning. Knollys, his Private Secretary, communicated his fury in a letter to Lord Crewe, the Leader of the Tories in the House of Lords:

> The King thinks he ought to protest in the most vigorous terms against one of his Ministers making such a speech – one full of false statements, of Socialism in its most insidious form and of virulent abuse against one particular class, which can only have the effect of setting 'class' against 'class' and of stirring up the worst passions of its audience. It is hardly necessary, perhaps, to allude to its gross vulgarity. The King cannot understand how Asquith can tacitly allow certain of his colleagues to make speeches that would not have been tolerated by any Prime Minister until within the last few years, which H.M. regards as being in the highest degree improper, and which he almost looks upon as being an insult to the Sovereign when delivered by one of his confidential servants.

At Limehouse, Lloyd George had been fighting his corner. Three months earlier, in the House of Commons, the Chancellor had outlined his plans for a 'People's Budget'. 'This is a war Budget,' he said. 'It is for raising money to wage implacable war against poverty and squalidness. I cannot help hoping and believing that before this generation has passed away we shall have advanced a great step towards that good time when poverty, and the wretchedness and human degradation which always follow in its camp, will be as remote to the people of this country as the wolves which once infested its forests.'

The Chancellor proposed to introduce old age pensions, and a range of measures to provide for widows, orphans, the sick and infirm. But in putting his ambitious proposals together – Britain's first steps towards a Welfare State – he faced an enormous deficit. The Army and most notably the Navy, in the race to build a fleet of battleships to match Germany's, had placed a great strain on the national purse. Land, and implicitly the aristocracy, was the source he intended to milk for income. He proposed a super-tax on all incomes above £5,000 a year, an increase in death duties, and a duty on coal royalties and undeveloped land.

'I claim that the tax we impose on land is fair, is just, and is moderate,' he said at Limehouse. 'They go on threatening that if we proceed they will cut down their benefactions and discharge labour. What kind of labour? . . . Are they going to devastate rural England by feeding and dressing themselves? Are they going to reduce their gamekeepers? Ah, that would be sad!' The ownership of land, he argued, was 'not merely an enjoyment', but a 'stewardship' which carried a fiscal responsibility. If the landowners and coal owners would not 'discharge their functions in seeing to the security and defence of the country, in looking after the broken in the villages and in their neighbourhoods', the time would come to 'reconsider the conditions' under which land was held. No country, however rich, could 'afford to have quartered upon its revenue' a class which declined to do its duty and which possessed a formidable powerbase in the House of Lords.

The Chancellor had set a snare to trap the Lords. In 1909, the second chamber had the right of veto: the peers decided which bills did or did not pass through Parliament. If they chose to, the Lords could block the 'People's Budget'. Historically, they had left finance bills alone: the last time the House of Lords had rejected a finance bill – in Charles I's reign – the result had been a civil war. If the peers were to break with tradition and throw out the People's Budget, as there was every indication they would, the King would be forced to dissolve Parliament. The Liberal Government would then go to the country, not simply on the question of the budget, but on their Lordships' power of veto. The constitution of Britain and the power and prestige of its ruling class were at stake.

★

Three days later, the Prime Minister, Herbert Asquith, arrived at Cowes to find Edward VII still furious. On 2 August he dined with the King at a banquet held in honour of Tsar Nicholas II. Writing to Lloyd George from the Admiralty yacht, the *Enchantress*, Asquith noted:

On my arrival here yesterday, I found the King in a state of great agitation and annoyance in consequence of your Limehouse speech. I have never known him more irritated, or more difficult to appease, though I did my best. He sees in the general tone and especially in the concluding parts, of your speech, a menace to property and a Socialistic spirit, which he thinks peculiarly inappropriate and unsettling in a holder of your office.

The Prime Minister went on to reprimand his Chancellor for upsetting the King.

The King, of course, lives in an atmosphere which is full of hostility to us and to our proposals; but he is not himself unfriendly, and, so far, he has 'stood' the Budget very well – far better than I expected. It is important, therefore, to avoid raising his apprehensions and alienating his goodwill . . . I have, as you know, heartily and loyally backed the Budget from the first, and at every stage; and I have done, and shall continue to do, all I can to commend it to the country. But I feel very strongly that at this moment what is needed is reasoned appeal to moderate & reasonable men. There is great and growing popular enthusiasm, but this will not carry us through – if we rouse the suspicions and fears of the middle class, and particularly if we give countenance to the notion that the Budget is conceived in any spirit of vindictiveness.

I am sure you will take what I have written in good part. My sole object is to bring our ship safely into port.

Political expedience was Asquith's excuse. Closer to the truth, however, was the fact that he and his Chancellor inhabited different social worlds. Like the King, Asquith balked at the sentiments of class hatred that Lloyd George had expressed. Half his Cabinet came from the landed establishment and six of them were peers. The Prime Minister, a self-made lawyer, was from a relatively modest background. The aristocratic Establishment was the world to which he aspired; he had no particular desire to turn it upside down. The ties of birth, marriage and friendship that bound the class Lloyd George attacked also bound the Prime Minister. He was married to Margot Tennant, the daughter of Sir Charles Tennant, a wealthy Glasgow chemical manufacturer. Margot's childhood had been spent in London's Mayfair. At the close of the nineteenth century, no other stretch of the capital could boast more Dukes, Marquesses or Earls.

Crystal chandeliers, polished floors and footmen were not of Lloyd George's world. A schoolteacher's son from a small town in North Wales, he had no ties of birth, marriage or friendship to aristocratic society, which he regarded as alien to his principles, and which he loathed. Two years after his Limehouse speech, in the autumn of 1911, staying with King George V, Edward VII's son, at Balmoral, he told his wife, 'I am not cut out for Court life. I can see some of them revel in it. I detest it . . . The whole atmosphere reeks with Toryism . . . Everybody very civil to me as they would be to a dangerous wild animal.'

Asquith was unable to steer the ship 'safely into port'. In the summer of 1909, powerful grandees came out against Lloyd George's People's Budget as they looked to protect their own interests. In the first week of August, many of them were gathered at Cowes Regatta, the social highlight of the summer season.

Throughout that week, the *Standart*, Tsar Nicholas II's yacht, and the *Victoria and Albert* were moored side by side in the centre of Cowes harbour. They towered over the fleets of lesser, but no less impressive yachts, clustered around them at a respectful distance. They belonged to Europe's royal families and to members of the British aristocracy, who had come in their hundreds to pay court to the King and the Tsar. *The Times* listed the names of the boats and their owners: Prince Henry of Battenberg's *Sheila*, the Empress Eugenie's *Thistle*, Lord Ormonde's *Mirage*, Lord Arran's *Isa*, the Duke of Leeds's *Aries*, Lord Brassey's *Sunbeam*, were a few among many. Billy Fitzwilliam was also there on his yacht, the *Kathleen*. Police boats patrolled around the clock to prevent unauthorized craft from entering the harbour, and a line of battleships guarded its entrance. 'This was the one and only time I ever saw Tsar Nicholas,' wrote the Duke of Windsor looking back on the event. 'Because of assassination plots . . . the Imperial government would not risk their little father's life in a great metropolis, therefore the meeting was set for Cowes on the Isle of Wight, which could be sealed off almost completely . . . I do remember being astonished at the elaborate police guard thrown around his every movement . . .' Behind the security cordons, Cowes was en fête; those without boats, like the Duke of Somerset and the Duchess of Manchester, had rented houses for the week.

'Ashore and afloat', as one observer recorded, 'there were dinner parties and balls. Steam launches, with gleaming brass funnels, and slender cutters and gigs, pulled by their crews at the long white oars, plied between the yachts and the squadron steps. By day, the sails of the racing yachts spread across the blue waters of the Solent like the wings of giant butterflies, by night the riding lights and lanterns gleamed and shone like glowworms against the onyx water and fireworks burst and spent themselves in the night sky.'

Yacht racing and socializing dominated the agenda; a constant round of lunches, dinners, dances, bridge parties and promenading on the lawns of the Royal Squadron Yacht Club. But beneath the certainties of social etiquette and the trappings of great wealth lay a profound uncertainty, an uneasy sense that the demons of revolution lurked in the chasm that divided the rich from the poor.

In the minds of many of those belonging to this social elite, Lloyd George had unleashed the demons in his Limehouse speech. Lord Rosebery, the son of the former Prime Minister, said the People's Budget was 'not a budget, but a revolution, a social and political revolution of the first magnitude'. Describing it as pure socialism, he claimed it represented 'the end of all, the negation of faith, of family, of property, of Monarchy, of Empire'. Lord Ridley, voicing the instinctive reaction of many of his class, believed the Government to be in the hands of a 'pack of madmen'.

Yet, at the same time, the peers' uncertainty was matched by blinding confidence. The thought that this period was the Indian summer of their social and political power was implausible to its contemporaries. They failed to understand the true nature, or the implications, of the currents that shifted beneath the surface of their England. While they sensed an acceleration in the pace of change, they elected to resist it, confident that they would win.

In November 1909, believing the country would support them, the House of Lords voted against the People's Budget, forcing the King to dissolve Parliament. In January 1910, in the election that followed, the Liberal Government was narrowly voted back in. Three months later, the Lords, accepting the country's decision, passed the People's Budget. It was too late: the Liberals' majority had been slashed and the Irish Nationalists and Labour MPs held the balance of power; a promise to curb the Lords' veto was the price that Prime Minister Asquith had paid for their support.

The Lords moved to defend their interests. Their right of veto meant they could throw out any bill the Government introduced to curtail their powers. It provoked a constitutional crisis that only the King could resolve, made more acute by his death – in the middle of it – on 6 May 1910.

Edward VII's son, George V, when he was Prince of Wales, had scarcely bothered to conceal his dislike of Liberals and Liberalism. After an encounter at Lord Londonderry's house, Edmund Gosse, the society poet and critic, described the Prince as an 'overgrown schoolboy, loud and stupid, losing no opportunity of abusing the Government'. While awaiting the results of the January election in 1910, he had made known his dread of a Liberal victory.

Humiliatingly, within months of his accession, the new and inexperienced King was forced to make a secret promise to the Prime Minister, that if the Lords would not destroy themselves he would use his royal prerogative to create an unprecedented 250 Liberal peers who would vote whichever way the Government told them. The King made one stipulation: that the Prime Minister, for the second time that year, should call an election, specifically to be fought on the question of reforming the House of Lords. In

1. Billy, 7th Earl Fitzwilliam, on a training exercise with the Wentworth Battery, Royal Horse Artillery, 1911

2. Troops guarding Wentworth House during the coal riots of 1893

3. The Marble Salon at
Wentworth House, 19

4. The Whistlejacket Room at Wentworth House, 1924

5 and **6**. William, 6th Earl Fitzwilliam, and his wife, Harriet, Countess Fitzwilliam, *c*. 1865

7. William, Lord Milton, photographed in the Pillared Hall at Wentworth House, *c*. 1860

8. Billy, later 7th Earl Fitzwilliam, as a boy in 1878

9. Lord Milton (*second from right, with headband*) and his expedition party after crossing the Rockies in September 1863. William Cheadle, his physician, is seated to his right

). Laura, Lord Milton's wife, fter the birth of their eldest daughter, *c.* 1870

11. A lithograph, dated 1869, taken from an original watercolour depicting the rugged landscape around Pointe de Meuron. The house where Billy was born is visible in the distance

12. The house in Pointe de Meuron where Billy, 7th Earl Fitzwilliam, was born

13. A group of male indoor staff at Wentworth House, 1912

14. The outdoor servants at Wentworth House, *c*. 1906

15. The housekeeper and a group of housemaids at Wentworth House, *c.* 1890

16. A ploughing team on the Wentworth Estate, *c.* 1900

17. Maud, Lady Milton, later Countess Fitzwilliam, dressed as Madame Le Brun at the Devonshire House Costume Ball in July 1897

making his promise, the King secretly hoped, as the Unionists in the House of Lords believed, that the country would vote with the Peers. It didn't: in December 1910, Britain backed the Liberals and their Parliament Bill – the proposal to legislate the aristocracy into impotence by abolishing their right of veto on finance bills, and by limiting their veto on other bills to a period of two years.

When the King's secret pledge to create 250 Liberal peers became known, as the historian George Dangerfield wrote, 'it was generally supposed that his promise to exercise it would be enough; under such a threat their Lordships would have to yield. Better to vote their death themselves, than to have it voted for them; better to die as they were, a decent corpse, than to die ludicrously swollen with Liberal peerages.' Yet to the last, it seemed as if the die-hards in the House of Lords would destroy the Parliament Bill, and in doing so heap ridicule on the Sovereign and the nation.

The peers resisted reform to the wire; finally, to the King's immense relief, on a sultry night in August 1911, more than two years after the People's Budget had sparked the constitutional crisis, the Parliament Bill passed through the House of Lords by a slender majority of seventeen. George V had Lord Curzon to thank: almost single-handedly he had succeeded in persuading a sizeable number of Unionists to defect to the Liberals in the final hours of the debate. The following day, the usually unflappable Stamfordham, the King's Private Secretary, wrote to Lord Curzon: 'What a relief all is well! The King is quite another man – and if I may say so, is deeply grateful to you for the very valuable service which you have rendered to save the situation.'

The crisis had passed. But, people wondered, had it not simply been deferred? In both the elections of 1910, it had been a close-run thing: the country, it appeared, had been split down the middle. The power of the peerage was substantially diminished; confidence had evaporated: the impression the crisis left was that the next bloodshed would come from a war not between nations, but between classes.

The signs were ominous: the character and strength of trade unionism had changed since its cornering by the legal offensive of the 1890s that culminated in Taff Vale. In 1906, the Denaby and Cadeby Main Collieries Company had finally lost its court action against the Yorkshire Miners' Association. The judge, in delivering the verdict, said that if he had found against the union, he would in effect be ruling that 'every strike was an actionable wrong'. Months later, steered by Lloyd George as President of the Board of Trade, the new Liberal Government had introduced the Trades Disputes Act, reversing the Taff Vale decision. Labour had regained its most powerful weapon; the legislation meant that trades unions could strike without fear of being bankrupted.

The stage was set for a titanic struggle between capital and labour, between the upper and working classes.

Between 1902 and 1909 trades union membership, spurred by Taff Vale and isolated parochial disputes such as the Bag Muck Strike, had risen dramatically. Among the most powerful of the unions was the Miners' Federation of Great Britain. The internecine rivalry that had characterized the relationship between the regional miners' unions in the late nineteenth century was a thing of the past. As the century dawned, so too did the realization in the ranks of the miners' unions that they possessed a devastating weapon: if they joined forces to halt production, they could hold the country to ransom.

In 1912 the miners would put their newfound strength to the test.

PART III

12

It was a midsummer morning in July 1912. At Wentworth, at eight o'clock, the temperature was already 70 degrees.

In the formal gardens behind the house there was not a blade of grass or a petal out of place. Bees drifted lazily along winding beds crammed with roses and white stocks. The scent of the flowers hung tantalizingly in the warm, still air. Wentworth was expecting a special visitor. For the first time in the history of the house, the reigning monarch, King George V, was coming to stay.

The most important task had been left – deliberately – till last. A long straight path, half a mile long and some ten yards wide, was the crowning feature of the formal gardens. Huge rosette-shaped flowerbeds lay along its centre; at its edges, the scalloped borders, framed by low box hedges, were planted with lobelias in rows of alternate colours: brilliant white, set against a glowing blue. Most striking of all was the colour of the path itself: in contrast to the sombre green of the topiary and the vivid natural colours of the flowers around it, it was a deep synthetic pink.

A solitary figure appeared by the stone urns at the bottom of the steps leading up to the West Front of the house. He was carrying a two-handled brush; a yard wide at its base, it had long, stiff bristles. Placing it behind him, his arms awkwardly stretched back, the servant set off up the path, turning from time to time to ensure the brush was flush against its border. 'That path, it was made from red ash, it came from Earl Fitzwilliam's mines,' Geoffrey Steer, a garden boy at Wentworth, recalled. 'It was red from fire. It was muck from the pit that had turned red from the fires that burnt on the slag heaps. They used pit shale – little bits of rock broken up into pieces – for the gravel on the drive at the front of the house. They didn't stripe that though, it was only the path that was striped. The brushman had to walk up it keeping the brush straight all the way to the top. Then he used to turn round and come back, always dragging the brush behind him, else his footprints would mark it. By the time he'd walked to the top and back it was about a mile. He'd take the width of a brush at a time. Up and down, down and up, until he'd done. It used to take him about five hours. It was the only way to do it. One width was light, and the other dark, from the brushing in different directions. Two colours, you see, light and dark.'

At the front of the house, vehicles of every description crowded the drive. In the Kennels across the Park the Wentworth foxhounds howled and bayed, disturbed by the commotion. Dog carts pulled by ponies, ancient barouche sociables and double victorias drawn by pairs of cobs lined up alongside gleaming new motor-cars at the entrance to the Pillared Hall. The luggage had arrived ahead of the guests. Scores of footmen and housemaids milled in front of the house, supervising its unloading, shouting instructions to the 'oddmen', the servants lowest in the pecking order whose job it was to carry the baggage to the long list of pre-allocated bedrooms. It took two men to carry the 'Noah's Arks', the large trunks that contained the guests' clothes. A house party of thirty-four had been invited for the King and Queen's stay.

In the State Dining Room, the preparations were almost complete. Three circular tables, covered in damask cloths and seating upwards of twenty people, had been placed beneath each chandelier. On the ten-foot-long Chippendale sideboard, there were rows of crystal decanters with silver labels denoting the different wines and spirits. Tropical lianas, cultivated in Wentworth's greenhouses, trailed from the chandeliers on to the centre of the tables; fresh grapes, specially selected for the depth of their silvery bloom, were piled in pyramids in gold dishes. Everything that adorned the tables – with the exception of the cut glass – was gold: the cutlery, the Fitzwilliams' racing cups, the tiny matchboxes. The head gardener and his assistants had arrived to add the final touches. Reaching cautiously across the tables, they wove spider's fern through the settings, threading it between the knives and forks and up the delicate fluted spines of the racing cups and ornamental dishes.

Using the minutest lengths of garden twine, they sewed rose heads and single chrysanthemums, grown in Wentworth's hothouses, on to the trellis of fern, covering the cloth between the settings with a lattice of flowers. They were watched by locals from the village, relatives of the household servants and the Fitzwilliams' colliery and Estate employees who had filed into the dining room throughout the morning. 'It was the custom at Wentworth,' the son of one of them recalled. 'Whenever there was a big do on, the locals were invited to inspect, to have a look round. It was because everyone had been involved in making everything look so beautiful. People took pride in the work that had gone into it.'

Upstairs, the housekeeper was completing her final rounds. Each bedroom had to be checked to ensure that stationery supplies were plentiful, the inkstands were full, and the wardrobes and drawers dusted and freshly lined. She had walked the full length of the house. Thirty-six bedrooms were required: in the top and lower wings in the North and South Towers in the Village, the name given to the wing at the farthest end of the house, so called because of its proximity to the village; in Bedlam, the suite traditionally reserved for bachelors, and, of course, the principal guest bedrooms in the central block of the East Front. A further forty bedrooms were needed for the guests' valets, ladies' maids and chauffeurs. It had been many decades since the house had looked so spruce. Following the death of the 6th Earl in 1902, Billy Fitzwilliam had spent a small fortune on modernization and refurbishment. The mustiness, the feudal style of the old Earl's last years had vanished. Bathrooms and lavatories had been installed; sofas and chairs had been re-covered and new curtains and furnishings bought. Gone were the smoky oil lamps and wall sconces; above the light switches in the bedrooms, discreet black and white enamel plaques boasted 'Electric Light'.

Walking briskly through the corridors, the housekeeper missed nothing. From time to time she stopped to adjust the arrangements in the vases of flowers or to knead the bowls of pot-pourri to release their aroma into the air. The smell permeated everywhere. The housekeeper had made the pot-pourri herself, following closely guarded recipes handed down by her predecessors. Scrawled above some of the recipes were the words 'NOT TO BE GIVEN AWAY'. The secret of one scent that lingered in the corridors and rooms at Wentworth is revealed in a recipe that has survived:

2 pecks of Damask Roses part blown, part in bud. Violets, orange flowers and Jasmine – a handful of each. Orice root sliced. Benjamin and Storax 2 oz each. A quarter of an ounce of Musk. 4 oz Angelica root sliced. 1 quart of the red part of Clove Gilly flowers. 2 handfuls of Lavender flowers. Half a handful of Rosemary flowers. Bay and Laurel leaves – half a handful each. 3 Seville oranges stuck as full of cloves as possible, dried in an oven, cooled and pounded. Half a handful of knotted marjoram. 2 handfuls of balm of Gilead dried. Chop all together and put the ingredients in layers in a jar with pounded Bay salt strewed between each layer.

By four o'clock that afternoon, the house was ready. The guests were due to arrive at five. In the Pillared Hall, the main entrance to the house, thirty footmen stood among the stone columns, chatting softly, waiting to escort the guests to their rooms. Behind the hall, in the Upper Servants' Room, the valets and ladies' maids who had travelled ahead of their employers to unpack their luggage stole a quick cup of tea. They introduced themselves to one another, as was the custom, not by their own names but by the titled names of their employers: 'Londonderry', 'Rosse', 'Scarbrough', 'Zetland', 'Harewood'; it solved the problem of having to remember the visiting servants' names.

Outside, on the lawn in front of the house, battalions of soldiers from the West Riding National Reserve had been arriving throughout the afternoon. 'The men had a good long march from the railway stations,' reported the local newspaper, 'but they made light of it and swung into the park in fine style.' They had come from all over Yorkshire: from Leeds, Bradford, York and the neighbouring towns of Barnsley, Rotherham and Sheffield. There were six battalions in total. Watched by a crowd of 40,000 that had gathered at the edge of the lawn, the soldiers had formed up into columns, flanked by mounted police and a battery of the West Riding Royal Horse Artillery. The place of honour, directly in front of the entrance to the Pillared Hall, was reserved for thirty 'Boys of the Old Brigade'. Standing bent and grey, their medals had been won in the Indian Mutiny, and at the Charge of the Light Brigade.

At precisely one minute to five o'clock, a bugle sounded, and an expectant hush fell over the crowd. A plumed officer on a grey charger galloped across the lawn, reigning his horse to a crunching stop on the drive. Seconds later a fleet of grand cars, moving at walking pace, came into view, As they drew to a halt at the entrance to the Pillared Hall, the royal standard unfurled from the flagstaff above, catching in the breeze.

It was not a social visit. The King and Queen had come to Wentworth on business. The day before they arrived, Billy Fitzwilliam had issued a statement to the Press:

> I am instructed by His Majesty that he wishes 'informality' to be the watchword. It is in no sense a state visit. The King and Queen have expressed a desire to see working men and working women in working conditions. We have impressed upon the owners of works and establishments to be honoured by the royal visit that a great deal of whitewash is not what is required.

In the course of their four-day stay, George V and Queen Mary planned to visit collieries, factories, engineering works and steel foundries. The highlight of the tour – a personal coup for Billy and a first for a British monarch – was to be George V's descent underground at Elsecar Main, Billy's own pit.

The Royal Tour of the North, as it became officially known, was radical in concept. It was also unprecedented. No British monarch had previously toured the industrial heartlands. Yet, historic though it was, the minutiae of the tour have not been preserved for the historical record. As in most matters relating to

Wentworth, the details are blurred. The correspondence between the King's officials and Billy Fitzwilliam in the months prior to the royal visit has been destroyed – both at Wentworth and in the Royal Archives at Windsor Castle.

The destruction of the Fitzwilliam side of the correspondence is not in itself odd; a reasonable assumption would be that the papers were among those burnt in the great bonfire of 1972. At Windsor, the Registrar of the Royal Archives explained why the King's correspondence has not been preserved: 'Many of the files from the Private Secretary's Office in the reign of George V were destroyed many years ago. They ran out of space. There was nowhere to store the papers.' Yet the suggestion is, from other historical sources, that George V's visit to Wentworth was instigated by worried courtiers. Mysteriously, as the Registrar at Windsor confirmed, important correspondence between the King and the Prime Minister in the months leading up to his visit to Wentworth – and directly relevant to it – was also deliberately destroyed: not for reasons of space, but due to the sensitivity of the letters. The aim of the Royal Tour of the North, as George V himself stated, was 'to see working men and working women in working conditions'. Why then were the stewards of the Crown so determined to hide the traces of the events that led to a four-day public appointment that on the face of it demonstrated an admirable engagement with the lives of the working classes?

It is necessary to look elsewhere. A Cabinet memo suggests that the tour was hastily arranged. George V, so it reveals, had never intended to go to Wentworth. He had originally planned to spend the summer conducting a series of state visits to his European cousins. At the Cabinet meeting at Downing Street on 6 March, the King's proposed tour of the 'royal houses of Europe' was one of the main subjects of discussion. 'After careful consideration of the matter in all its aspects,' the Prime Minister wrote to the King, 'it was the general opinion of the Cabinet that Your Majesty should be advised to postpone the visits until next year.' Chief in the Cabinet's reasoning was 'the unsettled social and industrial aspect at home'. It was a masterful flourish of understatement; the subtext was that the political situation was too precarious to permit the King to leave the country.

In the first months of George V's reign, Britain had been convulsed by strikes. In the summer of 1911, soon after his coronation, a pamphlet was circulated by radical trade unionists to soldiers serving in His Majesty's armed forces at garrisons in the north of England.

> Men! Comrades! Brothers! You are in the army. So are we. You, in the army of Destruction. We, in the Industrial army of Construction.
>
> We work at mine, mill, forge, factory or dock, producing and transporting all the goods, clothing stuffs, etc, which makes it possible for people to live.
>
> You are Working men's Sons.
>
> When we go on Strike to better Our lot, which is the lot also of Your Fathers, Mothers, Brothers, and Sisters, YOU are called upon by your Officers to MURDER US. Don't do it.

On 17 August 1911, the newly crowned King, staying with the Duke of Devonshire at Bolton Abbey in Yorkshire, was compelled to send a telegram from the grouse moors to Winston Churchill, the Home Secretary. Was he satisfied, he inquired, that order in the country could be preserved? Two hundred miles south, the Aldershot Garrison had been mobilized to the capital. Along St James's Street and Pall Mall, gunmakers had sold out of revolvers in twenty-four hours. 'The difficulty,' Churchill replied, 'is not to maintain order but to maintain order without loss of life.'

The country was in the grip of a national railway strike – a strike that, as the King described, caused him the 'greatest possible anxiety'. It had been preceded by a national dock strike and a national transport workers' strike. Collectively, they indicated a new mood among the working classes, one that would become increasingly belligerent as the year progressed. The King's distress – and his alarm – is evident in a letter his Private Secretary wrote to Herbert Asquith, the Prime Minister, on 6 September, shortly after the King returned from Bolton Abbey.

> The King is very much disturbed by the present unrest among the working classes and by the possibility, if not probability, of further strikes breaking out at any moment. He is afraid that if there were a renewal of recent occurrences, the disturbances might lead to political elements being introduced into the conflict which might perhaps affect, not the existence, but the position of the Crown – independent of other evils. He desires me therefore to urge most strongly on the Government the importance (& it is also their duty) of their taking advantage of the lull, and of Parliament not meeting until the end of October, to devise a scheme, which although not entirely preventing strikes (perhaps that is not possible) would to a large extent prevent a threatened strike from coming to a head, and might be the means of preventing 'sympathetic' strikes from taking place.

The Liberal Party had repealed the punitive Taff Vale Judgement of 1902. The Prime Minister was not prepared, as he perceived, to legislate against the grain of democracy. Five months later the storm the King had anticipated was unleashed.

On 1 March 1912, the country was faced with a situation that had never been experienced, never even dreamt of. One million miners went out on strike, the number downing tools unequalled in any industry in Britain or Europe. The closest parallel was the General Strike of 1905 in Russia. The miners were striking for a minimum wage – the 'fives and twos' – 5 shillings for a man per shift and 2 shillings for a boy. It was the gravest of all the challenges from organized labour: in the Prime Minister's words, British trade was as dependent on coal as 'we all of us' depend on agriculture 'for our daily bread'.

Within days of the start of the strike, industry began to stagger, then it stopped.

It is at this point that the letters between the King and his Prime Minister also stop.

In the Archives at Windsor Castle and at the Bodleian Library in Oxford, where Herbert Asquith's papers are deposited, the letters between the two men in the month of March 1912 are missing. In point of fact, there are very few letters for the entire first year of the King's reign.

George V's correspondence with Herbert Asquith has been systematically pruned. The King's letter to the Prime Minister, written on 6 September 1911, by his Private Secretary, is to be found in Herbert Asquith's papers. It is the only letter from the period. Stark in its revelation of the King's anxieties, it appears to have slipped through the net: after the correspondence between George V and the Prime Minister was destroyed at Windsor Castle, there was obviously a clear instruction to ensure that the originals among Asquith's papers were also destroyed.

The gravity of the crisis engendered by the miners' strike is apparent in the Cabinet's decision on 6 March – a week after it began – to advise the King to postpone his European tour. That George V and the Prime Minister regarded the strike as a threat to the very existence of the Crown, as opposed merely to its position, is suggested by the missing correspondence. Further clues lie among the fragments of historical record that remain. They are to be found in the private papers – and in the behaviour – of the Prime Minister and his wife.

Three weeks after the Cabinet meeting on 7 March, an extraordinary scene took place in the House of Commons. On 27 March, Margot Asquith recorded the following entry in her diary: 'Last night an emergency coal bill – the Minimum Wage Bill – was carried at 3 o'clock this morning by 213 votes to 48. I should say this is perhaps the most dangerous and unhappy moment of our or indeed anyone's political experience.'

Faced with the paralysis of industry and deadlock between the coal owners and the miners, Asquith was forced to rush a Minimum Wage Bill through Parliament in an attempt to resolve the strike. At 10.30 on the evening of 26 March, he opened the speeches at the Bill's third reading. It was by no means certain that the Bill would resolve the strike, or that Parliament would pass it. The historian George Dangerfield, based on the testimony of those who witnessed the Prime Minister's speech, described what followed:

He was on his feet, speaking not so much to the apprehensive faces around him, as to the miners themselves. He begged them to stay the havoc with which the country was confronted: he recited once again the efforts which had been made, how hopes had risen and hopes had been shattered. 'We laboured hard,' he said. He turned to the packed Labour benches. If their case for the five shillings and the two shillings was strong, would they not trust the district boards to provide these rates? Must the country be subjected to further hardship? 'I speak under the stress of very strong feeling,' he went on; and hesitating between words – he, who was always so impassive, so lucid – begged Parliament to pass the Bill. 'We have exhausted all our powers of persuasion and argument and negotiation,' he concluded, in low thick halting tones. 'But we claim we have done our best in the public interest – with perfect fairness and impartiality.' He stood there, struggling for words; and they would not come. The House watched him, fascinated and appalled: something was taking place before its eyes which not one of its members had ever expected to see.

The Prime Minister was weeping.

Asquith's were tears of exhaustion and humiliation. For the first time since the English Civil War, the sanctity of Parliament had been breached: the miners, a non-elected body, had forced the Prime Minister to legislate. Further humiliation threatened. The Bill had failed to stipulate the amount of the minimum wage – the 'fives and twos' the miners demanded: it was possible that it would not persuade them to call off the strike.

Here was power indeed. At the height of her Imperial wealth and glory, and for the first time in her history, the miners had combined to bring Britain to her knees. Syndicalism, a continental movement the revolutionary socialist ideas of which had struck a chord in some industrial areas, was blamed. Lord Cecil, the son of the former Conservative Prime Minister, believed the strike posed a 'profound danger to civilization'. It was 'part of a great conspiracy', an attempt, he said, to gain 'dictatorial powers over the industries of this country by a small band of revolutionaries'.

At Downing Street, Herbert Asquith's anxiety was echoed by his wife. In an entry in her diary, Margot confided, 'I was terribly harassed by the living danger and for H's anxiety over the strike.' Out of desperation, in mid-March at the height of the strike, when her husband was deadlocked in heated negotiations with the miners' trades union leaders – and behind his back – she endeavoured to arrange a secret meeting with Robert Smillie, the Vice-President of the Miners' Federation of Great Britain and a key figure in the negotiations. The day after meeting Smillie at a lunch party, hosted by the industrialist Sir George Askwith, Margot sent him a letter:

> I was pleased to meet you yesterday. You will keep your promise of being at the Westminster Palace Hotel at 3.30 tomorrow, where I shall meet you. The big question I long to ask a man of your ability, sympathy, and possibly very painful experience is: What do you want? Do you want everyone to be equal in their material prosperity? Do you think quality of brain could be made equal if we had equal prosperity? Do you think in trying or even succeeding in making Human Nature equal in their bankbooks, they would also be equal in the sight of God and Man? Equal in motive, in unselfishness, in grandeur of character?

Margot concluded her letter with a plea: 'I don't like to see my husband suffer in his longing to be fair, just and kind to both sides in this tragic quarrel,' she wrote. 'Keep your blood warm. Don't let it get cold. Use your great power for an honourable settlement. Destruction is a sad exchange for construction. Help my husband. He is a self-made man like yourself . . .'

Smillie reneged on his promise to meet her. Undeterred, she wrote again, imploring him:

> I don't see why anyone should know we have met. I am afraid I vexed you in my letter, which was written quite freely. (Perhaps you did not

get my letter?) Do the masters and the miners live at your hotel? Do let us meet again. I don't want to talk about the strike at all. It is only for the pleasure of discussing abstract ideas with a man whose temperament and views interest me. I am very sorry you have thrown me over. I've never been afraid of any individual, or any situation, or rumour, or gossip in my life; but can assure you that I would meet you at 3 Queen Anne's Gate, Sir Edward Grey's house, at 3.30. Even he need not know. I would just ask him if he would allow me to have private talk with a friend for 15 minutes. He would say 'Yes' and never even ask, nor would I tell anyone. If you won't do this, do answer my letter.

Smillie does not appear to have answered either of Margot Asquith's letters, yet the answers to the questions she sought were simple, expressed by John Cairns, a miner from Northumberland. 'Our men have been under the thumbs of the masters from at least 1870 until now and our men are more refined than they were forty years ago,' he said, 'they desire better homes, better food, better clothing, better conditions.'

The core issue of the miners' strike was wages, as it had been in the railwaymen's, dockers' and transport workers' strikes that had preceded it. In the winter of 1912, the British working man was poorer than he had been in 1900. Between 1896 and 1910, food prices had risen by 25 per cent, causing the real level of wages to drop. In presenting the case for a minimum wage, George Barker, a trades union leader from South Wales, illustrated his argument using the example of the average miner whose nominal wage was 27 shillings* for a six-day week living in a household of six. 'He does not work full-time,' Barker said,

there is the slack time, trade and general holidays to be taken into account, which will reduce the average from six days to five-and-a-half-per-week, and reduces his average wages from 27 shillings to 24 shillings 9 pence per week. Let us look now at the family budget, which will work out at something like this for a family of six persons. Rent 6 shillings

* £89 at today's values.

per week, coal 1 shilling and 6 pence, fuel 1 shilling, clothing and footwear per week 5 shillings, club doctor and Federation per week 1 shilling, making a total of 14 shillings and 6 pence. This leaves 10sh and 3 pence per week for food to feed six persons for a week. Allowing a bare three meals per day, eighteen meals per week – 126 meals – with 123 pence to pay for them, or less than 1 pence per meal per head. Have we overstated the case? No; if anything it is understated. There are thousands in this movement that are existing for less than 1 pence per meal per head.

In the event, the miners did not, as the Prime Minister had feared, continue their strike. Reluctantly, divided over the fact that the Minimum Wage Bill had failed to stipulate the 'fives and twos', they returned to work at the beginning of April. The crisis had passed, but it left a profound feeling of unease. The miners had returned not just with a sense of grievance, but with a sense of power. They were not alone. The transport workers, the dockers and the railwaymen had come out before them: it was felt that it was simply a question of time before they joined forces to mount the final assault of a General Strike.

George V's visit to Wentworth was triggered by the unprecedented industrial militancy that overshadowed the first twelve months of his reign; that it was a deliberately conceived public relations exercise designed to strengthen the position of his throne is suggested by an entry in the Archbishop of York's diary. It was he who first thought of the idea while staying with the King and Queen at Balmoral. Intrigued, George V asked the Archbishop to submit a memo. He recorded its substance in his diary: 'I urged the importance of his [the King's] coming into contact with the masses of his people, that it was not enough that they should assemble in the streets on ceremonial occasions to see him, but that he might, so to say, go to see them – move about with as little ceremony as possible through their own towns, villages and workshops.'

Cosmo Gordon Lang, the Archbishop of York, was a member of the Edwardian 'liberal' establishment; he subscribed to its belief that society would have to be modified if its essential features were to be preserved. As a close personal friend and adviser to George V, it was this belief that motivated him to suggest that the King should alter his modus operandi too. As prelate in one of the great industrial dioceses, Gordon Lang was sensitive to the suffering of the working class. Presciently, on the eve of George V's coronation, he addressed an audience in the Queen's Hall. 'The nineteenth century,' he told them,

> was concerned with the creation of wealth: the twentieth century will be concerned with its distribution. There is none of us, whatever may be his political views, who does not feel that this is a problem which needs adjusting. We cannot but be appalled by the contrast of increasing prosperity and great wealth and of great poverty, of increasing luxury and of great squalor . . . When I think of that great multitude of our working folk among whom I have laboured, whom I have learnt to revere, I cannot but see the picture of the monotony of toil which they are called upon to bear, of the uncertainty of employment which haunts them day by day, of the overcrowded houses in which we ask and expect them to rear British homes, of the mean streets from which every sign not only of the beauty of God's earth but of the comforts and conveniences that are common to ours are shut out . . . Our best self in the contemplation of this inequality says that these things ought not to be.

In the weeks immediately following the coal strike, George V's courtiers and advisers worked on the concept that Lang had outlined in his memo. The intention was to show the King's subjects that he sympathized with the plight of the working man, with particular emphasis on the miner. Wentworth was the obvious base for the duration of the royal tour. The Fitzwilliam family had a track record, stretching back over a century, that showed their concern for the welfare of their employees; the house, situated close to Sheffield and in the heart of the South Yorkshire coalfield, was located in a major industrial area – and it was maintained in a style that was appropriate for the King and Queen. No other coal-owning family could match these criteria.

The tour was orchestrated with the precision of a military campaign. Five-minute stops were scheduled for maximum effect: at one, at Clifton Park outside Rotherham, the King was to meet a fourteen-year-old boy who had had both his legs amputated after a bout of scarlet fever. A pair of artificial limbs, to enable the boy to walk again, was sent ahead seven weeks in advance of the visit with a personal note from the King attached.

Billy Fitzwilliam's brief as host of the royal tour was to show the King 'three million of his working people'. On the afternoon of 8 July, the royal train pulled in at Doncaster station. On the fifteen-mile journey to Wentworth, along streets festooned with bunting and the cross of St George, tens of thousands from the pit villages en route turned out to greet the royal party. At Conisbrough Castle, where the King and Queen stopped for tea with the Earl and Countess of Yarborough, 7,000 miners lined the castle's keep. Cosmo Gordon Lang was travelling in the King's car. As the open Daimler approached Wentworth, it was held up outside Rotherham by a crowd of thousands more. In his diary, the Archbishop records overhearing the following conversation:

'Na then, which is t'King?'
'It's little chap i' the front wi' a billycock hat.'
'Nay, he ain't seech a fine man as Teddy [King Edward VII].'
'Well, anyway, he's gotten him a fine oopstanding wife.'

At first, as Lang noted, the King and Queen 'seemed to be somewhat disconcerted by such free remarks', but as he described, the warmth of the welcome was overwhelming. On their arrival at Wentworth, 40,000 spectators were gathered in the Park. To the cheers of the huge crowd, the King and Queen descended from the royal car. Crossing the drive, they mounted the steps leading to the balcony beneath the portico from where they were to watch the assembled soldiers parade. As they did so, a lady-in-waiting bent down discreetly to remove a piece of pit shale from the pink drive that had caught in the Queen's long skirt.

13

Some hours later at Wentworth, a servant rang the gong for dinner in the Pillared Hall. A single metal disc, the size of a manhole cover, it was mounted on a wooden frame. He rang it once, using a long drumstick with a large felt-cushioned tip. The noise was ear-splitting, ricocheting off the stone pillars to the Marble Salon above. A sixty-foot cube, the room was a perfect echo chamber: the marble walls and floors transmitted the sound to the farthest reaches of the house.

Below stairs, the servants had finished their dinner. The custom at Wentworth was for the staff to eat early. 'An army fights on its stomach as they say,' recalled Elfrida, Countess of Wharncliffe, Billy's daughter. 'They were much happier, they liked it much better than in some other houses where they had to wait until the dining-room dinner was over and they didn't get their supper until 11 o'clock which I thought was disgraceful.' Dinner in the Steward's Room had been as formal an affair as the one that was about to take place upstairs. 'There were six separate dining halls for the servants, depending on your place in the hierarchy,' recalled Peter Diggle, the son of Colonel Heathcote Diggle, the manager of Billy Fitzwilliam's estates. 'The Steward's Room was the top dining room, reserved for the Upper Ten. It was terribly smart. They sat on Chippendale chairs.' The Upper Ten were the most senior servants in the hierarchy. They included the groom of the chambers, the housekeeper, the house steward, the butler, the under-butler, the head housemaid, the Fitzwilliams' valets and ladies' maids and those of their visiting guests. They dined in style: a footman served them at a table laid with fine china and glass; the men wore smoking jackets or evening dress, the women, long silk gowns. Precedence was strictly observed.

The Marchioness of Bath, in her memoir *Before the Sunset Fades*, a nostalgic record of country-house life before the Great War, explained the intricacies of the rules of precedence below stairs:

> A visiting servant ranked on the same scale as his master or mistress, and his place at the table was arranged accordingly. If, for example, a Duke came to stay, his valet would have the honour of arming-in the housekeeper and would be seated at her right; in the same way, the maid of a visiting royalty would go in to dinner on the arm of the hierarchical head, the house steward.

The servants of a commoner, however eminent, processed into – and left – the room last. It was a frequent cause of resignation, as Lady Augusta Fane described in her memoirs. 'One lady's maid,' she noted, 'told her untitled employer that she wanted to leave her service because "it hurts my feelings always to have to walk last from the Hall. I want to take a situation with a titled lady or at least an Honourable."' But as the memoirs of other aristocrats record, the servants' social vanity was equally matched by their employers'. 'I always remember the Duchess of Buccleuch and the Duchess of Northumberland sidling through the door together in their determination not to give precedence to the other,' recalled the Duke of Bedford. Consuelo Balsan, the American heiress married to the Duke of Marlborough and regarded as an arriviste by her aristocratic contemporaries, wrote of her own humiliation when, in deference to her elders, she failed to observe the strict codes of precedence. As a Duchess, the rules dictated that she should proceed first: 'After waiting at the door of the dining room for older women to pass through,' Consuelo wrote, 'I one day received a furious push from an irate Marchioness who loudly claimed that it was just as vulgar to hang back as to leave before one's turn.'

At Wentworth, on the night of 8 July, after the gong had sounded, the house party gathered in the Ante Room to the south of the Marble Salon.

In the presence of royalty, social etiquette reached its apotheosis. The King and Queen did not enter the room until the other house guests had assembled; only they could originate conversation; no one was allowed to sit down if the King and Queen were standing up. The party formed up to process across the Marble Salon to the State Dining Room. Billy Fitzwilliam led off with the Queen. They were followed by the King and Maud Fitzwilliam. The other guests processed in pairs behind them according to their position in the tables of precedence.

Besides the King and Queen, the house party numbered thirty-four. It was made up of courtiers, Yorkshire grandees and friends and relations of the Fitzwilliams. The guest list for the royal visit included:

Lord Stamfordham – Private Secretary to the King
The Hon. Henry Legge – Equerry to the King
The Hon. Clive Wigram – Assistant Private Secretary to the King
Sir Charles and Lady Fitzwilliam – Equerry to the King and his wife
The Archbishop of York, Cosmo Gordon Lang
Lady Eva Dugdale – the Queen's lady-in-waiting
The Marquess and Marchioness of Zetland – Billy's parents-in-law
Major and Lady Theresa Fletcher – Billy's sister and her husband
The Hon. Henry and Lady Mary Fitzwilliam – Billy's uncle and his wife
Sir Francis and Lady Bridgeman, Mr Frank Brooke and Miss Magdelene Talbot – Billy's cousins
The Earl of Scarbrough
The Earl and Countess of Harewood
The Earl and Countess of Rosse
Viscount and Viscountess Helmsley
The Hon. Edward Wood – the heir to Viscount Halifax
Mr George Lane-Fox, MP for Barkston-Ash, and his wife, Lady Agnes, daughter of Viscount Halifax
Walter Long, MP for the Strand division of Middlesex, and his wife, Lady Dorothy, daughter of the Earl of Cork

Miss Dawnay, the daughter of Viscount Downe
Henry Lygon, the nephew of the Earl of Beauchamp
Lord Charles Beresford, MP for Portsmouth and his wife, Lady Mina
Theresa, Marchioness of Londonderry

The list of guests reflects the small, exclusive world of the grand Edwardian house party where the degrees of separation could be calculated in fractions. The guests were tied by land, politics and marriage. If they did not know one another personally, they certainly knew of one another. But it is the vein of scandal that links them that is the most intriguing. The house party at Wentworth typifies the double standards of Edwardian life. The formality, the strict adherence to social codes, was a mask: behind it lay a tangled cluster of forbidden love – illegitimate children, illicit affairs and homosexuality.

Theresa, Lady Londonderry's, love affairs, for instance, linked her to two of the other guests. One of them was her sister's son: her nephew, Lord Helmsley. For several years, during the 1880s, she had had an affair with his father, who had been the best man at her own wedding. Her second son, Reginald, was thought to have been the product of this liaison. She was also rumoured to have had a brief affair with Edward VII, George V's father, who, when he was Prince of Wales, apparently seduced her at a shooting party. 'She was in love with Love,' wrote Theresa's confidante, Elizabeth, Countess of Fingall; 'she was deeply interested in the love affairs of her friends and very disappointed if they did not take advantage of the opportunities she put in their way. She used to say to herself: "I am a Pirate. All is fair in Love and War".' Lady Theresa's colourful emotional life was the rule rather than the exception in the fin-de-siècle years that extended to the beginning of the Great War. Aristocratic marriages were more or less arranged: it was understandable – and understood – that the socio-economic motives that lay behind them would lead the parties to search for love elsewhere.

But of all the guests staying at Wentworth, Lord Charles and

Lady Mina Beresford were perhaps the most notorious. They had come within a whisker of breaking the most rigid of the social conventions. 'What a man or woman might feel or do in private was their own affair, but our rule was No Scandal!' wrote the Countess of Warwick. 'Whenever there was a threat of impending trouble, pressure would be brought to bear, sometimes from the highest quarters, and almost always successfully. We realized that publicity would cause chattering tongues, and as we had no intention of changing our mode of living, we saw to it that five out of every six scandals never reached the outside world.'

Frances Warwick, married to the Earl of Warwick and one of the great beauties of her time, was Banquo at the table of the Wentworth house party. Twenty years earlier, along with Charles and Mina Beresford, she had been at the centre of a scandal in which Edward VII – at the time Prince of Wales – had also become embroiled. Charles Beresford and the Prince had been great friends until, in 1890, they had a spectacular and – within their circles – very public falling-out over the Prince's affair with Frances Warwick, Charles Beresford's mistress. Society was gripped by the quarrel: 'Wild rumours passed,' wrote Sir Shane Leslie, 'that they had met in the boudoir of a lady that they both admired and that Charlie had knocked his rival down. The truth was that he had pushed the Prince, who dropped into a sofa murmuring, "Really, Lord Charles, you forget yourself."' Beresford was angry with the Prince, not because he had taken up with his mistress, but because his wife, Mina, had been doubly humiliated. After discovering her husband's affair she had shown the Prince a letter that Frances Warwick had written to Beresford in an attempt to win him back. The letter was passionate and sexually explicit, described by the Prince as 'the most shocking letter [he] had ever read'. Yet such were its charms that, rather than banishing Lady Frances from court, as Mina Beresford had hoped, the Prince promptly claimed her as his mistress. It was Mina who was banished from court instead!

Eighteen months of the Prince's boycott, coupled with the favours he bestowed upon Lady Frances, proved too much for the

Beresfords. In June 1891, Charles wrote to the Prince threatening to make the scandal public and to expose the contents of Lady Frances's 'shocking letter'. 'Matters have now reached a state,' Beresford warned the Prince,

> that compels me to reflect whether I am to go on shielding a former friend . . . and see my wife deliberately insulted in vengeance for my turpitude. The days of duelling are past but there is a more just way of getting right done . . . The first opportunity that occurs I shall give my opinion publicly of Your Royal Highness, and state that you have behaved . . . like a blackguard and a coward, and that I am prepared to prove my words.

Pressure was – to use Lady Warwick's words – 'brought to bear from the highest quarters'. The Prime Minister, Lord Salisbury, fearful of a genuinely public scandal – one that would escape the confines of Society and prove damaging to the Crown – was forced to intervene: 'Ill-considered publicity,' he admonished Lord Charles in a letter, 'would be of no possible service to Lady Charles . . . it would do you most serious harm . . . I strongly advise you to . . . do nothing.' The Prime Minister persuaded the Prince of Wales to issue an apology to the Beresfords on condition that Lady Frances's letter was destroyed. Five years later, the young George's distaste at the whole affair is apparent in a letter he sent to his wife: 'My levee went off very well . . . there were a great many naval officers. Lord Charles Beresford was presented. I did *not* shake hands with him. It was rather unpleasant for me, but luckily he did not come very close.'

'All is fair in Love and War,' as Lady Theresa quoted. By the summer of 1912, the froideur between the King and the Beresfords had abated. Prior to his visit, George V had been sent a list of the people Billy Fitzwilliam planned to invite: the Beresfords were clearly acceptable.

The list of those who stayed at Wentworth during the royal visit is comprehensive, drawn from the handwritten one that Billy gave to his groom of chambers. We know which bedrooms the guests slept in; we know what they ate during their four-day stay. The descendants of the servants, through memories passed down by their parents and grandparents, have painted the scene. Yet that is almost all that is known about what happened inside the house, away from the public stage, during the the royal visit. Not only have the Archives at Windsor Castle and at Wentworth been destroyed, but so, it seems, have the private papers belonging to Billy Fitzwilliam's guests.

With the exception of those of the Archbishop of York and one other member of the house party, no records appear to survive to offer a personal account of the royal visit. There are no diaries, no letters, no mementos. There are, of course, many reasons why this should be the case. Some are particular: in 1919, a fire gutted Duncombe Park, the home of the Helmsleys, destroying most of the family's papers; Captain Frank Brooke was murdered by the IRA in 1920 and his house in Ireland burnt to the ground; at least six of the guests died childless – there were no heirs for them to pass their papers on to – and in the case of some members of the house party, the turbulent events of the twentieth century diminished their families: in the downsizing from house to house, the bulk of the past was thrown away.

But there are families descended from the guests at Wentworth who emerged from the twentieth century comparatively unscathed – in the sense that their historic homes remain in their possession, or have been handed over to the nation relatively intact. The Zetlands, Scarbroughs, Rosses, Harewoods and Londonderrys are among those who fall into this category. Yet none of their historic collections contain references to the Royal Tour of the North.

The coincidence of the void is extraordinary. One reason alone might explain it, evident in a letter written by a descendant of Sir Henry Legge, equerry to George V, who accompanied the King on his visit to Wentworth in 1912. 'Unfortunately,' he explained, 'we have virtually no letters, diaries or other written archive of Sir Harry, who would have regarded it as totally unethical to "tell tales" of his work over 3 reigns.'

The coincidence is otherwise inexplicable.

In light of the events that unravelled in the course of the King's stay at Wentworth, it is remarkable that so little appears to have been preserved.

14

Albert Wildman stood in a queue of men waiting to go down the pit. The cage came suddenly, swinging up from nowhere, juddering to a halt with a clash of metal. Blackened faces hurried past – miners coming off the afternoon shift eager to get home. It was the start of the night shift at Cadeby Main colliery, a mile from Denaby. The time was ten o'clock on 8 July 1912.

The queue shuffled forward into the cage: 'Fourteen . . . fifteen . . . sixteen!' shouted the banksman, thrusting his arm across a man's chest. Sixteen men made a load or a 'draw'. Wildman could see the dusk settling outside: the flywheel silhouetted against the darkening sky, a mist rising from the ribbon of road stretching towards the village. He was feeling out of sorts. Some 500 miners normally worked this night shift, but that evening only a hundred or so had shown up. The absentees had gone to the party at Conisbrough, a few miles from Denaby, to welcome the King and Queen. Albert would have liked to have gone too, but he had young children to feed: like most of the men working that night, he could not afford to miss a shift. A bell rang sharply. In an instant, road and mist were clipped away. As the cage gathered speed in its descent to the pit bottom half a mile below jets of air whistled through the floor, billowing coats and trousers and rustling hair. The men's lamps illuminated the slimy walls slipping past, streaking upwards, the sky above becoming a pinhead, then a speck. The floor began to bounce; the cage was slowing down: far above, the steel rope had tightened on the drum. The doors rattled open to a whitewashed cavernous chamber where scores of deputies, trammers, faceworkers and pony boys crowded, waiting to start the shift.

Albert Wildman, along with forty other miners, headed off for

No. 1 district – a remote area of the pit, a twenty-five-minute walk from the bottom of the shaft.

Eight miles away, at Wentworth, the King and Queen and the house party of thirty-four guests were half-way through dinner, seated at the three round tables in the State Dining Room. In the soft light cast by the candelabra the gold tableware and the crystal glass glittered. Military medals, pinned on the men's lapels, caught the light as they moved; diamonds, rubies and emeralds from the ladies' tiaras and jewels glinted in reply, as if flashing some secret aristocratic code.

More than twenty footmen in full-dress livery stood behind the guests waiting to serve the ninth of thirteen courses. Even by the standards of the late Edwardians it had been a sumptuous meal, prepared by French chefs drafted up to Wentworth from London specially for the occasion. It had begun with *Caviar Frais, Consommé Froid Madrilène, Saumon Truite et Mayonnaise, Filet de Boeuf Poêle, Poularde aux Perles de Périgord* and *Timbale d'Homard Royale*, with *Neige au Cliquot* and *Cailles aux Raisins* to follow. The ninth course, the main dessert, was the culinary highlight. A strawberry dish, with a base of crème anglaise and jelly, the pudding was served in baskets spun from sugar. It had taken the resident confectioner three days to weave the baskets. Perfectly proportioned, they had circular handles and a tiny lid that lifted to reveal the strawberries nestling inside. To complete the conceit, the confectioner had coloured the sugar paste to give it a grain, like dark oak. The remaining courses – a savoury, cheese, fruit and petits fours – were still to come.

Billy Fitzwilliam sat with the Queen on his right. Playing host to a reigning monarch was a first for the family. Queen Victoria's visit to Wentworth in 1855 had been cancelled owing to the ill-health of the 5th Earl Fitzwilliam. Before that, in 1789, George IV, as Prince of Wales, had been the most senior royal to visit the house. In the library at Wentworth, Billy kept a treasured leather-bound scrapbook, passed down through the generations, containing the newspaper cuttings from the Prince of Wales's stay. The 4th Earl Fitzwilliam had been his host:

> His Lordship in honour of his royal visitor gave the most splendid and magnificent entertainment that was ever witnessed in this part of England. Anxiously expecting to behold the illustrious visitor, not less than 40,000 people were assembled before the front of the house early in the afternoon. About four o'clock he returned from a morning visit to Lord Strafford and their highest hopes were fully gratified. He alighted from his horse amidst the huzzas of thousands, and, with the endearing affability which is his popular characteristic, he exhibited himself in the portico of the Saloon . . .
>
> After dinner – the Prince, Lord and Lady Fitzwilliam, His Grace of Norfolk, Sir Thomas Dundas and family and other gentlemen of distinction appeared again in the portico, and by means of a speaking trumpet held intercourse with the delighted multitude. A call of silence being made, the King's health was drunk by the Prince, and followed by loud and repeated acclamations . . . The spectators were all this while gratified by the Prince's presence, who for some time held up Lord Milton (a beautiful cherub, three years old) the only child of Earl Fitzwilliam, to see and be seen by the surrounding thousands.

More than a century had passed, yet in scale King George V's and Queen Mary's arrival had all but matched the Prince's visit in 1789. As dinner drew to a close, looking at the scene around him, Billy Fitzwilliam could congratulate himself; the royal visit was an affirmation of his family, testimony to its enduring wealth and strength.

The Prince and his entourage had danced till dawn; in 1912, it was not that late when the party began to break up. An early start was planned for the next morning: the first stop on the King's itinerary was a meeting with the fourteen-year-old boy to whom, seven weeks earlier, he had sent a pair of artificial limbs. It was to be followed by a tour of the surface workings at Silverwood colliery.

By midnight, the house was wrapped in silence and darkness.

★

Half a mile below ground, in the tunnels of No. 1 district at Cadeby Main colliery, Albert Wildman and William Humphries were laying a road. Aside from their clogs, they wore only a strip of cloth around their groins; the tunnel they worked in was just six feet high, the temperature in the pit approaching 95 degrees. As they sweated in the half-light, the props – the timber joints that held up the roof along the tunnel – creaked and cracked, shifting to the awesome weight above. 'Hundreds of millions of tons of stone and clay and shale and dirt,' one miner wrote, 'and higher still upon the table of it all, moves the busy world of men.' Albert should have been up at the coalface with his usual workmate, Joseph Boycott, but, because of the number of absentees, the pit deputy was a man short in No. 1 district. Wildman had been paired up with William Humphries instead.

The two men felt uneasy as they worked; the pit was so empty. Where normally there would be a hundred miners, there were no men working either side of them for 400 yards.

'We were getting along swimmingly with the work,' Wildman remembered. 'There was only another few hours left before the end of the shift. All of a sudden the air reversed, and it grew even hotter. The air was filled with dust, it all picked up from the tunnel floor. I can't tell you what it was like but it was fearfully weird. We didn't hear a sound, but the air, which had been blowing in one direction, suddenly began blowing in exactly the opposite. The sensation it gave me was just as though a big clock had been ticking and suddenly stopped.'

The two men carried on working, but Humphries, a more experienced miner, was frightened. He went off to ask the opinion of a couple of men working further up the tunnel. He told them what he had felt but, as he later reported, 'could not make anything of them'. Returning to Albert, they continued their work. After a bit, the flame in their lamps guttered to a thin blue plume – the sign of foul air. 'Work I could not,' said Humphries, 'I thought there was something really amiss in the pit, but where it was I did not know.' Increasingly anxious, he decided to walk to the top of the district to check the ventilation system that circulated air around the pit. On his way back to Albert, to his relief, he saw the light of a miner's lamp heading towards him along the tunnel. It was John Farmer:

When I got to Humphries, Humphries asked me if I'd heard anything or seen anything. I said, certainly not. I said I've just come off the east to the pit bottom and I'd neither seen nor heard anything, so he described to me what had occurred. As soon as he mentioned the wind reversing and the dust, I said, 'My God! There's been an explosion down the South Plane.' I said it would be wise for us to go down the plane forthwith. Well, we wanted to see: we hadn't any snap [food and water], we generally feel dry when we've had a run around like that. He wanted to see Wildman as regards coupling this road up. I said, 'Nip down and tell him and I'll wait of [*sic*] you and we'll go down the plane. Of course, when he came back I asked him if he was ready and he didn't answer as regards going down and he did utter these words, he says, 'If what you think is right there will be someone up before now if there had been anything the matter.' I says, 'Good God, have you never known a district cut off and another district at work and that district know nothing about it.' He said, 'I have,' and I said, 'Perhaps there is no individual down there can get up.'

The truth was that Humphries was too scared to go and investigate. More than half an hour had passed since he and Wildman had first noticed something was wrong. Farmer went alone.

When I got 200 or 300 yards I began to see pieces of lids and various coverings and timbers blown about, lying in awkward positions across the rails. And then I proceeded further down. When I got further down, I began to feel being all alone, I began to feel a little strange in the head. I shouted two or three times and it was silent as the grave. I thought it would be wise for me to go back and get assistance.

Farmer dispatched Albert Wildman to run the half-mile back to the shaft to get help. It was 4.30 a.m., an hour after the explosion.

Above ground, dawn was breaking over Denaby, the village where many of the Cadeby miners lived. Bunting from the previous day's festivities fluttered in a light breeze; in the alleyways between the back-to-backs, Union Jacks lay strewn over the cobblestones. As the sun rose from behind Scabba Wood, the village was woken by the most sickening of sounds: a sound every householder dreaded. Someone in one of the houses began to bang a poker against a fire grate, the signal that there had been a serious accident at the pit. Within seconds, the sound was replicated a thousandfold, as others took up their pokers to drum out the grim beat.

At Wentworth, the domestic army had risen early to prepare breakfast.

The kitchen men and the coal porters were the first to wake. Their job was to stoke the fires in the kitchen so that breakfast could be cooked and to rouse the lower servants – the housemaids, scullery maids and kitchenmaids. 'It was the handymen – the kitchen men – who woke us up,' recalled May Bailey, a scullery maid. 'We slept on the lower ground floor. When they carted the coal to the kitchen they used to knock on our windows. The handymen were always in the kitchen. They lifted all the big pans. There were these huge pans, set pots they called them. Like cauldrons, they were. We couldn't lift them, the men did that. They had all these big cookers like barbecues. The fires were underneath the grate, with the stoves on either side, like an Aga. The fires kept the ovens going, and the men used to keep them going. The head kitchenmaid would say, "We want some more fuel on the fire, rake it, I want it hot."' Breakfast was cooked over the fire: chops, bloaters, chickens, woodcocks and cutlets were roasted in rows on spits. 'They'd have twenty woodcocks in a row,' remembered May Bailey, 'all hanging down over the fire. The bacon was grilled in another part of the kitchen and there was one chef who had to make all the egg dishes.'

By seven, the housemaids and footmen were also up. Tea trays were prepared to be taken upstairs and presented to the ladies' maids and valets outside the guests' bedroom doors. Footmen toasted and ironed the newspapers, crisping them for the breakfast table. In the scullery, the maids washed the loose change the men in the house party had emptied from their pockets and left out the night before. Later, their valets would return the sparkling coins. Breakfast was to be served at eight. The King was due to leave Wentworth at ten o'clock.

Six hours after the explosion, underground at Cadeby Main, a rescue party had at last reached '14 level' in the South District, the place where it had occurred.

The devastation was described by Albert Wildman:

> We went slowly forward through the darkness. Suddenly one of the men shouted. We had come upon the scene of the disaster. At this point the pit was just one awful crumple. Lumps of roof and piles of 'muck' were in all directions, and fragments of shattered tubs were scattered all about. Suddenly we saw something white sticking out of the dust. It was the body of a man. He lay with his head on his arm as though he had tried to shield his eyes. We pulled him up out of the dust in which he was nearly buried and rolled him over. But he was quite dead. A little further on there were more bodies. Some were terribly shattered and scorched, while others looked as though they had passed peacefully away in their sleep. One boy – a lad of fourteen – we found lying with his arms around the neck of a pit-pony. Every hair was singed from the pony's body . . .

At 8.45, the pit manager confirmed that every man, boy and horse on '14 level' was dead. As Albert Wildman later told a reporter, 'My mate, Joseph Boycott, went down the workings and he's dead now. But for the King's visit, I should be dead also.'

Unaware of the manager's verdict, at the pithead a crowd of 200 women waited for news of their loved ones. The night shift had ended at 6 a.m. Seventy-six men had come out of the mine. All they knew was that thirty-five miners were missing. As the first bodies were brought up, the police formed a cordon around the shaft to hold the women back from the pit mouth. A local reporter was with them:

Some three hundred yards from the road is situated the shaft and plainly visible to the horror-stricken spectators was a continuous procession of ambulance men bearing corpses from the pit to the pay room, where the long tables were rapidly filled up with the bodies of victims wrapped in white sheets . . . at first the women were fiercely angry with the officials for keeping them away from the squat building of red brick into which the stretchers are carried. 'Why can't you let us see whether our men are dead or not?' one woman shouted, seizing a policeman's arm. 'If I was in your place I wouldn't block the way two minutes.' Another woman put an arm around her and led her gently away. 'It's no good taking on so,' she said. 'We'll know soon enough, God help us.'

Stretcher-bearers were bringing a new body out of the cage every two minutes. The suspense was awful.

On a stone by the road that leads to the colliery an old man has kept watch for many hours. Sometimes he mutters to himself and plucks at his beard, and every now and then he springs to his feet, and, confronting some little group of miners that are about to pass him, beseeches them to give him some news of his sons. He is incoherent with agitation – almost crazy. 'They're down there, both of 'em,' he keeps repeating. 'Don't say that they've put 'em in the dead house.'

By mid-morning, the body count had reached twenty-two. Then, suddenly, shortly after eleven o'clock, the procession of corpses came to a halt. The great wheels silhouetted against the sky above the pithead – the mechanism that wound the cage up and down the shaft – stopped turning. Shouts were heard coming from the vicinity of the lamp room next to the cage. Rumour of a second explosion ran through the waiting crowd.

It was true. Underground there was carnage. Forty-four men who had courageously volunteered to go down the pit to bring up the bodies from the first blast had been killed. Sergeant Winch was one of the few members of the rescue party to survive:

We had been working down the pit for a couple of hours recovering the bodies of those killed in the first explosion – loading them into a train to carry them to pit-bottom. I think we had recovered about twenty-four bodies. It struck me that our electric torches had been in use for rather a long time, and that it would be well to recharge them. That thought saved my life. Two other men came with me. We had not gone more than a hundred yards when there was a roar. I found myself groping on the ground in thick darkness and swirling dust. How many yards I had been thrown by the explosion I can't say. Dust. I have seen some terrible dust storms in India, but they were a trifle to the dust that swept over us. It was like a great black torrent. I groped my way about and suddenly I saw a tiny twinkle of light. It was from my electric lamp which was lying on the ground half-buried. There were hoarse shouts from behind us, and I got my lamp and we groped our way back to see if we could save anyone. We came across one or two who had been even nearer to the explosion than ourselves. They were badly cut about and we assisted them along the road. But there was no sign of the main body of rescuers. A huge fall had taken place close to where they were standing, shutting them in completely. It stopped up the way just like a cork pushed into a bottle. I believe that fall saved our lives, for while it crushed many of the rescue party, I believe that it dammed the flow of the after-damp which otherwise would have reached us and choked us before we got a hundred yards.

Frederick Smith and his team, volunteers from a neighbouring colliery, were also lucky to escape: 'For the most part,' he said, 'we were strangers to the pit, and half a dozen other men and myself took a turning which we thought would lead us to the victims of the first explosion. As a matter of fact, we lost our way, and that saved our lives. We went down a turning, and suddenly found we were cut off from the remainder of the rescue party. We were just about to turn round to get back to the main body, if possible, when the place was filled with a red glare. There was a dull rumbling noise and smoke and dust filled the air. Then came the gas. It made us turn sick and faint, but we held up, and in a few minutes the air had grown comparatively clear, and seizing our lamps, we retraced our steps along the road to discover what had become of our friends. We had not gone far before we came upon them. Bodies absolutely littered the ground. We had a pulmotor apparatus with us, and we did our best to revive one or two of them. Some of them were still alive and gasped feebly. One man suddenly exclaimed, "Lord help me, I am done," and collapsed. When we bent over him he was quite dead.'

Sergeant Winch and the two miners who had gone with him to get the chargers for the lamps, and Fred Smith and his men were among the few left alive on the shaft side of the fall. One hundred tons of rock had crashed from the roof in the explosion, entombing the rescue party: without proper digging equipment, it was impossible to reach the dead and dying on the other side. For the second time that day, as Albert Wildman had done some hours earlier, the men ran the mile to the pit bottom to raise the alarm.

News of the first explosion had reached the King at breakfast. Immediately, his Private Secretary wired a telegram to the colliery:

The King and Queen are shocked to hear of the terrible accident at your colliery, and perhaps the fact that Their Majesties were near to the scene in the midst of so much rejoicing, when they visited Conisbrough yesterday, brings home to them still more the sorrow and sadness which now prevail amongst you. I am desired to express Their Majesties' sympathy with the families of those who have perished, and with the sufferers in this grievous calamity.

There was no question of cancelling the morning's programme: after breakfast, it was decided that the royal show must go on. The King had left Wentworth at ten o'clock. In the space of three hours he saw nine pit villages – all in the vicinity of Cadeby. Throughout the morning, the royal party was kept informed of developments. Though overshadowed by the tragedy unfolding close by, the first morning of the tour was judged to be a great success. On the scheduled stops – at Clifton Park outside Rotherham and at Silverwood colliery – crowds of upwards of 50,000 turned out to greet the King and Queen. Similar numbers lined the roads along which they progressed. Everywhere they went, the brass bands from the collieries played the national anthem, the crowds spontaneously joining in. At Silverwood colliery, the royal party stopped for an hour to inspect the surface workings. They watched two windings of coal coming up from the pit, and saw it weighed and 'checked' before it passed on to the tippers. The colliery had arranged an eccentric form of transport for the Queen. 'For a greater part of the distance,' the local newspaper reported,

a railway platelayer's trolley was provided for Her Majesty, who, seated in a revolving chair, and with Lady Eva Dugdale and Lady Aberconway standing on either side, appeared to enjoy greatly the novel mode of locomotion. Excepting that a piece of cocoa-nut matting served as a carpet, the trolley was in proper working 'condition' and it was propelled along the lines by half-a-dozen men.

The highlight of the morning, as the *Yorkshire Post* floridly reported, was an unscheduled stop at a cottage in Woodlands, the model village that had been built for the workforce at Brodsworth Main colliery.

It was William Brown's, bearing the prosaic number 33, and the aristocratic address of The Park. Yet it was only a miner's cottage, with a trim little garden in front of roses and more common-place flowers carefully cultivated by the tenant. In the little garden there stood the collier's wife, Mrs Brown, and Mrs Aston, the next door neighbour, both with babies in arms, wistfully watching the Royal procession and the great people who made it up. Suddenly the Royal car stopped outside the garden gate and out stepped the King and Queen smiling. Both advanced towards the cottage door. The poor women, embarrassed, seemingly almost frightened, turned on their heels and rushed to the threshold of the house. Greatly amused their Majesties followed, piloted by Mr Greensmith, the local colliery manager, and in a second the party had disappeared into the house. News of the visit, which was obviously unexpected, quickly spread, and in less than a minute the cottage of the Browns was in a state of violent siege. In the middle of the crushing and squeezing could be seen the Archbishop of York, laughingly enjoying his own novel position as much as he appeared to do the unusualness of a Royal visit to a humble cottage, while members of noble houses who had accompanied the party looked on with great good humour. The crowd surged over the rose trees and flower beds of the trim garden in their anxiety to get a closer view of the Royal visitors, and Mr Brown's little plot was soon a wreck. For five full minutes the colliers and their wives clamoured round the house, cheering madly, and when the King and Queen emerged the crowd would hardly let them pass to their motor car, so demonstrative were these Woodlands villagers. The Royal pair were obviously touched and obviously pleased. The King's face was wreathed in smiles, and his Consort showed equal pleasure in her experiences, as she made her way back along the garden footpath to the car. A minute later the Royal party left for lunch at Hickleton Hall.

The lunch for the twenty members of the King's suite at Hickleton Hall, Lord Halifax's house, had been well planned. On 29 June, Lord Stamfordham, the King's Private Secretary, had written to Lord Halifax:

I fear I must ask you to consider the luncheon which you kindly give to Their Majesties on the 9th as a hurried meal to satisfy in the shortest time the cravings of more or less empty stomachs!! The tendency is to undertake too much in these 'tours' and it is most difficult to keep up to time and consequently the luncheon is a hurry . . . Their Majesties will be glad to meet anyone you wish to invite but if we are pressed for time it would be difficult for Their Majesties to talk to them but of course you would present them. *No tall hats and black coats.* We shall all be in ordinary county clothes!

Lord Halifax evidently satisfied the 'cravings of more or less empty stomachs': the printed menu for the lunch for his forty guests was as follows:

Chaud

Consommé à l'Impériale
Filet de Soles Frites
Côtelettes d'Agneau à la Macédoine
Poulardes en Casserole
Légumes
Pouding à la farola
Fraises à la Cowlper
Gelées Variées
Macédoine aux Fruits
Pâtissiers

Froid

Salade d'Homards
Poulets à la Langue de Boeuf
Jambon de York Sauce Cumberland
Galantines aux Truffes
Pressé de Boeuf en Aspic

Lunch, intended as a pleasant interlude in a gruelling schedule, became a crisis meeting. When the royal party arrived at Hickleton Hall, some three miles from Cadeby colliery, the latest news of the disaster awaited them. The death toll had leapt from an estimated thirty-five after the first explosion, to over eighty following the second. It was the worst colliery disaster in South Yorkshire since 1893 when 139 miners had been killed at Combs Pit in Thornhill. The tragedy at Cadeby dominated the conversation over lunch. In his diary, the Archbishop of York reveals that a number of the King's officials were uncertain whether, in view of what had happened, it would be wise for the King to keep to his plan to descend Billy Fitzwilliam's mine at Elsecar later that afternoon. The previous week, a miner had been killed at the pit by a fall of stone; that incident – and the dangers evident in the explosions at Cadeby – prompted the officials to urge the King to reconsider his schedule. But, as the Archbishop records, George V was adamant that the descent at Elsecar should go ahead as planned. 'Whatever happens,' he told them, 'I have got to show I want to do all I can at this time to see for myself, as far as I can, the risks to which my miners are exposed.'

By mid-afternoon, at Cadeby, 80,000 people were gathered on the hillside overlooking the pit. As word of the tragedy had spread, they had come from the nearby villages. A local reporter described the scene:

> . . . the ill-fated colliery stood out from the hillside of Cadeby black and stern and sinister and foreboding. The flags that had floated from the headgears the previous day to welcome a King and his Consort were gone and no touch of colour relieved the gaunt tombstone. All that long black terrible day the bodies took their solemn journey down that awful gantry. Men who went to their work hearty and strong at night came back stiff and cold at noon; men who gallantly rushed to the rescue were gently shunted, twisted and lifeless on the slabs at night-fall. The crowd that had flocked into the place in the heat of the afternoon grew and swelled . . . Motor cars and ambulance wagons streamed in continual procession up the hill to the hospital. Now the burden was a rescuer who had been 'gassed' lying back in the arms of a half-naked miner, with a nurse plying a paper fan with tremendous energy for the revival of the lungs; now it was a man desperately wounded, who writhed under the brown covering of the stretcher, and uttered moans or screams. An old, wrinkled woman with red-rimmed staring eyes shambled up and down the grass-bordered pathway, praying at the top of her voice. An ambulance wagon galloped up the hill, and as it pulled up the man inside began to shriek. The old woman thought she recognized the voice of her son. 'Oh God help him,' she cried and she ran forward. The man moaned again, his arms had been unstrapped and he beat the air with them. The old woman peered into his face. It was the face of a stranger. 'Thank God,' she said and tottered back against the wall. 'The Lord he knows everything. The Lord he knows everything.' One woman who had volunteered to help with the ambulance work came face to face

with the dead body of her own husband. Another woman whose husband was killed in the disaster had no less than fourteen children, the youngest an infant in arms.

There were still tens of thousands of people on the hillside and along the roads leading into the village when the King's Daimler, driven at walking pace and with no accompanying motorcade, approached the colliery. The car edged its way through the crowds lining the road, the men and women standing in stunned silence in rows four deep. As the King and Queen drove past, the men removed their hats and bowed their heads, the women dropping to the ground in deep curtseys. The King's visit to Denaby had not been scheduled. In his diary for that day, George V wrote:

At 6.45 May and I with Fitzwilliam and Legge motored off to Conisbrough about 10 miles to the Offices of the Cadeby colliery, as there was a terrible accident this morning, two explosions in which I fear 78 men lost their lives, including Mr Pickering (Govt. Inspector), splendid man. We went to inquire and to express our sympathy with those that have lost their dear ones. There was a large crowd of miners outside the Offices and they appreciated our coming to inquire.

At the entrance to the pit, the royal party was met by a group of officials and twenty miners who had been recovering bodies all afternoon. They wore their working clothes, their faces still black with coal dust. The local paper marvelled at the fact that the King and Queen shook their 'grimy hands'. In the pit office they were shown plans of the mine and told of the force of the explosions. They had been caused by 'gobfires' – the spontaneous combustion of the layers of dust and muck that lay between the seams of coal. Both explosions had occurred after gobfires had ignited pockets of methane gas that had built up in that section of the pit. Billy Fitzwilliam, who, in his early twenties, had worked underground at his own pits before qualifying as a mining engineer and for whom safety was paramount, had anticipated the explosions. Though he owned a stretch of land under which the coal at Cadeby was mined, he had been unable to convince the colliery manager to install better safety measures: 'They hadn't got enough ventilation,' his daughter Elfrida recalled. 'My father had warned them: "You must have more ventilation, you haven't got enough. You've got too much dust. Too much coal dust. That is the biggest danger of the lot." He always said, "Watch Cadeby. There will be a terrible blow-up one day." And he was right.'

Both the King and the Queen were visibly shocked by what the miners and pit officials told them. When the Queen emerged from the pit office she was in tears. Later that evening, Lady Mary Fitzwilliam, one of the guests at Wentworth, wrote in her diary, 'Today the deep shadow was cast over us all of the awful mine explosions at Cadeby mine near Conisbrough: so many killed. After their heavy day's work was over the King and Queen started again for Cadeby to see the poor people and to show their deep sympathy. It has really saddened us all – one could see how the Queen had cried.' The miners and their families were touched by the King and Queen's visit. The local paper described the scene as the royal car drove away from Denaby.

> Their obvious sympathy with the sufferers had a remarkable effect upon the spectators, many of whom, as the Royal party left the village, involuntarily burst into cheers which, although somewhat misplaced, denoted their warm appreciation of the kindliness which had prompted the King and Queen to visit the stricken village. Their visit touched the hearts of the villagers and women sobbed aloud as they drove away.

Lord Halifax at nearby Hickleton Hall was more cynical. Mindful of the impact of the disaster in terms of the King and Queen's public relations, he wrote in a letter to a friend,

> Their visit to the pit after the explosion has done a quite untold good. They, the miners and all the people, were much impressed by the King going down the pit in the afternoon after the accident in the morning. And I am told the women were so moved when the King and Queen came to the scene of the accident in the evening and spoke themselves

to the miners that they were ready to go down on their knees and kiss the Queen's feet.

For two days – night and day – the women of Denaby kept vigil at the pit. They refused to leave until the bodies had left the Pay Station, the makeshift morgue. Fifty still remained, waiting to be identified – and waiting for coffins. The undertakers in the district had run out: their stock had been filled by the first batch of dead. On the Wednesday, the day after the explosions, the Coroner visited the Pay Station:

> A horrible sight met my gaze. There outstretched on the tables were the bodies of the victims, each tenderly covered with a white cloth. The first I saw was the body of a fine muscular man. His face was bronzed, and he seemed to be asleep. The next was a body, the face of which was almost beyond recognition. The poor fellow must have met an awful death. There were several others in a similar state, whilst one man, I shall never forget him, had no legs at all. His clogs were lying underneath the table. And so I proceeded viewing the mangled frames of men – men who had died doing their duty.

The disaster had created sixty-one widows, and left 132 children fatherless. There were no death benefits at Cadeby Main colliery: the management made no provision for a miner's family in the event of his accidental death underground. The widows' housing was tied to the colliery: the loss of their husbands meant the loss of the roof over their heads. For the majority, the future now depended on private donations and parish relief. In the coming months, people gave generously, not only from the district, but from all over the country. But still the bereaved families were left to subsist on a pittance – 5 shillings for each widow, and 1 shilling for every child under fourteen.*

The night before Denaby buried her dead, Billy Fitzwilliam held a party in the Park at Wentworth. It had been planned as a

* At today's values 5 shillings is approximately £16 and 1 shilling, £3.

celebration to mark the end of the King and Queen's visit. With the morning's burials pending, it became a wake.

It was a beautiful summer's night. The sweet smell from the mounds of grass that had been cut, ready for haymaking, drifted across the Park from the surrounding fields. Twenty-five thousand people were gathered in front of the house, stretching as far as the eye could see. They had come from all over the district. On the high balcony, beneath the portico, the King and Queen sat facing the crowd in the middle of the row of house guests. To their right, on a raised crescent-shaped platform, the Sheffield Symphony Orchestra, hired by Billy specially for the occasion, and 300 choristers, dressed in white, waited for the light to fall. When the sun had almost set, the choir began to sing. Their voices were drowned by the crowd joining in:

When Britain first, at heaven's command,
Arose from out the azure main,
This was the charter of the land,
And guardian angels sang this strain:
Rule, Britannia! Britannia, rule the waves.
Britons never, never, never shall be slaves.

'It Comes from the Misty Ages', the chorus from Elgar's *Banner of St George*, followed.

Dusk had fallen. The recital ended with Handel's *Messiah*. As the choir sang the 'Hallelujah' chorus, 600 miners, bearing flaming torches and walking four abreast, appeared beneath the North and South Towers that marked each end of the house. The miners worked at Billy Fitzwilliam's pits. Parading in, with great precision, swinging round in front of the King and Queen, they executed two figures of the Lancers, including the grand chain. The crowd pressed forward into the light cast by their torches. When the music stopped, George V stood up, gesturing to them to come closer. 'My friends,' he shouted, 'the Queen and I are very glad to meet so many miners from this district here tonight, and I wish to tell you how delighted we have been with the beautiful torchlight procession and the excellent singing of the choir. It has been a great pleasure to us to visit your homes and see you at your daily work. We are deeply touched by the enthusiastic reception given to us wherever we have been during the past four days – a reception which we shall never forget and which has made us feel that we are amongst true friends.' The crowd cheered. 'One shadow,' the King continued, 'and a very dark one has, alas, been cast over the joy and brightness of our visit to the West Riding by the terrible disaster at Cadeby, in which so many brave men lost their lives; I am sure that you know that the Queen and I feel deeply for those who mourn for their dear ones. Again we thank you most sincerely for your hearty welcome, and we wish you goodnight and good luck.'

For the moment the neighbourhood was united in grief. The anger and retribution would come two months later when the Government launched an official investigation into the disaster.

The explosions at Cadeby Main could have been avoided. The inquiry found that the union officials were right to accuse the pit management of having sacrificed the lives of the victims on the 'altar of output'. South District, where the explosions had occurred, was – so the investigation revealed – particularly prone to gobfires. A fire had broken out two nights before the disaster. The Inspector of Mines concluded that the pit manager, Mr Chambers, should have withdrawn the miners from that district until the gobfire had been made safe. His failure to do so, after it was first reported, meant that the miners working the night shift on 8 July had been placed in 'grave and unnecessary danger'.

There was no question of the pit manager being prosecuted. Health and safety legislation in the days before the Great War was minimal: broadly, safety issues were left to the discretion of the manager of the individual pit. At the inquiry into the disaster, with the final death toll standing at ninety-three, Mr Chambers gave a series of monosyllabic replies in answer to the investigator's questions. He showed no remorse:

'Mr Chambers, you said that if these men were withdrawn you would have a pit of gobfires and nothing else?'

'Yes.'

'That means you would not get any output, is that it?'

'That is so.'

'Would there not be great consideration expected to be given to the men more than to the output?'

'If you have to have a pit at all you must have men down.'

For managers like Mr Chambers – and there were many like him – the high injury and death toll among miners was simply a way of life. Almost 2,000 miners had been killed and 160,000 injured in 1911. In the pursuit of profits, the men were expendable.

But the tragedy at Cadeby Main, covered extensively in the national Press, had raised the political stakes. Editorials appeared, pointing to the glaring injustice in the coalmining industry. In the *Yorkshire Post*, one of the most widely read northern newspapers, the following challenge was posed:

> Every ton of coal represents so much in money to an idle royalty owner or drawer of fat wayleaves who does nothing: it represents so much in money to the capitalist who has put brains into the concern as well as gold; it represents so much money to the collier and – so much life. An arithmetician could calculate for you in terms of gold, silver, copper, blood, bone and breath the value to a decimal fraction of each ton of black diamonds that comes to the surface . . . For every 137,000 tons of coal one collier is killed, and the question is ought not this killing part of the trade be extended to the royalty owners and the mine-owners?

The King and Queen left Wentworth on the morning of Friday 12 July. The Archbishop of York, the man who had thought up the idea of a Royal Tour of the North, sent a letter to his mother a few days later: 'All my hopes,' he wrote, 'have been more than fulfilled. I can testify to the delight of the people on seeing him and Queen Mary in the midst of them in their own familiar surroundings. I feel sure that these tours did much to create and sustain their sense that he belonged to them and they to him in a very human and personal way.'

On his return to Buckingham Palace, the King sent a thank-you letter – written in his own hand – to Billy Fitzwilliam:

My dear Fitzwilliam
I send you these few lines to repeat how greatly the Queen and I appreciated the very kind hospitality shown to us by you and Lady Fitzwilliam during our charming stay at Wentworth. Our visit to the West Riding was a new experience to us and if I may say so a most successful one and chiefly due to the admirable arrangements which you made and carried out. We shall never forget the splendid reception given to us by the thousands of people we saw during those few days wherever we went. I was very glad to have been able to see so many miners and their families and was especially interested in going down the Elsecar Mine; the different mills and factories which we visited were also most interesting and gave us an insight into the daily life of the people which we were so anxious to get.

Lady Fitzwilliam and you made us most comfortable in your beautiful house and the Queen and I wish once more to express to you both our warmest thanks for all your kindness.

The heat here for the last three days has been very great. I am glad we were spared that last week.

Believe me, very sincerely yours, George R.I. [Rex Imperator]

The Cadeby disaster had overshadowed the royal visit. Yet in the King's letter to Billy Fitzwilliam, it was as if it had never happened. The Queen, in a brief letter to the Archbishop of York, did not mention the disaster either: 'I am delighted,' she wrote, 'to hear that our visit to the West Riding was so much appreciated and I hope it will do permanent good. We were intensely interested in everything we saw and are gratified by our kind welcome from all classes. Believe me, yours very sincerely – Mary.'

In 1914, the class war that had threatened to erupt in the early years of George V's reign would be forgotten as the country united behind the war against Germany.

15

Within days of the outbreak of war, the front lawn at Wentworth was transformed into a troop training ground.

Two batteries of the Royal Horse Artillery – 400 men and forty-eight gun carriages – thundered and rattled up and down the length of the great house. The soldiers were stylishly turned out. Wearing black gold-frogged jackets fitted tightly at the waist, they sported plumed shako caps: these were the Wentworth batteries, personally raised by Billy from his farms, factories and pits. He had equipped the men out of his own pocket, spending thousands of pounds on their uniforms and their mounts: the finest hunters in the county.

In that sweltering summer of 1914, as Commanding Officer of the Wentworth Batteries, Billy prepared his troops for battle. At his instigation, they were among the first to use motorized artillery. Motor-cars were one of Billy's main interests. Since 1905, he had bankrolled the manufacture of the Sheffield Simplex, a luxury touring vehicle intended to rival the Rolls-Royce. At the outbreak of war, he ordered a fleet of them to be driven over to Wentworth from his factory at Sheffield. After a morning spent practising traditional gun drills and manoeuvres on the lawn in front of the house, the men dismounted to the open-top cars. Criss-crossing the roads through the Park, they progressed in single-column cavalcades, gun-carriages in tow. There was space for four gunners in each of the cars: standing smartly to attention, two stood in the front, and two at the back. Within months, barbed wire and trench warfare would render these specialized drills obsolete.

Billy would not see the war out with his men. In the autumn of 1914 he was called up to serve on the General Staff in Flanders as Assistant Director of Transport. In the last days of October, the outdoor servants and the household staff assembled on the steps beneath the great portico at Wentworth to wave him off and wish him luck.

Ninety miles south, at Milton Hall, near Peterborough, a palatial Elizabethan mansion owned by the Fitzwilliams for 400 years, a drama was about to be played out which would prove of far more significance to the family's destiny than events on the international stage.

16

3 November 1914. The ninety-second day of the war. King's Cross railway station was teeming with armies on the march. Khaki columns snaked through the crowds, NCOs and orderlies jostling alongside, frantically counting heads and ticking off the long lists of men and supplies. Clad in sober dress, the troops marched in silence: their cornets, tubas and drums had been left behind.

Vendors at the news-stands shouted the headlines of the war: 'Gallantry of London Scottish', 'Allies' Steady Progress', 'Many German Deserters'. The dreadful casualty lists printed that morning told a different story: stark beacons in a fog of censorship, it was evident, even to the civilians on the platforms, that matters at the Front were grave.

Toby Fitzwilliam, Billy's twenty-six-year-old cousin, eased his way through the crowds. Wearing the service dress of an officer in the Mounted Brigade, he was taller than most of the soldiers around him, and slighter: a round-shouldered, slightly hunched figure with thinning blond hair. Moving against them, he headed towards the platforms from which the trains disgorged their loads of troops.

The soldiers were en route to the southern ports to join the battalions of Territorials being rushed to the Front. The very fact that they were being sent to the line at all was an indication of the critical state of the war. The first battle of Ypres was in progress. Three days previously, on 31 October, the British Expeditionary Force (BEF) had come perilously close to being defeated at Ghievault. They would call it Ypres Day: in the years to come, the men who fought and survived would wear blue cornflowers in their lapels in remembrance of those who fought and died. At lunchtime on Ypres Day, Sir John French, the Commander-in-Chief of the BEF, had little doubt that 'the last barrier between the Germans and the Channel seaboard was broken down'. His soldiers at Ghievault had been outnumbered by four to one: a heroic last stand by the Worcesters, the Scots and the South Wales Borderers had proved him wrong. But for how much longer could the line be held? The battles of Mons, Le Cateau, the Marne and the Aisne had taken a heavy toll. Whole brigades had been reduced to the strength of single battalions, battalions to the strength of companies, and some companies to little more than platoons. In the space of three months, 86,000 of the 100,000-strong BEF that had set out in August, confident of victory by Christmas, had been wounded, killed, or were missing in action. In a matter of months, the BEF had suffered a casualty rate of 90 per cent.

In the coming days, Toby Fitzwilliam's regiment would also cross the Channel to the Front. 'All leave was prohibited, we were going over at any moment,' he later recalled. 'I went to see my Commanding Officer and explained the situation and said I felt I must see my mother and father before I went overseas.' The Colonel of Toby's regiment was an old family friend. Knowing Toby's circumstances, he had been sympathetic. He had given him special leave to return home to Milton Hall to make one final attempt to be reconciled with his parents.

That morning, the wind was in the north at King's Cross, confounding the ingenuity of the Victorian engineers. Smoke from the steam trains that had collected in the steep narrow tunnels that led into the station, dug deep under the Regent's Canal, blew through the double mouth of the terminus. Toby stood waiting for his train at the point where the smoke gathered – in swirling, choking clouds, above the barriers to the platforms. He felt he was embarking on a pointless journey. He held out little hope of being reconciled with his parents: in the preceding weeks, they had not even wanted to say goodbye.

In the space of six traumatic months, Toby had become the black sheep of the Fitzwilliam family. The eldest son of George Fitzwilliam, the 6th Earl's nephew, in the spring of 1914 he had been banished by his father from the 23,000-acre estate at Milton. Toby had not spoken to his parents since. Despite his repeated efforts, his father and his mother, Evie Fitzwilliam, had refused to see him.

'I believe, as I pointed out to Mother, if I saw you both together I could in a very few minutes clear up so many misunderstandings,' he implored his father in a letter written at the end of May. 'Misunderstandings that are making my life miserable and which I am certain you and Mother would like to have removed. I am absolutely sincere in this and I believe I could convince you of my sincerity if you would let me put the whole of my case before you. I am, your loving son.'

George's reply had been terse and unforgiving:

> You have insulted your mother.
>
> You have sent her a half-hearted apology which you never meant except so far as it suited your purpose.
>
> You are not to go to Milton under any pretext whatever.
>
> Yrs George W Fitzwilliam.

Beneath his signature, he had added a postscript: 'You've put the lid on it this time.'

It had been longer still since Toby had heard from his mother. The very thought of her last letter, even after the passage of time, made him wince.

The journey from King's Cross to Peterborough was painfully slow. The trains were running to military timetables. The Great Northern line served the big army camps beyond Grantham at Belton Park and Harrowby, and further north at Ripon, Clipstone and Catterick. Toby's route was clogged with passenger trains commandeered to carry reserves to their units and the battalions to the ports; thousands of Belgian refugees, fleeing from the German advance in Flanders, had placed an additional strain on the service.

Progressing slowly at speeds that at times amounted to little more than a shunt, Toby knew he would be hard-pressed to get up to Milton and back to his regiment at Winchester within the twenty-four hours allocated for his leave. Depressingly, as the hours dragged by, he had plenty of time to reflect on the coming meeting – and the whole ghastly business that had led up to it.

Toby's rift with his parents had been caused by his marriage. His crime in their eyes had been to marry for love. Five months earlier, against their wishes, he had married a girl called Beryl Morgan. The ceremony was followed by a reception at 4 Grosvenor Square, Billy Fitzwilliam's house in Mayfair. Neither of his parents had attended.

The so-called 'insult' was the reason they gave for their absence. Yet such were the bitterness and anger on both sides that the row had long since escalated beyond rationality. The 'insult', the slight against his mother for which Toby could not be forgiven, had been made when he had returned her wedding present.

In what his father called 'a damned insolent message', three weeks before the wedding, on 19 May, Toby had sent him a note:

My dear Father,
On my return to London today from Oxton I found a silver tray waiting for me from Mother. Will you please point out to her how impossible it is for me to accept a present from one who feels towards the girl I love and am shortly to make my wife as recent letters show that Mother feels towards Beryl.

I have returned the tray to Garrards and asked them to keep it pending further instructions from you or Mother.

Six months on, his father's accusation still rankled. According to the manager at Garrards, Evie had expected her present to be sent back. Contrary to his father's charge that, following his 'damned insolent' note, Toby had merely sent her 'a half-hearted apology', one that he had 'never meant', he had in fact written a grovelling letter of apology:

My dear Mother
I am so sorry to hear from Father that he considers my letter insolent, and I take this immediate opportunity of apologizing to you and to him

for having written a letter which should even appear to bear any signs of ingratitude or insolence.

One word in explanation of my hasty action.

Beryl means to me more than all that the world and its contents can mean to anyone and I have felt very very deeply the letters which I have received from you, my mother, about her, and I thought that in accepting a present from you it might be taken as some sort of tacit admission on my part of the truth of some of these statements.

I adore Beryl with all my heart and soul. I am convinced that the girl I love, if it were possible loves me even more than I love her.

Think then what a letter from you must mean which tells me that she is marrying me, not because she loves me but for what she thinks she can get out of me.

Whether Beryl and I will ever be able to convince you how much we mean to each other only the years to come can show, and I am sure they will show it.

In the meantime I can only repeat that if the letter I wrote to father appeared or was insolent, I retract it and apologize for it most sincerely and I should like to have the first opportunity of telling you personally how sorry I am.

Evie did not allow him the opportunity. The following day, Toby went to see her at the Berkeley Hotel where she was staying on one of her periodic visits to London. She refused to see him: sending a note via a servant, she told Toby that she was busy with engagements until her return to Milton Hall.

Where Evie led, George followed, so Toby believed. He did not blame his father for the rift. He was convinced that it was his mother who had turned his father against him. If there was to be any chance of making it up with his parents before he left for the Front, he would have to be reconciled with Evie first.

Toby had sent a telegram to Milton Hall to let her know he was coming. Knowing his father would not be there, he was dreading the meeting. Evie was notoriously quixotic, her moods unpredictable, often unfathomable. Even at times when their relations had been harmonious, there was little intimacy between them. Years later, in front of a packed courtroom, a barrister would grill Toby about his relationship with his mother: 'There are some people with whom it is easy to discuss intimate and personal matters and some people with whom it is not. How did you feel, with your mother, about discussing that sort of thing?' 'It is awfully difficult to explain the relations between my mother and myself,' Toby replied. 'Do you know, I never got to know her well, never really got to know her well; I was very frightened of her.'

Few people ever knew Evie well. Her life, loves and ultimately her lies form the core of the third Wentworth mystery. In 1951 it would unravel in a court case fought between her two sons: Toby and his younger brother, Tom. In his summing up, the judge presiding over the case would describe Evie as 'a beautiful woman possessed of very considerable charm, personality and character'. In every other respect, his verdict was damning; she was, he concluded, 'temperamental', 'obstinate', 'intransigent', 'unreasonable', 'quarrelsome' and 'capable of displaying considerable hardness and obstinacy in important matters'.

Toby's train, bearing the apple-green and black insignia of the Great Northern Railway Company, pulled into Peterborough, the station nearest to Milton Hall, shortly before lunch. It had none of the grandeur of the cast-iron cathedrals of York and Edinburgh further up the line. There were very few people about. The rain, dripping off the clapperboard awning and down the spindly pillars that ran the length of the platform, lent it a desolate air: the effect was of an empty pier in midwinter in an unfashionable seaside resort.

What was to follow in the course of the next few hours was predicated, as in all family rows, by what had gone before.

In the spring of 1914, Toby had deposited a file of correspondence with his father's solicitor. It contained the letters Evie had written to him and his then fiancée, Beryl Morgan, during their engagement. Some of the letters had been so vituperative that Toby had felt compelled to caution the solicitor in the attached note. 'I trust letters of the sort which Miss Morgan and I have received lately will now cease,' he wrote. 'If not I feel that some sort of steps must be taken to put a stop to them.'

The file Toby lodged with the solicitor has survived. The letters reveal that, as he embarked on his first meeting with his mother in six months, he had every reason to feel the way he did. More intriguingly, they offer one of the few glimpses into the character of Evie Fitzwilliam – the woman on whom, almost half a century later, the fate of the Fitzwilliam family would turn.

Toby Darling, I find I need not go to the Girls Club tomorrow so we can have the day to ourselves. I am so looking forward to meeting Beryl, Much Love, Thine, Mother.

To begin with, in the autumn of 1913, Evie had been delighted at the news of Toby's engagement. 'My dear Beryl,' she wrote, dashing off a note of congratulations to her future daughter-in-law, 'Toby has told me the news and I am delighted and hope you will both be very happy. I am much looking forward to seeing you tomorrow and hope you will get here early.'

Beryl's first visit to Milton was a resounding success. To celebrate the engagement, George and Evie gave a party for the Fitzwilliam Hunt. 'My father was secretary of the Fitzwilliam Hunt of which George Fitzwilliam was master,' Margot Lorne, whose family lived at nearby Tansor Court, recalled. 'My parents and I therefore knew George and Evie and their children intimately. We were asked over to Milton to meet Beryl and we went. They had a big meet with the hounds, where she was introduced to all the farmers and the people of the Hunt as Toby's fiancée. And then we had a dinner party to celebrate. There were one or two tables, I should say there were about thirty people present. There was no doubt that Evie was delighted at the engagement. She told us so and obviously was. She said, "Both George and I love her".'

So enchanted was Evie with Beryl that she insisted she return the following weekend. 'Beryl Darling,' she wrote, 'I am counting the days till Friday and want you much! Can't you get rid of Toby for a few days so that I have you to myself!! He really must let me have a bit of you. Yours very loving, EWF.'

Beryl and Toby had become engaged within weeks of meeting.

In the late summer of August 1913 they had met at a country-house dinner party given by the Weigalls, who lived in a large half-timbered mansion in Lincolnshire. 'Beryl wasn't extremely pretty, but she was very attractive,' a cousin recalled. 'She had the most wonderful kindly nature. She was terribly bright and terribly nice. It was not surprising that Toby fell for her.'

The date of the wedding was fixed for late autumn. Evie, thrilled at the prospect, set arrangements for an elaborate society wedding into full swing. In the days following the announcement, she and Beryl spent many happy hours together closeted over material samples for the bridesmaids' dresses – and Beryl's own wedding dress – which was to be a special gift from Evie. 'For a time all appeared to be going well,' Margot Lorne remembered. 'Mrs Fitzwilliam, I know, gave Beryl some jewels. Suddenly, I heard that there had been a row. The jewels were demanded – and handed – back.'

'A pathological occurrence' – to use the words of a senior QC, spoken almost half a century later – had taken place. Within weeks of Beryl's first visit to Milton, a series of poison-pen letters began to arrive at the house. Written on the back of a postcard for anyone to read, they were addressed to Beryl Morgan c/o Mrs Fitzwilliam. The information they contained came as a bolt from the blue to Evie.

One of the postcards has been preserved:

> What luck you gave up being a teacher in Clifton to be paid companion to Mrs Weigall. Your sisters who married Bristol business men and your lowly relatives, the baker etc here must be pleased and proud at such a grand match for you. How did you ever manage to pass amongst people so very different to those you were born and always lived with.

Evie had taken what little she knew of Beryl's background on trust. At Toby's insistence, Beryl had told her that her grandfather owned a 'small property' in Gloucestershire and that her mother came from a 'good old Devonshire family'. In the terminology of the day, a 'small property' was the expression used to describe a modest landed estate: Evie had inferred that Beryl came from solid gentry stock.

Alarmed, and wishing to make her own inquiries, Evie wrote to Mrs Weigall, the woman at whose house, so she had been led to believe, Beryl was staying as a guest. When Mrs Weigall failed to answer her letter, Evie instructed George to hire detectives to investigate Beryl's background. Their inquiries revealed that the substance of the poison-pen letters was true: Beryl's grandfather, far from owning a small property, was a tenant farmer in Gloucestershire, and her mother, the daughter of a draper from Exeter. Beryl was not, as she had claimed, a guest at Mrs Weigall's house: she was, as the anonymous postcards had stated, an employee – a paid governess to the Weigalls' eight-year-old daughter.

Shocked at her discovery, Evie insisted the wedding be postponed for a year. In a dramatic change of tone, she sent her future daughter-in-law a poisonous letter of her own. 'My Dear Beryl,' she wrote archly, dismissing the 'Beryl Darling' of old:

> I am sorry you have had all this worry but it had to be. By putting off the wedding it will give you both time to look round and know one another better. Do you feel I wonder that you can live with Toby for the rest of your life in a small cottage on £1,000 a year?
>
> That is what it would have to be, for even if Toby did succeed to this place, unless he married money he could never live here as the succession and death duties would be so big. Certainly the son who does succeed will have to marry money, otherwise it will go back to the head of the family at our death. When your wedding does take place, surely one of your married sisters can arrange for you to be married from an hotel in London? I hate all this swagger and would like you to have a simple wedding in accordance with your own social position.
>
> If you have 7 bridesmaids it means 7 presents Toby has to buy and he has not got the money nor has his Father . . .
>
> Had you been a Duke's daughter you were entitled to it, but being like myself 'a nobody' I would like simplicity as I do hate climbing.

It was an extraordinary letter, coming as it did from a former chorus girl.

Beryl's 'social position' had touched a raw nerve. Thirty years earlier, Evie's own marriage had scandalized society. When she and George Fitzwilliam first met, she had been a 'Gaiety Girl' appearing in the second row of the chorus in a production of *Little Jack Shepherd* at the Gaiety Theatre in London. In the mid-1880s, to be 'on the stage' was worse than being a 'nobody'. Girls of good breeding were forbidden even to look at an actress, as Lady Warwick recalled:

> In those days etiquette for girls was very, very strict. I can remember walking with my chaperone and being suddenly told to 'look the other way now, dear, and take no notice'. The reason was that some man we knew was passing in the company of a lady friend whom it was impossible for us to know. No man in such circumstances would take the slightest notice of anybody in his own world whom he chanced to meet.

In smart social circles, to marry an actress was regarded as a heinous offence. George Fitzwilliam was an officer in the Royal Horse Guards when he married Evie: 'A fellow marrying like that is asked to go,' recalled Lieutenant Colonel Burns-Hartopp, the Senior Subaltern in George's regiment. 'He is asked to send in his papers. If an officer married an actress, he had to go. It was true of all the Guards regiments.' Forced to resign his commission, George was condemned by his relatives for his bohemian lifestyle and for bringing the family into disgrace. 'George hasn't one ounce of family pride or feeling in his constitution,' his cousin, Charles Fitzwilliam, exclaimed angrily in a letter to his uncle.

Even in 1914, the social stigma attached to actresses still lingered, evident in an anecdote Lady Warwick recorded in her memoirs: '"Just imagine," remarked a very exclusive grande dame to me one day,' she wrote. "I found a portrait of my niece on one page, and opposite to her was the chorus girl whom that fool — is going to marry! Why should one rub shoulders with a creature like that, even in a weekly paper? What are we coming to?"'

'My mother's reactions to things were so sudden it was like a thunderstorm rolled up,' Toby remembered, 'then it would disappear and the sun came out. You just did not know where you were.'

Following her outburst over the anonymous letters, Evie's relationship with her future daughter-in-law appeared to recover. 'Darling,' she wrote to Beryl two weeks later, 'I'm not one bit angry but I've had nothing to write and absolutely no time. I have had to write reams and reams every day about Cooks until I am sick of saying how many there are in the kitchen etc and still we are without a Cook. Will you come to us on Saturday for a week. I must teach you Bridge. Thine.' Two days later, came another note: 'Darling, Do be an Angel and get me 3 yards of good white Crepe de Chene and send to me at once; pay about 6/- or 7/- a yard for it and I will pay you back. I also want a champagne colour wooley [sic] jacket from Debenhams. Will you go there and try one on and tell them to send it to me on appro. I have an account there. I don't like a collar to my coats. Thine.'

At the end of November, Evie invited Beryl to spend Christmas at Milton. Yet despite the invitation, Beryl sensed a high-handedness in Evie's manner that suggested all was not well. Hoping to clear the air, she resolved to confront her future mother-in-law. At the beginning of December, some weeks after she had received a particularly chilly reception at Milton, Beryl wrote to Evie. 'My dearest Mum, I have been thinking very deeply about things,' she ventured. 'I feel I must write you this letter and I can only hope you will not misunderstand me when you have read it – but I don't think you will. I can see that things are really no different to what they were when I came to Milton last and I can't help feeling that Mr Fitzwilliam is not so pleased that Toby and I are going to be married one day as he was at first. Don't you think he would be happier if I did not come to Milton for Xmas or indeed until he really wants to welcome me as a future daughter-in-law. It is not that I do not want to come, far from it, as you know how empty Xmas would be for me without Toby, but I could not be happy with you myself, feeling as I do that I should in some way be spoiling either yours or Mr Fitzwilliam's happiness. If there is still any other reason that hurts or worries either of you please tell me as now you have thoroughly gone into the matter of those cruel letters I feel there still must be something and misunderstandings are so hard to bear. Words will never be able to express how awfully sorry I am that things are in this state. Please Mum do not misunderstand all I mean in this letter, it is not written in any anger whatever but simply that I feel that neither of you can really want me at Milton at present.'

There was no 'misunderstanding'. The simple truth, though Evie did not communicate it, was that she did not want her son to marry the granddaughter of a draper. 'I remember my father telling me that he and my aunts were scandalized by Evie's attitude,' Deirdre Newton, one of the Fitzwilliams' Dundas cousins recalled. 'Such hypocrisy, they said, you could never find. Beryl and Toby were very happy together. She was delightful. My father and his sisters were always very [*sic*] in defence of her.'

Beryl, it seems, did spend Christmas at Milton, but Toby, sensing his parents' antipathy towards her, was becoming anxious. In common with other would-be heirs to large estates, he was dependent on his father for an income. Though he was working as an assistant to Walter Long, the Conservative MP, his salary was negligible: it was his private income which kept him in the style to which he was accustomed.

From the age of twenty-three, Toby had received an allowance of £800 a year from his father, approximately £50,000 at today's values. On his marriage to Beryl, George was proposing to increase the allowance to £1,000 a year: what worried Toby was that its payment depended on his father's whim.

Knowing his parents' capriciousness and concerned about their ambivalence towards Beryl, in the spring of 1914 Toby wrote to George to ask if his allowance could be paid on a formal basis. In a letter to the family solicitor, he explained the reasons behind his request. 'I feel I could never place a wife of mine in such a position, that if any time she or I had a difference of opinion with one of my parents, my father could entirely deprive us of funds and a living. I admit that such a possibility is very remote but I also am certain that it ought not to exist.' In addition, Toby wanted a small amount of money to be formally settled on Beryl so that she, and any children they might have, would be provided for in the event of his death.

Evie's reaction to Toby's request was extremely hostile. Blaming Beryl and her relatives for putting Toby up to demanding a marriage settlement, she sent him a furious letter:

My dear Toby
I am sure you have been most ill-advised by Beryl and her people about this money business.

You ought to know your father well enough now to know that he would always do the right thing. If you marry her now you will estrange yourself from us forever. I really thought you had at last met someone who really cared for you for yourself but it seems it is not so.

You had much better break it off before it is too late. You can ask Beryl to show you my letter to her.

At the same time, Evie had written a second letter. It was the one she wanted Toby to see:

My dear Beryl
I think that both you and your people are very ill advised to even suggest settlements. I feel disgusted with the whole thing, as people in your position in life don't think of settlements but just insure their lives. I come of the same class of people as yourself so I am not writing of what I do not know.

When I married Mr Fitzwilliam nothing was ever mentioned about money nor thought of, we just lived in our own happiness.

I should have thought that you would have known Mr Fitzwilliam well enough by now to know that he is the most just and generous man that ever God put breath into and that once you had belonged to us your future was secure, but all this has upset everything.

As you think best to take the line you are doing I must explain to my friends and relations the reason why.

The people I have told so far were flabbergasted and tell me they had no settlements whatever. Mrs Faudal Phillips had no settlement, Sir

Charles Fitzwilliam tells me he made none and he tells me that none of his brothers had money settled on their wives and I can mention many others . . .

I can only think that it was your people who have persuaded you, anyway I hope it did not come entirely from you otherwise I fear for Toby's future happiness, as you have taken this line you must do exactly as you like, only don't now ask me to be present at the wedding because I have finished with it all.

Yrs, Evelyn W. Fitzwilliam

If Toby marries you he will estrange himself forever from us.

Toby was devastated. Without foundation, the woman he loved, the mother of his future children, had been insulted by his own mother. 'I would write to Mother myself in reply to her letter,' he told his father, 'but I fear I dare not trust my powers of self-restraint, so will you please point out to her that I cannot take her suggestion as to breaking off my engagement.' Assuring his father that Beryl was no fortune-hunter, he reiterated their love for one another: 'Beryl and I have become more and more to each other every day in fact were our engagement to be broken off now my life and ambitions in which I see so much future help from Beryl would be ruined and for Beryl myself I honestly believe that not only would all the happiness of life be taken from her for ever but I think even worse might happen.'

Siding with Evie, George sent the following reply to his son: 'I do not intend to discuss the business any further as I am damned sick of the whole thing as I have always been. So long as you do not engage in any business competitive to any I am already engaged in and so long as you are not politically opposed to me your allowance will be paid regularly. I agree with your mother in what she has written as I saw her letter.'

The letter George referred to was the last letter Evie wrote to Toby before his wedding. Thwarted in her attempt to prevent the marriage, she gave full vent to her spleen:

'Under no circumstances will I ever have Beryl here again,' she began:

I am very very sorry indeed for you as you have been let in for this marriage and I feel convinced that were you to break it off she would sue you for breach of promise.

When she first came here and saw this place with you alone she thought she was in for a real good thing, but when she saw we were opposed to the whole thing, she suddenly insists upon settlements. I have tried to trust her but failed, the reason being that when I first knew her (having first explained to her I was nobody) I asked her who her people were. She told me her grandfather owned a small property in Glos and that her mother came of a good old Devonshire family. Her grandfather was a farmer and her mother was the daughter of a draper in Exeter, so why should she try to deceive me? There is no necessity for it to me. You can show her this letter if you like. She may have told you the truth and if so why not me? I have no intention of ever meeting her again if I can possibly help it and my sympathies are with you entirely in having to marry her. She must know by this time that she will ruin your life by so doing.

The torrent of accusations against Beryl – of her lies and deceit – was, as it transpires, remarkable.

A closer investigation of Evie's background suggests that her whole life was constructed on a lie. Though she openly confessed to being a 'nobody', she was in fact quite literally a nobody. It is doubtful whether anyone ever knew who Evie Fitzwilliam really was.

To her friends in the smart Northamptonshire hunting set, to her Fitzwilliam relatives and to the wider world, according to the entries she and George submitted to *Burke's Peerage and Baronetage* and to *Debretts*, Evie claimed she was the eldest daughter of one Charles Stephen Lyster.

She rarely talked about her childhood: on the very few occasions when she did, Evie gave the impression that it had been an unhappy one. In the mid-1880s, when she was appearing as a chorus girl in London's West End, Kate Rickards was her closest friend: 'She told me that her father had been a doctor,' Kate recalled. 'I think they [her parents] were dead and she was brought up by a brother or a stepbrother . . . she was very unhappy at home and I think she ran away from home, or left home.'

In the early twenty-first century, electronic search engines make it possible to reveal what no one in Evie's lifetime – and for many decades after her death – could have known: her identity, it appears, was false.

Evie was born in 1867. There is no record of a Charles Stephen Lyster, the man she claimed as her father, in the UK Census Records between 1851 and 1881. A search of the medical directories listing doctors practising in Britain in the mid- to late nineteenth century also draws a blank. Nor does Evie herself appear in any official records under her given name – Daisy Evelyn Lyster. Her birth, despite the fact that the registration of births became mandatory after 1837, was not recorded; in the 1871 and 1881 Census records for the United Kingdom there is no one of that name. On her marriage certificate, issued in 1888, 'Lyster' was the name she gave: it appears that she had even deceived her husband, Toby's father, George.

Evie's chauffeur was waiting for Toby when his train pulled in to Peterborough station. Meeting him on the platform, the chauffeur handed him a note from his mother, which read:

Dear Toby
Please don't for one moment think that I asked to see you because I did not. If you want to come and say goodbye you can do so.

Toby almost turned on his heel to catch the next train back to London. There, he could at least snatch a few hours with Beryl before his regiment left for France.

He did not. So convinced was he of his own moral rectitude in the rift with his mother that he decided to go on to Milton. Not for his own sake, but for hers. 'My feelings were, if I went out to France and got shot,' he later recalled, 'if I had not gone to see my mother she would have been the one to suffer.'

The chauffeur drove Toby to Milton Hall. It was a fifteen-minute journey from the station, five of them along the two-mile drive that led up to the imposing Elizabethan house. Passing the familiar landmarks in the park – the follies, the great oaks, the hedges that traversed the flat grazing fields – it was strange to see the landscape he knew so intimately. He had been brought up to believe that one day it would all be his. Yet now, after six months' absence, it did not feel like coming home. His mother had sworn that she would 'never have Beryl here again': even if he were to be reconciled with his parents, which he doubted from the tone of Evie's note, for as long as his wife was banned from Milton, he could not bring himself to regard it as home.

To Toby's surprise, Evie greeted him warmly. After giving him lunch, she showed him around the hospital that she and George had set up in a wing for officers wounded at the Front. 'My mother was very correct and very nice,' Toby remembered. 'She did not raise any of the old rows.'

After a harmonious few hours together, Toby left Milton to return to his regiment. What he did not know then – and would only discover after he joined the long lists of casualties on the Western Front – was that Evie's charm had been a sham.

Years later, when a barrister questioned him about the meeting, the pain at the recollection of its outcome was evident in his monosyllabic replies.

'There was nothing in the nature of a reconciliation?' the barrister asked.

'No,' Toby replied.

'I think you were rather badly wounded in France, were not you?' the QC continued.

'I was shell-shocked.'

'Were you in hospital for some time?'

'Yes. In London.'

'Did either of your parents come and see you there?'

'My father came to see me, yes.'

'What year would that be?'

'Just before Christmas, 1914.'

'Your mother did not come to see you? In fact, I do not think you ever saw your mother again?'

'I never saw my mother again, no.'

'We know that during the war your children were born.'

'Yes.'

'I have not got the exact dates. About 1917?'

'1916 and 1918.'

'Did your mother ever see your children?'

'No, never saw them.'

Evie lived for more than a decade after her last meeting with Toby. Until her death in March 1925, despite George's entreaties, she never forgave her elder son. 'Evie was a woman of very strong character, just as George was a very weak character,' Margot Lorne, the daughter of the secretary to the Fitzwilliam Hunt, remembered: 'She completely dominated him, and he gave in to her every wish. They were obviously devoted to each other. She was a woman of extremes. She made friends quickly and easily, then just as suddenly dropped them and would be rude about them. She had a very vindictive and stubborn streak in her character. Once her mind was made up nothing could move her. I know that she remained vindictive towards Toby and Beryl from the time they married until she died.'

Evie's vindictiveness began as soon as Toby left Milton – his last visit to the house in her lifetime. As he risked his life fighting at the Front, she gave instructions to her friends and to the household staff that his name should never be mentioned in her presence. Nor was it to be mentioned in the family. Toby's younger brother, Tom, was ten years old at the time. 'I went to school in 1914 and the war had started and Toby was never there after that date and his name was never mentioned,' he recalled. 'I asked where I could get his address because I wanted to write to him, and I think I was told that the butler had his address and I got it from him.'

Evie's unnatural cruelty towards her elder son did not end there. To the shock of her friends, her vindictiveness appeared to take the form of a vendetta – even if it meant destroying her own reputation in the process. In the weeks after Toby left Milton, she cast doubt over his right to succeed to the estate by telling her friends that he had been born before she and George married. 'A little time after the outbreak of war in 1914 I heard it said in the neighbourhood that Evie was saying that Toby was not legitimate,' remembered Margot Lorne. 'I heard that Toby was going to be proved illegitimate in order that Tom should succeed. She told everyone. Everyone was very fond of Toby and this shocked people greatly, because it so obviously came as a consequence of the row over the marriage. I would say this story was not generally accepted, but was attributed to vindictiveness on Evelyn's part. This complete change of attitude caused a great deal of very adverse comment. I remember my parents coming back from Milton one day very upset because she had told them that Toby was illegitimate.'

Evie had set a time bomb ticking under the House of Fitzwilliam: almost half a century later, it would explode.

PART IV

17

Wentworth, January 1920, barely a year after Armistice Day: the house was under siege.

Thousands of black-suited men, scarves muffled at their throats against the piercing cold, stood along the border of the lawn. Hundreds more crowded the raised grass bank at its southern edge, directly opposite the house. Many bore the wretched scars of war: empty sleeves, wooden legs, black patches worn over blind eyes.

In the grey January sky flocks of crows circled, scattered by the disturbance. The men waited, shadowy figures, flitting among the trees that edged the lawn. Winter had dulled its emerald sheen, yet still, eleven acres in extent, it stretched before them like a piece of stencilled silk. Thick parallel lines, hand-rolled by the Fitzwilliams' groundsmen, were etched on its surface: razor-straight, they each ran to a point on the 600-yard-long façade.

As the men stood watching the house, their breath condensed on the sharp air. They were fortunate to have come home from the Great War. Fifty thousand Yorkshire miners had served in the trenches; more than 5,000 had been killed in action.

Tension from the cold, the anticipation, the knowledge that they were forbidden to be there, rippled through the crowd. It was a Sunday morning. The rules at Wentworth on the Sabbath were strict, posted on noticeboards in outbuildings and workshops dotted around the Estate. The immediate vicinity of the house was categorically out of bounds: 'On Sundays, the Park gates are all to be closed to horses, carriages and vehicles of every description.' No one had foreseen an invasion by foot.

The miners had come across the surrounding country, climbing into the Park over stiles a mile south at Greaseborough, or slipping through the turnstiles at Doric Lodge and Lion's Gate. By lunchtime, 10,000 had gathered at the edge of the lawn.

An echo of war drifted across the ranks of men: coming from the direction of the Riding School behind the North Tower, a lone voice called 'A-TTEN-TION'. It was followed by the dull rumble of hundreds of feet on sawdust.

Up at a window of the house, Billy and his guest for the weekend, Field Marshal Earl Haig, watched anxiously. They were old friends: Billy had served under Haig in the Boer War and on the General Staff in Flanders. Both men were profoundly unsettled by what they saw. Along the perimeter of the lawn, the smudgy winter colours had been obliterated by dense lines of black. It was clear to Billy that they were miners; he knew from the way some of them squatted, the pose all colliers assumed to eat their 'snap' underground at the pit. Jack May, the groom of chambers at Wentworth, was on duty that morning. 'They did not know what to do,' he told Billy's cousin later. 'They did not know why they had come. They were frightened. They thought the miners were going to storm the house.'

The two Earls debated whether to call in troops to disperse the crowd. The house was surrounded: across the Park, through the gaunt branches of the great oaks, they could see the dark silhouettes of thousands more men, massing from all directions to join their former brothers-in-arms.

It was a situation both Haig and Fitzwilliam feared, and one they had anticipated for more than a year. The Great War had destroyed their peace of mind.

In 1919 the spectre of revolution haunted England's ruling class. Within months of the Armistice, the class conflict of the pre-war years had again erupted. Thirty million working days were lost as a result of industrial disputes, fought out in a world transformed by the apocalypse on the Western and Eastern Fronts. Ancient continental dynasties and empires had fallen; the red flag flew over Moscow: it was only a matter of time, people felt, before Bolshevism would subsume Britain.

Earl Haig's anxieties had fixed upon the returning armies: the demobilization of four million men. The year began ominously. In the month of January alone there were fifty mutinies in the British armed forces. 'For the manufacturer of revolution there is no more incendiary material than soldiers returning from war,' wrote Haig's biographer Duff Cooper, a Lieutenant in the Grenadier Guards during the First World War. 'They have grown careless of danger and accustomed to risks. The peace to which they have long looked forward is likely to disappoint them. The homes are never worthy of heroes. They see others who have not endured the same hardships enjoying greater prosperity, and they are easy to persuade that they have much to gain and little to lose.'

In the five years of war on the Western Front, five out of every nine in the Army were killed, missing or wounded. The question that preoccupied Haig and the heads of British Intelligence throughout 1919 was whether something else had been lost in the carnage. Lord Annan, writing in his memoirs, *Our Age*, described the 'ideal' of an Englishman, one that he and his contemporaries had been taught to admire as children in the years before the First World War. 'It went back to the eighteenth century', he wrote. 'Wellington embodied it, Waterloo exhibited it. According to this code an Englishman should be guided by an overpowering sense of civic duty and diligence. Every man's first loyalty should be to the country of his birth and the institution in which he served. Loyalty to the institutions came before loyalty to people. Individuals should sacrifice their careers, their family, and certainly their personal happiness or whims, to the regiment, the college, the school, the services, the ministry, the profession or the firm.'

In 1919, Britain's intelligence chiefs believed that the old prewar loyalties had been buried in the Flanders mud. That summer, Sir Basil Thomson, Head of the Intelligence Section at the Home Office, called on Haig to ask his permission to use officers in British Army units as government informers in order to obtain forewarning of 'internal unrest'. Haig refused. 'I said that I would not authorize any men being used as spies,' he wrote in his diary. 'Officers must act straightforwardly and as Englishmen. Espionage amongst our own men is hateful to us army men.'

Hateful also to Haig was the thought of having to use troops in the suppression of civil disorder. 'It is not their duty to act as policemen,' he had argued with the hawks at the Home Office. As he stood with Billy Fitzwilliam watching the men gathering on the borders of the lawn at Wentworth, there were five days to go until 31 January, when he was due to leave his post as Commander-in-Chief of the Home Forces. The likelihood, as it had seemed throughout 1919, of being driven to employ force against some of the very men who had fought for him in France was one of the main reasons behind his willingness to relinquish his command. There were 10,000 miners massed around Wentworth House; might this be his own eleventh hour, a hideous postscript to the victory he had won in 1918 at the eleventh hour on the eleventh day of the eleventh month?

In the scores of pit villages that ringed the house, and in coalmining regions across Britain, the rumble of revolution had been loudest of all.

Colonel Mitchell, a landowner in Wath, a village a few miles from Wentworth, railing against the popularity of the 'Bolshevik anthem', 'the Red Flag', observed in a letter to the local newspaper, 'Chatter about revolution is becoming so respectable now-a-days that nobody feels very much shocked or annoyed at hearing this rather mournful ditty sung.'

The lifting of wartime financial controls had caused a sharp escalation in the cost of living; in the course of the year, prices had doubled from pre-war levels, placing a strain on family budgets. The rash of strikes that had broken out in the country's biggest industries – textiles, shipping and among railway workers – were primarily disputes over wages: once wage increases had been agreed, the disputes had been quickly settled.

But the miners' union, the MFGB, was fighting for more than wages: its battle was political. Stoking the fear of revolution, blatantly, unashamedly, within months of the end of the First

World War, the MFGB declared its objective: to depose the coal-owning aristocrats and confiscate their pits. The more radical of its representatives wanted to seize their land. Calling for the redistribution of wealth and the levelling of social injustice, the union urged the Government to place Britain's collieries under 'joint control and administration by the workmen and the state'.

The MFGB had embraced Communist doctrine; so, it seemed, had its members.

Across Britain's coalfields, district after district balloted in favour of nationalizing the collieries. There were 1¼ million miners; their dependants included, it was estimated that the industry touched more than 5 million people, a tenth of Britain's population. It was a community the Government and the coal owners ignored at their peril.

The Whistlejacket Room became a temporary HQ and OP. Located on the raised principal floor at the centre of Wentworth House, it commanded the best view over the lawn outside on that bleak Sunday morning in January 1920.

The room was symbolic of all Billy Fitzwilliam stood to lose. Forty feet square, its splendour was breathtaking. Eight doors decorated with Palladian pediments led into it. The walls and the ceiling, a brilliant white, were sculpted with stucco panelling embossed in gilt, depicting vases of flowers, heroes from Homer's mythology and eagles with spreading wings. A sumptuous Aubusson rug lay across the glazed wooden floor, polished with beeswax from the apiary in the grounds. Gold glittered from the furniture: a pair of gilt candelabra, seven feet high, holding twenty-four candles, stood at opposite corners; flush against one wall there was a long gilt settee, its cushions covered in Prussian blue. There were twelve matching armchairs positioned around the room. Most striking of all, though, was its centrepiece: Stubbs's portrait of the famous racehorse Whistlejacket, commissioned by the Marquess of Rockingham.

The Fitzwilliams were descended from the Marquess through the female line. Family legend, according to a visitor to Wentworth in the late nineteenth century, explained the portrait's unusual composition:

> There is neither shadow nor background in the picture but it was intended that some portrait-painter should place King George III on the horse's back, and that a landscape painter should put in the background. But, when the Marquis heard how nearly the picture had been destroyed by the horse, who caught a sight of his own portrait just as it was finished, and would have furiously attacked it, he preferred keeping it in its present state in memory of the occurrence.

The scale of luxury, the sheer beauty of the Whistlejacket Room, were replicated 300 times over in the other rooms at Wentworth House – paid for and maintained by the profits from coal.

The previous February, when the result of the miners' ballot to nationalize Britain's collieries had been announced, Billy Fitzwilliam had moved to defend his interests. Field Marshal Earl Haig had rejected the use of covert methods to fight Communism. Billy welcomed them. His horror of publicity, combined with an acute sense of realpolitik – that he risked further jeopardizing his wealth by making public pronouncements in favour of the private ownership of the coal industry – dictated that his war against Communism was waged covertly.

In essence it was a battle for hearts and minds: overnight, the churches and chapels in the towns and pit villages around Wentworth became one of the first fields of engagement. The Rector of Barnsley, a radical socialist, fired a warning shot. 'Nothing,' he said, preaching from the pulpit to a packed congregation, 'is likely to revive the spirit of revolution so much as the sight of the extravagant follies of the rich, more especially when riches represent the profits of war, at a time when others were sacrificing all, even life itself.'

Billy retaliated, using the power he wielded in his own churches. Twenty vicars in the parishes around Wentworth were dependent on the Earl for their livings. Under their auspices, he arranged for an Oxford don, Professor Wilden-Hart, to tour the parish halls lecturing on the dangers of Bolshevism. The *Mexborough and Swinton Times* carried a report of a well-attended lecture at Swinton Church Hall:

> The lecturer said that the Russian workmen had never suffered as much as they were doing at the present moment. The workmen were confined to their factories by force, the right of meeting was prohibited, all Socialist papers were suppressed, and any Socialist who did not agree with the terroristic policy of the Bolsheviks was at once imprisoned or killed . . .
>
> The Professor went on to say that the Bolsheviks had abolished God, and had forbidden children to say their prayers, therefore it was not surprising to find that archbishops had been massacred and mutilated, bishops had been buried alive, and priests and monks had been massacred wholesale . . .
>
> Reading from captured German documents, the lecturer then startled his audience by declaring that Bolshevism was not Russian at all, but was a German-made instrument . . . The majority of the Bolshevik leaders, he said, were German Jews.

Billy did not confine his crusade against Communism to South Yorkshire. At the start of 1919, he revived a secret society that had lain dormant during the Great War. With the unedifying name of the Mineral Owners' Association of Great Britain (MOAGB), its members were some of the richest and most powerful men in Britain. So secretive was the organization that later that year a Government inquiry failed to elicit their names.

The association was established on a pact: should it ever be disbanded, its records would be burnt precisely twelve months after. The society closed in 1947; a year later the documents were duly destroyed.

Nevertheless, a few papers have survived. They reveal that in the years between the two World Wars over fifty peers joined the MOAGB. 'Mowbray and Stourton, Buccleuch, Carnarvon, Leeds, Northumberland, Scarbrough . . .', the list reads on, a throwback to the Middle Ages, a roll-call of the country's wealthiest aristocrats.

Between them, they owned great swathes of Britain; they also, as mineral royalty owners, owned a sizeable proportion of the country's largest and most lucrative export: coal.

The principal aim of the MOAGB was to stop the Government nationalizing the collieries. Based on intelligence supplied by its network of informers in the coalmines and exploiting its members' close links to the Press barons and to the Cabinet, in March 1919 the Association launched a public relations campaign to convince the nation that the country's pits should remain in private hands. But within weeks of the launch, it went disastrously wrong: by the summer of 1919, the men Billy had chosen to defend were among the most vilified in Britain.

Six months later, looking out from the Whistlejacket Room across the thousands of men surrounding his house, Billy knew that relations between the coal owners and the miners had never been worse.

The bad blood stemmed from a Royal Commission that had mesmerized Britain. Its outcome had enraged the MFGB: the miners, in the words of a member of the union's Executive Committee, had been 'duped, deceived and betrayed'. It had also shaken Billy Fitzwilliam and the members of the MOAGB to the core. Eight peers of the realm, representatives of Billy's association, had been coerced to appear as supplicants to plead their cause.

The stage for their humiliation was the King's Robing Room at the House of Lords.

18

The Duke of Northumberland, twenty-first in the Dukes' table of precedence, the owner of five stately homes, a quarter of a million acres and a townhouse in London's Kensington, stood in the witness box, facing twelve Commissioners, seated at tables arranged in a horseshoe around him.

Under subpoena and against every fibre of his aristocratic being, the Duke had been compelled to answer a question that few, if any, had ever dared ask him. Precisely how much income did his coal royalties bring in per annum? At his answer – £69,194* – the assembled audience gasped.

Behind the Duke, members of the public and Press crowded every inch of the room. Hundreds had been turned away. The setting was magnificent: the carved ceiling owed its inspiration to Cardinal Wolsey's closet at Hampton Court; frescoes depicting the Arthurian legend, among them 'Generosity', 'Courtesy', 'Mercy' and 'Courage', were painted on the walls. The Winterhalter portraits of Queen Victoria and Prince Albert, almost nine feet in height, flanked the Cloth of Estate. But for the handwoven royal blue carpet, a pin could have been heard to drop.

Leaning forward, looking the Duke directly in the eye, Commissioner Sir Leo Money, representing the Miners' Federation of Great Britain, began his interrogation.

'Don't you think it is a bad thing for one man to own as much as you do?' he asked.

'No. I think it is an excellent thing,' replied the Duke.

The assembled public and Press roared with laughter. It was excellent entertainment. Class war had come to court.

Commissioner Herbert Smith, President of the Yorkshire

* £2 million at today's values.

Miners' Association, continued the cross-examination. 'If this Commission recommend nationalization,' he asked, 'you would use your influence in the House of Lords to defeat it?'

'Certainly. What has this Commission got to do with me?' the Duke replied.

'The House of Lords has always opposed reform in the country,' retorted Smith.

'That is a matter of opinion. I do not agree.'

'Will you give me any reform that they have voted for that has brought about better conditions for the people?' challenged Smith.

'I think there have been many,' said the Duke.

'Why do you oppose nationalization?'

'Because it is only a blind – perhaps it is correct to say a stage to something more revolutionary.'

It had been the Earl of Durham's turn to be interrogated before the Duke of Northumberland. He was the owner of Lambton Castle and one other stately home; the coal royalties from his 12,411 acres brought in an annual income averaging £40,000 a year.*

Lord Durham was cross-examined by Commissioner Robert Smillie, the President of the MFGB. The true extent of the union leader's revolutionary intentions swiftly became clear.

'I suppose it may be taken that the land, which includes the minerals and metals, is essential to the life of the people? Do you agree?' he asked him.

'If you like, I accept that. They cannot live in the air,' Durham replied.

Pressing the Earl, Smillie said, 'You do agree that land is essential to the life of the people, but you will not accept the proposal that if the land is in the hands of a limited number of people, practically they hold the lives of the people at their disposal?'

'The lives of the people who live on my land are as happy as those on any other land, and it makes no difference whether I own it or not,' the Earl replied sharply.

Flicking through a sheaf of notes on the desk in front of him,

* £1.2 million at today's values.

Smillie continued, 'I will quote a constitutional lawyer, Blackstone, who says, "It is a received and undeniable principle of law that all lands in England are held immediately of the King." Do you deny Blackstone's authority? If he is correct, you cannot hold the land you claim to own?'

'That is your opinion. My family has owned land for a great many years and no one has disputed it.'

'We dispute it now!' retorted Smillie. There was loud laughter from the spectators.

Rising to his audience, he went on, 'I will quote another. There is a very old Book which says, "The earth is the Lord's, and the fulness thereof." I am not exactly sure of the author but it appears in the Bible, upon which you have promised to tell the truth and the whole truth this morning. Would you deny that authority? The reference is Psalm Twenty-four, verse one.'

'I prefer another authority,' replied Durham. '"Render unto Caesar the things which are Caesar's, and unto God the things that are God's." Matthew, chapter twenty-two, verse twenty-one.'

'That is exactly what I want to be done at the present time,' said Smillie, 'because if "the earth is the Lord's, and the fulness thereof", it cannot be the property of individuals!'

'Is this an ecclesiastical examination?' asked the Earl.

It was not. Lord Durham and the Duke of Northumberland were appearing, under subpoena, before a Royal Commission set up by the Prime Minister, David Lloyd George, to conduct a forensic inquiry into the state of Britain's coal industry. Its remit was to examine every aspect of it: wages, the length of the working day, the miners' housing and social conditions, but most crucially its future. Should the industry be nationalized or not?

The Prime Minister had been forced to set up the Commission in order to avert a national coal strike. The panel of twelve Commissioners, presided over by the Chairman William Sankey, was made up of representatives from all sides of the industry: capital (the coal owners) and labour (the miners' trades union representatives) were in equal balance. For the first time the miners, through their union leaders, had the opportunity to challenge the coal owners on a very public stage. Private ownership of coal was in the dock: capitalism, with particular emphasis on the English aristocracy, was on open trial.

Of the 116 witnesses called to appear before the Commission, among them coal owners, Government officials, trades union leaders and the miners themselves, it was the mineral royalty owners, the men whom Billy Fitzwilliam had formed his Association to defend, who drew the most fire.

Following the evidence of the Earl of Durham and the Duke of Northumberland, six other peers were compelled to testify against their will: the Marquesses of Bute and Londonderry, the Duke of Hamilton, and Lords Dynevor, Dunraven and Tredegar. Between them, during the Great War, they had earned over £2 million pounds (£61 million at today's values) in royalty payments.

Mineral royalties were the dividends paid per ton of coal by the colliery operators to the owner of the land under which the coal was mined. To the shock and incredulity of the British public, the Commission revealed that, whereas the miners were paid less than a shilling per ton of coal, the mineral royalty owners received more than a shilling for every ton they mined.

The country was gripped by the inquiry: in exposing the issue of mineral royalties, one of the most inflammatory in the industry, the Royal Commission ceased to be purely about coal; in effect, it became an investigation into the injustices of the British class system.

The mineral royalty owners, as Billy Fitzwilliam's Association reflected, were invariably upper-class. In the years between the Reformation and the turn of the twentieth century, the pattern of land ownership in Britain had barely changed. In the late 1870s, 7,000 individuals, the majority of them aristocrats or members of the landed gentry, owned almost four-fifths of the British Isles. Twenty-nine peers owned a staggering 4,600,000 acres. In 1919, this group, together with the King and the Church Commissioners, were the biggest owners of coal. Less than 5 per cent of the mineral royalty owners mined their land themselves, preferring to lease it to the colliery companies. As a consequence, their huge revenues were earned from doing nothing – bar having had the good fortune to inherit their land.

The inquisition of the Dukes, Marquesses, Barons and Earls had no historical precedent. Never before had individual members of the British aristocracy been so publicly humiliated, so rudely challenged.

The miners' representatives played to the public gallery. Using every trick of class rhetoric, weaving speciously constructed arguments incorporating details which at times were irrelevant to the Commission's line of inquiry, they humiliated the mineral royalty owners. The effect was devastating: by the pointed use of ridicule, the peers became the laughing stock of the proceedings, the spectators thrilling at the pricking of their power and mystique.

A farcical note was struck from the beginning. Robert Smillie had asked the Chairman of the Commission to request that 'certain Dukes and Earls' send the titles and charters 'justifying their possession of certain land in the country' to London for the Commissioners to examine. The Chairman waived the request when it became clear that several railway vans, if not a special train, would be required to transport the documents.

The issue came up during Smillie's cross-examination of the Earl of Durham. The transcribers in the Robing Room were careful to annotate the moments when the public laughed.

'I want to examine you as fairly as I can without bitterness of feeling of any kind.'

'About a railway van?' (Laughter)

'Do you agree that it would require a large van to carry your title deeds?'

'It is an exaggeration.'

'Would it require a railway van to produce them?'

'A portion of a railway van, no doubt . . .'

'Now that you have had the title deeds examined, does that indicate that you have any doubt at all? Any doubt about the validity of them?'

'Yes. No. And I hope I never shall have.'

'Was it only recently this examination was made?'

'About a fortnight or three weeks ago, when you practically made a demand that my title deeds should be produced in this room. You caused a great deal of inconvenience in suggesting that these title deeds should be sent up. Otherwise they would have remained in the depository. I don't read them every Sunday.' (Laughter)

'They have not been sent up?'

'No. But if the Chairman says I am to bring them I will.'

'And the Chairman may say that. (Laughter) You say you did not read them yourself?'

'No.'

'You depend upon your agent keeping you read up in matters of this kind?'

'Yes. For many years past.'

'A good many people would be delighted to read their title deeds from day to day if they could manage to secure any.' (Laughter)

'You don't suggest I should give them my title deeds?' (Laughter)

'I have a feeling that you have no title deeds which justify your ownership of land or minerals, and that being the case I would suggest you ought to give it back to the State, who is the proper owner of it, if I am correct.'

Commissioner Smillie proceeded to draw the Earl's attention – and the public's – to the deplorable state of the miners' houses in his own district.

'Are you aware,' he said, 'that in Durham and Northumberland there have been serious complaints about the conditions of houses? I put it to you that in very few of the houses you would like to live.'

'I would prefer to live where I am living,' replied the Earl.

Beneath the flourishes of comedy and class rhetoric, the undertones were grave. For the private owners of the coal industry, the inquiry, with its royal imprimatur of objectivity and impartiality, was more damaging than anything that had gone before. In its forensic exposure of an industry riddled with abuses, the chief asset of which the aristocracy owned, it undermined the supremacy of the ruling class.

The country was both appalled and startled by its findings.

'There are houses in some mining districts,' the Commissioners reported, 'which are a reproach to our civilization. No judicial language is sufficiently strong or sufficiently severe to apply to their condemnation.' There were more casualties in Britain's mines in 1918, it was revealed, than there were in the Gallipoli campaign, and for the children of miners, the infant mortality rate was higher than in any other section of the population: 160 per thousand, as compared with 96.9 among agricultural labourers and 76.4 for the upper and middle classes.

Particularly disturbing was the testimony of the Financial Adviser to the Coal Controller, who gave evidence of widescale profiteering by the coal owners during the war. The total profits and royalties of the coal-mining industry in the years 1914–1918 amounted to £160,000,000 – £25 million more than the total pre-war capital of the industry. Many of the coal owners, it emerged, had succeeded in concealing further profits by the capitalization of reserves or other readjustments of capital.

What caused the public revulsion was that the swollen profits had been wrung out of low wages for the miners and high prices paid by the consumer. Further, the Commission concluded, wastefulness and inefficiency engendered through the private ownership of the mines had seriously hampered the national war effort.

In the course of the hearing, it became clear that the nationalization of the mines offered the only really adequate method through which to raise the miners' standard of living and to safeguard the interests of the consumer. In an interim report, submitted to the Government at the end of March 1919, the Chairman of the Commission, Mr Justice Sankey, concluded, 'Even upon the evidence already given, the present system of ownership and working in the coal industry stands condemned, and some other system must be substituted for it, either nationalization or a method of unification by national purchase and/or by joint control.'

Billy Fitzwilliam was lucky to escape the Inquisitors. Following the King and the Ecclesiastical Commissioners, only the Duke of Portland and the Marquess of Bute owned more coal than he did.

During the Great War, Billy's mineral royalties, combined with the profits from his two collieries, had yielded an income well in excess of £100,000 a year.* Yet he had not been called before the Commission.

The miners' leaders, Robert Smillie and Herbert Smith, were careful in their choice of the Peers they subpoenaed to attend. For political reasons, they chose mineral royalty owners who were historically unpopular among the miners in their districts and whose family's track record in industrial relations and social welfare was poor.

The Fitzwilliams' record was exemplary. Unusually, they were both mineral royalty owners and coal owners – the term used to denote the men who owned and operated Britain's collieries. The standard of safety in the Fitzwilliams' mines and the housing and social conditions in their pit villages were unequalled anywhere else in the country. Arnold Freeman, a writer, visited Elsecar in July 1919, shortly after the Royal Commission submitted its final report. So shocked was he by what he had seen of the miners' living conditions in Scotland and South Wales that he wrote in overblown terms of what he saw at Elsecar:

> They are all decent workmen's cottages, many of them ivy-covered, most of them neat, clean, attractive . . . Lords are the natural targets for the slings and poisoned arrows of every demagogue, every agitator on the make, every Bob on the bounce – and I have thought of them as rather expensive luxuries for a democratic country to indulge in. I looked at them from afar off, through glasses coloured by prejudice perhaps. Now that I have studied the work of a real live earl at first hand, I have to admit he justifies his existence . . . Elsecar is a small flower-embosomed town . . . almost the first thing that strikes the eye is the number of its gardens or allotments. I have never seen a town in all my life with such a number in proportion to its size – probably more than one for every householder, for some of the miners have two or three. And gardens are fine antidotes to Bolshevism.

* £3 million at today's values.

It would take more than gardens, as Billy realized, to save his coal. In January 1920, the consequences of the previous summer's Royal Commission had come to a dramatic head: a General Strike threatened, triggered by the Government's failure to depose the coal owners. The Prime Minister, David Lloyd George, had betrayed the miners.

At the outset, he had promised so much. 'If they throw themselves into this inquiry and present their case,' he had told the House of Commons in March 1919,

> they will achieve great things for their industry . . . they will get a Miners' Charter, which will be the beginning of greater and better things for them. And they will have the satisfaction when they have got these things of knowing that they obtained them without inflicting any hurt upon hundreds of thousands of other men and women engaged in honest toil like themselves.

They did not get those things. Lloyd George got exactly what he wanted. The miners got nothing.

The Commission's interim report, submitted three weeks into the inquiry, had been necessary to head off a national coal strike. On the day it was published, the Government announced that it accepted its findings – the nationalization of the collieries – 'in spirit and in letter'. The strike was called off: the MFGB interpreted the Government's announcement as a signal that it would introduce legislation to end the reign of the coal owners and bring the mines under state control.

As it turned out, the union was misguided. The Commission's strength – a panel of Commissioners drawn from all sides of the industry – became its weakness. When it came to submit its final report in June 1919, the panel failed to agree. Lloyd George, motivated by his dislike of the trades union movement and in defence of private property, used the rift between the Commissioners as an excuse to reject the idea of nationalization.

'Was it a huge game of bluff?' Vernon Hartshorn, a Labour MP and a member of the Executive Committee of the MFGB, demanded angrily. 'We did not ask for a Commission. We accepted it. We gave evidence before it. Why was the Commission set up?' he asked. 'Was it never intended that if the reports favoured nationalization we were to get it? Why was the question sent at all to the Commission? That is the kind of questions the miners of the country will ask, and they will say: "We have been deceived, betrayed, duped."'

In the months following Lloyd George's decision, the Cabinet and the coal owners waited nervously for the backlash as the Executive Committee of the MFGB conferred with trades union leaders in other industries to find a means of forcing the Prime Minister's hand.

Revenge, when it came, was sweet. Or so the MFGB's leaders thought. In December 1919, the Trades Union Council agreed to support its bid to call a General Strike to coerce the Government into nationalizing the mines. In a year dogged by fears of a Bolshevik-inspired revolution, Britain now faced its first true test of working-class revolutionary intent. If the coalminers and the union members in the country's other key industries supported the decision of their leaders, the workers, rather than Parliament, would dictate the governance of Britain.

To proceed with its bid, the MFGB needed the consent of its 800,000 members. Delegates in the coalfields were asked to ballot the miners on the question as to whether, at the next Special Trades Union Congress, scheduled for the second week in March, the union should propose a 'General Strike in the event of the Government continuing to refuse to nationalize the mines'.

This request, dispatched to every colliery in the country, was sent out on 9 January 1920: two weeks before the day that 10,000 miners surrounded Wentworth House.

Throughout the last days of January, as the discussions took place in the districts, it emerged that the miners, far from being united by radical politics and the collective sense of betrayal that Vernon Hartshorn had claimed, were divided. The anticipated echo of political radicalism did not resound.

At Wentworth, Billy Fitzwilliam monitored the discussions

through the network of trusted informers he had set up at his pits – favoured men whom he relied upon to keep him abreast of what was happening on the ground. The Yorkshire miners, he was told, would vote against the call for a General Strike.

It was the reason why, on the morning of Sunday 25 January, after hours spent deliberating in the Whistlejacket Room with Field Marshal Haig, he ruled out the option of calling in troops to defend the house.

Running with his instincts, he decided to take a risk.

19

Shortly after a quarter to two, Jack May, the groom of chambers at Wentworth, slipped quietly out of the Whistlejacket Room. Three footmen waited in the corridor outside, standing statuesquely along its length. Softly, speaking to each man in turn, May whispered their orders.

Some minutes later, a dray, pulled by a carthorse, made its way slowly along the gravel drive in front of the house. Upwards of twenty 'outdoor' servants, the men responsible for maintaining the Park and grounds at Wentworth, crammed the base of the wagon, sitting shoulder to shoulder, facing outwards.

A murmur ran through the crowd. Under the watchful gaze of thousands, the dray came to a halt beneath the portico outside the entrance to the Pillared Hall. Jumping down from the cart, the men unloaded stacks of fence posts, the sort used to mark out the paddock at the races. They were not white but striped, like a Venetian barber's pole, in black, yellow and green, the Fitzwilliam racing colours. Some of the men carried coils of thick tasselled rope, woven from black and green silk.

Walking twenty paces out on to the lawn, they marked out a square. Perfectly proportioned, it encompassed an area large enough to hold 400 men. They worked quickly, slotting the posts into metal bases and hooking the coils of silk rope on to the brass rings mounted at their sides. When they had finished, each man took up position at one of the posts. Tiny figures on an expanse of green, the servants were dwarfed by the scale of everything around them: the 10,000-strong crowd, the façade of the house, the great portico towering above. The Fitzwilliam family motto was carved in gold on its entablature: 'Mea Gloria Fides' – My Glorious Faith. Higher still, on the stone-carved parapet, was a marble statue of Minerva, the Goddess of Wisdom and War, her head inclined towards the lawn below.

A lone bugler sounded the 'General Salute'. At the windows on the piano nobile, the gloved hands of footmen flashed white against the darkness behind as they reached in unison to release the bolts on the doors leading to the terrace from the Marble Salon.

From the direction of the Stable Block came the sound of marching feet. Rounding the corner of the façade under the North Tower, Billy Fitzwilliam came into view, a single figure at the head of a column of 400 men. At the same moment, Field Marshal Earl Haig stepped out on to the balconied terrace beneath the portico.

A deafening roar rose from the crowd.

As Billy led his troops into the square marked out by his groundsmen, the miners held station along the perimeter of the lawn.

The moment of danger had passed.

The risk Billy had run was to proceed with the afternoon's arrangements as planned.

Weeks before, as a mark of his esteem towards the local veterans from the Great War, he had invited the Field Marshal to honour a troop of ex-servicemen with a General Inspection.

On the makeshift parade ground, ringed off from the crowds by the silk tasselled rope, the 400 men dressed in their best mufti, wearing flat caps and trilby hats, stood smartly to attention. Every one of them worked for Billy. There were miners from his collieries at Elsecar and Low Stubbin, factory workers from the chemical works and the Simplex car factory in Sheffield, tenants and labourers from the Estate farms. Like thousands among those watching, they bore the scars of war. But they had at least come home. One hundred and eighty-three of the Fitzwilliam employees had been killed in action. Some of the veterans wore their sleeves turned up, proudly displaying the gold watches Billy had given them for winning the Military Medal. He had also donated £17,000* to the dependants of the dead and seriously wounded.

Earl Haig moved to the head of the column to address the men.

* £520,000 at today's values.

At a nod from Billy, the head groundsman raised his arm, a signal to the servants to unhook the ropes.

It was also a signal to the watching crowd. Surging forward, thousands of miners came streaming on to the lawn, swelling up to the square, some of them sprinting at full stretch, hoping to catch the Field Marshal's words. Haig's speech was a plea for unity in the face of class war and industrial strife. Thanking the men for their support in 'the most trying ordeal the country has ever had to face', he swiftly moved that the 'spirit of comradeship present in all arms, branches and classes of the service' be applied to the current crisis. 'Band together as firmly now as you did in the darkest hours of the war,' he urged. 'Together you stand for the safety of your country. Together you are better situated to obtain all you are reasonably entitled to.' Closing his speech with a caution, the Field Marshal warned, 'Each one of us must bear in mind that most excellent motto: "United we stand, divided we fall".' Gesturing towards Billy, who stood facing him at the head of the column of veterans, Haig praised his host: 'He has striven his utmost to further the cause of freedom and justice and to secure the victory of Right.'

Ten thousand voices boomed 'Hip, hip, hooray!' They were followed by a single cry: 'To the King!' The 400 veterans stiffened their backs, sharply raising their right hands to their caps, the rapid motion rippling from the square through to the farthest reaches of the crowd, as thousands of men joined in the salute.

The fears of that morning had been groundless. The miners had crossed the fields to Wentworth, not in the spirit of rebellion, but in search of meaning and guidance.

That winter, a collective depression hung heavily over the pit villages in the district. Falling wages, the high cost of living, the futility of the Royal Commission had thwarted wartime hopes that things would change for the better, that the poverty, disease and danger the miners encountered at work and in their daily lives would be alleviated. Instead, they faced a string of broken promises. Where was the 'Nation in a molten state' that the Prime Minister had spoken of in 1918, the Nation that would never 'return to the old ways, the old stupidities'?

What hurt most was the feeling that the carnage and sacrifice of the Great War had been in vain. Grief, and the sense of hope that had been crushed, seeped through the neighbourhood finding its expression in the unveiling of war memorials. At ceremony after ceremony, in village after village, Laurence Binyon's 'For the Fallen' was chosen as the most appropriate reading:

> They shall grow not old, as we that are left grow old:
> Age shall not weary them, nor the years condemn.
> At the going down of the sun and in the morning
> We will remember them.

For the miners who worked for Billy Fitzwilliam, among the thousands gathered at Wentworth that Sunday, it was a pilgrimage to their patriarch. 'Billy Fitzbilly' or 'Lordie', as they called him, was more than a provider, he was their protector. He was all they had. In the absence of a Welfare State, they were dependent on him in almost every aspect of their lives: at work, in the conditions and regularity of employment underground at his pits; at home, in the standard of housing in his tied cottages, and of education at his schools. Even their social lives depended on the Earl, reflected in the myriad of sports and cultural activities available in his pit villages. In bad times, only he could cushion them from the vagaries of their trade.

Billy had been right to trust his instincts. In ruling out the option of calling in troops, he had correctly judged that the miners did not pose a danger to either him or his house. It was a brave step, one that in the circumstances few coal owners would have taken. But he belonged to the small minority among the coal aristocracy who believed – and rightly – that the Bolshevist threat did not come from the miners as a whole.

His intelligence had been correct. When the coalfields voted on the question of whether to call a General Strike to force the Government to nationalize the pits, almost half the country's miners, including those from South Yorkshire, voted against the MFGB's proposal. The radicalism of the union's Executive was at odds with its membership, a confusing contradiction that would impact with tragic consequences in the decades to come.

Billy Fitzwilliam's personal crusade against Bolshevism was motivated by his desire to protect not only his own interests but, as he believed, those of his miners too. He saw himself as the custodian of a way of life. As radical as he was reactionary, he regarded it as his duty to wield his wealth and power with a conscience: to provide the best possible living and working conditions for the men he employed. A benevolent paternalist to the core, the protection of his interests and the protection of his men were in equal balance. The one followed from the other, or so he believed. If he could protect his miners, he could protect himself.

But could he protect them? What neither he nor his miners could know was that 1919 was the year of no return: the world beyond Wentworth was closing in.

20

Two small boys, oblivious to the gathering political storm, balanced on a silk-covered footstool in a room on the top floor of the South Tower. They had moved the stool from its usual position by the fire and placed it beneath the bison's head that hung above the door. Slowly, concentrating rigidly, the younger boy stretched his leg, aiming his toe at a low wooden nursery chair positioned a few feet beyond. Dressed in a heavily starched linen sailor's suit, he was overweight. The suit hung awkwardly, accentuating his tubbiness. His soft brown hair, unflatteringly long, curled in wisps at its collar. Taking a deep breath, he leapt from the stool to the chair and vaulted on to the banister rail at the top of the stairwell. Reaching over with a cry of victory and peals of laughter, he grabbed the chair and slid down the rails, perching on the banister curl at the bottom of the stairs.

Peter Fitzwilliam, Billy's only son, and his cousin, Armand Smith, were playing a game. 'It was our favourite game,' Armand recalled, 'we had to get from one end of the house to the other without touching the floor. I suppose we were about eight or nine. We played it for hours. You could stand on any of the furniture – there were low chests and seats in the window recesses along the corridors which helped – but if you fell off, you had to start all over again. We allowed ourselves a prop, a small chair, which was very useful, though it made it more difficult sometimes because you had to pull it with you all the way.'

The games with Armand Smith during the winter of 1920 were among the rare moments in Peter Fitzwilliam's childhood when he was able to be a child. In the family photograph albums that survive – the personal albums of Maud Fitzwilliam, his mother – as a young boy, he never smiles. Most of the photographs are of him on his own. In the few pictures there are of Peter with his parents and his sisters, he looks stiff and uncomfortable. They are staged images of a young heir, not portraits of a child. At the age of two, he is shown cutting the clod at the sinking of his father's colliery; at three, shaking hands with an old Fitzwilliam servant at a garden fête. Most poignant of all perhaps is a photograph of Peter when he was four. Dressed in a specially tailored uniform, wearing a heavy greatcoat and puttees – the full battledress of a British soldier in winter – he solemnly salutes a march past of troops at Wentworth on their way to fight in the Great War.

Peter was destined to become the 8th Earl Fitzwilliam, in the words of his friend, Sir Henry 'Chips' Channon, the 'Fabulous Lord Fitzwilliam'. Yet the man is as elusive as the boy. It was after his death that the bonfires at Wentworth began. Like his father and grandfather before him, Peter's life has been erased, its minutiae, his correspondence and records burnt by his successors.

Memories are all that remain of him. Between the years 1918 and 1926, when their father was Vicar at Wentworth, Armand Smith and his sister, Joyce, glimpsed into the world of his childhood. 'We saw it through a gauze. We were only children,' said Armand Smith almost eighty years later, 'but still, we were left with the impression there was something odd about the household. It was not a clean-running fish.'

21

It was in the autumn of 1918 that Joyce and Armand Smith moved into the Vicarage at Wentworth. 'My grandfather lived at Barnes Hall, Grenoside, a few miles from Wentworth House,' Joyce Smith recalled. 'He had nine sons and hunted with the Fitzwilliam Hounds and was the starter for the point-to-point races. He was getting old and wanted my father near him. The Fitzwilliams were cousins of ours and Lord Fitzwilliam wanted to help out. So he offered my father the living at Wentworth – to our disgust!'

Joyce and her five brothers and sisters came from Cartmel, a sleepy rural village in Cumbria, where their father, Godfrey Smith, was the Vicar. 'We were very happy at Cartmel. We didn't want to go to Wentworth. We were the poor cousins! We'd never come into contact with the sorts of things that Wentworth did, the grand social life – big house parties, cricket matches in the summer and dances, that sort of thing. In the weeks before we left we were warned by our governess, "You can't do this there, you won't be able to do that there, you'll have to be on your Ps and Qs all the time." We were dreading it. Our governess, you see, she'd come into contact with stately homes before, she knew what sort of thing to expect.'

Nothing their governess had told them prepared the Smith children for their arrival at Wentworth. 'The thing that struck us most forcibly when we got there was how filthy everything was – with coal dust – mines all around us. Everything black. Then, when we went up to the house, it was the grandeur, the riches, the sheer scale of the place. The first morning I was told, "Daddy has to go up to 'The House' to take prayers and you can go with him if you like." So I went. We walked through the lovely gardens to the chapel entrance. All the servants came in to Prayer and "the family" sat in a gallery with its own entrance. I was fascinated.

Then my father said, "I must take you to see Whistle Jacket." So we went up some stairs and along carpeted passages to find what sounded so exciting, a jacket that whistled! It was so disappointing to discover that it was only a huge painting of a horse! But the grandeur was beyond anything I had imagined. From that moment, I longed to be invited up to Wentworth House.'

Joyce did not have to wait long for the invitation. 'One morning, Lady Fitzwilliam called on my mother at the Vicarage and said, "We are going to get a dancing teacher for the children and make a little dancing class. Would your Joyce like to join it?" Well, of course I thought this was absolutely wonderful!'

Every Friday afternoon, during the winter of 1919, Joyce and her brother were taken up to Wentworth by their governess. 'It was a child's dream. You arrived at the front door, an insignificant-looking entrance under the great steps beneath the portico. It was opened by the butler and you went through into this pillared hall, filled with pillars, rather like going to church. There must have been twenty or thirty of them and all round the walls there were elk's and buffalo's heads. At the end of the hall there was this lovely staircase, running up two sides. I always used to make my governess go up one side and I'd go up the other. The carpet was white and you were practically ankle-deep in it. It had been specially woven to fit the sweep of the stairs. We were shown up to a bedroom with a purple carpet and yellow silk walls where the footmen took our hats and coats. This bedroom had its own bathroom and loo. We thought it very impressive. Very few people had that then.'

Peter and Helena Fitzwilliam, aged nine and eleven, were the same age as Joyce and Armand. The dancing class for the four children was held in the Ante-Room to the south of the Marble Salon. It was forty feet by twenty-two feet, with a huge fireplace guarded by two griffins carved from stone. The ceiling was a copy of the Inigo Jones ceiling at Forde Abbey. Alongside the famous pair of Reynolds's canvases, *The Adoration of the Shepherds*, portraits of the Fitzwilliam family lined the walls. The servants had prepared the room in advance: Joyce remembers the marble and mosaic console tables, the yellow silk-covered sofas, the black and gold

Louis Quinze chairs, stacked neatly against the walls to make space for the children to dance.

It was here that Joyce first met Peter Fitzwilliam. 'I longed to meet him. After all, he was the only son and heir. My brother and I were in awe of the idea of him. Everything for miles around was going to be his.' At the first dancing class, in a routine that would be followed precisely in the coming weeks, after taking off their hats and coats, Joyce and her brother were shown into the Ante-Room by the butler, where they were instructed to sit on the Louis Quinze chairs while they waited for the Fitzwilliam children to be brought down from the nursery wing. At exactly two minutes past two, a footman came in to announce their arrival. 'Seconds later,' remembers Joyce, 'Peter and his older sister, Helena, appeared in sailor suits, accompanied by Nanny and their governess. Lady Fitzwilliam had brought a woman over from Sheffield to teach us. She was quite young and she had to curtsey when they came into the room. She called the children Lord Milton and Lady Helena. I thought this very peculiar. They were only children, they were nine and eleven! Peter struck me as a very fat unhappy little boy. He was a sort of Little Lord Fauntleroy. Overfed, terribly nannied all the time in case he caught a cold or got his feet wet. Later my mother told me that Nanny had complained to Lady Fitzwilliam when she heard that Armand and I had been invited to the dancing classes. She was horrified at the idea because these children from the Vicarage were certain to have colds and germs and pass them on!'

The Fitzwilliams' nanny and governess remained in the Ante-Room for the duration of the dancing class while the children were taught the hornpipe and the Lancers, and to waltz and polka. 'If Peter was doing anything he shouldn't, which he often was, his governess would gabble at him in French, rapid French. I think they all spoke French when they were alone. Lady Fitzwilliam did too. I suppose it was so that the servants wouldn't know what they were saying. When the class finished, we had tea in the nursery. Everything was so special. It was brought up and served by the footmen on Rockingham china. There were always footmen and butlers in all directions. Before sitting down to tea, the first time I went, Nanny asked me if I would like to wash my hands, and what sort of soap I liked. I said, "Oh, Pears soap." I just said it for fun because I liked looking through it, you see, it was transparent. She immediately produced it out of a drawer. I was frightfully impressed. If I'd said some other type of soap, I suppose she would have produced that too. Peter was awfully sweet, very polite and playing host, and he showed me to the loo, and I remember he said, "There you are, Joyce," and flung open the door. Poor boy was immediately ticked off by Nanny – she didn't think it was proper of him to open a loo door for a lady.'

At the dancing classes and on the days when Peter played at the Vicarage, Joyce and her brother got to know him well. 'Armand and I liked him very much, but he was soft. He wasn't allowed to be anything but soft. All round the Vicarage gardens, beyond the shrubbery, there were these tall trees, and Armand used to go along the tops of them, swinging from one to another, like a monkey. Peter would watch him from below with Nanny. He wasn't allowed to climb trees. In the summer holidays we always camped in the shrubbery, made our own camp and slept out at night. Peter was never allowed to join us. I remember saying to my father, "Can't we get Peter here without Nanny to play with us?" But his mother wouldn't let him. He did not have a proper childhood. He was a very kind gentle sort of person, but so sheltered. He was wanting to spread his wings one felt, even when he was a little boy.'

For the couple who had everything, Billy and Maud Fitzwilliam had waited thirteen years for the thing they wanted most of all: a son and heir.

A succession of daughters had followed their grand Society wedding at St Paul's Cathedral in the summer of 1896: Elfrida was born in 1898, Joan in 1900, Donatia in 1904 and Helena in 1908. 'They thought they couldn't have a son. It made them feel rather miserable, I think,' recalled their granddaughter, Lady Barbara Ricardo. 'In those days, an heir was everything. It clouded the early years of their marriage. It made them terribly unhappy.' In 1908, Billy's frustration and disappointment at the birth of yet another daughter, Helena, became evident moments after she was born. When the monthly nurse took the baby in to show its father, he turned his back and said, 'Don't you point that thing at me.' Years later, when Helena was eleven years old, she told Joyce this story, solemnly adding, 'If you call a baby Marie Gabrielle the next one is a boy. That's why my middle names are Marie Gabrielle, because they wanted a boy so badly.' Billy and Maud's longing for a son touched all their daughters. Joyce was deeply embarrassed when Elfrida, Peter's oldest sister, told her, 'If you ever want to be sure of getting an heir in your family, when you're having sex you must stand upside down, that's what you must do, stand on your head.' Joyce was fourteen at the time: 'I was very embarrassed, not because I was shocked but because I didn't understand. I had to ask her what sex was.'

Peter was born on New Year's Eve in 1910. 'His birth meant everything to my grandparents. It was the most important thing in their lives,' recalled Lady Barbara. 'They simply doted on him. After so many years of trying to have a son, when one finally came, they were absolutely thrilled.' To celebrate the arrival of their son and heir, Billy and Maud gave Peter the traditional family christening, one that Billy himself, because of the mysterious circumstances surrounding his birth, had been denied. In February 1911 Peter was christened in the private chapel at Wentworth swathed in a medieval piece of silk that William the Conqueror had awarded to one of his ancestors for valour at the Battle of Hastings in 1066.

The public celebrations that followed the christening were comparable to a coronation. As if to trump his predecessors, Billy invited 60,000 people to attend a party in the Park at Wentworth. In the event, after word spread through the neighbourhood, more than 100,000 showed up, the majority miners and their families from the pit villages around Wentworth. Billy spared no expense: there were marquees and beer tents, funfairs and brass bands. Oxen were roasted on spits, 4,000 gallons of tea and beer were drunk, and four tons of bread and cakes and tens of thousands of sandwiches and meat pies consumed. Painted in gaudy lettering around the curves of the helter-skelters and merry-go-rounds, even the fairground attractions proclaimed they were 'suppliers to the nobility and the elite'. The day ended with a spectacular fireworks display specially orchestrated by a team from the fireworks manufacturers, Brocks. Set to music, it consisted of a series of pyrotechnical portraits. One showed a British dreadnought bombarding a ship from a 'continental power'; in another, the Niagara Falls rolled 'its waters down in limpid fire'. The climax of the display was a double portrait of the Earl and Countess Fitzwilliam, drawn in Catherine wheels and Roman candles.

'Anything Peter wanted he had to have,' said Lady Barbara. 'My grandmother was so thrilled when she had him that he was frightfully spoilt as a consequence. Of course my grandfather was thrilled too, but he didn't approve of the way she spoilt him the whole time. It used to make him quite cross.'

Peter was a shy, sensitive boy. Fat, physically gauche, withdrawn and lacking in confidence, he was his father's opposite. Machismo was the strongest trait in Billy's character. A trained and distinguished soldier, he had been decorated in both the Boer War and the Great War. Speed and sport, particularly hunting and horse-racing, were his great passions. In the 1920s, life at Wentworth revolved around horses. During the hunting season, Billy hunted six days a week. 'He rode out with the Wentworth Pack on Mondays and Fridays, on Tuesdays with the Badsworth, a pack that hunted the ground west of Doncaster, and Thursdays with the Grove,' his cousin, Charles Doyne, recalled. 'On Fridays, when the day's hunting was over, his chauffeur would drive him to Holyhead to catch the overnight boat to Ireland. Another chauffeur met him at Dublin docks and drove him down to his estate at Coollattin. He'd get there just in time for the Meet and off he'd go with his Irish pack.' Billy's love of hunting was equalled only by his love of horse-racing. The household accounts show that, in the years after the First World War, the Stud at Wentworth, with its stallions, hunters and brood mares, cost more to keep up than the house. 'We were all mad about horses,' Billy's eldest daughter, Elfreda, Countess of Wharncliffe, recalled. 'Mother was a great horsewoman. Terrific. I think she made us all the horse people we were. We girls all hunted from the age of two. I did five days a week on a horse, two horses a day, and one day a week on Hobson's choice. We were all hard riders – fitter than fiddles and hard as nails.'

Peter was the exception. When he was two years old he was taken to the opening meet of the Fitzwilliam Hounds, held on the lawn in front of Wentworth House. Twenty-five years later he wrote, 'A rather fat spoiled little boy was dressed up in a red coat, white breeches, hunting boots, spurs and a huntsman's cap, and placed on top of a very quiet and very old pony, which was held by a groom, threatened with instant execution if anything should happen. The small boy was supported on both sides by a nurse and a nurserymaid, and he proceeded to cry continuously for at least half an hour, which was the entire time he was on the pony's back. The Hounds then moved off to draw and the small boy was taken upstairs and comforted by his nurse.'

Horses became an early source of friction between father and son. 'In the nursery there were horses everywhere. There was a rocking horse and there were little model horses all over the place,' Joyce remembers. 'Everyone in the family was very horse-minded, except Peter. He was frightened of horses. He hated riding – especially hunting – and refused to go. In this respect he was a great disappointment to his father. You felt terribly sorry for him really, he was so inept as a little boy. He was mad keen on Cricket – it was the one thing he was rather good at as a boy – and I remember a sad thing happened. His great ambition was to play for Yorkshire and the team used to come to Wentworth. They had a cricket pitch on the lawn in front of the house. One summer – Peter was about eleven, I suppose, maybe not as much – as a treat he was allowed to open the batting for the Yorkshire team. There was great excitement. We were all sitting in a row of chairs at the edge of the lawn and Peter went out to bat. First ball, pretty well, he was bowled out for a duck. He came back half-way to where we were sitting and stopped. And I know he was crying. I felt so sorry for him. He didn't want anyone to see him. He was so disappointed. He really was a sweet boy. Very modest. He wasn't at all "I am the great I am". I think he got sick to death of having to try and be the great I am.'

Almost from the moment he was born, Peter was expected to be the 'great I am'. As soon as he could walk, he accompanied his father to public functions: to civic ceremonies in the district and to the host of social engagements that revolved around the Fitzwilliams' business interests. From the age of four, on Christmas Eve, it was Peter who handed out the family's presents to the long line of village children that queued up in the Marble Salon. Compelled by his parents to assume centre stage, he was constantly on parade, the obligation to play a part no less relentless in the formal atmosphere of life at home.

Joyce Smith remembered Peter's tenth birthday party on New Year's Eve in 1920. 'There was a huge house party. All sorts of grand people were there. I hadn't the least idea who any of them were. As a special treat, the children were allowed to join the grown-ups for dinner. Peter appeared in an Eton suit. He had a white waistcoat and tails, the same kind of get-up as men's tails, with beautiful studs down his front. Though we were only children, we were escorted into dinner! We all met in the small ballroom to the side of the Marble Salon, and then you walked in pairs in procession with your person across the hall. There were these lovely long tables, banked with flowers and set with gold cutlery, and all these men waiting. The footmen stood behind the chairs, one for every two chairs. They had yellow striped waistcoats. Yellow was the Fitzwilliams' colour. All the cars were yellow, everything was yellow.'

After dinner, there was dancing in the Marble Salon and games. 'Then, at that sort of party, conversation was very rare,' recalled Lady Marjorie Stirling, a close friend of Billy's and a guest at Wentworth during the 1920s and 1930s. 'We relied on games and practical jokes during house parties. At most country seats time was devoted to very energetic, endless games – energetic physically, like Murder or Sardines. All over the house; it must have been awful for the host and the hostess, but it was quite fun, sometimes great fun . . . Some houses absolutely revelled in practical jokes: apple-pie beds and creatures in baths. One or two families were known for it. Sometimes you couldn't take it any more; you thought twice before going again.'

Practical jokes were frowned on at Wentworth. In the 1920s, Sir Richard Sykes was sent home and banned from the house after running over a pheasant in the Park and putting the mangled bird in a girl's bed. But at 'energetic games' the Fitzwilliams – with the exception of Peter – excelled. Wentworth was the perfect place to play them. As a young boy, Charles Doyne remembered watching one of the house favourites. 'There was quite a party and they collected all the jerry pots. They had a curling competition, sliding the chamberpots across the polished marble floor in the Marble Salon. Some were prize Rockingham – quite a few were shattered to pieces.' Another popular game, as Joyce described, was 'The "Fox" Hunt'. 'One of the young men of the house party was chosen to be a fox and there was a hunt. He was given ten minutes start to go anywhere in the house. Then the rest of the house party hunted him. In full cry! When they caught him, they stripped him. There was a kill! They took all his clothes off. Scragged him, and brushed his hair up the wrong way. He came back into the dining room looking like nothing on earth.' There were other games too. Bert May, whose father, Jack, had become the butler at Wentworth, and whose wife, Margaret, worked as a housemaid there, remembered her complaining one day about the mess she had cleared up. 'They'd had a paper chase. The toilet rolls were unravelled all around the house. To this room, to that room, to the next room, and all the way back again. She started work at seven in the morning and it took her till lunch time to clean it all up.'

Vicar Godfrey Smith and his wife Katharine found their eight years at Wentworth difficult. There was a darker side to life at Wentworth House. Behind the façade, family life was not all that it seemed. 'It was terribly difficult for my parents,' Joyce remembered. 'They both knew they were under the wing of these people whose private lives they believed to be most immoral.'

From an early stage in their marriage, Billy and Maud had led separate lives. In 1913, Billy had been cited as the third party in a high-profile society divorce case. A few days before the case was due to be heard his reputation – and his marriage – had been saved when, unusually, the parties opted to withdraw the proceedings. Billy's detractors claimed that to avoid a scandal he had paid the couple a large amount of money not to divorce.

Throughout his marriage, among his family, his staff and in the villages around Wentworth, Billy's philandering was well known. 'He was very keen on hunting – of all kinds,' his cousin Charles Doyne remarked dryly, a memory Lady Barbara Ricardo, his granddaughter, shared: 'He had many girlfriends. He was especially fond of actresses and chorus girls!' One long-standing affair with a former Variety girl, Rosie Boot, married to the Marquess of Headfort, became the subject of family legend. 'He used to take her on his yacht. It was a beautiful boat, huge, with State Rooms and lots of bedrooms,' Griffith Philipps, Billy's grandson, recalled. 'When the tender launch carrying the guests left shore, the Captain used to scrutinize its occupants with a pair of binoculars to see whether it was the Marchioness of Headfort or the Countess Fitzwilliam coming on board. Depending on which it was, he would order the crew to rearrange the furniture in the time it took for the launch to reach the yacht. The Marchioness and the Countess liked the state rooms furnished in a different way.'

Stories that assumed a similarly legendary status circulated among Billy's servants. Years after his death, Robert Tottie, the deputy agent at Wentworth, recalled a conversation with Billy's former chauffeur, Jim Swift. 'In the 1920s there used to be a wind-up phone connected from the Big House to Jim's house in the village. His Lordship used to call him in the middle of the night. "Hello Jim," he'd say. "Maudie's locked her bedroom door again. Come on, we're going down to London." It was the middle of the night. London was four hours away. But off they'd go!' It seems Billy also regarded the servants as fair game. Bert May remembered the gossip his wife, Margaret, brought back from the Big House. 'Lordie was a bit of lad. There was one girl, a housemaid, they called her Marina. A big fine lass, good-looking girl and all. She used to go up to his room. He thought the world of her, old Lordie. They said he wanted to buy her a house in London.'

The Fitzwilliams moved in a fast set. Drawn from the hunting field and the enclosures of England's smartest racecourses, their friends included wealthy second- or third-generation aristocrats, the heirs to great shipping, industrial or banking fortunes. It was a world where extra-marital love affairs were regarded as the norm. 'You didn't marry a person, you married into a social group in those days,' Peter Diggle, the son of Colonel Diggle, one of Billy's closest friends, recalled. 'But you married for life. Everything else was peccadilloes. You had your code and you stuck to it.' Maud Fitzwilliam, the daughter of the Marquess of Zetland, who had married Billy when she was seventeen, was also rumoured to have had affairs with various men. One relationship of long standing was with Peter's uncle, John Diggle. 'Billy's flirtations made it very difficult for Maud,' Peter, who remembers Maud with great affection, recalled. 'She was a very lonely person in many ways. She was often on her own. But she was a tremendously warm person, very kind, with a great sense of fun and rather mischievous herself. There was a touch of vulgarity about her sense of humour. I remember she once said of her unmarried daughters, "They don't lead very satisfying lives. They've too many unused things in their drawers." A very risqué double entendre at the time!'

Growing up at the Vicarage in Wentworth, as Joyce grew older, she became aware that her parents felt compromised by the Fitzwilliams' lifestyle. 'My mother was a very cosy person, a very comfortable person. Rather stout and pink-cheeked, the sort of person you wanted to hug. But quite different from the Fitzwilliams. I don't think they liked her very much. They were never at ease with her. She was hardly ever invited to parties at the house. I'm sure Lady Fitzwilliam felt the difference, that she belonged to a different kind of life, a different kind of society altogether. I daresay she felt she disapproved of her. Which she did. My mother came from a long line of clergymen. She was very moral, very disapproving of what she called "immorality". My mother told me that Lord Fitzwilliam had lots of girlfriends. She felt that Lady Fitzwilliam was much too easy-going with the men – I'm sure only because he was so flirtatious. I think in that layer of society, people accepted these things, thought of them as perfectly normal, though a bit of a nuisance perhaps, or a bit embarrassing. My parents weren't used to it. They used to worry dreadfully because they had to teach morality in the parish, and there were the Fitzwilliams, the heads of the parish, being as they thought, most immoral, a lot of the time. My father did all the services at the church in the village. Everyone who was C of E turned out for them. They all knew about Lord and Lady Fitzwilliam's carryings-on. I don't think they missed much. Wentworth was feudal. They were all in the pay of the Fitzwilliams. The whole village was. I don't think there was anybody independent, except perhaps a few of the shopkeepers and the postmistress. Even the doctor was paid by them. Well, of course, the servants of the house, the miners and the men who worked on the farm all gossiped among each other. It was a funny artificial kind of life in the village. It was like a double life really. It upset my mother dreadfully, she was never happy there. She knew this double life was going on.'

It was the illegitimate children at Wentworth that caused the Vicar's wife the most anguish, the offspring of the 'double life' lived by scions of the Fitzwilliam family for generations. 'When we were there the sons of the old Lord Fitzwilliam had illegitimate children living in the village,' Joyce remembered. 'Two of them taught at the school, and there was another family – a widow who had two daughters – they were supposed to have Fitzwilliam blood. As I grew up and could understand anything, I was led to believe that it was a "droit de seigneur". Because they were Fitzwilliams, you couldn't refuse them.'

At the turn of the twentieth century, in the pit villages around Wentworth, to be born illegitimate, regardless of the identity of the father, marked a child for life. 'The fact of my illegitimacy, of my being a bastard, caused me more mental anguish in the first years of my life than any other influence,' Fred Smith, from Kiveton colliery, wrote.

The old adage that the sins of the father fall upon the children has no better example to prove its truth than the example of the bastard. He is the victim; he suffers the penalty of a sin committed before he was born. In a village where every cupboard skeleton is the common knowledge of all, where every tongue that has a weakness for wagging, has plenty of material to wag about, the existence of an illicit sexual union is not made a pleasant one. As I grew up the epithet 'bastard' was thrown at me as a method of putting me into my place at the bottom of the social strata. If the user of the word was within striking distance, I was always struck. On the principle that bastards always beget bastards, I was looked upon as a potential ravager of all the females in the village. Up to my seventeenth year I had not been on speaking terms with any girl except in one case and she immediately cut me on learning the facts of my birth. The grand dames of the village many times within my hearing, prophesied that I should end my days on the gallows.

Ironically, the Smith family were themselves the product of illegitimacy: Joyce's mother, Katharine Smith, was a direct descendant of Lavinia Fenton, an actress who had played the part of Polly Peacham in the first production of Gay's *Beggar's Opera* in 1728. Lavinia had lived in France for twenty years as the Duke of Bolton's mistress, having three illegitimate sons by him before becoming the Duchess of Bolton late in life. It was one of Joyce and her brothers' and sisters' favourite family stories. 'We thought it was great fun! We had a baton sinister in our coat of arms! We loved our Polly! It was where our noble blood came from. But my mother would never talk about this descent. She didn't like having to disclose that she was descended from illegitimate children. She wasn't allowed to think of it as fun. She had been brought up to think of it as something you mustn't tell anybody because Polly's sons and their sons and grandsons had gone on to be Admirals and clergymen and it was not on.'

During her eight years at Wentworth, Katharine Smith, in spite of her own sensitivity to the taboo of illegitimacy – or perhaps because of it – devoted her energies to looking after one particular single mother in the village. Her name was May Bower.

The year the Smith family moved into the Vicarage, May, then in her early twenties, was living opposite in a two-bedroomed cottage with her parents, grandparents and her two-year-old son, Edgar. The Bower family was one of the poorest in the village. To help them out, in 1918, Katharine Smith took May on as a junior housemaid. As Joyce remembered, leftovers from the Smith family's meals and her brothers' old clothes were always sent to the cottage across the road. In taking May and Edgar under her wing, Katharine was forcing herself to confront daily, and under her own roof, the suggestion of the 'double life' she so loathed.

The village rumour was that Edgar Bower was Billy Fitzwilliam's son. A few months after his birth, in the winter of 1916, he had been baptized at Wentworth Church. His father was stated as 'unknown'; unusually for a boy of his class, he was christened with two middle names, 'William Wentworth', names no villagers would normally dare choose. They were the names traditionally given to every Fitzwilliam son. Almost nine decadess later, Gracie Woodcock, an old lady of ninety who lived at Wentworth all her life, exclaimed, 'It was a lot of rot! People in the village used to say Edgar was Fitzwilliam's boy. But May was so plain and so simple, it couldn't be true.' Gracie's view was the exception: in the years after the First World War most of the village believed that Billy Fitzwilliam was the father of May's child. 'It weren't her face or her mind he were after, were it?' said one old miner. 'Lordie were never known to be very select in love.'

May Bower was nineteen when Edgar was born. Her family came from a long line of Estate employees; her father and grandfather were miners at the Fitzwilliams' pits, her uncles and cousins hunt servants at the Dog Kennels, the eighteenth-century building that housed the Wentworth pack of hounds. When Edgar was conceived, May was working as the gatekeeper at Doric Lodge, one of eight gatehouses that stood along the perimeter of Wentworth Park. 'The gatekeepers were expected to be on standby around the clock,' recalled Gordon Hempsey, whose grandmother had been a gatekeeper at Mausoleum Lodge on the Greaseborough side of the Park. 'At the end of the nineteenth century, to stop the carriages being interfered with on the through run, his Lordship dug these trenches through the Park with a grating over them. They put wires in the trenches and these ran down to the Lodges. When the carriages passed over a plate, a bell would ring at the Gatehouse. Out my Grandmother would come, mop cap on, apron on, and then depending on what mood his Lordship was in, sixpence or a shilling would fly through the air on to the grass. She'd then spend the rest of the day trying to find it.'

Doric Lodge, where May Bower worked, was one of the gatehouses most frequently used by the Fitzwilliams. It stood on the old coach road from Wentworth towards Sheffield, the quickest route up to the house coming from the city, and from the village and the pit at Elsecar. In 1915, the year before Edgar was born, Billy, suffering from nervous exhaustion, was given extended leave from his wartime duties as Assistant Transport Director at the British Army's supply depot at Calais. He did not return to France until the end of 1916.

Whether the rumour that Edgar Bower was Billy Fitzwilliam's son was true or merely a figment of his mother's or Wentworth's imagination will never be known. There is no evidence to suggest that he was, but nor is there anything to prove that he was not. Yet whatever the truth of Edgar's provenance, the question mark over his identity determined the horrendous arc of his life. At best, it is the story of a handicapped boy rejected and abandoned by the village – a misguided closing of ranks to protect the Fitzwilliam family name. At worst, if Edgar was Billy's son, the Fitzwilliams did nothing to save him from his truly appalling fate.

More than fifty years after Edgar was last seen in the village, the men and women who had played with him as children remembered him well. 'He used to haunt our lives,' Joyce recalled. 'He lived with his mother in the cottage opposite the Vicarage gate. He would come out and shout at us and make strange noises. My mother wanted us to be kind to him, but we found him very tiresome. You couldn't talk to him. You couldn't understand him. We thought he was mental.' Mrs Bradley, a former schoolmistress, also remembered Edgar:

During the school holidays, myself and a number of other children from the village would meet at Woodcock's farm. We played games, joined in the usual farm activities and sang songs together in the evening. Edgar Bower, who lived close by, would join us and yet not be one of us. He obviously liked being with us but, because of his handicaps of speech and hearing, remained an onlooker. The most vivid memory I have of Edgar is of the awful sounds he made when distressed or trying to say something. As evening approached, his mother would come to fetch him for bed. But he would disappear, running across the fields to the hills. In the distance we could hear the most dreadful noises – a mixture of moaning and screaming. Chris, the oldest Woodcock son, would go and persuade the boy to come home. But it was quite a task. Chris was the only one who could do anything with Edgar. It was difficult to communicate with him, or to know how much he comprehended. I was left with the impression his mother was unable to cope.

Edgar, so the village thought, had been born deaf and dumb. In 1922, when he was six years old, the Estate officials at Wentworth decided that it would be better for all concerned to send the boy away. He was sent to the Royal School for the Deaf at Derby. His school fees were paid by Billy Fitzwilliam via one of his charitable trusts: whether his motive in doing so was simply an innocent gesture of kindness to a handicapped boy in the village, or a tacit acceptance of paternal responsibility, is not known. Edgar stayed at the school in Derby until he was sixteen years old, returning home to the village in the school holidays. 'He is a backward type of boy,' the headmaster reported in the Easter term of 1932, Edgar's last before leaving the school.

I am very doubtful whether he can ever become self-supporting. He has had a course of boot-repairing in our shop here and shapes fairly well at the practical side. I don't want you to be under any misapprehension as to the type of boy he is. He is quite clean in his habits, well made physically and knows how to look after himself. He has done nothing in school work and has a wry kink somewhere.

In the months after Edgar left the Royal School for the Deaf, the record is blank until, that is, August 1933, when, at the age of seventeen, he was certified insane at Wentworth by Dr Mills, the village doctor, who was appointed by the Estate. Edgar was sent to the West Riding Paupers Lunatic Asylum at Wakefield, a vast and forbidding Victorian building that accommodated up to 2,000 patients. He remained there for the next fifty-three years of his life.

Edgar Bower was not insane. According to his Admittance File at the asylum, he was committed because he had been 'observed pulling out the hairs on his arms and grimacing'. No other grounds for insanity were given. A Statement of Particulars, taken shortly after Edgar was admitted, reveals that he was neither suicidal nor a danger to others. No form of mental illness was diagnosed; his 'attack of insanity' had been temporary: according to the document, it had lasted for a mere 'few days'.

A few days that turned into most of the rest of his life.

'I was frightened the first time I saw him. He was like an alien. He was doubled over and could barely walk. His nails were all long and bent,' remembered Lily Fletcher, a hospital social worker for Wakefield Social Services, who met Edgar in 1987 when he was seventy-one years old. 'I'd read his patient history. It was a ghastly history. You could see from the file that no one had visited him in fifty-odd years. He was on every medication going. The only thing they didn't do was give him a lobotomy. He'd been verbally, sexually, physically and mentally abused. You couldn't get him into a bed. He used to sit in his chair all night. The psychiatric staff called him "The Dummy". He was no dummy. No dummy at all. That first meeting, I gave him a pen and paper. In cases like his, sometimes it's the only thing you can do.'

Edgar, as Lily discovered, was not deaf. Though he was speech-impaired, the staff at the Paupers Lunatic Asylum, later renamed

Stanley Royd Psychiatric Hospital, had not thought to give him a pen and paper in fifty years. Lily was the first person to find a means of communicating with Edgar; through this simple method her patience enabled him to give voice to thoughts and feelings that no one had given him the time or the opportunity to express since the day he had been locked away.

The first word Edgar wrote down was 'Mother'.

May Bower had been dead for sixty years. She had died in 1928 from scarlet fever in an isolation hospital near Wentworth while Edgar was at the Royal School for the Deaf. In 1988, though he knew his mother was dead, he asked Lily to help him write a letter to her. Sixty years after her death, he gave it a title: 'Mother said I would go home':

Dear Mother
What did I do wrong? Why was I taken away from my home, my family and friends? I know at times I have been naughty and difficult, but you see I didn't understand other people's attitudes towards me and they didn't understand my handicap. They thought I was deaf and dumb. I could hear what people were saying, but for some reason I couldn't speak. You see I cannot use my tongue properly. I have a voice, a proper man's voice, but I have difficulty speaking like other people, something I so very much want to do. I remember how we all lived together in our cottage, you, grandmother, great grandfather and great grandmother. The tales you all used to tell me about our ancestors, who all worked on the Estate. I know you were only 18 when you were taken advantage of, but you gave me a lot of love and care and we were all so happy. You know Mother if I hadn't been taken away when I was a young boy, I'm sure the Estate would have cared for me and found me work.

May Bower had told Edgar that he was Billy Fitzwilliam's son. 'When he told me,' Lily said, 'he said his mother had said to him, "You go to school. You'll be all right. They'll look after you. There'll be money when you come home."' As Lily began to unlock the story of Edgar's life, she was profoundly shaken by what she discovered. 'The thing that haunted me, the thing that I couldn't get out of my mind, was that someone must have cut out his tongue.'

If Billy Fitzwilliam was the father of Edgar Bower, the advice May had given her son was correct. Historically, the Fitzwilliams had looked after their illegitimate children in the villages around Wentworth, though always on their own terms. Over the centuries, a convention had emerged: male Estate employees were persuaded to admit paternity and to marry the mother of the child. The pay-off was a good job, a decent house and an understanding that the Estate would look after the family for the rest of their lives.

So why was this convention not followed in Edgar Bower's case? The answer, possibly, is to be found in May's religious beliefs. The Bowers were Quakers who believed that God married people, not the magistrate or the priest: according to their faith, the social aspect of a marriage – the umbrella of respectability – was of little significance. May was a devout Quaker and it is conceivable that her religious faith caused her to reject the offer of an Estate-arranged marriage.

Had the offer been made, and refused, it was May's failure to conform that partially sealed Edgar's fate. Because she flouted the conventions of the village, the community was no longer bound to accept her child. When Edgar returned to Wentworth from the Royal School for the Deaf in 1932, May Bower had been dead for four years. No one wanted to look after him; his severe handicap, his reputation as a difficult, troublesome child, and the rumour and taboo surrounding the identity of his father, determined that the village closed ranks and rejected him. Had Katharine Smith still been living at the Vicarage she might have taken him under her wing as she had done when he was a child – or at least seen that he was found a home. But the Smith family had long since gone; they had left the village in 1926.

The one person who might have looked after Edgar was unable to. Four years before she died, May had married an outsider to the village, a man from London called Charles Garwood. They had two children, Albert and Gladys, born in 1925 and 1927. After May died, Garwood had struggled to raise the two younger children on his own; in the late 1920s, he had been forced to send Albert, Edgar's half-brother, to an orphanage in Rotherham.

Fifty-three years after Edgar left the village, it was Lily Fletcher who uncovered the secret it had tried to conceal. 'I believed Edgar,' she said. 'After he told me he was the Earl's son, I got hold of a copy of his birth certificate. That's when I found out that his name was Edgar William Wentworth Bower. I then went back to check his hospital file. It was very odd. There was no mention of his middle names. He was admitted to the asylum under the name of Edgar Bower. The hospitals always recorded the full name of a patient. They were always very strong on that. I can only think that the village doctor who certified Edgar must have deliberately left those names off his admittance form.'

An error of omission on the part of Dr Mills, the Estate doctor? The action of a loyal retainer anxious to protect the Fitzwilliams' reputation? Or, conceivably, did the doctor omit Edgar's middle names, sacrosanct in the village at the time, because he knew he had no right to bear them? Following the great bonfire at Wentworth in 1972, the Estate archives that could have revealed the answer have not been preserved; the old villagers, who might have known, are now mostly dead. But among those still alive – still anxious to protect the Fitzwilliams' reputation – there is one point on which they are adamant: the family played no part in the doctor's decision to certify Edgar insane.

The truth, it appears, is more prosaic. In 1933, when Edgar returned to the village after leaving school, Charles Garwood, his stepfather, was working as gardener and chauffeur to Dr Mills. 'The doctor sent Edgar away because Mr Garwood was his gardener. He didn't want to lose him,' Gracie Woodcock explained. 'Too much of Garwood's time would have been taken up with looking after Edgar. It was easier to send him away.'

All his life, as Edgar repeatedly told Lily, he had wanted to go home. 'It was the love of Wentworth and his mother that sustained him all those years,' she recalled. 'He must have been an extraordinary person to have coped with what he had been through. When I first got him, he used to stand in the corner of the room banging his heels against the wall. I couldn't understand why he did this, then I found out they had these metal shoes at the hospital. They were a form of punishment. The shoes were chained to the wall; patients were made to go and stand in them when they misbehaved. Edgar was always being punished. It was all there in his hospital file. Every time he was in trouble, he was never able to put his point of view. There was no one to represent him. All they did was increase his medication: he was drugged up to the eyeballs. How on earth that man kept the picture of his mother and the village in his mind for all those years, goodness knows. But it was the thing that carried him through.'

Lily's patience and persistence changed the course of Edgar's life. In the autumn of 1988, under the Care in the Community initiative – a Government proposal to close Britain's Victorian asylums – Stanley Royd Psychiatric Hospital, previously the West Riding Paupers Lunatic Asylum, was due to be closed. Lily resolved to try to get Edgar a place at the Residential Care Home in Wentworth. Ironically, the Home was at the Vicarage, the place where May Bower had worked as a housemaid for the Smith family, opposite the cottage where Edgar had grown up.

In the spring of 1988, Lily took Edgar back to the village: his first visit in fifty-five years.

'When we pulled up outside the Home, an awful thing happened,' she remembered. 'He ran straight across the road to the cottage and tried to open the door. There were people in the front parlour, I had to pull him away. He was terribly upset, he was shaking all over. I took him over to a low wall and sat him down. Then he asked me for a pen and paper.'

Seeing his old home for the first time triggered Edgar's memories of his mother's death. Situated on an oak-lined avenue at the edge of the village, the cottage stood along the road leading up to Wentworth Church. Edgar had last been there in September 1928 when he had walked behind May Bower's coffin as it was carried up the avenue to the graveyard to be buried. Sitting on the wall with Lily, his memories came flooding back. 'Everybody was feeling sorry for the two young children, nobody cared for me, they thought I didn't understand,' he later wrote. 'I was twelve years old and I had lost the love of my life.'

'We went up the churchyard afterwards,' Lily remembered, 'and we looked for his mother's grave. I'd given Edgar some flowers to put on it but we couldn't find it. Then we went into the church and we saw one of the churchwardens and he said he'd look into it and let us know. We went back outside and had a wander round and we found an old grave, it must have been about 1870 or so, and it had the name Bower on it, so we put the flowers on there instead. An eerie thing happened. I discovered afterwards it was as if we had left a signal to the village. It got them going, didn't it – there was whispering behind doors. That grave hadn't been tended for years. People saw the fresh flowers, they knew no one local had put them there, and they started making inquiries at the church. Who'd put them there, who'd come back?'

'Bower': the name was on the grave. 'They knew,' said Lily. 'The older ones – the ones who'd played with Edgar as a child – guessed. When I asked them later what had happened in the months before he was sent to the Asylum, they just shrugged their shoulders and shook their heads. "We didn't know anything," they said, "he just disappeared." I asked them if they knew Edgar was the Earl's son. Some said one of the stocksmen on the Estate was his father. Others said he had been made to take the blame. I didn't push it, I didn't want to jeopardize Edgar's chances of coming home.'

In the autumn of 1988, Edgar moved into the old Vicarage. 'I moved back home on October 16th 1988, nearly sixty years to the day when you died. I do so wish you could be here, Mother,' he wrote, 'but we will meet again. I have asked to be buried with you, and I did "come home", just like you said I would.'

Soon after Edgar moved to the old Vicarage, Lily Fletcher contacted the Wentworth Estate, the agency responsible for overseeing the Fitzwilliam family's descendants' interests in the area, to ask their permission to allow May Bower's grave to be opened on his death, in order that he could be buried alongside her. Edgar had no financial assets. In the terminology of the pre-war era, he was a 'pauper': the costs of burying him in the churchyard at Wentworth were over and above the standard funeral arrangements covered by the Department of Health and Social Security. After consulting the Fitzwilliams' descendants, the agent for the Wentworth Estate agreed to pay the full costs of the funeral in the form of a grant from Wentworth Charities, a long-standing family trust. 'Such matters to be covered by the Trustees' grant,' the agent informed Edgar in a letter, 'would include a service in Wentworth Church, provision of a burial within Wentworth churchyard utilizing the grave presently occupied by your mother and the provision of a gravestone. I do hope this sympathetic view held by the Trustees,' he continued, 'will reassure you that efforts will be made to ensure that you will be laid to rest with your mother following a service in Wentworth Church.'

Edgar Bower died in February 1996, aged seventy-nine. Godfrey Broadhead, who had worked for the Estate for almost fifty years, was charged with making the arrangements for his funeral. Some months after Edgar's death, he left a message for the agent at the Wentworth Estate office: 'Mr Broadhead is arranging for the headstone which will be put in place in July,' the secretary noted in a memo to the agent. 'He wondered if the inscription should be: "In Memory of Edgar Bower" or "In Memory of Edgar William Wentworth Bower". Broadhead thought perhaps the first option may be the best.'

Godfrey Broadhead was in his eighties. He had grown up at Wentworth: he knew – and was close to – the older residents in the village who had worked for the Estate in the early decades of the twentieth century, the men and women who would have known whether the rumour that Billy Fitzwilliam was Edgar's father was true. Broadhead told his daughter what he knew of Edgar Bower's story. But at the dawn of the twenty-first century, among the descendants of the village families who worked for the Fitzwilliams for generations, the old loyalties, the old taboos linger. 'It's a matter for the Wentworth Estate,' Godfrey Broadhead's daughter said after his death. 'I couldn't possibly say. My father told me things in confidence which he would not have wanted people to know.' Asked whether her father had ever denied the rumour, she said again, 'I cannot say.'

The headstone above Edgar's grave in the New Churchyard at Wentworth bears two names – 'Edgar Bower'. Not the four names with which he was baptized. The only gravestones inscribed with the names 'William Wentworth' are in the Fitzwilliam family plot. Even in death it appears that things did not go right for Edgar. The confusion, rumour and counter-rumours continue. 'He ain't buried with his mother,' one woman in her nineties said. 'They put him in the wrong grave. I know for absolute certain that he was buried in the wrong one.'

PART V

22

On the evening of Saturday 1 May 1926, at 19.40 hours according to the Admiralty logs, the *Neuralia*, a Royal Navy transport ship, steamed out of Devonport en route for Liverpool docks. On board were two detachments of troops: the 1st Somerset Light Infantry and the 1st South Wales Borderers. One hour earlier, at 18.45 hours, the *Nevasa* had sailed from Portsmouth carrying the 1st Duke of Wellington's regiment, its destination the port of Leith in Scotland. The two troop ships were the first to be mobilized. Britain was girding for war – not against an external aggressor, but against herself.

'Everything I care for is being smashed to pieces at this moment,' the Prime Minister, Stanley Baldwin, told the House of Commons in an Emergency Debate. 'Despotic power . . . has been put in the hands of a small executive in London. This irresponsible power is a gross travesty of any democratic principle . . . threatening the basis of ordered government, and going nearer to proclaiming civil war than we have been for centuries past.'

The country stood on a knife edge. Hours before the *Neuralia* and the *Nevasa* sailed from the naval bases on the South Coast, the 'despotic power', the General Council of the Trades Union Congress, had issued an order to its own troops; if the Government failed to meet its demands, at precisely one minute to midnight on Monday 3 May, 9 million workers, it instructed, were to down tools and come out on a General Strike.

The threat of coordinated industrial action on such an unprecedented scale had triggered the mobilization of Britain's armed forces. Successive governments had been haunted by a fear of revolution since the end of the First World War; in the years up to 1926, the Home Office Directorate of Intelligence, in conjunction with Special Branch, had been required to issue weekly reports on 'revolutionary organizations in the UK'. Official anxiety had focused on the trades union movement – an extra-governmental body, capable of acquiring extensive political power not through the ballot, but through force majeure. Coordinated strike action was the eventuality post-war governments had dreaded the most, a spectre first raised in 1919 when the newly formed 'Triple Alliance' – the unions representing Britain's miners, railwaymen and transport workers – had pulled back from the brink of launching a General Strike. Seven years later, in the spring of 1926, the fear had become a reality: the Government regarded the TUC's ultimatum as the precursor to political revolution.

'Enemies to the Parliamentary Constitution system,' Winston Churchill, the Chancellor of the Exchequer, told the nation, 'threatened the subversion of the State.' The position, he warned, was now extremely uncertain:

> It is a conflict which, if it is fought out to a conclusion, can only end in the overthrow of Parliamentary Government or in its decisive victory. There is no middle course open. Either the Parliamentary institutions of the country will emerge triumphant, and the nation, which has not flinched in the past through many ordeals, the nation, which indeed has always shown itself stronger and nobler and more generous in its hours of trouble, will once again maintain itself and be mistress in its own house, or else, on the other hand, the existing constitution will be fatally injured.

The crisis had been provoked by Britain's million miners. On 30 April, the day before the War Office mobilized the armed forces, every colliery in the country had closed. It was the coal owners who had shut them down. 'The owners are the provokers of this quarrel. They are the men who served notice upon their workmen. It is not a strike; it is a lock-out,' the Labour MP George Barker exclaimed angrily in the House of Commons. 'How is it,' he asked, 'that the owners have not been censured for locking out a million men? We have a million men in this country who are prepared to go to work tomorrow if they can only get a reasonable living wage.'

The coal owners were not offering a living wage. Until the miners agreed to accept wage cuts, the mines would remain closed. Six weeks earlier, the Samuel Report, the third Government inquiry into the state of the coal industry in seven years, had concluded that, due to the depressed economic conditions, wage 'revisions' were necessary. It was the verdict the coal owners had been waiting for: seizing the opportunity, they proposed to reduce the miners' average weekly wage to little more than 30 shillings* – less than it cost to keep a man in the workhouse. They also proposed to increase the length of the working day. The coal owners' terms, so the miners and their representatives believed, were nothing short of belligerent. 'I do believe in the class war,' said George Lansbury, the future leader of the Labour Party,

> I believe the class war is responsible for the starvation of my kith and kin, people who are the bone of my bone and flesh of my flesh, down in the coalfields of Britain. The only thing that is being asked today by the Government and the capitalists is that the workers should sacrifice. I hope to God that the workers will be able to stand out and with their women defeat the most nefarious campaign that has ever been waged against them.

The TUC hoped the threat of a General Strike would force Baldwin to guarantee the miners a 'living wage'. But there was no question of the Government caving in to the ultimatum: a fundamental principle was at stake. In 1919, Lloyd George had expressed it succinctly: 'If a force arises in the State which is stronger than the State itself, then it must be ready to take on the function of the State itself, or withdraw and accept the authority of the State.'

Behind the scenes in Whitehall, the Cabinet, in liaison with the Chiefs of the Defence Staff and the Chiefs of Police, prepared for civil war. All military leave was cancelled; soldiers suspected of Communist leanings were placed under observation, and troops

*£58 at today's values.

dispatched to guard 'vulnerable points', a pre-determined list of strategic sites that included explosives factories, oil depots and power stations across the length and breadth of Britain. Five battalions of troops were mobilized to potential sites of conflict in the coalfields, and to the dockyards in the main shipping ports, to ensure the flow of essential supplies. Priority destinations included Glasgow, Newcastle-upon-Tyne, Bury, Bradford, Cardiff and Hull. 'It should be impressed upon all Commanding Officers,' the War Office cabled the Home Commands, 'that early and accurate information as to the possible trend of events and as to the temper of the populace in any particular area is of paramount importance. To this end selected officers should be employed by officers in command of bodies acting in aid of civil power to move about in plain clothes and keep in close touch with the civil authorities and with the populace generally.' Anticipating the likelihood that insurgents would target telegraph poles across the country, the War Office was leaving nothing to chance. Commanders in the field were notified of the Emergency Wireless Scheme, a secret network of wireless stations to be used 'in the event of a serious breakdown of the normal means of inter-communication'. They lay off Britain's coastline, on Royal Navy ships positioned to operate as makeshift communication centres of the last resort: if the telegraph wires were brought down, key signals staff were to be ferried out to the ships to relay enciphered messages back to Whitehall.

The battle lines had been drawn, the outlook appeared ominous. Twenty-four hours after the War Office mobilized the armed forces, it had no option but to send a telegram to the Admiralty. The loyalty of some sections of the Army appeared to be in doubt: 'The M.T. [Military Transport] Drivers of transport detailed to take the Aldershot Brigade to Yorkshire are unreliable and may join strikers,' the cable read. 'Prepare to take the Brigade by sea.'

'There are very few light hearts in England today,' Baldwin told the House of Commons, speaking hours before the TUC's deadline ran out. 'The only people who are happy in this situation are those who envy us or hate us, because they see the home of democratic freedom entering on a course which, if successful on the part of those who enter it, can only substitute tyranny.' That evening, Lord Salisbury, the son of the former Conservative Prime Minister, ran into Lady Sybil Middleton at a cocktail party. 'All of Europe is watching,' he told her, 'absolutely shivering in their shoes with fright in case we should go under, for they realize that if we do, nothing could save them.'

On the front line, in the pit villages, the day the crisis broke, the enemy – for the most part – was asleep, enjoying a collective lie-in.

In the Fitzwilliams' pit villages little stirred. In the absence of the dust and smog that normally choked the air, overnight the mining communities in the neighbourhood of Wentworth had turned into prosperous-looking rural settlements. At Elsecar and Greaseborough, and in Harley and Jump, along row after row of the yellow-stone cottages, flowers trailed from the baskets hanging under the eaves of the slate roofs. In the front gardens, the roses were in bud. It was a bright spring morning: the green-painted doors and guttering, and the white window frames, the ubiquitous two-colour signature of the Fitzwilliam Estate, glistened in the sun.

Arthur Eaglestone, the miner at the Fitzwilliams' New Stubbin colliery, described the sounds that usually woke him in the morning. He lived at Netherhaugh, a small hamlet that straddled the main road to the pit:

Clip-clop! . . . Clip-clop! . . . Someone is walking in the dim and shadowy corridors of the mind . . . it fades and dreams away, drifting to a point of nothingness . . . A hammer plaything – some one fooling with a hammer, in the darkness too . . . shurrup! . . . sleep! . . . it isn't light . . . it isn't dawn . . .

I open my eyes at last and gaze into the darkened room, marking the blurred outline of familiar furniture, and noting how the gas lamp in the street below throws up a sickly, yet none the less accommodating circle of illumination. A little light invades the room, shining on the brass knob of the bedstead foot, the white painted washstand and the chair with trousers slung across . . . Cold it is . . . and misty too . . . b-r-r-r! I bury my nose beneath the sheets . . . dark, quite dark.

Clip-clop! . . . Clip-clop! There it is again – the sound of clogs, collier clogs. It must be five o'clock, or thereabouts; a little later perhaps, for the morning shift begins at six with a promptitude unvarying and institutional . . .

. . . Some one whistles now between his teeth. Occasionally the footfalls are lighter, much more sprightly, with a tripping quality. These are the boys I guess, and I am not long left guessing. A mellow little voice comes up, singing? I know not what . . .

Other sounds woke the hamlet: the blast of a ship's foghorn blown at the pit top to mark the start of the shift; the echo of others – 'buzzers', as they were called – from the pits in the valley below. For the deep sleepers, there was the 'knocker-up'; a human alarm clock, he used a long pole to rattle the window panes of the households that paid him a few pennies each week.

On the morning of 1 May, with the collieries closed, none of these sounds disturbed Netherhaugh: much later than usual, the hamlet was woken by the clanging of a handbell. That day, the same sound roused every mining community in Britain. In the midst of a very twentieth-century crisis, the eighteenth century had wandered in. Few people had radios and newspapers were not always widely read. The time-honoured method was necessary to communicate the State of Emergency that George V had proclaimed the night before. To the cry of 'Hear ye, hear ye, hear ye', the bellmen paced the pit villages, pausing only at street corners to read the proclamation from the King:

'GEORGE REX IMPERATOR,' they shouted:

Whereas by the Emergency Powers Act 1920, it is enacted that if it appears to Us that any action has been taken or is immediately threatened by any persons or body of persons in such a nature and on so extensive a scale as to be calculated, by interfering with the supply and distribution of food, water, fuel, or light, or with the means of locomotion, to deprive the community, or any substantial portion of the community, of the essentials of life, We may, by Proclamation, declare that a state of emergency exists:

And whereas the present immediate threat of cessation of work in the Coal Mines does, in Our opinion, constitute a state of emergency within the meaning of the said Act:

Now therefore, in pursuance of the said Act, We do, by and with the advice of Our Privy Council, hereby declare that a state of emergency exists.

Given at Our Court at Buckingham Palace, this thirtieth day of April, in the year of our Lord One thousand nine hundred and twenty-six, and in the Sixteenth year of Our Reign. GOD SAVE THE KING.

The King's Proclamation awarded draconian powers to Baldwin's Government. The authority of Parliament was suspended and civil liberties swept aside. Anyone suspected of attempting to cause sedition or mutiny among His Majesty's forces or among the civilian population was liable to instant arrest and imprisonment. Interfering with or impeding the supply and distribution of vital commodities – food, water, light, fuel and electricity – was also an imprisonable offence. Freedom of speech was withdrawn and 'seditious' literature banned.

In the Fitzwilliam villages, the King's Proclamation caused alarm. '"If tha' goes out, tha'll get *nowt*!" That's what Fitzbilly's miners used to say,' recalled the son of one miner working at New Stubbin pit in 1926. 'They wanted nothing to do with the General Strike. No one, my dad said, ever got rich from going out on strike. 1926: that were a really bad job. People were afraid.'

In the days leading up to the strike, a deputation from New Stubbin and Elsecar had called on Billy Fitzwilliam at Wentworth. They told him they did not want to strike. 'You must,' he told them privately, 'or you will let the others down.' Elsecar and New Stubbin were 'happy pits', an expression used locally to describe pits where relations between the management and the miners were harmonious. In the difficult years after the First World War, while the miners at both the Fitzwilliam collieries had come out in the national coal strikes of 1919, 1921 and 1925 – as they were bound to do through the unionization of the industry – neither pit had been subject to the one-off disputes and wildcat strikes that had hit other collieries during the mid-1920s. As Arthur Eaglestone, writing of his years at New Stubbin during this period, recalled, 'There was never a major dispute while I was at the pit, a tribute to the commonsense and flexibility displayed by both the management and the men's representatives.' Billy was popular among the miners. When he visited his pits, it caused, as Eaglestone wrote, 'a condition of high excitement that set the wires tingling into every quarter of the workings . . . Earl Fitzwilliam always reminded me of Charlie Markham. He had the same informal approach and was regarded generally by the miners (not without affection) as "a bit of a lad".' 'He was generous when things went wrong,' remembered Jim McGuinness, a miner from Elsecar. 'Lordie was liked. He looked after you. He was good at thinking of ways to keep his miners happy.'

Ironically, given that the 1926 dispute was about wages, the miners at New Stubbin and Elsecar were paid less than miners at other pits in the neighbourhood. 'Wages-wise we were worse off, but you see Fitzbilly's mines were perfect,' Ralph Boreham, a miner from Elsecar, whose father and grandfather had worked there before him, explained. 'Everything was safe. Even the King went down our pit. Some of the others around, the roads weren't much higher than a chair. But Fitzbilly used to keep them high, so the miners could walk. And all the air were fresh. Air was moving through, you see. You were safe. You could breathe.'

'We knew our place. You had security. You had your cottage,' one miner recalled. It was not that the men at Elsecar and New Stubbin were unsympathetic to the cause of their fellow miners, or that they did not support their fight – Arthur Eaglestone, though writing under a pseudonym, had risked his job to expose the treacherous, badly paid conditions under which all miners of the period worked. But they were fatalistic and had more to lose than most.

It was with a sense of foreboding that Arthur Eaglestone, on the evening of 3 May, presented himself for guard duty at New Stubbin colliery. He and a number of other men had been appointed to protect its coal and timber stocks for the duration of the strike. Rotating in shifts, they patrolled in pairs:

Bearing each a formidable stick, we circled, that first evening of inaction, the half mile length of the sidings that connected the colliery with the railway station. The air was ominously quiet. The setting sun threw enormous shadows from the headstocks and the serried stacks of timber. There was no wind. The grasses, the wild parsley, with which the wagon road was bordered, were perfect as an etching. Soon darkness fell, the stars emerged, and in and out of the silent avenues of loaded trucks we paced speaking softly. Was this the beginning of the Twentieth Century Revolution? We walked, and sat, and smoked, and talked till midnight . . . In spite of outward appearance, all was not well. All that the ear apprehended – the chuffing of a locomotive, the rhythm of the winding engine, the impact of a hammer, the rattle of screens, even the tramp of colliers' feet – had vanished. When the church clock struck midnight, and its stroke resounded across the valley to where we stood under the shadow of the coal-drops, it carried with it impressive undertones. The town was not asleep. It lay silent, brooding in the darkness.

His disquiet was voiced by others. 'Here we are in the throes of revolution and it's unpleasant,' wrote Sir Walter Riddell, Principal of Hertford College, Oxford. 'We're dependent for news mainly on what the Government choose to tell us by wireless and their official paper: and there is an uneasy, and I suppose inevitable, suspicion they don't tell all. Rumours are countless and mainly depressing.' Lady Manners, writing from Cobham in Surrey, had seen the soldiers moving along the Portsmouth Road: 'Yesterday 20 tanks went up to London. Today, 40 charabancs filled with troops, steel helmets and all. I felt like crying. It brought the war straight back. They all looked such babies too and one felt would be of no use . . . The atmosphere is all of war.'

In London, people were gloomiest of all. 'Its citizens looked very strained and over-tired,' Riddell reported on his return to Oxford, after spending a few days in the city. 'The whole place,' he wrote, 'was painfully war-like – reduced lights, theatres mostly shut, barbed and boarded buses, Specials [constables] by the score and at certain places knots of rather hostile strikers.' In Mayfair and Belgravia, many of the residents believed they would soon be facing the barricades. 'I don't think I ever felt anything was so beastly as this strike,' bemoaned Mabel, Countess Grey, 'the whole atmosphere reminds me indescribably of the war . . . without any of the glamour or the glow of patriotic feeling . . . I don't think anyone can doubt a very well-organized really revolutionary bolshevist element.'

On Tuesday 4 May, the first day of the General Strike, Government officials in Whitehall waited nervously for the enciphered reports from the GOCs in the Home Commands to come in. At 14.30 hours, the War Office issued its second situation report of the day; the first had gone out at 09.00 hours. Marked 'Secret', its circulation was confined to the Cabinet, the Civil Commissioners, Chief Constables and the Army Chiefs.

'General Situation,' it reported, 'No change':

5th Infantry Brigade was ordered at 12.00 hours to commence as soon as possible the move by road to Northern Command. 5th Brigade H.Q. and 3 Battalions proceed to Catterick, 1 Battalion to Beverley. The units are due to arrive on the night 5/6th May.

1st and 2nd Battalions, Scots Guards, temporarily at Pirbright Camp, have been ordered to return today to London.

2nd Battalion Black Watch have been ordered from Fort George to Stirling.

HQ 8th Infantry Brigade, 2nd South Stafford Regt, 2nd Hampshire Regt, 1st Wilts Regt and 14/20th Hussars all under orders to move at 24 hours notice.

The country held its breath.

23

Two hundred miles north of Whitehall on the afternoon of 4 May, Billy Fitzwilliam was playing polo in a field in front of Wentworth House. The clipped cries of cavalry officers, the soft applause from polite, white-gloved hands, were noticeably absent. Broad Yorkshire dialect echoed across the pitch: 'C'm on, Tartar, you bugger.' 'Eh up, Walt, o'er here.' 'Put one in't bakka't net!'

Billy, his horse towering above the others, was teaching his miners to play polo on their pit ponies. Some of the ponies were barely taller than a large dog. Twenty-four hours earlier they had been shackled in pit gear a quarter of a mile underground; in their heavy bridles, the bonnet fortified around the eyes and along the nose, they might have stepped from the Bayeux tapestry. Freed of the harnesses, the ponies skittered and scrambled across the field. A tall man could stand astride the smallest, a Shetland called Caesar.

The last time the ponies had come up from the pits was the previous summer. Year round, except for two weeks in August when the collieries closed for the holidays, they were stabled underground. Caesar was one of the miners' favourites. At New Stubbin colliery he had saved many a man's – and a boy's – life. Arthur Eaglestone was working underground with the pony the night his reputation was made:

Caesar had been restless for something more than an hour and a half, wandering hither, thither (within the limitation of the place), swinging his head slightly from side to side, and turning sharply well within his own length. The rattle of chains, the clinking of metal, had exasperated us. 'Damn thee,' said Sturgess the trammer, 'damn thy hide! Be still! Did ye ever see sich a hoss in all thi life? A bloody clothes hoss ud make a better pony nor 'im!' 'He's put out about something,' I said. 'He's strange. He may be ill for all we know. It may be belly ache.' 'Belly ache be buggered, if 'e'd belly ache 'e'd roll abart an' make a noise. Be still – damn your rags.'

Seconds later, the props cracked, bringing down the roof, tons of dust and rubble falling like sand, burying the two men and the pony. Luckily, a rescue party was on hand to dig them out.

Billy had organized the polo match between Elsecar and New Stubbin collieries. The players, boys aged between thirteen and sixteen years old, were the pony drivers at the two pits. The voices of the younger ones had not yet broken; many still wore short trousers. All their faces were bleached. It had been a long winter on the day shift. Six days a week, they had gone down the mine before dawn and come up after dark.

It had been Billy's idea to teach the boys to play polo. The previous evening, he had ordered the ponies to be brought out of the pits. In the past, when the ponies came up for their annual rest, they had always been let loose in fields outside the Park walls. Breaking with tradition, he had instructed that for the duration of the strike they were to be put out to grass in a field alongside Wentworth House itself.

Early that morning, hours before the polo match began, a line of upwards of thirty boys stretched along the edge of the field, feeding the ponies bits of carrots and turnips pinched from allotments, or titbits they had saved from home. Every boy had his own pony, the one he worked with day in and day out. Some of the boys had whistled or called as they approached and their pony had come sprinting down the line. 'The horses knew the boys not by their features,' one miner recalled, they had only seen them with blackened faces; they recognized them by their 'whistle, voice and smell'.

The polo match and the decision to put the ponies in a field within yards of the house were symbolic gestures on Billy's part: a signal of unity and solidarity with his men. 'My father adored his miners,' his daughter Elfrida remembered. 'He was passionately interested in mines and mining. It was more important to him than anything else to do with the Estate.'

Billy depended on his miners; it was where his money came from. But he also had a genuine empathy and understanding with them. Most of the boys working at his pits had started work in the mines the first Monday after their thirteenth birthdays. As Billy knew, the drivers and their ponies had a particular place in a miner's psyche – and in his heart. In the first decades of the twentieth century, pony driving was the first job a miner did down the pit, one of the ways he learnt his trade.

For every miner, the first shift was a rite of passage, a descent from childhood that stayed with him for the rest of his life.

Jim Bullock was one of the few miners to write an account of what it was like to be a pony driver at a West Yorkshire mine in the early decades of the twentieth century. Two months after his thirteenth birthday, in the spring of 1917, he said goodbye to his mother and set off up Princess Street to Bowers colliery, a coalmine employing several hundred miners in the village of Bowers Row, near Castleford: 'My mother put her arm around me and said, "Be careful," ' he remembered. 'I was the only one she had left. All my brothers were fighting in the First World War.'

The time was 8.45 p.m. Jim's first shift was the night shift; his wage, 1 shilling (5 new pence). Wearing a pair of shorts and a new pair of clogs, he was barely five feet tall; he carried a two-pint Dudley filled with water and a snap tin containing two rounds of bread and dripping, his food for the night.

'When I went to work that first night,' he wrote later, 'history was repeating itself, for generation after generation of Bullocks had made the same journey. They had all undergone the same experience, but whereas most of them had made their descent into the depths of the earth in the comforting presence of their father, I went alone.' The advice his father had given him, as hundreds of others had given to their sons before him, came in the form of a poem. Jim had learnt it by heart:

> If the mice move out, move out with them
> If the rats run, your life is nearly done.
> When the roof begins to trickle,
> Father Time is sharpening his sickle
> When your pony baulks, then death stalks,
> If your lamp goes out, don't muck about.

No one spoke to Jim as he went down in the cage. When he reached the pit bottom, a group of older boys jumped on him and dragged him into a 'passby', a small enclosed space set back from the main tunnel road. 'There used to be all sorts of tricks played on young boys. When we first went down the pit we all had to go through our initiation ceremony, during which they used to pull our trousers down and examine our little sparrow. The size of that was very important. If we were well endowed, we were looked on with great respect; if we had a poor weedy little thing, they used to cover it with fat and make fun of us for days, or they used to paint it and hang a bit of bank on it and all sorts of things.'

'Bank' was muck and shale: a new boy was told that if he hung it on his penis, it would make it grow.

It was the dark, not the older boys, that scared Jim the most. From the pit bottom, a Deputy, a senior official at the pit, escorted him along a warren of tunnels to the place where he was to work. 'Despite everything I had been told, I was still not prepared for the overwhelming darkness, the stifling atmosphere, the deathly silence, the unusual creaks and the cracking sounds that broke the silence.'

The darkness could – and did – send men mad. 'There is no night so dark above, that the outline of an outstretched hand cannot be seen before one's eyes,' Arthur Eaglestone wrote,

> but down below the world, all darkness here is utter, final and controlling. Let your lamp go out and in IT floods upon the dying spark, overwhelming in intensity and volume. The blackness swims around you, thick and fluid almost, takes you by the legs, the throat, the eyes;

presses with a sinister intention upon your shoulder blades; it seems to flurry in your hands; engulfs your body wholly, and drives your little soul upon itself in the remotest and most secret of fastnesses . . . Pinch your cheek if that is what suffices, touch your empty eyes, then, pull your hair . . . It is all of no avail – of no avail . . .

Jim followed the Deputy through the tunnels for more than thirty minutes, stumbling to keep up. The roads were not flat or straight; there were twists, turns, inclines, places where the height of the roof dropped, so that not even Jim could stand. Corve rails, for moving the tubs of coal, ran along their length – easily traversed by an experienced miner, but for a small boy who had never been down a pit before, the sleepers, set two feet apart, were perilous in the dark. There were other hazards: the roads were strewn with debris from the sides and roof, and in places, wooden pit props jagged, buckled by the weight above.

The Deputy did not tell Jim where they were going or what he would be asked to do. Two miles from the pit bottom [the shaft] he stopped by a line of empty tubs and a mound of dust. What followed, Jim remembered for the rest of his life. 'As soon as the Deputy had showed me where I was to work and how many tubs I had got to fill with dust, he said, "Oh! you'll be interested to know that this is where your John Willie got killed." I can never, never forget that. As he went away and I saw his light slowly going into the distance, I was left completely alone.'

Purposely, to inflict the maximum psychological terror on the thirteen-year-old boy, the Deputy had taken Jim to the exact spot where, five years earlier, his much-loved elder brother had been crushed to death by a fall of rock. Jim was eight years old when he was told what had happened to John Willie. 'He had finished his own job and he was actually on his way out of the pit when another miner who was just going to set a girder said, "Give us a lift, John Willie, will tha?" And John Willie being what he was, immediately took his coat off and was just walking towards the girder when the whole place collapsed. The fall instantly killed him and the man whom he was going to help, as well as two pit ponies. There were two hundred tons of rock on top of them, and this all had to be shifted before they could bring the bodies back to the surface.'

The morning John Willie died, he had been due to take Jim and his younger sister to Scarborough for their annual summer treat. The two children were woken by a knock at the door at the house in Princess Street, a few hundred yards from the colliery. It was the first time Jim had seen his father cry. 'When my father was told that John Willie was trapped, we heard him breathing heavily and then a sort of half-stifled sobbing, and him saying, "Oh Lord, it is hard, help us now. If ever we needed Thy help we need it this morning, but if it is Thy will, if it is Thy will, then let Thy will be done," and then he stumbled up the stairs. He passed us in our bedroom without even seeing us. Tears were running down his cheeks and he looked like a man mortally wounded.'

As Jim worked alone on his first shift, shovelling the coal dust into the tubs, two miles from the pit bottom, the only light coming from his flickering oil lamp, he was terrified. 'I have never known a night that lasted as long as that one; I thought it would never end. I was frightened to death. I had John Willie's face in front of me that night, as plain as day. I kept thinking, Good Lord! if he got killed here, what might happen to me. I dared not hang my lamp in case it toppled over, I dared not put it on the floor in case it rolled over, I dared not turn the wick up, in case it smoked, I dared not turn it down for fear it went out.'

It was six hours before the Deputy returned to take Jim back to the bottom of the shaft. Leaving the thirteen-year-old new boys alone in the dark on their first shifts, the bullying and the terrorization were common to all pits – an underground baptism to toughen the boys up. They were never warned; no one told them it would happen. It was something that had to be endured; to talk about it would have been to express fear, a sign of weakness, a failure of manliness.

Jim did not tell his mother anything of his night, though he remembered the horror of it for the rest of his life. 'When I got to the pit top, I handed in my lamp and rushed home in the darkness. My mother was already up, cooking the breakfast – only that morning, instead of bread and jam, I could smell bacon and eggs. I thought that now I was really a man. As she fussed over me, I looked with pride at my black body and legs. Nobody – and I mean nobody – could persuade me to get washed until I had been outside to let all my younger mates see me on their way to school. I felt really superior – they were just school kids whereas I was a worker. I had arrived. I was important. I was a contributor to the family exchequer.'

From shovelling pit muck, Jim graduated to pony driving, a job given to all the new boys underground. Two weeks after he started down the mine, he was taken to the stables at the bottom of the pit shaft. Bowers colliery had 150 ponies; each had its name over its stall and any rosettes it had won at local shows. They had come to the pit wild from the Welsh hills to be broken in by the boys themselves. Underground, they were not ridden, but driven by verbal commands. Jim's family had been pony trainers at Bowers Row for generations. 'The ponies were put on a long rope and taught all the ordinary commands, such as "Whey!" (that means stop); "Get on a bit" (go forward a bit); "Come over" (step over one set of rails to the other); and "Back a bit". At "Come here" they would lift their legs up and spin round in their own lengths, because the roads were too narrow to do anything else. When we said "Back, shuv", the pony would put its bottom against the back end of the tub and start shoving it back. This was called britching. They were also taught to open doors with their heads, which was called trapping.'

Pony driving was important work. The ponies' job was to pull the lines of corves, the tubs that carried the coal to and from the coalface. Rippers, the men who worked alongside the hewers, filled the empty tubs; the ponies then hauled them back to the cage to be sent up out of the pit. Hewers and rippers were paid by contract at so much per ton. Their wages were dependent on the pony drivers – the speed with which they could get the corves up to and back from the coalface. If a boy was slow, he was often physically beaten. At most pits the roads through the tunnels were poor. The journey up to the face was often a mile or more, debris from the roof and the sides of the tunnel littering the rails on which the corves ran. In temperatures that could reach upwards of 90 degrees Fahrenheit, as one pony driver described, 'The pony was always in extremis, and the tubs were often derailed.'

Traipsing the tunnels alone, the boys depended on the ponies for companionship; if their lamps went out, as they frequently did, a pony could guide them home. 'The ponies knew their way around their own district of the pit and could always find their way back to the pit bottom. They did this by travelling against the air which was being fed down by the shaft,' Jim remembered. 'If you got caught in the dark, you grasped your pony's tail and tried to get your head just below the level of his back while he walked slowly – never offering to kick you – straight back to the pit bottom.' Jim was given a pony called Tim. 'I could write about Tim for pages. He used to chew tobacco like a man; he would go mad for mints, he would pull his lips back and grin at me. If I were not going fast enough when we were on our way to the pit bottom, he would shove me in the back. He would drink out of my bottle and take crusts from my bread when I was eating my snap. When I was down that pit for hours and hours alone with my pony I had no one but him to talk to, so I used to chat to him. He would shake his head up and down as I asked him all sorts of questions; he seemed to listen as I carried on long conversations about football and all sorts of subjects.'

The pony drivers' dependency on their ponies sparked fierce rivalry between the boys. Wherever they congregated, at street corners or down the mine, as Fred Smith from Kiveton colliery recalled, they would argue over the abilities of their respective charges: '"I know that Dan can take three empties up 6c gate." "Why, he couldn't pull an old hen off the nest," another would counter. "Tha wants to see Linnet take four fullens on 83's cross gate," and so on it would go. "I'll bet thee he can't" and "I'll bet thee he can".'

The number of tubs a pony could haul determined a boy's standing in the pit, both among his contemporaries and in the eyes of the older men. The boys also knew that they depended on the animals not just for company, but for their lives. To an inexperienced or inattentive pony driver, the roads, with their steep inclines and sharp descents, could be fatal. The ponies often pulled as many as five loaded tubs, weighing up to 600 cwt each. 'The worst accidents,' Jim remembered, 'would happen when the full tubs were coming down the gradient and the driver missed his lockers. These were bits of wood or steel which the driver put into each wheel to make the wheel slide like a brake. If you missed a locker, the tubs started going faster. If you missed one, you could easily miss the lot. The tubs would then run and run, until finally they ran over the pony and invariably broke his back.'

In 1925, seventy-three boys under the age of sixteen were killed in Britain's coalmines and a further 15,241 injured. When the tubs ran, all too often the pony driver, as he tried to correct his error, would fall under the wheels. Made of sharp steel, they scythed through limbs and necks. There were other instances where a wrong move could have disastrous consequences: hooking the tubs up behind the pony, Jim explained, was one: 'You would hang them on the pony's chain and when you told him to stand up a bit, he would stand up about two or three inches. Then the driver put his hand in between one tub and the next, to link the two tubs together. If the pony set off without being told while the driver was doing this, he would probably have his fingers cut off.'

Cruelty to the ponies was a dismissable offence. At Jim's pit, one boy was sacked for pulling out a pony's tongue with a switch. 'Fortunately,' as he recalled, 'lunacy of this kind was exceptional.' But from time to time, there was a stubborn pony that had to be thrashed. 'The older lads would get the tail chain, pass it into the link on the bridle, very tight, so that the pony had something pulling on its left- or right-hand side, tightening all the time, so that he would start spinning. This was done when the road was about 12 feet wide in the passby, the pony spinning and spinning until finally it became dizzy and dropped on the floor. While one of the big lads sat straight on its head the other would just knock hell out of it with a pit prop or pick shaft. They let it stand up and put it back in the tubs to see if it behaved any differently. If it did not, they would do the same thing again.'

The ponies were often killed, or so seriously injured they had to be put down. 'I remember one occasion when a pony was "britching",' recalled Frank Johnson, a pony driver at a mine near Doncaster. 'The rails were fishplated together and it must have got its back foot fast and its hoof was ripped off. I had to report it. The horse-keeper came from the pit-bottom and put a cap on the horse's head.' The cap, called a 'peggy', had a hole in it, positioned between the horse's ears. Two or three miners would sit on the pony to hold it down, while the horseman dazzled it with his lamp as he placed the 'peg' in the hole. It was the most humane way of killing the pony in the cramped conditions underground; as Frank Johnson described, 'The peg was hit with a hammer directly into the animal's brain. It killed them instantly. We used to have to fetch dead ponies on trams, which were like tubs with no sides. The pony drivers cried like babies when their ponies were killed.'

The pony drivers at Billy Fitzwilliam's pits remembered the strike of 1926 for the rest of their lives. 'I should not be living now were it not for that strike,' said Arthur Clayton, a ninety-nine-year-old miner who worked at Elsecar. 'It lengthened men's lives. There were no holidays with pay. We were like young ponies let out to grass.'

For the duration of the strike, Wentworth House became the focus of the neighbourhood. Joyce Smith, then aged seventeen, was home from boarding school for the Easter holidays. 'Lord Fitzwilliam's idea was to entertain his men. He turned the Park into a pleasure ground. There were games and competitions with prizes and all sorts of things to help the miners. I think they were all very sorry for each other. He did a lot to try and help them.'

Handicap races were run for the pit ponies and rosettes awarded for the best turned-out; Maud Fitzwilliam gave £5 to every boy who had a pony with no scars. Football matches and tug-o'-war contests were organized between the two collieries and a fête was held in the gardens at the house. 'There used to be great heaps of coal, tubs of it, and if you guessed the weight it were yours,' a miner from Elsecar recalled. 'Then there was this greasy pole with a ham on top of it. And you'd go skimming up it and if you got this ham it were yours.'

The start of the General Strike coincided with the opening of the cricket season. Cricket was a consuming passion in the pit villages. 'We'd play cricket on the dirt road between the terraces. We'd play the street down below us. Everyone would come out and watch. It were a great event,' remembered Ernest Whitworth, who grew up at Rawmarsh where many of the miners at New Stubbin pit lived. 'The men were stood along the side of the road and the women used to sit out on the chairs. We'd have a post as a wicket, a bit of board. There were no stumps. We couldn't afford them, or a proper cricket ball. Someone would stitch it out of something, an old piece of horse hide out of the knacker's yard was often used.'

At Wentworth House, the cricket pitch was in the middle of the front lawn. On 1 May, the day after the collieries closed, Billy opened the pitch to the Elsecar and New Stubbin colliery teams. To the delight of the players, as one remembered, he issued a challenge: 'He said if anybody hit a cricket ball from the middle of that lawn while they were batting and broke a window at the house there were £25 for them! It were more than four months' wages! And there were all them windows to go at! It took some doing though. The distance from the crease to the house was a good few hundred yards.'

No windows were broken at Wentworth House that spring – either playing cricket, or in anger. Nor was there much trouble anywhere else. The Government had misjudged the country's mood.

24

Five days into the General Strike, on 9 May at 15.00 hours, the War Office issued its fourteenth Situation Report. The word 'Secret' was stamped in red ink across it. It was for the eyes of the Cabinet – and the top civil and military commanders – only. Britain was under a State of Emergency, her armed forces mobilized, but as the report reveals – some of the detail unworthy even of a line in a local newspaper – with the exception of Northern Division, the commanders in the field had precious little to communicate.

SECRET
SITUATION REPORT NO 14 Issued at 1500 hours on 9.5.26
General Situation – Quiet throughout the country.

Northern Division. Quiet but decidedly troublesome. Twenty-five telegraphs were cut near Blaydon – some bus services were withdrawn as a result of interference. In the Northwest area strong pickets have stopped private cars and refused them passage without permit. Much false news is being spread by strikers' Councils of Action. In the Blaydon district the Chairman of the Council is a Communist. More trouble with food supplies is anticipated next week and more Special Constables would be welcomed.

North Eastern Division. Quiet generally. Buses and trams started at Hull but have been stoned by mob. Police raided printing works at Shipley and found much seditious literature. About 48 buses running in Bradford.

North Western Division. Quiet generally. At Liverpool Docks unloading with Volunteer labour proceeding satisfactorily. Engineers reported on good authority to be returning to Messrs Patins and Beyer Peacock's works on Monday.

Eastern Division. Quiet generally. No further trouble at Ipswich, but Specials have to be worked in large parties. Buses all day without interference.

South Western Division. Quiet generally. Some trouble in Plymouth consequent on trams restarting, manned by Volunteers. Railway men are dribbling back all over the district.

South Midland Division. Quiet generally. Trams running all day in Reading and Huntley and Palmer's tin box workers have all returned.

Midland Division. Quiet generally. It is expected a considerable number of railway men will dribble back on Monday

North Midland Division. Quiet generally. Grimsby tramwaymen have returned to work.

Western Command Report. Situation throughout the command remains unchanged. Railway traffic shows a marked increase. No organized disturbances have occurred.

Eastern Command Report. Situation generally quiet. Attempts to interfere with road transport show more signs of organization. Attempts to stop petrol lorries from the Thameshaven Area were made on May 8th by digging up the roadway. The Corningham Oil Depot is now guarded by troops. There were organized interferences with buses on the Harrow Road on the afternoon of 8th May. A violent assault on a soldier, when off his guard, was made at Woolwich yesterday afternoon by an individual armed with a knuckle-duster.

London District Report. Area quiet generally. During the passage of the food convoy yesterday from the Docks many thousands lined the streets from Canning Town to Stepney: – the general behaviour of the crowds was most good natured, and there was quite a lot of cheering. From remarks overheard, comments were made to the effect that 'The sooner we chuck it the better'. In Camden Town, the women appear prominent in arousing resentment against Police, and more particularly against Special Constables.

'Quiet generally'. The 14th Situation Report echoed those that had preceded it.

In Mayfair and Belgravia, members of the aristocracy, among the most fearful at the start of the General Strike, began to relax, delighting in their temporary civic responsibilities. 'Most people enjoyed it I think!' wrote Lady Bentinck to Lady Halifax in India. 'All our friends were "Specials" or working at the Docks and stations. The Oxford boys were driving very skilfully with delicious notices chalked on the front, such as "Flappers are Welcome" – "The Tortoise" and "On the Streets Again, but Don't Tell Mother" and so on! Sonny T. has charge of the Westminster Tube station, with Sir Victor Warrender as ticket collector.' Lady Sybil Middleton, also writing to Lady Halifax, gave a further tally of mutual friends who had momentarily traded places. 'Lord Portarlington was head porter at Paddington, Sir Rennell Rodd in order to set a good example went as Dustman but he dropped a big dustbin on his foot and was thereby put out of action for the remainder of the strike. [Lord] Edmund Grey went to the Docks and hauled at a rope as he said it was the only thing he could do – so you see the old and distinguished had a variety of jobs!'

By the end of the first week of the strike, it was the activities of the 'racing hogs', the aristocratic owners of the 'fastest cars in England', that were causing the most alarm among Lady Halifax's correspondents. 'The Horse Guards Parade is a great car-park where Rex Benson, Lord Curzon and one Reggie Seymour send out racing hogs to distribute the *British Gazette* all over England,' wrote Mabel, Countess Grey. The *British Gazette*, a news-sheet edited by Winston Churchill, was a propaganda vehicle for the Government. Distributed countrywide by the 'racing hogs', even they, according to Lady Middleton, were unnerved by the speeds they reached: 'Rex is a pretty dashing driver himself but I believe some of the times that the fast cars did in the middle of the night fairly made his hair stand on end. I know one going to Liverpool and back averaged 60!'

Leading society ladies had queued up to volunteer. 'I was in despair as it was so difficult to get a job,' wrote Lady Bentinck, who, like so many women of her class, had rarely, if ever, cooked a meal or done a day's paid work in her life. 'There were 3 eager females for every job! At last I got into a newspaper office which has been commandeered for the *British Gazette* – it was next to the *Herald* office where the *Worker* was being printed and we had police on the roof with revolvers as it was thought the strikers might come in and wreck our machinery! But nothing occurred, everybody was far too orderly. I was busy frying bacon and eggs for volunteers, who luckily were hungry otherwise they couldn't have faced the horrors I produced.'

Debutantes, whose presentation at Court had been postponed by the General Strike, were drafted to marquees in the London parks where they worked around the clock, washing dishes and serving meals. 'Instead of me, it was the workers of England who came out,' recalled Lady Mary Clive in her memoirs.

For eight ecstatic days I enjoyed the privilege of spending the evenings in a canteen in Hyde Park. My cousin Imogen and I were allowed to walk there together, seen off by dubious parents, torn between the obvious duty of sacrificing their young on the Nation's altar, and fear that their young might get their looks ruined by a passing brickbat. We served in a large marquee near the Park Lane edge, and our patrons were chiefly the men out of the lorries which were parked from Marble Arch to Hyde Park Corner. I think they slept in their lorries. They certainly looked very grimy.

The lorry drivers were volunteers, working-class men who were opposed to the General Strike and whom the Government had deployed to deliver milk and other essential goods. 'When they were not eating they sat as good as gold in corners, poring over disintegrating copies of the *Tatler* and *Bystander* which somebody had thoughtfully sent to bolster up the supporters of capitalism.' An eccentric blend of hymns, sermons, dance music, grand opera and French lessons blared from loudspeakers that had been put up in the tent as a further bolster to morale. Flirtation, as Lady Mary Clive remembered, was encouraged. 'It was of course a positive duty for us in this hour of National Crisis to keep on good terms with the Nation's toughs, and every time we got off with one we felt we were helping to avert the Revolution. There was no false modesty or coyness about our response to their advances. We met them more than half-way.' But 'half-way', as she pointed out, was quite enough. 'Our triumph was sometimes tempered by waves of panic that we had gone too far, and that they really would try to take us to the cinema or escort us home or otherwise impinge upon our private lives.' Some of the girls, finding the work too taxing, coaxed their servants to come and help in the tents. 'The washing water was like minestrone and the drying cloths, which one would otherwise have relied on to clean the plates, were always soaking wet in spite of the labours of somebody's footman who had got into the park by climbing over the railings and who was made to stand the whole afternoon in front of the oil stove as a sort of human towel-horse.'

An element of burlesque was also to be found among those drafted to more serious duties.

On Monday 3 May, Lady Sybil Middleton, who was staying with her in-laws at Lowood in Scotland, travelled south with her son, Henry, and one-year-old baby, Molly, to be near her husband, Lambert, who had volunteered as a Special Constable. 'As soon as Lambert enrolled, I came up to bind his broken head if need be,' she wrote to Lady Halifax. 'We came by the last night train and I put Molly in my suitcase in which she travelled and slept comfortably.' Lambert Middleton was one of eighty volunteers attached to the CID unit at Scotland Yard responsible for rounding up Communist subversives. Lady Sybil told Lady Halifax,

He spent one very lengthy day, from 9.30 to 7.30 standing outside a Communist office watching it and trying to capture a badly wanted Communist. His hat was well pulled over his eyes (I made him leave his eyeglass at home so that under no circumstances should he be tempted to use it) and eating peas spitting [*sic*] the skins in the gutter – a thing he said he had never done in London before. By the middle of the afternoon he was so tired that he asked to sit on the pavement and started drawing coloured pictures. They did end by arresting a young man called George Miles who is one of the youngest and most fiery of the Communist leaders. They talked to him for half an hour. Lambert said he was such a good-looking boy very well educated and talking perfect English without any accent at all. This boy said that the failure of the General Strike was the best thing that could happen to the Communist Party as the strikers would be so disgusted with their leaders that they would go in their 1,000s to the Communist Party. Perhaps he is right. The detective who was with Lambert thought not. The last day he was on duty, he was sent in the pouring rain to mingle in the crowd in the East End at a Communist Meeting. He did not get back till 1 a.m. and he brought back the detective he was working under to stay and have breakfast here, and it turned out to be a Sergeant Dew, the son of the detective who arrested Crippen. So you see we have been moving in high criminal circles.

'The position as a whole is still one of deadlock,' the BBC reported in the ten o'clock bulletin on the morning of 12 May. Two short hours later came the noon bulletin: 'General Strike ceases today.'

Lady Mary Clive was in Selfridges watching the ticker-tape machines with a crowd of people when the news came through. 'The shop girls fell into each other's arms as unanimously as though they had been drilled,' she later wrote, 'and we all grinned and laughed insanely. We were as good as saved. Nothing was going to happen. Everything was going to be just as it had always been.'

The TUC had caved in. As Thomas Jones, the Deputy Secretary to the Cabinet, observed, 'The General Strike could not succeed because some of those who led it did not wholly believe in it and because few, if any, were prepared to go through with it to its logical conclusion – violence and revolution.' The General Council of the TUC had opted for a compromise. In the days leading up to 12 May, it had held secret negotiations with Sir Herbert Samuel, the man who had been in charge of the Government inquiry that had triggered the strike. Samuel's report had concluded that the miners' wages should be cut, but it had also recommended widespread reform of the coal industry. After meeting Sir Herbert, the General Council judged that he could be used as an intermediary to persuade the Prime Minister to make the reductions in the miners' wages contingent on reform: specifically, nationalization of the mineral royalties and the introduction of better working conditions. This was the argument the General Council presented to the MFGB, the miners' trade union: ultimately though, its heart was not in the strike.

While the trades unions sought radical change to the social, political and economic fabric of the country, they unequivocally rejected the use of violence as a means to this end. So too did their membership. During the nine days the strike lasted, not a shot was fired, nor a single person killed. A total of 4,000 people were arrested in sporadic outbreaks of violence and hooliganism. But this was a trivial number given the millions of strikers. At no stage was there an indication of the Bolshevist-inspired revolution that, for almost a decade, the Establishment had so feared. The extent of Communist activity was negligible. An MI5 report, published after the strike, reveals that just 192 men were prosecuted for sedition. Of these, 121 were arrested on a probability – for making a speech or for possessing seditious documents 'likely to cause disaffection' – rather than for a flagrantly seditious act.

It was the final tally in a dispute which both Baldwin and Churchill at first feared would threaten to subvert the State. Yet, the 3 million men who came out in support of the miners had made no demands for themselves. They had not sought to challenge the Government, still less to overthrow the constitution. They had simply wanted the miners to have a living wage. It was a paradox that the leading politicians of the day failed to recognize. Instead, they chose to interpret its outcome as a victory in what they believed to be the ongoing class war. 'The result of the GS altogether delights one; for it shows that this old England of ours retains its spirit unimpaired,' wrote Lord Birkenhead, Secretary of State for India, to his friend Lord Irwin.

Everyone is asking why this GS collapsed so quickly. Fifty contributory explanations are available, but I recall the lines of Edgar Allan Poe:

> A wind blew out of the sea,
> Chilling and killing my Annabel Lee,
> My beautiful Annabel Lee.

A wind blew from the whole of England, chilling and killing the spirits and the pretensions of those who were challenging constitutional government and Parliamentary institutions. More and more they became conscious how numerous were their enemies, how few and in many cases how unwilling were their friends. The collapse was very sudden. I was one of the few Ministers who received the ultimate Trades Unionists' surrender. It was so humiliating that some instinctive breeding made one unwilling even to look at them. I thought of the Burghers of Calais approaching their interview with Edward III, haltered on the neck.

The day after the General Strike ended, the miners voted to strike on. One million men in the coalfields refused to concede defeat. Taking their dependants into account, millions more were caught up in the dispute. 'This coal trouble is more serious than the strike proper, I think,' reported Lady Henry Bentinck to Lady Halifax, 'however everyone seems to take it very lightly and dance every night and are busy with Ascot clothes!'

The coal strike that followed the General Strike would transform Britain beyond recognition. 'Everything was going to be just as it had always been,' Lady Mary Clive had written gleefully when the TUC had caved in. Only time would reveal this, but it was Britain's historic ruling class that was about to be 'haltered on the neck'. After the coal strike – destined to last almost until Christmas 1926 – nothing would ever be the same again.

'We are not prepared to have our wages reduced under present conditions,' Herbert Smith, President of the MFGB, told the Prime Minister at a meeting at Downing Street the day the General Strike collapsed. 'I am compelled to say this,' he added, 'because my people are down.'

Between 1921 and April 1926, a miner's average earnings had fallen from 19 shillings and 2d a day to 9 shillings and 4d*; the average length of his working week, from six days to four. Britain's colliers were, in the words of the Labour MP for Pontypridd,

*From £32 to £18 at today's values.

George Hall, at 'rock bottom'. 'The level of wages is such,' he continued, 'that it is almost impossible for our people to live.' It was not Communist propaganda. What he said was true. Harold Macmillan, the future Conservative Prime Minister, in a letter to Winston Churchill, written from Stockton in April 1926, wrote of 'the appalling conditions' in his constituency, which lay in the heart of the Durham coalfields.

The 'appalling conditions' in the North-East were replicated in mining communities across the country. In the spring of 1926, Miss Brodigan, the Warden of a London-based Charitable Trust and a staunch Conservative, visited the district of Blaina and Nantyglo in South Wales. Writing to the Prime Minister, she described the 'desperate plight of the place', submitting a detailed account of the conditions in the district in the hope that he would take action to alleviate the distress:

Blaina and Nantyglo form an urban area of 16,700 inhabitants in the Ebbw Valley, South Wales. There are no local industries whatever except mining. Up to 1921 there were 11 pits working, employing 4,500 men. In that year, 7 were closed down because they were not paying, and a further 3 in the years up to 1924. One only, a modern one, with good electrical machinery was kept going. Up to last December, however, it could only work on 2 and sometimes 3 days a week and out of the 4,500 Blaina miners, it could only employ 1,500. About 900 found work in the various pits down the Valley towards Newport, some having as much as 2 hours' walk to and from their work.

A few men emigrated to Australia and a few to America, but owing to the long coal strike there, came back to Blaina. About 1,500 remained permanently unemployed: some struggled on, gradually using up their savings, a large number turned to the Poor Law Guardians for help.

Housing conditions became worse and worse. The local Council issued orders for repairs to property but none of the owners had the wherewithal to carry them out. An outbreak of typhoid in one group of houses revealed a condition of things in that particular area which the County Medical Officer of Health described as 'worse than the black hole of Calcutta'. Quite two thirds of the straggling town from Blaina to Nantyglo consist of desperately dilapidated old cottages with bulging and cracked walls and only too often with cracked and leaking roofs as well.

The doctor says the clothing of the children, especially their underclothing, is in a very bad condition and is in some cases almost non-existent. She is very much concerned about the nursing and expectant mothers whom she sees at the Welfare Clinic and says the women do not let the children suffer but are thoroughly underfed themselves. The same suggestion of continuous under-feeding came from the Hospital. The House Surgeon, a Sligo man, compared the district to Connemara in the old days and the Matron told me that the patients come in so much under par that after one or two unfortunate experiences they now keep them for two or three days' good feeding before putting them under an operation.

The poverty and hardship were the consequences of an industry in crisis. The huge coal exports that for a century had helped maintain Britain's balance of payments were shrinking at an alarming rate. In 1870 the UK had produced half the world's coal; by the mid-1920s it was producing little more than one-fifth. While the development of alternative fuels – oil and hydro-electric power – had reduced the demand for coal, it was the emergence of new producers, able to undercut the price of British coal, that had hit her markets hardest. By 1926, 40 million tons of British coal, formerly supplied to the Empire, was being dug out in Africa, India and China at one-third of the cost of British coal at the pit mouth.

Most damaging of all was the disintegration of the European export markets. In a bitter twist of historical irony, the Versailles Treaty, designed to punish Germany, dealt Britain a devastating blow. In striking at the coal industry, with its millions of dependants, it struck at the country's heart. Under the terms of the Treaty, Britain and her allies had stipulated that a proportion of Germany's reparations should be paid in deliveries of free coal. France, Belgium and Italy, previously large importers of British coal, were the main beneficiaries. By the mid-1920s, British exports to Italy alone had fallen by 3.5 million tons from their pre-war level: over the same period, German coal exports to Italy had jumped from under 1 million metric tons to 4.4 million, the majority of which was reparations coal.

Quite how damaging the Versailles Treaty was to the British coal industry became evident in 1923 when French and Belgian troops occupied the Ruhr after Germany defaulted on its coal deliveries. That year, with production halted in the German coalfields, Britain's exports leapt briefly to an inter-war high of 98 million tons. The boom was short-lived; by 1925, the Dawes Plan, an American-led rescue operation to stabilize the Deutschmark, had kick-started the German economy, driving coal production in the Ruhr from strength to strength. As European markets were flooded with cheap German coal – on top of the free reparations coal – in Britain, the terms of Versailles tipped the mining industry into a slump, knocking mines and the miners out of work.

For industrialists and economists alike, in the grim economic conditions of the mid-1920s, the price of coal became the Holy Grail. If the cost of production could be reduced by cutting miners' wages, so could the cost per ton of British coal: pre-war export markets, so the argument ran, would recover and unemployment would fall. The assessment, as it turned out, was flawed: in the bleak decade between 1925 and 1935, wage reductions served to depress the home markets further, causing more unemployment than they cured.

The truth was that neither politicians nor industrialists were prepared to grapple with the reality that the coal industry, on which Britain's imperial wealth and power had been founded, was haemorrhaging, in slow, mortal decline.

The dual issues of Coal and Class had become inextricably entwined.

25

A breeze blew through the marquees at Wentworth. It came from the south, smelling of industry: of tar, sulphur and the metallic tang of steel. A mile away, at Parkgate, the steelworkers and factory hands had returned to work. Dense clouds of smoke belched from the foundries into the late spring air, the roar of industry competing with the clear chimes from the church clocks in the villages nearby.

It was a Saturday morning, the fourth week of the coal strike, and 1,200 children, the sons and daughters of the New Stubbin colliers, stood outside the marquees waiting to be fed. A remnant from the Great War, the Fitzwilliams' agent had bought the former hospital tents as a job lot. A decade earlier they had stood in a line of others along the cliffs above Calais – Casualty Clearing Stations for British soldiers wounded at the Front. Now, under Billy's instructions, they had been put up along the southern edge of Wentworth Park, close to Greaseborough and Rawmarsh, where many of the miners from New Stubbin lived. For as long as the coal strike lasted, Billy had undertaken to provide his miners' children with one midday meal a week. Five miles away, at Elsecar colliery, a further 1,300 children were being fed.

The officials at New Stubbin pit had marshalled the children into a queue. Boys and girls up to the age of thirteen, they clutched the mugs and basins they had brought from home. As they waited in line, each child was given an orange. It was strange fruit to most of them; few, if any, had tasted one before. A few years earlier, a teacher at Rawmarsh Junior School had asked a group of ten-year-olds to write about their parents. The results of the classroom exercise reveal that, even before the coal strike began, family life in the Fitzwilliams' pit villages revolved around the struggle to survive. Food and work dominated their barely literate accounts. The descriptions were short, in some cases little more than a sentence, but they were the first thoughts that came into the children's minds:

'I hawe gotta father and some fathers has dide [died] and the ladys get some roses and daffodils and croces and tulip and put on the graffes.'

'My father gos to work. Wehen he comes home his has black has sut. he coms home at afternoon. When he comes home he has is dinner. he goes to wrk at nighte. When he comes home he bringht some moony back. My father goes to work to get some mony to get some food whit it.'

'My father gos to wak [work] for mony to keep ues we bay food for to aet our Nell she waks at keethli [Keighley]. We had not inuf to keep us all So. She went a waye so we cud live aply [happily].

'I have got a mother at home and she warks hared and when she woshes some time is mase her pooly and then she mite die and my father will go in the cab and then myt bey some flower eles my anty will bey some.'

Inside the main marquee, the air was clammy and fetid. It smelt of overcooked porridge and the sweat from the bodies of scores of women. Four weeks into the strike, soap was an unaffordable luxury. Clouds of steam rose from the gruel pans that simmered on industrial-size gas burners; a long trestle table stretched down the length of the tent where an army of miners' wives, working at an efficient pace, was buttering bread.

Feeding 1,200 children was a military operation. Besides fruit, the children were to be given 'water gruel', teacakes and sandwiches. It was Maud Fitzwilliam who had taken charge of the proceedings. Working beside the miners' wives in the long assembly-line, she stood out from the others. Most of the women wore white pinnies over their drab dresses; the fine fabric and the pale spring colours of the Countess's dress marked her out at a glance. 'The Fitzwilliams were liked. Nobody ever called them nought. You never heard people call 'em bad names. They were really nice people, kind people, they looked after you,' remembered May Bailey, who lived in Greaseborough, and whose father and brothers worked at New Stubbin pit. May's memories were echoed by others. 'If anyone went without it was their own fault,' Gracie Woodcock from Wentworth recalled. 'There was always a rabbit or a pigeon, they only had to open their mouths. My husband used to go down every week to the Big House with a cart and he used to come back with great hunks of sheep and calves to give to the poor.'

During the grim months of the coal strike that lay ahead, the Fitzwilliams' generosity would be tested to the limit. On that first Saturday morning in the marquees, Maud turned to the woman next to her to reassure her: 'I'll slay the last bullock in Wentworth before the children should want,' she told her. 'We called her Lady Bountiful,' Bert May, the Fitzwilliams' butler's son, recalled.

It was said without a trace of irony.

From the moment she arrived at Wentworth, Maud Fitzwilliam had devoted much of her time and energy to charitable activities. In Billy's grandfather's time, formal procedures had governed the way the family looked after the needy in their pit villages. 'When the Vicar took Morning Prayers, as he did every weekday at 9.30 a.m. in the House Chapel for residents, visitors and staff, the old Earl expected him to bring what he called "The Soup List",' remembered Marguerite Verini, the former Principal of Hughes Hall, Cambridge, whose father was Vicar at Wentworth from 1898 to 1912. The 'Soup List', as Verini described, was the daily tally of the sick and the poor. After Morning Prayers the Earl would instruct his staff to arrange for provisions to be sent round to the families. In 1902, when Billy succeeded the 6th Earl, Maud Fitzwilliam had dispensed with this tradition: she took charge of the arrangements personally, identifying those families in need of assistance and delivering the provisions herself.

She became a familiar figure in the district. Most afternoons, she toured the pit villages, driven by her chauffeur in a yellow Rolls-Royce. Pregnant mothers and the mothers of newborn babies were automatically included in her daily round. 'All the mothers would get milk and her special gruel and a dozen or two eggs,' remembered May Bailey. The servants at the house packed the Rolls-Royce with all sorts of provisions for the poor – food, clothes and, on some occasions, even live chickens. Unannounced, the Countess would stop off at the miners' cottages, often staying to have a chat and a cup of tea. 'Lady Maud was always in the villages, popping in and out, dropping something round,' Rita King, a miner's daughter from Greaseborough, recalled. 'I remember my grandfather grew chrysanthemums. He won first prize most years at the flower show up at the house. One morning Lady Maud came down the path. "Are you there, Maleham?" – that were his name – she says. "I've brought you this." It were a lovely little silver cup. She said, "You may as well have it. You've won the bloody thing often enough."'

Favoured tenants and employees were treated to the same food as invalids at Wentworth House. Beef tea and calves' foot blancmange – or its variant, calves' foot custard – were thought to be especially restorative. The calves' foot 'blammonge' was made following a special house recipe:

Put a set of Calves feet, well cleaned and washed into 4 quarts of water and reduce it by boiling to one quart, strain it and let it cool. When cold scrape off all the fat, cut it out of the bowl avoiding the settings at the bottom, and put to it a quart of new milk with sugar to taste and boil it for a few minutes. It may be flavoured with cinnamon or lemon peel *before* boiling; if flavoured with rose water or peach water *after* boiling. When boiled 10 minutes, strain it through a fine sieve and stir it till it cools. When only blood warm, put it into moulds, first dipped in cold water.

The Wentworth House gruel, a thin water-based porridge, was another favourite of Maud's. During the coal strike, it was made

18. Miners from the Fitzwilliams' collieries outside the gates to Wentworth Park, *c.* 1910

19. Main Street, Wentworth village, 1905

20. Loversall Street, Denaby, 1903. The blockhouse containing the privy middens can be seen on the right-hand side of the street

21. Police evict miners and their families from tied housing during the Bag Muck Strike at Denaby in January 1903

22. Faceworkers hewing coal

23. A deputy below ground, 1912

24. A group of miners and a young child take a break while digging for coal during the 1912 strike. During industrial disputes the miners lost their coal allowance. Often, whole families would turn out to 'pick' the coal, an essential fuel for heating and cooking

25. A young miner. In the first decades of the twentieth century boys began work undergroun at the age of thirteen

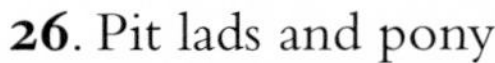

26. Pit lads and pony

27. Queen Mary, accompanied by her Ladies-in-Waiting, views Silverwood colliery from a trolley, July 1912

28. George V and Billy, 7th Earl Fitzwilliam, enter the cage to descend underground at Elsecar colliery, July 1912

29. The morning of 9 July 1912. An ambulance wagon passes through the crowds gathered on the road leading to Cadeby colliery, following the disaster at the pit

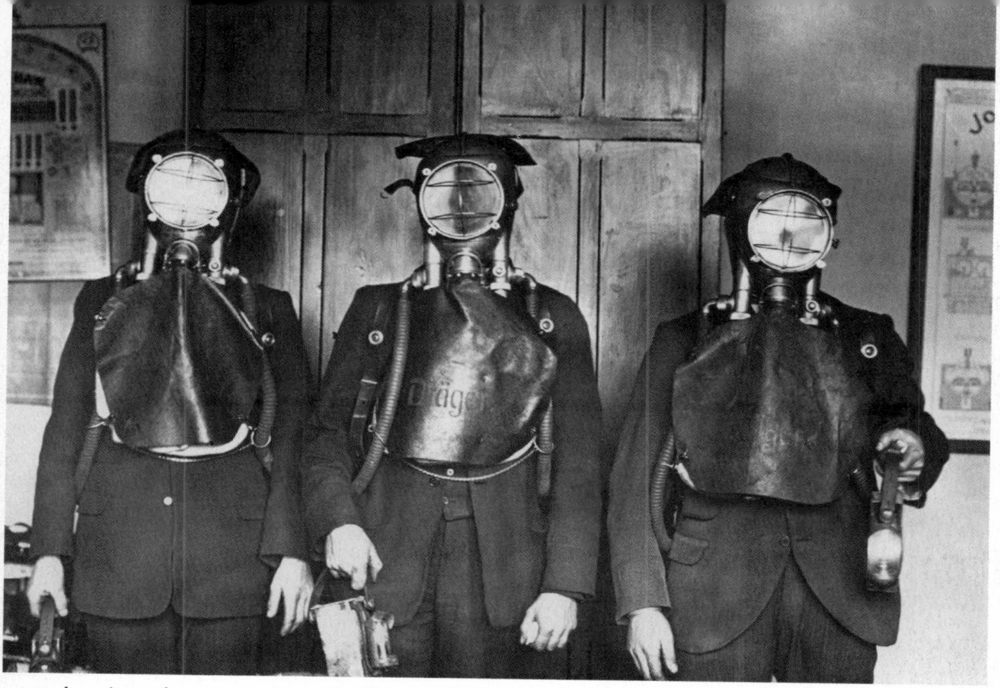

30. A miners' rescue team, similar to those deployed after the explosions at Cadeby. They are wearing Draegar smoke helmets. Hamstead colliery, 1908

31. The Cadeby colliery disaster created sixty-one widows and left 132 fatherless children. For many of the women, forced to survive on compensation payments of little more than 5 shillings per week, visits to the pawnshop became routine

32. The house party staying at Wentworth during the King and Queen's visit in July 1912

33. The Wentworth Battery, RHA, in training in Wentworth Park in the summer of 1914

in the kitchens at Wentworth, from where it was transported on flat drays to the marquees to be reheated. In 1926, May Bailey was working as a scullery maid up at the house. 'They had these huge set pots in the kitchen – like great cauldrons they were, and it were my job to scrub them. I didn't like scrubbing them set pots. They were used for making Countess Maud's gruel. The oatmeal used to stick to the bottom and it were a hell of a job getting it off. I were a lackey for better end – you know the cook, housemaids and chambermaids. I were at bottom! Them pots were on the go round the clock. That gruel went out at all hours.'

The Fitzwilliams' generosity towards their miners was not motivated by socialist principles; in Billy's case, it stemmed from a loathing of trades unionism and a near-feudal sense of his obligation to his men. In 1911, in the midst of an industrial dispute at Elsecar, he had issued a statement: 'Acting upon what has been a tradition in the family, Lord Fitzwilliam has declined to negotiate the dispute with representatives of the Yorkshire Miners' Association. He states that it is a matter between himself and his men, and that if the men are left alone, there will be a prompt settlement.' In 1926, although Billy's sense of realpolitik prevented him from airing his views in public, privately his position was as vehemently anti-union as it had been in 1911, and during the troubles of 1919. It was not just a question of politics; the issue had an emotional resonance to him. He believed that trades unionism threatened to poison his relationship with his men. By helping the miners during the long months of the coal strike, he was fulfilling the obligation he believed he owed to every man who worked for him. His grandfather had expressed it simply: 'the protection,' he had said, 'which is due from me to him.'

In addition to feeding the miners' children, Billy helped his men in other ways. Jobs were found for them on other parts of the Estate. Up on the family's grouse moors in the Pennines, an entire forest was planted by the miners from New Stubbin and Elsecar pits during the summer of 1926. Billy also allowed his colliers to mine coal from the old surface workings on his land. A source of free coal made a big difference to the miners: at home they were dependent on coal for heating, hot water and cooking. In neighbouring pit villages, the miners were forced to pick through the slag heaps to find what coal they could. 'Most people ran out of coal, which they needed for cooking on the fire – that was if anybody had anything to cook,' remembered Luke Evans, a miner from Aldwarke Main, a colliery close to Wentworth.

I used to go to Hickleton tips about five miles away on an old bicycle that had not got any tyres on the wheels. I would fill two bags with coal and push one bag through the frame and one on the top bar of the bicycle. This was a full day's work from early morning until late at night. Sometimes I would sell one bag of coal for one shilling. The number of people at Hickleton tips grew into hundreds; people came long distances with their horses and flat drays to collect coal. Men worked in teams and as darkness approached some would stay all night to guard their precious find.

In some districts, whole families resorted to picking through the sewage tips in search of any lumps of coal that had been thrown into the midden trenches.

As the strike dragged on, conditions became desperate in the Yorkshire coalfields and in other mining regions across the country. The government estimated that 1.7 million families were affected by the coal strike. 'It was clog and boot time if you like, not much to wear, no money at all,' Ernest Kaye, a miner from Birdwell, near Barnsley, remembered. 'We went to school as normal, some were worse than me, wearing just one shoe, with big holes in their jumpers.' 'I can remember the 1926 strike,' Jack Parkin, a miner from Carlton, a colliery village near Wentworth, recalled. 'One word sums up the village at the time: bloody destitute.'

The miners at New Stubbin and Elsecar collieries were better off than most. In the last week of August, Billy Fitzwilliam made an extraordinary announcement: instead of giving their children one meal a week, all 2,500 of them were to be fed every day.

In London, negotiations between the Government, the miners'

leaders and the coal owners were deadlocked. The strike had two more months to run.

'The owners are fighting Socialism,' wrote Lord Londonderry, one of the wealthiest coal owners in the north of England, in a letter to Winston Churchill, the Chancellor of the Exchequer, in the fifth month of the strike. 'The Federation [the miners' union] is nothing but a Communist Central Office. We want a victory over the strongest Communistic force in the country. You will have to fight Socialism in the very near future,' he warned the Chancellor, 'and the Miners' Federation is one of the powerful army corps in the field against us.'

The tragedy of the coal strike lay not simply in the hardship suffered by the miners but the fact that the Government allowed it to be hijacked by the warriors of class war.

During the eight months it lasted, it was the coal owners who were the most belligerent. In the years between the Great War and the Second World War, the Conservative and Liberal share of the electoral vote did not fall below 60 per cent; the Communist Party's share averaged 0.3 per cent. At the time Lord Londonderry was writing, in September 1926, while a number of the miners' union leaders were Communists, there was no evidence to support the theory that the men they represented were bent on overthrowing parliamentary democracy and forcing a revolutionary Communist Government into power. On the contrary, their docile conduct during the coal dispute, like that of the 3 million-plus men who had come out in sympathetic protest with them in the General Strike, ought to have shown that, far from posing a challenge to the constitution, the majority of miners were fighting solely for the principle of a living wage.

From the outset, the coal owners – the men who owned and operated Britain's collieries – were determined not to give ground. 'It would be possible to say without exaggeration of the miners' leaders that they were the stupidest men in England if we had not frequent occasion to meet the owners,' Lord Birkenhead, Secretary of State for India, and a member of the Coal Committee appointed by the Prime Minister to resolve the dispute, remarked to his friend Lord Irwin in May 1926.

During the negotiations to end the strike, the coal owners were represented by their association, the Mining Association of Great Britain (MAGB). In contrast to the aristocratic, often flamboyant, super-rich mineral royalty owners – the men who owned the land from which the coal was mined – the coal owners were a shadowy, provincial body of men. Their strongholds were the dour granite buildings, stained by dirt and damp, the civic megaliths to the industrial revolution that crowded the centre of the 'new' towns in the Black Country, the Yorkshire coalfields and at the heads of the Welsh valleys. Coal, iron and steel represented the whole of their lives; as Dr Outram concluded in his study of the forty-four men who in 1926 made up the Central Committee of the MAGB, 'their status in society, and in their communities depended entirely on coal; if it failed their moderate wealth and power was at stake. They had nothing else.'

Of the forty-four members on the MAGB's central committee, nearly half were JPs; twelve had served at one time as county or urban district councillors; seven were Deputy Lieutenants of their county. With the exception of one, their public activities were confined to their county and their industry, a record that fell far short of many of the wealthy northern manufacturers. Despite an average fortune of £112,000 each,* few, if any, of the committee members had followed the contemporary practice of dedicating parks or buildings to their localities. While the majority had inherited their mines and their wealth, they shunned – or were shunned by – 'society'; as Outram discovered, they stood apart from the political social elite. Few had been to the 'right' schools – Eton, Marlborough or Harrow; their families had chosen to send them to grammar schools or to minor public schools like Fettes and Clifton instead. A university education was the exception and only a handful had a record of military service. Their births, deaths

* Approximately £4 million at today's values.

and marriages were not reported in *The Times*; most had married the daughters of men from similarly provincial backgrounds to themselves. Only four maintained a London residence. In the terminology of the day, the coal owners were 'players' rather than 'gentlemen' – men of practical skills gained through experience or technical training, with few outside interests and whose chief concern was business. Deeply conservative in their outlook and in their politics, they regarded the strike as a challenge to their very existence. As the months wore on, they became determined to destroy the miners' union, the MFGB.

Crucially, the MFGB wanted the Government to guarantee the miners a minimum wage. In the mid-1920s, wages were still determined at a district level. The rates at every colliery – and for the different jobs underground – varied across the country. The drastic halving of the miners' average earnings between 1920 and 1926 had resulted not so much from cuts in wages as from the reduction in the length of their working week. If the coal owners could not sell their coal, they simply switched the pits to 'short-time'. It was a felicitous equation; at a moment's notice, they could cut their overheads by cutting the number of shifts. The consequences for the miner were brutal: if the coal owner stopped the pit, he did not get paid.

An agreed national minimum was the surest way of conferring 'a living wage', a cushion against the iniquities of 'short-time'. But during the months of bitter negotiations to resolve the strike, the coal owners would not concede it. Evan Williams, the President of the MAGB, refusing to give credence to the miners' distress, accused the MFGB of demanding a national minimum wage for the sole purpose of achieving its political objectives, 'the nationalization or socialization [of the mines] by means of the power which national agreements give them to threaten to hold up the whole country and make an industrial question a political issue'.

The coal owners' use of the rhetoric of class war obscured the real issue: the poverty and hardship the miners were being forced to endure. Their success is evident in the letter Miss Brodigan wrote to the Prime Minister following her visit to Blaina and

Nantyglo in South Wales. There, as she reported to Baldwin, the County Medical Officer had described the miners' living conditions as 'worse than the black hole of Calcutta'. Yet in the covering letter attached to her report she felt compelled to stress that her findings had not been coloured by the politics of the Left – quite the reverse. 'I spent last Monday and Tuesday at the Rectory there, where the rector is a strong unionist and his wife an ardent member of the British Fascisti,' she wrote. 'I think therefore that had there been anything serious to say against the local labour councillors I should have heard of it. As a matter of fact the rector and his wife described the miners as honest, decent men.' Miss Brodigan also felt bound to declare her own Tory colours and to emphasize that she had found no evidence of class hatred among the miners themselves. 'They struck me as a particularly moderate body of men, without any bitterness against anyone,' she assured the Prime Minister, 'just thoroughly depressed and worried about their future and fatalistically certain that however the coal dispute ends it will leave them with even more unemployment than before.'

In the autumn of 1926, with the coal owners and the miners' leaders proving equally stubborn, Winston Churchill, the one man in Baldwin's Cabinet who had the vision to see beyond the rhetoric of class war, took charge of the Government's efforts to resolve the dispute.

Churchill's reply to Lord Londonderry had been stern. 'You say that the Owners are fighting Socialism,' he wrote. 'It is not the business of Coal Owners as Coal Owners to fight Socialism. If they declare it their duty, how can they blame the Miners' Federation for pursuing political ends? The business of the Coal Owners is to manage their industry successfully, to insist upon sound economic conditions as regards hours and wages, and to fight Socialism as citizens and not as owners of a particular class of property.'

Throughout the autumn, Churchill fought to convince Baldwin that the Government should force a compromise on the coal owners. Appalled by their intransigence and shocked by the poverty in the mining districts, he argued that they should be pushed into meeting the miners half-way. Adamant that the Conservative Party should not be seen to align itself with the interests of one class, he vented his frustration in a letter to the Prime Minister. 'It would seem quite impossible for us to avow impotency when confronted with recalcitrant owners,' he wrote. 'We have legislated against the miners, broken the General Strike, imported foreign coal, and kept the ring these long five months. We can hardly take the purely class view that owners, however unreasonable, are sacrosanct and inviolable.' The solution Churchill proposed was to keep the mechanism of district wage settlements in place but to set – through legislation – a national minimum for the districts below which no coal owner could go.

Churchill's was a lone voice in the Cabinet. Even Lord Birkenhead, who had been so withering in his condemnation of the coal owners, rallied to their defence. In a telegram to Churchill, sent in mid-September, he said, 'I am not happy with your attitude. Why should we impose upon owners national settlement if they are strong enough to obtain district settlements? Why should we enable men's leaders who have done their best to ruin England to escape without the brand of failure?'

'Moscow Gold', perhaps the most inflammatory issue of the coal strike, had played into the coal owners' hands. In the course of the dispute Russian trades unions contributed £1,200,000* to the miners' welfare funds – almost three times as much as the amount contributed by British trades unions. 'The Moscow influence and the Moscow money have been powerful enough to drown the voice of reason and good feeling,' Churchill later wrote to his political ally, Sir James Hawkey. The Bolshevik donations revived the fear of revolution that the General Strike should have quashed. The coal owners remained 'sacrosanct and inviolable'; after seven months the Coal Committee concluded that it would be better to leave the miners and the owners to fight it out between themselves: the majority view was that to legislate against the coal owners would be to yield to force majeure.

* £46.4 million at today's values.

In November 1926, the miners, driven by poverty and hunger, returned to work. The coal owners won their victory: they returned to less pay and longer hours. The strike had cost the Treasury £30 million; Britain's coal exports for the year 1926 were a paltry 26 million tons.

It could have been so different. When the Prime Minister opened the Emergency Debate at the start of the General Strike, he had begun his speech with a reprimand to the managers of the coal industry: 'The whole machinery requires in my view a radical overhauling. I think that when we are in a position to deal with these matters in a calmer atmosphere, that must be one of the first subjects to which we devote ourselves.' His criticism was echoed by the Leaders of the Opposition. 'If wages are depressed, it is not the fault of those who are working in the mines,' said Lloyd George, 'it is something which is inherently wrong in the whole of the industry. That is accepted by the Government today. It was accepted by the previous Government, and it has been accepted by three inquiries.'

The industry had not, as Churchill had urged the coal owners, been 'successfully managed'. It was inefficient and antiquated; the lack of investment, the taking of quick profits, the labyrinthine wage and price structures, the appalling labour relations and the poor safety conditions at many pits had all contributed to its decline.

The coal owners' persistent summoning of the demons of revolution in the years after the First World War masked their refusal to put their own house in order, just as it masked the acute distress in the mining districts during the months of the coal strike.

As Lloyd George pointed out in the Emergency Debate, three Government inquiries had been commissioned into the state of the coal industry: the Sankey Inquiry, by his Government in 1919, and the Macmillan and Samuel inquiries commissioned under Labour and Conservative Governments in 1924 and 1925. Each had concluded that the restructuring and reorganization of the coal industry was a national imperative. Each had called on the Government of the day to direct the brains of the nation to draft legislation to place the coal industry on a secure footing. Each had pointed a finger at the coal owners, judging that they were largely to blame. And all had failed to deliver. Extraordinarily, given that coal was Britain's biggest industry on which her balance of payments depended, successive Governments – Liberal, Labour and Tory – had balked at forcing the coal owners to reform. The misguided and obsessive preoccupation with the war between the classes meant that, for all political parties during the 1920s and early 1930s, the defence of the coal owners' interests became synonymous with the defence of the realm.

In 1924, Arthur Eaglestone, the miner at Billy Fitzwilliam's New Stubbin pit, wrote an article for the *Adelphi* magazine. It was a bitter polemic, written at the time of the French occupation of the Ruhr when the British coal industry was experiencing a brief boom. He railed against what he perceived to be the class-prejudiced characterization of the miners in the tabloid press:

'Well?', it was entitled.

There are one and a quarter millions of us. What are you going to do about it? We are human as yourselves. 'If you prick us, do we not bleed? If you tickle us, do we not laugh? If you poison us, do we not die? And if you wrong us, do we not revenge?' Who are you, reader of these lines? And what your information? Are we still the worshippers of whippets? – hoary wife beaters? – the drinking den loungers? – the rapacious condottiere of the Picture Press? Do you remember our President's cloth cap, and hold it against us? Or that, earning fabulously, we squandered our wealth in riotous living, in grand pianos and chinchilla furs? Thus the daily, thus the Sunday Press!!! . . .

But there is a daily round which still remains curiously unreported. Split thumbs are not romantic things. Chronic rupture offers small delight even to the reading public. A bursted eye is a little boring – (you will readily understand that I am excluding the recipient?) A crushed foot? Any damn fool can crush his foot! And when the collier, emerging into God's own sunshine, finds that his eyes are streaming tears, and that his eye lids are uncontrollably fluttering – well, it's only nystagmus! And doesn't he get 'compo' dammit?

Well then . . .

'What are you going to do about it?' The answer to Eaglestone's question was, absolutely nothing. No steps were taken in the ten years after the General Strike to restructure the coal industry or to improve working conditions.

It was a catastrophic failure of government, one that would have tragic consequences for the miners. In the decade after the General Strike, conditions in the coalfields steadily worsened as lower wages and longer hours combined with unemployment to create widespread hardship. By 1931, 432,000 miners – 41.6 per cent of the workforce – were unemployed. The owners had the whiphand and kept it; the global slump that followed the 1929 Wall Street Crash, in combination with the wage cuts they had imposed, depressed trade in the coal regions, creating a pool of unemployed labour that ensured wages remained low. The miners' defeat in the 1926 coal strike determined that it was they who paid the price of Britain's economic ills. 'Through forces utterly beyond their individual control,' wrote the novelist John Galsworthy of their predicament in the early 1930s, 'a heart-breaking process is going on among a million in one of the best classes of our people . . . idle, hopeless and increasingly destitute.'

In the end, the owners' victory destroyed them. 'We never forgot 1926. The wicked 30s came after,' a miner from Sheffield recalled. 'Them as went through them, they'll never forget them days. They were hard times. We were on the poverty line.'

It would be more than a decade before power passed into the hands of the miners' representatives. When it did, Wentworth House would become a target for their revenge.

26

It was four years later, mid-April 1930. The senior members of the Fitzwilliam family were gathered in the private chapel at Wentworth, a square, simply decorated room, fitted out in oak. Its centrepiece was a large bronze eighteenth-century chandelier; oil paintings of the Twelve Apostles hung above the oak quarter-panelling on the plain white walls. Sunlight streamed through the spun glass in the Venetian window behind the altar, the light refracting in luminous circles on to the faces of the servants seated in the pews.

Morning Prayers at Wentworth were always well attended. The pews for the household staff were unusually arranged: inlaid into the oak panelling, they ran in a single row around the walls of the chapel, framing the chequered marble floor. This exceptional layout had been purposefully designed: it offered the servants, seated sideways to the altar, a clear view of the family seated above them in the raised gallery that faced the transept. 'Morning Prayers were a chance to get a good look at them,' May Bailey, the scullery maid, recalled. 'When we were working in the house, we didn't see much of the family. We were below stairs. They were up in the heights. If they passed you anywhere, you always stood. You never moved. You just stood with your eyes cast down at the floor. At Prayers, we tried not to stare but we used to like looking at them. It were nice to see them. They seemed such a happy family. We'd think of our lives compared to theirs and of course naturally we used to think, Oh, I wish it were me.'

Besides the junior staff, the senior members of the household were also present; Alex Third, the dour head gardener who had won a DSO in the Great War; Mrs Lloyd, the housekeeper, who was known among her charges – the housemaids and undermaids – to be vicious with her tongue, and Jack May, the butler. As ever, he was immaculately turned out. 'By golly, he always looked a treat,' his son Bert recalled. 'When he polished his shoes, he used to polish the instep. Me mother always used to say, "When your Dad's cleaned me shoes, it'll last me a month." I tell you something else about Father. When he put his boots on, he used to put his foot up on a chair to lace them and the laces had to be flat – not just twisted and tied any old way – they had to be flat on the top.'

Spring had come early to Wentworth that year; in the gardens that stretched beyond the courtyard outside the chapel, the magnolias and rhododendrons were in full bloom. It had not lifted Billy Fitzwilliam's mood. The country was in the grip of the worst economic crisis in living memory: he had been forced to put both his pits on short-time.

Of far greater concern to him, though, was the behaviour of his son.

Peter was seated with his father. He had left Eton at seventeen. Some six months away from his twenty-first birthday, he was now an officer in the Scots Greys. The fat, unattractive little boy had grown into a lean and handsome young man, well over six feet tall. His eyes were hazel-coloured; his hair, worn slicked back from a pencil-straight side parting, a deep chestnut brown. The diffident, troubled expression that had haunted his face as a child was still evident in the heavy set of his brow. It conferred a smouldering appeal: he might easily have been mistaken for one of the matinee idols whose faces adorned the billboards outside the new picture palaces in the nearby towns.

Seated alongside each other, there was little resemblance between father and son – except in profile, in the gentle, aristocratic curve of the nose. Billy was almost fifty. In recent years he had gained weight. Flecks of grey tinged his side whiskers and his luxuriant Edwardian moustache; his hair had receded beyond the crown of his head and the chiselled features of his youth had become puffed and jowled. Physically, Peter had grown into the son that his father could at last be proud of; to Billy's delight, he had even developed a late but passionate interest in horses and hunting. Yet in every other respect, the boy was a source of grave anxiety to Billy.

The tension between them, a feature of his childhood, had continued. In recent years their relationship had been a stormy one, as Peter had persisted in defying him at every turn.

It was indeed a tense moment when, half-way through the Vicar's address, Peter stood up and left. His feet clattering on the oak floor, he strode up the steps to the door leading to Chapel Corridor – the family's private entrance from the house. Below, along the servants' pews, all eyes were raised as it slammed shut behind him.

It was not the first time Peter had walked out. Charles Booth, the steward's boy at Wentworth House, regularly attended Sunday Matins at the village church. 'I was a choir boy. We sat in the stalls opposite the Fitzwilliams' pew,' he remembered. 'Peter used to sit there and glower at us. Many a Sunday I've seen him get up and walk out half-way through. Browned off he was. Up he jumped and out he went. He didn't stand on ceremony the way his father did.'

From his early teens, Peter had rebelled against his parents' values and the lifestyle at Wentworth House. Shunning boys of his own social class, most days, during his school holidays from Eton, he would set off across the Park on his bicycle to the pit villages of Greaseborough and Rawmarsh, or to the farm labourers' cottages north of Wentworth along Burying Lane.

The villages hugged the boundaries of the Park wall. An almost seamless extension of it, the ranks of two-up, two-down cottages were built in the same coal-blackened yellow stone. Here, Peter sought refuge from the formality of life at home. 'He was a grand fellow, nothing stuck up about him, he was a real grand bloke,' Walker Scales, the butcher at Greaseborough, recalled. 'He were just the opposite to old Lordie, he were rough and ready. He were one of us.'

Walker first met Peter by the ponds at the bottom of the Park. 'There were five of us lads from the village – we were about fourteen or fifteen years old, I suppose – and we spotted him on his own. We were going to have a bit of fun. We were going to throw him in the dam. We went up to him, and he were straightforward with us, a good mixer, friendly like. And he said,

"Come on, let's all go swimming." It were a blisteringly hot day and it were against the Estate's rules to swim there. There were reeds under the water and the big house didn't want the young uns drowning. So in we went. Then we used to see him all the time. Played football together, knocked about the lanes. Went drinking with him. He were a down-to-earth young man.'

Peter also made friends among the young miners at his father's pits – boys in their mid-teens who were working as pony drivers underground. 'He were a friend of mine,' remembers Walt Hammond, a ninety-year-old miner who spent his working life at New Stubbin colliery. 'Everybody thought well of young Lordie. He were all right. Course we liked him! He were spending money on us!'

Most of the pit boys gave their wages to their mothers to ease the family budget. Swiftly, Peter gained a reputation among them – at his father's expense – as a latter-day Robin Hood. Every Sunday afternoon, as Walt described, he would take the New Stubbin junior football team to Bassindale's, the sweetshop at Wentworth, where Billy had an account. 'We could have whatever we wanted. To a certain degree, like. The shopkeeper would be in a right fluster. He used to say, "I can't serve you all at once, I'll take you one at a time." Course, everyone used to choose chocolate. They didn't get it much. Our mothers only gave us a ha'penny a week for spice [sweets].'

May Bailey, the scullery maid at Wentworth, also remembers Peter. 'He'd mix around. He'd go in't Rockingham Arms and he'd have a drink, have a chat, and he'd go to pits. If anything happened at pits he'd go, if someone was fast down pit, he'd go.'

Cycling around the pit villages on his own, Peter's accessibility and his genuine friendships with the miners were in pointed contrast to his father's patrician style. In the early 1930s, on the Sunday afternoons when Billy was at Wentworth, a feudal ritual was enacted. Riding in a pony and trap, with a servant or one of the senior household officials in tow, he toured his villages. 'Everyone used to come out in front of their houses. It would run like a ripple down the street,' Walker Scales recalled. 'You'd hear the cheering and shouts of "Quick, Old Lordie's coming" and you'd all run out to the porches. The men nipped their caps and everyone waved and cheered. There was an old joke that ran about. Anyone who wasn't seen to wave would be finished at the pit on Monday. Course they weren't.' A triumphal progress was Billy's chosen style: 'He never went anywhere on his own. He was always accompanied by someone from his retinue. Even when he went out riding, he'd have a groom with him to open and shut gates, or to knock on someone's door,' recalled Peter Diggle, whose uncle ran the Fitzwilliam estates.

'God lived in t' big house, didn't he? And when God came tot' village, you kowtowed,' said one old miner. Peter's friendships in the villages soon caused tongues to wag. As Walt remembers, the older generation were unsettled by what they regarded as his over-familiarity: it eroded the mystique and confused the old feudal rules. 'There were a lot of talk among some,' said Walt, 'they'd say Old Lordie were far out in front. Peter were too rough and ready.'

Billy was equally disapproving of his son's friendships with the miners' children. Realizing that it was more than just a passing phase, he put Peter on a tight rein. He reduced his allowance and ordered a block to be put on his account at the village shop. At home, increasingly, Peter's conduct became the subject of family rows. 'There was a boy up at the farm by the flour mill called Albert Sylvester,' remembered Bert May. 'We called him Cocky. Cocky Sylvester. He was a bit of a daredevil. I don't know what age Peter would have been when he met him, fifteen or sixteen, something like that. Well, they stuck like glue. They went everywhere together. One day, they were up at Wentworth House on the drive by the entrance to the Pillared Hall. There were two flights of stone steps there, the curving ones. Ay, there must be more than twenty steps. And young Lordie said to Cocky, "I bet you daren't ride down those steps on my bike." "I dare," he says. "Go on then. You can take it home with you if you do." And Cocky did. There was hell to pay. His father was furious. It were a brand-new bike that he'd been given for his birthday.'

The row over the bicycle was the first of many involving Cocky Sylvester.

The Sylvester family had come to Wentworth from the Potteries in the late 1870s when Cocky's grandfather had been hired as a stonemason to work on the building of the New Church, commissioned by the 6th Earl Fitzwilliam as a memorial to his father. Cocky, the son of a miner, had left school at fourteen. When he and Peter became friends he was working as a loader at Newton Chambers, the ironworks outside Sheffield. 'His Lordship regarded him as a bad influence,' Bert May remembered. 'Lord Milton was coming back to the house at night blind drunk. His Lordship thought it were Cocky who'd introduced him to drinking. After that, he forbade him to see him.' Ignoring his father's ban, in the evenings, Peter would sneak out of Wentworth and go round to Cocky's house in the village. 'My grandmother lived behind the shop on Main Street. My mother told me she used to get besides herself with worry over Lord Milton's friendship with my father,' David Sylvester recalled. 'He would be in and out of her house as if it were his own. He used to walk in through the back door. One of her jobs in the village was to lay out the bodies. They didn't use undertakers in those days. My uncle was a joiner and he made the coffins. When someone in the village passed away, he and his men would go and collect them and take them round to my grandmother's. She used to wash and prepare the bodies for burial. She'd put two old pennies on their eyes to close them before rigor mortis set in. Often as not there'd be a corpse on the kitchen table. She hated the idea of Lord Milton seeing these bodies – which he did because he'd just walk straight in through the back door. It worried her sick the way he'd turn up. My mother said she couldn't come to terms with the fact that it were him coming in. He were like royalty to her. It frightened her. She was a timid sort of woman. She knew that he was coming to her house without his father knowing. She thought it would get the family into trouble.'

Sitting round the kitchen table in the cramped cottage, Peter and Cocky planned their drinking expeditions. 'Lord Milton must have been kept on a tight financial stick by his father,' David Sylvester recalled. 'When he came round to my grandmother's she saw things that were hidden from the Earl. Whether he discovered,

I don't know. Peter would bring things – clothes and objects that he'd taken from the house. He and my father would take them to a pawn shop over Rotherham way. It paid for their drinking. Ay, pinching and pawning Lord Milton was.'

Over cups of tea and sandwiches, reluctantly supplied by a nervous Mrs Sylvester, Peter and Cocky would also plot the seduction of the local girls. Deliberately escaping the narrow confines of Wentworth, their elected hunting grounds were the rougher pit villages of Greaseborough, Rawmarsh and Netherhaugh.

'Ooh, Lord Milton were lovely,' May Bailey remembered. 'He were so handsome, lovely manners. All the girls wanted to go courting with him.'

Every Friday and Saturday night, rain or shine, a courting ritual, known locally as the 'bunny run', took place in the fields and lanes that linked the villages around Wentworth. 'I started down the mine when I was fourteen and I saved up till I was sixteen to buy my first made-to-measure suit,' Jim McGuinness, a miner from Elsecar, recalled. 'It were biscuity brown with a stripe and 26-inch bottoms and it cost me 39 shillings and sixpence. I couldn't keep it off. I used to wear it on the bunny run. You never took a girl out for a meal, or anything like that. There weren't restaurants or bars in them days. Not round here. All the lads and lasses used to meet in the lanes outside the village. We had a circuit. We'd walk to Hoyland and then up New Street across the fields round the top. You used to keep patrolling until you saw someone you liked. The good bunnies would run! There were that many of us – about a hundred or so. You had to be careful though. Some of the older ones in the village complained. They thought the kids were getting up to too much mischief. So the Police introduced on-the-spot fines. Me and the girl I was courting, we got stopped and it cost me 19 shillings – 9 shillings and sixpence each. I had to pay for her you see. I were only holding her hand! You couldn't kiss in public in them days, you could only hold hands. We'd walk round the fields and then you'd walk a girl home. It were lovely.'

There was one girl, Madge Green, the daughter of a horseman at New Stubbin pit, whom all the boys liked. 'She was a notable girl! The girl of the village!' said Walker Scales. 'She had lovely bubbly blonde hair. A bit of a girl, she was, a bit friendly to the lads!'

Madge lived at Netherhaugh in a small miner's cottage close to Cortworth Lodge, the gatehouse by the entrance to the track leading up to the Fitzwilliams' mausoleum, a splendid eighteenth-century building that stood on the crown of a hill in the Park. To make ends meet, Madge and her mother ran a shop in their front room, selling odds and ends: packets of biscuits, cigarettes, boxes of matches. 'All the boys in the village knew Madge,' May remembered. 'She were full of life. I wouldn't have been surprised at any boy taking Madge on, because she would have gone with them. Her father died when she was young. She had such a lonely life with her mother, once she got out, she sort of let herself go a bit. This cottage where they lived, a little bit further down you came to Cortworth Lane. Well, the lads used to play football there. She'd happen go down and have a kick of the ball with them. They all knew her. "Come on, Madge," they'd shout. "Where are you going, Madge? Come on over here." She were liked, she were great fun.'

To May's surprise, when Peter was seventeen, he started taking Madge out. 'There was another girl in Greaseborough, her mother kept the "Beer Off". You know, the place where the women went to get a jug of beer to take home. Doris Hare was her name. I always thought she'd be the one he'd pick because she was smarter than Madge. She had a bit more money, her mother had a proper business.'

May was living at home with her parents in Greaseborough at the time. She had left her job as scullery maid at Wentworth House for better-paid work as housekeeper to a local estate agent. Twice a week, she went to night school to learn millinery, hoping to achieve her dream of leaving service and getting a job at a hat shop in Rotherham. Madge Green was in her evening class. 'Lord Milton used to fetch her. He had a little green car with a hood and he used to be blowing the hooter outside night school. And he'd call out, "Madge" and they'd fly away. We were all jealous.

If I'd had the chance I should have gone off in the car with him. Why not? Let's face it, he were a Fitzwilliam. We all looked up to the Fitzwilliams, didn't we? I mean, they were the be all and end all, weren't they?'

It was not long before Madge became pregnant. 'One day, suddenly, Madge and her mother disappeared. The little house and shop were shut up. They'd flit. It were all done so quickly. They were there one minute, the next minute they'd gone.' Their disappearance, as May remembered, was the talk of the village. 'They'd been sent down, hadn't they? It would be to keep people quiet. But everybody knew! We all knew she were expecting, that's why they'd left. There were nasty talk. People in the village said, 'She's done what she shouldn't have done and it's come home to her and it'll have learnt her a lesson.' 'She's asked for it,' they said. Well, she hadn't asked for it. What would she be, fifteen or sixteen? That would have been her age.'

May's upbringing was typical of other girls in the villages around Wentworth in the 1920s. 'I didn't know about sex when I was fifteen. It were never discussed, not even with the girls at school. When I started to be unwell, when I had me curses, I didn't know what it was. My mother had never told us. Never told us what to expect. I said to my Mother I'd got this blood. "Well, you'll be like that every month," she said. And I says, "Why?" And of course I wanted to know this and that and everything else. All she said was, "While ever you've got your curses you're alreet." She took some old shirting belonging to the boys, and cut me a square. "Now then," she said, "I'll give you plenty of old material every month. You'll have to soak 'em and wash 'em. And that's it." When I were older, she'd say to us, "If you bring any trouble home, it'll be the workhouse for you." You were threatened with that. After I started courting, it was, "You can't come in late. You've got to be in for such a time. Who have you been with? I've told you not to go with them." You had it drilled into you. You were frightened to bring any trouble home.'

Pregnancy before marriage, particularly in the close-knit and conservative 'family pits' like the Fitzwilliams', was rare. 'I only knew one other girl, apart from Madge, that fell,' May recalled. 'She lived down Scrooby Street. I remember her being pregnant. She were only young and she said she didn't know. She told her Mother that she didn't know they were doing anything wrong. The doctor said to her, "Well, where did it happen?" She said, "Well, up against Grayson's Gate." It were a farm gate at the top of the village. Later on – it weren't very nice – it became a code word round the village. People talked about having a bit of "Grayson's Gate". The boy that was going with her, he said he would marry her. And they did. They got married. Poor old Madge. She were never going to marry Lordie. I felt sorry for her because there were only her and her mother, things were hard enough in them times. Nobody thought less of Lordie because he'd got a girl into trouble. Oh no, no, NO! They didn't blame him for it. They all liked him. They said he were a naughty boy. But a grand lad. He didn't only have Madge though, there were quite a few. People said she weren't the only one he got into trouble. There'll be a few more. I know that.'

In the space of three years, Peter had three sons by girls from his father's pit villages. Billy's Heads of Department – the men who ran the Estate and who were privy to the family's most secret business – were entrusted with the delicate task of providing for them. In Madge's case, money was sent via an intermediary: 'The Vicar at Greaseborough, old Brotbeard, let it slip out somewhere along the line that Earl Fitzwilliam paid him money every month,' May remembered. 'He used to send it on to Madge and her baby. They were living down South somewhere.' While the children were financially taken care of, the human cost was high; two of the girls were forced into loveless marriages by their families – compelled to marry husbands who had been procured for them by the Estate.

It is doubtful whether Peter ever had any contact with his sons. To this day, one of them, a man now in his mid seventies, does not know that he is the son of the 8th Earl Fitzwilliam, as Peter became. Such was the shame in his family, he was never told. His mother's first cousin, an elderly lady in her late eighties still living in Greaseborough, remembered their shame. 'When — got into trouble it were the talk of the place. It were there for the whole world to see. It upset my aunt and uncle because they were very much Lord Fitzwilliam's tenants. My uncle was a miner and they lived in one of their cottages. They were really ashamed. We were the hoi polloi, weren't we, compared to the Fitzwilliams. It was the class system, wasn't it? Me grandfather worked for His Lordship as foreman saddler in Elsecar pit. He used to earn coppers going down to the ponds in the Park to help Their Ladyships put their skates on. I remember him telling me a story about one of His Lordship's hunters. It went into the pond and got stuck, frozen in. They covered over its carcass with a tarpaulin. They couldn't move it, while the ice was there, so they covered it and it was like a settee. The ladies of the house sat on the dead horse to put their skates on. Me grandfather were a miner, his son were a miner and His Lordship were their boss. It was all "Yes, Mi' Lord, no, Mi' Lord." When Her Ladyship came round they used to curtsey and all that. My aunt and uncle were ashamed their daughter was such a loose-living girl and ashamed because she had swum out of her sea.'

In the course of his late teens Peter had crossed every class barrier: upon his coming of age, at his father's insistence, those barriers were to be rigidly maintained.

27

'Dear Jim,' Billy addressed his agent, Colonel Landon, in a letter written on 8 May 1931:

> Peter's 21st birthday is on the 31st Dec next and the occasion should, we feel, be appropriately celebrated amongst the tenantry and workpeople connected with our family and the estates in England and Ireland.
>
> Lady Fitzwilliam and I want the help and advice in this matter of our friends, and we shall be very grateful for your views and assistance. Will you think things over and jot down what you suggest might be most suitable in the way of entertainment to mark the event . . .
>
> We will then meet and talk over the recommendations with a view to a programme being prepared for fuller consideration by Her Ladyship and myself . . .
>
> I am, as always, Yours very sincerely, Fitzwilliam.

Peter's twenty-first birthday party was set to become the next round in the clash between father and son. 'It were his father who were pushing for it,' Walt Hammond, Peter's friend from the Rawmarsh football team, recalled. 'Lord Milton were a pubs man. Low-key like. He didn't want a fancy party. It weren't his style.'

Billy wanted to celebrate the birthday on a grand Edwardian scale. Traditionally, the coming of age of a Fitzwilliam heir had been a landmark in the life of the community as much as it had been in the life of the eldest son: he intended the party to serve as a reminder to Peter of his duties and obligations as the future Earl.

On this occasion, Peter had no choice but to demur. He was to be given no say in the planning of the party: instead, the precise form of the entertainments was to be decided by Committee.

★

10 June was a muggy summer's day in London: the skies were overcast and a persistent light drizzle fell.

The members of the Milton Committee, the men appointed by Billy to organize Peter's birthday celebrations, caught the early morning train from Yorkshire. They were the heads of department from the Fitzwilliam estates, among them the managers from the two collieries and the chemical works and the land agents and comptrollers from Wentworth and from the family's subsidiary estates in the North and East Ridings. In their mid-fifties and upwards, they were mostly ex-military: men with impeccable war records, they carried the rank of Captain or above.

Their newspaper of choice on the journey down was *The Times*. Aside from the raising of the German Fleet, scuttled at Scapa Flow in 1919, the news that morning was unremarkable. The previous evening, the Third Court of the Season had been held at Buckingham Palace: a page and a half of the broadsheet was devoted to detailed descriptions of the outfits worn by each of the 200 debutantes and their chaperones as they had been presented to the King and Queen. The Court Circular, taking up three column inches, carried the usual announcements: 'The Hon. Mrs Sidebottom has arrived at Claridges from the country'; 'Lord Sydenham apologizes for his failure to answer correspondence owing to ill health'; 'The Misses Dunns, accompanied by Lady Paget, have taken a house at South Place for the Season'. Following the presentations at court, there was a momentary lull in the social calendar: Ascot was over, the Lawn Tennis Championships at Wimbledon were yet to begin. On a rainy afternoon, the picture houses at least offered some entertainment. *Dance, Fools, Dance* was playing all over London: the hit of the summer, Joan Crawford, according to the reviewers, 'looking more beautiful than ever in her most exciting talkie to date'.

A close scrutiny of the unusual number of both small and large advertisements told a hidden story. All kinds of goods and services were being offered at knockdown prices: in Hyde Park, a nine-bedroom Regency house was up for sale at the 'sacrificial price' of £3,400; at Harrods, under the blazing headline 'Reduce Housekeeping Costs', 'best Norfolk Ducklings' had been slashed from 10 shillings to 5 shillings each, and a bundle of fifty spears of asparagus reduced to a shilling; the White Star Shipping Line was offering an eighteen-day cruise around the islands of Scandinavia 'from £23'. Britain was feeling the pinch: the global slump that had followed the Wall Street Crash of 1929 had sent the economy into a spiral. Across the country, almost 3 million people were unemployed.

The Milton Committee convened punctually at eleven o'clock at 10 Grosvenor Street in Mayfair, the London headquarters of the Fitzwilliam empire. Lavish celebrations – not economies – and Edwardian-style class gradations would dominate the discussion: a minimum of 15,000 people were to be invited to Peter's coming-of-age celebrations, the style of entertainment offered to each guest to be determined by their social rank. 'There are,' Captain North informed the assembled men, 'various classes of persons to be catered for:

Classes 1 and 2: the Officials, Heads of Department and Household staff, numbering 302
Classes 3 and 4: the Estate employees and the Colliery and Chemical Works employees (other than Officials), numbering 3,990
Class 5: the farm tenants, 261
Class 6: the cottage and other tenants, 1,268
Class 7: the leaseholders, of which there are 1,300

Lastly, in two further classes of their own, named rather than numbered, were the local gentry and the 'county' – the Yorkshire aristocracy.

Only Classes 1 and 2 and Classes 3, 4 and 6 could be expected to rub shoulders together: according to social convention – and to avoid giving offence – separate entertainment was to be arranged for the remaining classes.

Class segregation, as one villager recalled, had always been imposed at Wentworth. 'Once a year you went up to the Big

House to pay your rent. You were given a meal in return. The different classes had different rent days; they got different meals and ate in different rooms. You were either a farm tenant, a house tenant or a cottage tenant. House tenants regarded themselves as better than the other tenants. They were offered wine. The farm tenants got whisky and the cottagers had beer. Farm and house tenants ate off china plates in the Upper Servants rooms. The cottagers were fed in the Lower Servants Hall. At cottage grade you ate off a wooden plate made of elm. It had the initials "EFW", standing for Earl Fitzwilliam, burnt on to it and a number. It came – and stayed – with your cottage. You brought it out once a year to take up to the big house for rent days. It was double-sided with a flat top and a small edge to it. One side was for your main course and then you turned it over and it was dished for a pudding on the other side. EFW was stamped on everything. It was even on the snow shovels. Every cottage tenant was given a shovel. It hung on a peg outside their back doors. They had obligations to "Lordie" that the farm and house tenants didn't. There were four acres of roof on top of Wentworth House, and flat at that. At first snowflake, the cottagers were expected to report to the house with their shovels. They had to go up to the roof and shovel the snow as fast as it fell.'

The Milton Committee had been assembled for each of its members to submit his proposal for the birthday celebrations. Captain North began by suggesting a total of six separate parties, to take place over the course of a week. On the night of the birthday he proposed a ball in the Marble Salon at Wentworth for the household staff and senior Estate officials, to be preceded during the day by a funfair in the Park for the cottage tenants, miners and factory hands. To avoid the risk of the classes mingling, he suggested that a dance floor be laid out in the Riding School in order that stragglers from the party in the Park could continue to enjoy themselves in the evening while the ball for Classes 1 and 2 was going on in the main house. The leaseholders, he argued, should have a separate garden party and the farm tenants, a separate ball of their own. In addition, he proposed two further balls: a 'Gentry's Ball' and a 'Grand Ball' for the 'county'.

Admiral Hugh Douglas, Billy's elderly cousin and the former agent at Wentworth, proposed that the miners and factory hands should be treated to 'Meat Teas' and a 'Concert and Social' in heated marquees, as well as a funfair. For the 'home' circle – the Estate and household staff – he proposed a buffet supper in the Pillared Hall, after which the 'stretchers for drunks' would be called. Come the evening, he thought it prudent that the lower classes should be given the chance to sober up: 'sandwiches and temperance drinks' only were to be on offer in the Riding School. He was also in favour of staging character-building games: 'Tugs of War between townships – 10 a side – each member of the winning team to be presented with an engraved pewter pot.'

In 1931, even among the Fitzwilliams' aristocratic contemporaries, there were few families in England who could afford to host a party on the scale that was being proposed.

'*Tout passe, tout casse, tout lasse*,' the Duke of Portland mourned in the prologue to his memoirs, written in 1937. Cushioned by his huge revenues from coal, comfortable in the turreted Welbeck Abbey, the Duke observed the unravelling of the England he had known. 'Hardly anything in life is the same today as it was in my youth,' he wrote.

> Then there was a happy sense of stability and security; but now, it seems to me, there is little or none of either . . . Large country estates, which had been in the possession of the same families for years without number, have been and are still being broken up, and the houses attached to them sold to individuals, most of whom have had little or no connection with the land.

The Duke was writing of a class in crisis: in the years immediately before and after the Great War a quarter of England, some 6–8 million acres, had changed hands, a transfer of territorial holdings unrivalled since the Norman Conquest and the Dissolution of the Monasteries. The assets of the aristocracy – land and the iconic seat of their power, the grand country house – were being stripped.

'A silent revolution', as Edward Wood, the heir to Lord Halifax, told the House of Commons in 1924. was in progress: 'We are, unless I mistake it,' he continued, 'witnessing in England the gradual disappearance of the old landed classes.'

Five years later, the decimation of stock market portfolios in the Wall Street Crash had served to make matters worse. As estate after estate tumbled on to the market, the glut of houses meant that many were impossible to sell. One, Sudbrooke Holme in Lincolnshire, was to be purchased by a film company to be burnt to the ground 'in order to produce a spectacular scene on the cinematograph'. Members of the aristocracy conjured their own fantastical visions: 'If I close my eyes for a moment, I can see before me a great castle now in the hands of caretakers, its reception rooms are shrouded in Holland coverings, its servants' quarters given over to dust and cobwebs,' imagined Lady Warwick, the former mistress of Edward VII, writing in 1931. 'Then my thoughts turn to a certain house in Park Lane, and I see the phantom of a dead woman, sitting solitary at a great table in a vast dining-room, with phantom flunkeys in attendance.'

A shortage of servants and the tragic slaughter of the scions of the aristocracy in the First World War are among the nostalgic and sentimental reasons offered for the dissolution of Britain's stately homes. But prior to the Wall Street Crash, the primary cause of the 'decay' had been more prosaic; the English aristocracy had been undone by the refrigerator and the steam engine.

In the last quarter of the nineteenth century the cultivation of the prairies and grasslands of the New World, combined with the development of fast purpose-built refrigerator ships and cheaper rail transport, led to a global glut of grain products and chilled meats, causing the prices of British agricultural produce to plummet. In 1870, Britain had been a thriving agricultural nation, virtually self-sufficient in what she produced and consumed. By the inter-war years, she had become heavily dependent on imported foodstuffs of all kinds.

For the landed classes with their broad acres, the consequences of the agricultural depression which bit deep over fifty long years were catastrophic. During the period, the continuous contraction in the amount of land under cultivation sent rental values and the profit on yields into freefall. Many estates were burdened by mortgages secured in the boom years of the 1860s; the resultant collapse in the capital values of land pushed the landowners into negative equity. Rising interest rates, the fixed costs of estate maintenance, combined with traditional commitments – the jointures, settlements and annuities that the aristocratic tenant-for-life was bound to pay out to family members and retainers – meant that estates were saddled with outgoings that could not be reduced. After 1906, straitened landowners found themselves politically assaulted as a succession of governments, with increasing severity, imposed taxes on both their capital and their income: in the years between 1914 and 1930, death duties, for example, rose from 15 per cent to 50 per cent.

A collective psyche had also played its part in the great sell-off: the fear that the future of property was politically vulnerable coalesced with the belief that a bigger and – crucially – a safer return could be secured by stripping landed assets to invest the proceeds elsewhere. Equities and overseas investments were the preferred choice: the former was liquid, the latter free of British taxes. The Wall Street Crash, followed as it was by the collapse of the world's stock markets, made a mockery of the putative foresight: family heirlooms flooded the sale rooms as those hit hardest struggled to raise cash.

But it was the divestments of the super-rich that most shocked their contemporaries, nowhere more evident than in the heart of the capital itself. One by one the London palaces of Imperial Britain's wealthiest families were abandoned, surrendered to the auctioneer, to tenants or to demolition crews. In the early 1930s, Lord Harewood, the Duke of Sutherland, Lord Curzon, Lord Derby and Lord Brooke put their London houses on the market. The mansions belonging to the Duke of Devonshire, Lord Lansdowne and Lord Dorchester had already gone; those of the Duke of Buccleuch, the Duke of Norfolk and the Duke of Westminster would follow shortly. 'Nearly all these great houses were thrown open every season for large social gatherings,' the Duke of Portland recalled of the years before the Great War.

> Now, except four, they are closed, and the pictures and other works of art which they contained have, generally speaking, been scattered all over the world. At present, only Londonderry House, Apsley House, Bridgewater House and Holland House remain as private residences . . . Vast and, in my opinion, hideous buildings have taken the place of Grosvenor House and Lansdowne House, and another, if possible more hideous still, that of the beautiful Dorchester House; while from a social point of view, restaurants, cabarets and night-clubs have risen in their place. Sic transit gloria mundi – a glory which, in this instance, I fear can never be revived.

Lady Frances Warwick, a convert to socialism, chastised her aristocratic contemporaries for failing to face up to the fact that the world had defeated them. 'Times change, and we must learn to change with them. It is in this clinging to what is dead, either in practice, thought, or custom, that the real danger lies,' she wrote. 'The Stately Homes of England have had their selfish day. Nothing could be better than that they should make atonement, in emptiness and disrepair, in the hope that a nobler future awaits them.'

In the midst of this unravelling, the lifestyle at Billy Fitzwilliam's various residences astounded his guests. Margaret Sweeny, the future Duchess of Argyll, who stayed at Wentworth in the early 1930s, marvelled at the 'magnificent reception rooms', the 'liveried footman standing behind each chair', the 'scene of unforgettale splendour'.

Far from breaking up his estates, Billy had bought new ones. The fifty-room Grosvenor Square townhouse was still the family's London residence: in addition, in the decade after the First World War, he had acquired two other houses in Mayfair.

In the spring of 1931, the Fitzwilliams' glory at least was undiminished.

★

On 10 June, at the end of the morning, the Milton Committee adjourned to Claridges, where a private dining room had been booked for lunch. Over Grapefruit Supreme, Truite Saumonée Carmen, Volaille Grillé Diable, Haricots Verts à L'Isigny, Pommes à La Fourchette, Fraises Parisienne and Pâtisserie, they continued to discuss the proposals for the party to celebrate Peter's twenty-first. They had divided into two camps: those who felt the celebrations should be of benefit to the community, or at least bind it closer together, and those who wanted to celebrate the birthday in high Edwardian style.

The old world was opposed to the new, the heads of department representing the Fitzwilliams' landed estates siding against the managers of their industrial interests. Mr Danby, the manager at New Stubbin colliery, voiced his frustration:

> I want to suggest, instead of attempting to give a party for the four thousand people employed at the collieries, together with their wives and children, which in itself seems to me rather an impossible job in midwinter, that the Elsecar Market Hall should be converted into a really nice concert hall with rooms suitable for small social events and that it should be called the 'Peter Milton Hall' or the 'Lord Milton Hall' and that a Sports Ground be donated to New Stubbin colliery and that we put up a small pavilion, and make a cricket and football pitch.

Mr Hebden, the manager of the South Yorkshire Chemical Works, agreed. Putting in a bid for his own factory, he further suggested that 'to permanently mark the occasion, the Company should build a suitable canteen for the use of the Staff and work-people'. He also proposed that an extra day's pay be given to all the Fitzwilliams' employees.

Alfred Wright, the manager of Billy's London office, was out on a limb on his own. Reading his eccentric proposal to the Committee, he suggested setting up a trust fund to distribute prizes of £25 each to thirty-two men and women. The men's prizes were to be awarded for 'Long Service' – 'to those who could demonstrate good behaviour towards his employer and the same quality towards his fellow workmen' – and 'Good Tenantry' – 'for the best-kept farms including hedges, ditches, gates and husbandry'. The women's prizes were to be allocated for the

> four best-kept homes, the four best examples of embroidery, needlework, or other handicraft, and for the four women whose families can show the best records in any of the following directions: (a) the greatest number of children with the greatest aggregate ages who have the greatest aggregate period to their credit of good honest work to the satisfaction of their employers (2 prizes); (b) the greatest scholastic or musical or artistic achievements (2 prizes); (c) outstanding nursing or secretarial service (2 prizes); (d) the four women who can prove to the satisfaction of the judges and jury that they have never quarrelled with their husbands and have consistently shown the best good temper towards and camaraderie with their husbands; the judges to consist of two ladies and a gentleman and the jury of three ladies and three gentlemen, a Counsel to be employed on both sides to cross examine the applicant. This might be productive of considerable amusement.

After considering the Milton Committee's recommendations, Billy concluded that Peter's birthday should be celebrated over the course of a week. Beginning with a ball at Wentworth House for the Yorkshire gentry, a further two balls were to be held, one for the farm tenants, the other for the Fitzwilliams' 4,200 employees. The biggest party of the week was to be on the day of the birthday itself; scheduled to take place in the Park at Wentworth, over 15,000 invitations were to be sent out. There was to be a fairground in Menagerie Paddock and scores of buffet tents to feed the guests. Three thousand bottles of Audit Ale – beer that had been specially brewed and laid down in the vast cellars at Wentworth at Peter's birth – were to be distributed, and an ox roasted. Throughout the week, in the afternoons, cinema shows and concert troupes were to be staged for the children at the Fitzwilliams' two collieries and at the chemical works. All employees were to be given a day's holiday and a day's pay. Lastly, to commemorate the coming of age, New Stubbin colliery would receive a sports ground and a cricket pavilion; Elsecar colliery, a new market hall; and the chemical works, a new canteen.

The cost of the celebrations was estimated by the Committee to run to tens of thousands of pounds. Privately, a number of its members believed the entertainments to be in poor taste. The slump that had followed the 1929 Wall Street Crash had decimated the British coal industry. In the summer of 1931 almost half the miners in the neighbourhood of Wentworth were unemployed.

28

The train bore me away, through the monstrous scenery of slag-heaps, chimneys, piled scrap-iron, foul canals, paths of cindery mud criss-crossed by the prints of clogs. This was March, but the weather had been horribly cold and everywhere there were mounds of blackened snow. As we moved slowly through the outskirts of the town we passed row after row of little grey slum houses running at right angles to the embankment. At the back of one of the houses a young woman was kneeling on the stones, poking a stick up the leaden waste-pipe which ran from the sink inside and which I suppose was blocked. I had time to see everything about her – her sacking apron, her clumsy clogs, her arms reddened by the cold. She looked up as the train passed, and I was almost near enough to catch her eye. She had a round pale face, the usual exhausted face of the slum girl who is twenty-five and looks forty, thanks to miscarriages and drudgery; and it wore, for the second in which I saw it, the most desolate, hopeless expression I have ever seen. It struck me then that we are mistaken when we say that 'It isn't the same for them as it would be for us', and that people bred in the slums can imagine nothing but the slums. For what I saw in her face was not the ignorant suffering of an animal. She knew well enough what was happening to her – understood as well as I did how dreadful a destiny it was to be kneeling there in the bitter cold, on the slimy stones of a slum backyard, poking a stick up a foul drain-pipe.

George Orwell, *The Road to Wigan Pier*

At the height of the Great Depression, George Orwell left his part-time job as a bookshop assistant in London to tour the industrial slums of the North. After spending some weeks in the mill towns of Lancashire, he caught a train to Barnsley. Orwell had been commissioned by the publisher Victor Gollancz to write an account of working-class life in the areas of high unemployment. Barnsley, barely four miles from Wentworth, was one of them. 'It is a kind of duty to see and smell such places now and again,' he noted, 'especially smell them, lest you forget that they exist; though perhaps it is better not to stay there for too long.'

Over the course of a month spent travelling around the South Yorkshire coalfield, Orwell recorded the living conditions in the mining communities. *The Road to Wigan Pier* provides a graphic account of the hardship in the neighbourhood of Wentworth. 'I have inspected great numbers of houses in various mining towns and villages and made notes on their essential points,' he wrote. 'Here are one or two from Barnsley':

House in Wortley Street. Two up, one down. Living room 12 ft by 10 ft. Sink and copper in living room, coal hole under stairs. Sink worn almost flat and constantly overflowing. Walls not too sound. Penny in slot, gas-light. House very dark and gas-light estimated at 4d. a day. Upstairs rooms are really one large room partitioned into two. Walls very bad – wall of back room cracked right through. Window-frames coming to pieces and have to be stuffed with wood. Rain comes through in several places. Sewer runs under house and stinks in summer but Corporation 'says they can't do nowt'. Six people in house, two adults and four children, the eldest aged fifteen. Youngest but one attending hospital – tuberculosis suspected. House infested by bugs. Rent 5sh. 3d., including rates.

House in Peel Street. Back to back, two up, two down and large cellar. Living-room 10 ft square with copper and sink. The other downstairs room the same size, probably intended as parlour but used as bedroom. Upstairs rooms the same size as those below. Living room very dark. Gas-light estimated at 4½d. a day. Distance to lavatory 70 yards. Four beds in house for eight people – two old parents, two adult girls (the eldest aged twenty-seven), one young man and three children. Parents have one bed, eldest son another, and remaining five people share the other two. Bugs very bad – 'You can't keep 'em down when it's 'ot'. Indescribable squalor in downstairs room and smell upstairs almost unbearable. Rent 5sh 7½d., including rates.

Studying house after house from top to bottom, Orwell saw the true extent of hardship – a level of poverty he suspected that many families were at pains to conceal from their own communities.

It is in the rooms upstairs that the gauntness of poverty really discloses itself. Whether this is because pride makes people cling to their living-room furniture to the last, or because bedding is more pawnable, I do not know, but certainly many of the bedrooms I saw were fearful places. Among people who have been unemployed for several years continuously I should say it is the exception to have anything like a full set of bedclothes. Often there is nothing that can be properly called bedclothes at all – just a heap of old overcoats and miscellaneous rags on a rusty iron bedstead. In this way overcrowding is aggravated. One family of four persons that I knew, a father and mother and two children, possessed two beds but could only use one of them because they had not enough bedding for the other.

Bedding was unaffordable on the average dole allowance of 32 shillings* a week. One miner, who had a wife and two children – one aged two and the other ten months – gave Orwell a precise breakdown of the family's weekly expenditure.

	s. d.
Rent	9 0½
Clothing Club	3 0
Coal	2 0
Gas	1 3
Milk	0 10½
Union Fees	0 3
Insurance (on the children)	0 2
Meat	2 6
Flour (2 stone)	3 4
Yeast	0 4
Potatoes	1 0

* £72 at today's values.

Dripping	0 10
Margarine	0 10
Bacon	1 2
Sugar	1 9
Tea	1 9
Jam	0 7½
Peas and cabbage	0 6
Carrots and onions	0 4
Quaker Oats	0 4½
Soap, powders, blue etc	0 10
Total	£1 12 0

Malnutrition, caused by a diet consisting primarily of fats, carbohydrates and sugar, was rife in the pit villages around Barnsley. 'You see very few people with natural teeth at all,' Orwell observed,

> apart from the children; and even the children's teeth have a frail bluish appearance which means, I suppose, calcium deficiency. Several dentists have told me that in industrial districts a person over thirty with any of his or her own teeth is coming to be an abnormality . . . In one house where I stayed there were, apart from myself, five people, the oldest being forty-three and the youngest a boy of fifteen. Of these the boy was the only one who possessed a single tooth of his own, and his teeth were obviously not going to last long.

In the years between 1930 and 1936 unemployment levels in the South Yorkshire coalfield did not fall below 45 per cent. By the summer of 1931, the Fitzwilliams' miners joined the shocking percentage claiming the dole.

'They were rough times,' Ralph Boreham, a miner's son from Elsecar pit, remembered. 'We were lucky. We weren't a big family, there were just me and me brother. "Now then, boy, what are you going to do when you leave school?" the Headmaster used to ask us. "We're going to pit, Sir." "'Cos tha' strong in the arm and weak in the head," he'd say. You were lucky to get a job in them days. When I were at school there were some kids, their mothers had put their names down at the pit for a job before they were ten years old. There was one at Platts Common, up the road from us. They shut it down. Thirteen hundred men thrown out of work. The council turned them out of their homes. They couldn't pay their rent. They had to emigrate. They went to Doncaster. It were a bad job. Elsecar pit were working one week on, one week off. The off week you were on the dole. It were sad. All the men wanted to work. Earl Fitzwilliam used to give the miners anything he didn't want, to get shot of it. The family next door to us got a harpsichord. Neighbours said, "It'll be growing grass out of it." Pitmen didn't go shouting and picketing. They just went gardening instead, to keep themselves. Keep their family. Everybody had a garden then. You lived off it. Mind, there was some as still thought they were a cut above the rest. One miner, they called him "Tommy Two Eggs" 'cos his wife 'ud always brag, "He has two eggs every morning before he goes down t' pit." Course he never did, two eggs were unheard of. There were a market on Hoyland Common. Me mother used to go there on a Friday night. She'd buy three pounds of beef cheek for a shilling. Deputies at the pit, the overmen, they thought they were better than you. Some of their wives 'ud say to her, "Would you bring us back some meat for the dog?" Dog n'er saw meat. They aten it.'

The psychological impact of unemployment was often hardest to bear. Walter Brierley from Denby Hall pit, forty miles north-west of Wentworth, was unemployed between the years 1931 and 1935. 'Though both my wife and myself are physically healthy, walking as we do about the Derbyshire countryside on Sundays and somedays in the week,' he wrote,

> the prolonged strain of living on the edge of domestic upheaval, and the fact that our social urge has to be repressed, has ruined our nerves and given us an inferiority complex. For myself, the dependence on the state for money without having honestly earned it, has made me creep within myself . . . there are fools, unintelligent fools, who believe that the fault of a man's being unemployed lies at his own door. This is especially so in isolated, gossip-ridden villages like the one in which I live, where, if

one does not stand at street corners or go rapping on the wet benches in the public houses, one is afraid to come out, ashamed, idle.

The work ethic was engrained in the miners' culture. Until the years of mass unemployment, idleness had been something to deride. 'Capacity to work was *the* criterion: a good workman being honoured everywhere by implicit assent,' Arthur Eaglestone remembered. 'The most heinous of accusations lay in the terrible phrase: "He doesn't like work!" I remember as a boy I looked upon men so branded with an apprehensive eye. In Rotherham the tradition of publicly shaming a lazy good-for-nothing who had shirked a day's labour, by trundling him through the streets in a wheelbarrow, still lingered.'

Ridiculing the idle was not exclusive to the Fitzwilliams' villages; it happened in every pit village in the West Riding. Jim Bullock, from Bowers Row colliery, remembered one miner known as 'Lazy Bill'. He wrote:

I could give you his last name, but for the sake of his relatives, I will not. Lazy Bill used to spend more time talking than working, always talking about the wonderful dreams he had. His workmates got completely fed up with him, and the manager got so tired of hearing complaints that he finally sent for Bill to come to his office and sacked him. Now he had a large family, because he had never been idle in that way, but in those days there were no relief benefits, no Social Security. The stark reality of his being sacked had to be faced by his wife.

To make ends meet, as Jim recalled, she resorted to taking in washing and ironing and doing housework for the neighbours. 'I have never seen anyone get as low as she did. She went about looking miserable,' he remembered, 'without interest in herself or anything else.'

The ultimate fate of Lazy Bill was a story told and retold in Jim's village; a salutary tale for would-be shirkers.

One day, just at the top of our street, Lazy Bill was knocked down by a bicycle and killed. They put him on an old door, one which was laid against the fences. When they took him in his wife was getting the tea ready for the kids, and she did not show the slightest bit of emotion. Years ago some wit wrote – and it was quoted quite often then:

> They brought him home dead on a shutter,
> But she just kept on cutting bread and spreading the butter.

This was not the end of Lazy Bill's story. His wife was so fed up with him that she expressed the wish to have him cremated, because she did not want the bother of tending his grave and she could not afford a headstone. She was not going to walk down to the churchyard to take him flowers, because he just was not worth it. The subscription towards the cremation was the first we had in the village, but the thing the villagers could not understand was the widow's one request. This came when she was asked what she wanted the authorities to do with the ashes: 'I want them, I'm taking them home,' she said.

The neighbours soon found out the reason for this strange request. She put his ashes in an egg-timer, stood back and looked in real satisfaction as she said to the neighbours, 'There now, I've got him just where I want him. He's never worked for me. He's never worked for the kids while he was alive, but I'll make sure he'll work for us now he's dead, because every time I boil an egg, he'll have to work in that egg-timer, and he won't do any grumbling either.'

In the slump years of the early 1930s, Billy Fitzwilliam, at considerable cost to himself, saved his miners from the humiliation of long-term unemployment. At the start of 1931, to artificially maintain the prices, quotas had been set to limit the amount of coal each colliery could produce. Billy could easily have met his weekly quota by shutting down one of his pits; instead, to save the men's jobs, he kept both pits open by operating them on alternate weeks.

In the weeks they were not working the men at New Stubbin and Elsecar were entitled to claim the dole. In order to qualify for unemployment benefit, a miner had to lose three days' work in every six. Working the collieries one week on, one week off, was an enlightened strategy on Billy's part, one that was in marked contrast to a number of other coal owners. In some mining regions, the bitterness and bad feeling generated by the 1926 Strike had continued: out of spite, to deprive the miners of the dole, the coal owners were operating their collieries on a four-day week, with the result that, in some areas, the miners were worse off for working. B. L. Coombes, who worked at a pit in the Brecknock Beacons in Wales, described this practice:

> I remember we were working only four turns every week for over six months, and yet not once getting eligible for the dole during that period, because we had to lose three in six to get paid. Often it was very difficult for the company to work the fourth shift, but they did so, and the men worked that shift at a loss, because had they not worked it, they would have qualified for three days' dole. My feelings were not very pleasant when I had to go to work for eight shillings and I would have had fourteen and sixpence – three days' dole – if we had not worked that night, while we knew that the colliery was bound to be idle again before many days. All that spring and summer I was working, but was not a penny better off than if I had been on the dole.

The human cost of the misery inflicted by the Great Depression was hard to measure; but by the summer of 1931, its impact on the Exchequer was all too calculable. On 11 July, Clive Wigram, George V's Private Secretary, who, twenty years earlier, had accompanied him on his visit to Wentworth, wrote a stark letter to the King: 'We are sitting on the top of a volcano, and the curious thing is the Press and the City have not really understood the critical situation. The Governor of the Bank of England is very pessimistic and depressed.'

The eruption came exactly one month later. On 11 August there was a dramatic run on the pound as foreign investors scrambled to remove their money from the City of London. Ramsay MacDonald's Government was already grappling with a deficit in the forthcoming autumn budget; the flight from sterling threw it into crisis. Interrupting his holiday, the Prime Minister returned to Downing Street where he was met by a committee of bankers. Britain, they told him, 'stood on the edge of the precipice'.

'Deficit' had been the political catchphrase of the preceding months. Earlier in the summer, two committees, the first headed by the future Conservative Prime Minister Harold Macmillan, the second under the chairmanship of the eminent financier Sir George May, had concluded their reports. Macmillan's focused attention on Britain's balance of payments with the rest of the world. Hitherto, it had been assumed that the country lived by trade, exporting manufactured goods and raw materials which paid for the foodstuffs and other imports that came in. In fact, Britain's trading account had not shown a credit balance since 1822. It was the 'Invisibles' – shipping and banking – that had always put the balance right. These were the very things that had been hit by the global Depression: receipts from shipping were £50 million less in 1931 than in 1929, and the return from foreign investment £70 million less. In the same period, the volume of Britain's exports had almost halved. Macmillan's report emphasized this decline; when May's report was published, alarm intensified. Owing to the Depression, the yield from taxes had gone down, whereas expenditure – specifically on unemployment benefit – had rocketed. May's report identified an immediate budget deficit of £120 million. It recommended that £24 million of this deficit should be met by increasing taxation: the remaining £94 million should be met by slashing unemployment benefit.

Faced with the flight from sterling, on 12 August MacDonald summoned his Cabinet to Downing Street. One way of propping up the pound was to secure loans in Paris and New York. But foreign bankers were unwilling to lend the Government money unless the budget deficit was resolved. Forced into a corner, the Prime Minister proposed cutting unemployment benefit by 10 per cent – a cut that nine members of the Cabinet were not prepared to make. As the country's gold and currency reserves continued to drain away, the Government collapsed. On the evening of

23 August, MacDonald went to Buckingham Palace to hand in his resignation to the King.

Once again, labour – the impoverished working class in Britain's old industries, a large percentage of them miners – was being asked to bear the cost of capital's mistakes.

Historians would condemn the crisis of the summer of 1931 as the 'bankers' ramp'. The flight from sterling on 11 August was not precipitated by the budget deficit – the millions being paid out in unemployment benefit – but by the speculative activities of London's bankers.

In the years after the Great War, striving to restore the City's position as the financial centre of the world, the bankers had borrowed money from French depositors at 2 per cent and lent it to Germany at 8 or 10 per cent. In the summer of 1931, a period of political tension between France and Germany, the French, objecting to the fact that their money was being used to help Germany, withdrew it from London. Simultaneously, a financial collapse in Central Europe caused the German banks to renege on their international loans. The London bankers were caught out, facing short-term foreign liabilities estimated at over £400 million. It was the Bank of England's decision to allow them to draw on the gold reserve that had caused sterling to run down.

The upshot was a National Government and a National Emergency. On the evening of 23 August, George V, refusing to accept MacDonald's resignation, had urged the Leaders of the Opposition to rally to the Prime Minister. The following day a coalition government was formed 'to deal with', as the official communiqué stated, 'the National Emergency that now exists'.

A week later, the Milton Committee held an emergency meeting of its own, convened in secret, behind Billy's back. The question its members debated was whether the National Emergency presented the opportunity to tell the Earl to his face what many of them had privately felt for months: that, in light of the economic crisis in the country and in the neighbourhood, the planned celebrations of Peter's coming of age were in poor taste. It was a time, they concurred, to conceal wealth, not to flaunt it.

The publicity could prove detrimental to the family's interests: if the celebrations were to go ahead, the Fitzwilliams would be caught in the 'glare of a spotlight on a dark stage'. The minutes of the meeting reveal their conclusion: 'In view of the present financial crisis in the Country we recommend the cancellation of the festivities, and suggest a Garden Party to farm and principal tenants in the Summer, if opportune.' For the remainder of the meeting, the Milton Committee debated which of them should break the news to Billy.

Billy was furious when he was told. He would not hear of the birthday celebrations being cancelled. Making a small concession to the Committee, he reluctantly agreed to reduce the number of parties from six to one large, spectacular, party on the day. He was adamant the commemorative donations to the collieries and the chemical works should go ahead as planned. The projected cost of the celebrations was £8,500 – more than £350,000 at today's values.

'It were the last hurrah at Wentworth. A feast of Bacchus!' Walker Scales, the nephew of the butcher who supplied the ox for roasting, recalled.

Shortly after lunch, on New Year's Eve 1931, the day of Peter's birthday, the gates to Wentworth Park were opened.

The guests arrived early, in one-pony traps, farm carts and on foot. Some came on bicycles; a handful, the senior officials at the Fitzwilliams' pits and factories, came in cars. Miners from the outlying pit villages had transport laid on for them: standing up in rows, they arrived in open-top charabancs, their hands clutching the sides to prevent them from tipping out on to the pot-holed, dirt-track roads.

To discourage gatecrashers, the Estate officials had insisted that lapel badges be sent out with the 15,000 invitations. Moments after the Park gates were opened, so great was the crush that the Fitzwilliams' outdoor servants gave up trying to filter the crowds. The uninvited – miners and their families from all over the district – had come regardless, as Billy knew they would. By mid-afternoon, there were upwards of 40,000 people trampling over the lawn and fields in front of Wentworth House.

Everyone from Wentworth village had turned out: Dr Mills, wearing a heavy tweed coat and yellow chamois gloves; old Miss Bartlett – one of the spinsters of the village, renowned for taking a shorthand note of the Vicar's sermon every Sunday – sporting her best sable tippet. Even the molecatcher was there. 'You never saw him without his shovel and traps,' a former stewards' room boy, Charles Booth, remembered. 'He was one of the village characters. You'd see him round Wentworth all the time. He carried this long shovel over his shoulder and had his mole traps slung round his neck. He was a very tall man, always dressed the same, in knee britches and a trilby hat.'

As dusk fell on the clear winter's night, the 'frost-fringed trees', so the local paper reported, 'added a note of enchantment'. Along the copse at the edge of the lawn, a giant projection screen had been put up: emblazoned in the Union colours were the words 'Welcome to All'. To the marvel of the crowds, every so often the red, white and blue lights flickered and the words 'Long Life and Prosperity to Lord Milton' would appear instead. 'Coloured lights were magic to us then,' Charles Booth recalled. 'When I were a little lad, we used to walk five or six miles to the hills above Sheffield, just so as we could see the lights. Me Mother used to take us. It were something to look forward to at the weekend. When they put traffic lights up at Hoyland Cross, it were a novelty. We'd go down and watch 'em too. Just to see 'em change.'

The classlessness of the party was applauded by the Press. 'The freedom of Wentworth House and its Park was extended to all: the great house itself open to all comers, numbers only permitting,' the *South Yorkshire Times* reported. 'Throughout the afternoon and early evening, the classes mingled. Despite the inclement weather, all were dressed in their Sunday best.' Young girls wore crisply starched white pinnies over their dresses; small boys fidgeted in their stiff collars and scratchy cloth jackets.

Ralph Boreham was one of them: 'Me father and grandfather worked at Elsecar pit. On 't birthday, the pitmen got a photograph of Lord Milton. It were like a plaque with fancy lettering, you know to mark the occasion. Some had it framed. Me mother took me and me brother to the party, me Dad and Grandad went separately – so as they could have a drink. I must have been about ten. I'd only ever been in the Park at Wentworth once before. The time before was with me mates. I remember, we followed this posh bloke, all dressed up fancy. He were smoking a big fat cigar. We trailed him all the way down through the village, waiting for him to drop it. When he did, bad old bugger trod on it, grinding it into 't ground. It were no good to us then, were it? On't day of birthday, we went through the gates at Wentworth Park and the first man we let on, he were laying there drunk. They called him Roland Locke. He were a Jehovah's witness, teetotal like. He used to go round with an accordion preaching on Sundays. Me mother said, "Eh up, Roland. What tha' doing here like this?!" "Ay," he said, "it's different, lady. It's free!" There were some great big stables just down the Park, before you got to the Big House. And it were filled, totally filled, with barrels of beer. All the pitmen and workmen were there knocking it back. They roasted a bullock and there were all these special men turning it round. Lord Milton had the first slice. You were given a big slab of meat in a sandwich dripping with fat. It were beautiful. On the lawn in front of the house, there was a wooden frame. It must have been o'er a hundred foot high. It were for fireworks. When it were dark they lit it up. The whole thing went off. It were wonderful. I've not seen nought to match 'em since.'

The fireworks were spectacular. 'The setting occupied several hundred yards along which dim diminutive figures hurried with torches,' the *Sheffield Daily Telegraph* reported.

At the opposite end of the line, mythical jugglers began throwing up balls of fire to left and right in pastel shades of green, pink and pale blue, and then followed a fireworks boxing match that created unbounded amusement, rousing the hearty cheers of the crowds. Wonderfully realistic were the firework dovecotes, to and from which fiery pigeons winged their way across the Park. The finest art of the pyrotechnician

> was surely embodied in a remarkably life-like picture in fireworks of the personality of the day, Lord Milton. 'A Fine Old English Gentleman' played by the band was a fitting accompaniment. The most wonderful spectacle of all was the concluding number, an air and sea battle in which the attacking airship was brought down in flames.

The Elsecar Colliery Brass Band, stationed in front of the house, accompanied the display. Mendelssohn's 'Spring Song', Romberg's 'Desert Song', the 'Waltz Song' and selections from Gounod's *Faust* were among the pieces of music chosen. When the display ended, the 40,000-strong crowd joined in singing the 'Londonderry Air' and 'We Won't Come Home Till Morning'.

'Ay, that party were a treat,' Ralph remembered. 'Everyone had a good time. Too good. At end of the night, there were that many drunks, all laid out in the Park asleep. They were all over the grass. They fetched some horses and a flat cart and tipped them out on't road outside the gates. It were middle of winter. A freezing cold night. There were one poor bloke from Jump – it were a Fitzbilly village – he went home after and sat on't fire. He were that drunk. He made a right mess of hisself. He got some real burns.

When it were time for us to go home, me mother took us the long way round. On't road, it were about a mile's walk to Elsecar. It were too dangerous to go back through Wentworth though, there were that many drunks. We went out of the village past the vinegar stone – for keeping the plague away – and down across the fields along "Forty Stiles". The woods by there were where the King's Troops mustered in the Civil War. She took us all the way round. A couple of miles it were. Up in't hills, on't tops, we could see great bonfires burning. Up at Hoober Stand, Hoyland Low – all over the place, a big circle of them. They'd lit beacons in Lord Milton's honour, all wired up with the wood properly placed so they'd burn.'

For Peter, the birthday celebrations were an ordeal.

The long day began at ten o'clock with a ceremonial tour of the district. Peter travelled with his mother and father in the front car in a fleet of yellow Rolls-Royces, the family's house guests and his sisters following behind. The whole of the eight-mile route, via Rawmarsh, Greaseborough and Elsecar, was lined with people who had turned out to wave the Wentworth party on. In the villages, the streets were festooned with bunting, painted in the Fitzwilliam colours: the district was en fête, every employee enjoying a day's paid holiday, plus a special birthday gift of a brand-new ten-shilling note.

The entire morning had been taken up with speeches and presentations at the opening ceremonies of the buildings and recreational grounds built to commemorate the coming of age. At every stop, Peter opened the proceedings by cutting a ribbon with a gold pocket-knife given to him by his father.

Geoff Steer, the former garden boy at Wentworth and the son of an Elsecar miner, remembered standing outside Market Hall on the main street in the village. 'There were a great gang of us, hundreds crowding the street outside the hall, all waiting to see Lord Milton. The car pulled up and he went inside. And we waited. Waited for Lord Milton to come out. But he never did. He went out a side door at the back. He didn't want to face us. He weren't one for creeping.'

Reporting on the speeches and presentations, the newspapers described Peter as looking 'awkward' and 'embarrassed'. It was Billy who stole the limelight. At the two collieries and at the chemical works, one after another, the officials and trades union leaders used the occasion to pay tribute to the Earl's generosity in the difficult times. Speaking at New Stubbin pit, Mr Humphries, the secretary of the local branch of the Yorkshire Miners' Association, thanked Billy on behalf of the men: 'As a Trades Union Secretary, I do believe we have in Earl Fitzwilliam the finest idealistic employer in the country today,' he said to long applause from the gathered miners. 'He is a man with some humanity, a man within our hearts, and quite different from some members of the upper class. I appreciate him for the humanity and kindness he has shown to his people.' Humphries was followed by Alderman Tomlinson, who echoed his sentiments. 'We have had reports throughout the years of the generosity of the family. We have said, when things were very bad, that if this country had more employers of the character and calibre of Lord Fitzwilliam there would be better relationships between employers and employed, capital and labour.' At Elsecar, the message was the same: 'The world is passing through a very troublous time,' one of the pit officials said, speaking before a crowd of thousands of miners and their families.

> To keep collieries going needs sacrifice if the workmen are not to suffer too greatly and Lord Fitzwilliam has made that sacrifice. He could have shut down Stubbin or Elsecar and still have got his quota out. He could have shut down the afternoon shift but there would have been a lot of men dismissed. He could have been better in pocket but he has not dismissed a single man. At the same time the work has been supplemented, and we have got the fullest benefits of the Unemployment Act. If he gave notice to half our men, it would be a dreadful thing for this district. I hope better times will soon be here and our pulley wheels will spin as in the former prosperous years.

Billy, confident, affable, his long speeches contrasting with his son's muttered brevity, paid tribute to the miners in return. Looking back to his youth, when he had experienced working underground at Stubbin and Elsecar pits, he thanked them – as 'a mining amateur' – for having taught him everything that he knew. 'Ever since,' he told them, 'it has always been my ambition to use the best machinery, the safest means: for safety to come first before profits.' He spoke with pride of the fact that under his stewardship the number of miners employed at the family's mines had increased from 700 to 3,600.

To Peter's embarrassment – and to the amusement of the crowds – Billy recalled the first time he took Peter to the pit. 'I remember when, wielding a tiny spade, a small bewildered boy dug a small hole in the ground. It is a long time since I brought Lord Milton to dig up the first sod which paved the way to the New Stubbin colliery. I thought at that time that if he digged [*sic*] in life as he did on that occasion, he would do well!'

As a local newspaper reporter transcribed, Billy closed his speech with a homily to his son:

> There are two men in the house now and one will have to turn out. It is not going to be me. He [Lord Milton] has to learn his job. You have given him a wonderful reception. You have given him the welcome which Yorkshiremen give to one another; a feeling that can only be learnt by experiencing it. I agree that games make a land, teaching patience, which makes Englishmen good in business, reasonable and unconquerable in war – and also in love. (Laughter) I hope he will not have as much war as I have had, and I hope that he learns the game with you. He has to realize that he belongs to a miner's family, the same as we always intend to be. (Cheers) I have taught him all I can; you can teach him now. If he knows how to go into the grievances of the men with them as a man he will have nothing to fear in the future.

After the loud applause finally subsided, Peter stood up to speak. He had very little to say: 'I am overwhelmed by the welcome you have given me,' he began. 'You have made me realize how you respect my father and I only hope I can follow in his footsteps. I hope times will get better, and that there will be a lot of smoke from our chimneys, for they say that where there is a lot of smoke there is prosperity. I wish you all the very best of luck.'

'He made a short speech, then he left,' Walt Hammond remembered. Walt and a group of young miners – Peter's old friends from the Rawmarsh football team – had got up especially early to reserve a place at the front of the crowd. Standing a few yards from Peter, they had hoped to be able to congratulate him personally on his coming of age. 'We never spoke to him. I never saw him again. He got married soon after. He went from us. He'd done with us then. Miss Olive Plunket, that were her name. She were a lady, well thought of she was. Don't think he were a bloody angel, mind. If he were, he had two sets of wings.'

In April 1933, to the delight of the gossip columnists, Peter married Olive 'Obby' Plunket, thought to be one of the most beautiful debutantes of her generation. The younger daughter of the Right Reverend Benjamin Plunket, the Bishop of Meath, she too was hugely rich. Her father had recently inherited a Guinness fortune from his uncle, along with St Anne's, an imposing mansion situated at the mouth of the River Liffey, overlooking Dublin Port. Newspaper editorials crooned at the 'fortuitous alignment of these two great noble houses'.

Obby *was* beautiful. Slim and petite, she had coppery-blonde hair. Her eyes were mesmerizing, a startling aquamarine in colour. Warm-hearted and full of joie de vivre, with an adventurous spirit that Peter found attractive, she shared his main interests: horses and speed. As a child, growing up at the Bishop's Court in Navan, one of her favourite games was to prance around pretending to be a horse. Nicknamed 'hobby horse' by her nanny, the name, shortened to 'Obby', had stuck. Like Peter, she was easily bored: friends of the couple recalled weekend house parties at Wentworth when the two of them would pace about, complaining how dull things were and wondering what to do next. Spur-of-the-moment trips would be organized, with the house party decamping by private plane to Le Touquet and Paris.

'Grandpa didn't want Peter to marry Obby. He didn't approve of her,' Lady Barbara Ricardo, Billy's granddaughter, recalled. 'He didn't think it would work. I suppose my grandfather recognized Obby for what she was. She was always a bit of a flibbertigibbet. It was my grandmother who was so keen on her. She doted on Peter. Went along with whatever he wanted. If he wanted to marry Obby, she wanted him to.'

The wedding, at St Patrick's Cathedral in Dublin, was the society wedding of the decade: the 800-strong guest list read like a volume of *Debrett's*. Tens of thousands lined the five-mile route from St Anne's to St Patrick's: 'At the west end of the Cathedral,' the *Dublin Times* reported, 'every window was crowded with heads and the roofs clustered as thickly as flypapers in summer.'

The bride wore a dress of ice-blue satin with a fourteen-foot train. Her tulle veil, tinted a delicate shade of blue to match her dress, fell in luxurious folds from a coronet of orange blossom. In her hand, she carried a bouquet of pale pink and creamy-white orchids that had been specially grown in the greenhouses at Wentworth and shipped to Dublin overnight. The twelve bridesmaids – all but three of them titled – wore diamanté-embroidered silk dresses in varying shades of St Patrick's blue, each carrying a bouquet of yellow roses that had also been cultivated at Wentworth. When the service was over, it took ten minutes for the police to clear the crowds to enable the cars to leave for the reception. Three of the Fitzwilliams' Rolls-Royces, bearing the family crest, had been shipped over from England to transport the bridal party.

A single event marred the day. En route from St Patrick's to the reception at St Anne's, the wedding cavalcade was held up by a funeral cortège. Peter and Obby's car was forced to stop while the hearse passed directly in front of it. It was a bad omen: in Ireland, according to superstition, it meant the marriage was doomed.

Some days later, at Coollattin, the Fitzwilliams' Irish estate, the portent appeared to come true. 'I was sitting in the drawing-room at Coollattin with my mother and my sister,' Lady Barbara remembered, 'when suddenly, in walked Obby. We were all astonished to see her. Peter had left her in the middle of their honeymoon. He had gone off somewhere else.'

Barbara was thirteen at the time. Her mother, Elfrida – Peter's sister – told her to leave the room. 'I remember Obby was terribly upset. We were all frightfully shocked. What could she possibly be doing there, what could have happened? I was too young then to be allowed to know. I left the room, as my mother asked. It was obviously a matter for the grown-ups.' Years later, when Barbara was older, her mother told her what had happened. 'Obby was a Bishop's daughter! Poor thing probably hadn't been told anything much about sex. There was Peter. He had had all those girlfriends – some of them very experienced. It was probably not very interesting for him! He got bored and left. Poor Obby, I think she had a very grim time with him.'

PART VI

29

The silhouette of Wentworth House was clearly visible. The moon was full, the sky cloudless, the night bitterly cold. That evening, 12 December 1940, a hard frost had fallen at dusk, encasing the roof in ice. The statues crowning the central block on the East Front glistened steel-white. Beneath them, thinly etched across the breadth of the portico, the Fitzwilliams' motto, 'Mea Gloria Fides' – My Glorious Faith – shimmered, blue-gold. The eighteenth-century shutters in the state apartments were closed; in the hundreds of windows along the two wings, and in the upper reaches of the house, the newly made blackout curtains were drawn. The ice continued its creeping advance as the temperature dropped: glinting in the moonlight above the blackness below, it confounded the labours of the army of seamstresses that had dressed the house for war.

Ten miles south, flying at 10,000 feet, Nazi bomber crews attached to the elite Kampfgeschwader 100 – the 'Pathfinder Squadron' – were making their final approach. Their flight path had been set by a radio beam, transmitted from a secret location in Europe. A continuous audio tone sounded in the cockpits to keep the pilots on course. Flying in formation, following the silver ribbon of the River Sheaf, the foothills of the Pennines stretched below. They were within seconds of their target. Marking off their position on neatly folded night navigation maps coloured deep magenta and green, the pilots waited for the continuous tone to alter. German Bomber Command had positioned a second beam to guide the Pathfinder Squadron in; at the point where the two beams intersected, an alert would sound in the cockpits: the final signal to the pilots to release their bombs.

The Kampfgeschwader's target was Sheffield. In the first year of the war, the 'Steel City', dogged by recession in the 1930s, had geared up to full capacity. By December 1940, it was of critical importance to the defence of Britain. The Vickers works on the edge of the city operated the only drop-hammer capable of forging crankshafts for Spitfires; Hadfields Steelworks was the only factory in the country producing eighteen-inch armour-piercing shells. The authorities had been expecting an air raid throughout the summer: barrage balloons floated above the city and on the crescent of hills that ringed it the anti-aircraft batteries were permanently manned.

On the night of 12 December 1940, the Kampfgeschwader dropped their bombs shortly after 7 p.m. First to fall were the parachute flares, magnesium bombs that ignited in the air, casting a fierce iridescent glow, as if a thousand arc lights were being trained on the city below. Then came the incendiary bombs – phosphorous exploding ones – deliberately designed to ignite fires as markers for the wave upon wave of Heinkel bombers following behind. Arcing to the east of the city, the squadron headed back for Occupied France. As the pilots executed a turning circle, four miles north-east of Sheffield, they discharged the last of their bombs over Wentworth.

'I was on the bus coming back from Rotherham,' Charles Booth, the former steward's room boy at the house, remembered. 'When the air raid started, they stopped the bus at Greaseborough and told us to get off. I had to walk the rest of the way home through Wentworth Park. It was about a mile and a half across to the village. I suppose I must have been a lad of about eighteen or nineteen. Terrified, I was. There wasn't a soul about, eight o'clock on a winter's night and it was bright as daylight. There were magnesium bombs littered all over the place, burning very bright, bright as a summer's day. They made a swishing noise coming down – sssssssssssssh, ssssssssssssssh. They were coming in showers, hundreds of them. I could see the knars on the old oaks as clear as my hand. You could hear the bombs crunching in the distance and the drone of the aeroplanes. Up on the hills the searchlights were going and the gun batteries blazing. There was a red sunset glow in the sky over Sheffield. I thought of all those poor people there.

You knew they were getting a pasting. One of the pubs, a place called Marples, received a direct hit. There were hundreds in there. They're still there. All they did was pour lime down the crater to cover the corpses. We wondered if it was us in the village next.'

The bombs were felt throughout the South Yorkshire coalfield. As far as ten miles away, at Conisbrough, the ground shook. 'Our kitchen door was a solid two-inches-thick wooden door,' Alicia Dufton recalled in her memoirs. 'It rattled loud and ominously during the blitzes, as did the contents of the pantry and the ornaments on top of the piano.'

At Wentworth, five miles closer to Sheffield, the pristine interior seemed to quiver with imminent destruction. Thousands of crystal beads in the chandeliers in the state rooms trembled and the loose Georgian frames rattled in every window of the house; the fine porcelain, displayed in glass-fronted cabinets, and the hundreds of bibelots that adorned the occasional tables, struck their own notes. 'Everything was moving. It was like a giant space ship about to take off,' Bert May, the butler's son, recalled. 'The noise was deafening. Everything were going off. All the china and crystal were singing, and then there were these bangs and crashes as bits and pieces came down from the walls. Pictures, bits of plaster, you name it. My father told me one of the bison's heads came down in the Pillared Hall.'

The Heinkel bombers that followed in the wake of the Pathfinder Squadron bombed Sheffield for nine hours. Two days later the bombers returned. In the course of the two raids, 785 people were killed and 589 seriously injured; in the centre of the city, thousands of buildings were destroyed. The factories and steelworks had been saved at the cost of high civilian casualties: years later it would emerge that the RAF, using powerful transmitters, had 'bent' the Germans' directional radio beam, diverting the Pathfinder Squadron's marker away from the strategic targets and on to Sheffield's residential and business centre instead.

Wentworth had a narrow escape. Three bombs barely missed the house, landing within yards of the state apartments in the walled garden behind the West Front. 'A stick of bombs came down by the greenhouses. None of them went off,' Charles Booth remembered. 'The next morning, they called in an army bomb disposal team to diffuse them. They had to blow one of the bombs up. It blew out every pane of glass in the greenhouses. Great white pavilions they were – like the ones at Kew Gardens. On a winter's day it was like the Amazon jungle in there – full of bananas and tropical fruits. That were the end of them after that.'

The phoney war was over: before long, the vaulted state rooms and the stone-floored corridors at Wentworth would echo to the tread of marching boots.

'The war turned my grandparents' world upside down,' Lady Barbara Ricardo recalled. 'It was when everything began to unravel.'

In the months following the declaration of war, thousands of country houses across Britain were requisitioned by the Government, or donated by their owners for wartime use. *Burke's Peerage* estimated that some 10,000 were commandeered: used for a variety of purposes, they were converted into schools, military headquarters, hospitals, repositories for national treasures, homes for evacuees and secret intelligence establishments.

Wentworth was one of the first of England's stately homes to be requisitioned. Early in 1940, it became the temporary headquarters of the 10th Battalion, the Duke of Wellington's regiment. To the Fitzwilliams' relief, the first year of occupation had been tolerable, even enjoyable. 'It was rather like having guests to stay,' Billy's daughter, Elfrida, Countess of Wharncliffe, recalled. The house had not been overrun: the 10th Battalion was a new battalion manned by a skeleton HQ Company Staff and only a handful of the Duke of Wellington's senior officers were billeted in the wings. The other ranks, 'the licentious soldiery' as one of the regiment's officers referred to them, were accommodated in the stable block where the stalls that once housed the Earls' hunters were turned into makeshift dorms. 'We were very comfortable. We had use of his Lordship's billiard table,' remembered Patrick Hewling, the Regimental Medical Officer, who was billeted in a wing along the East Front. 'Lord Fitzwilliam visited our mess, usually on a Sunday morning before lunch and had a drink with us. He liked a little "military gossip". He very often brought a bottle of his excellent port as a present to our mess for consumption after Sunday dinner . . . It was a very happy billet. The Fitzwilliams were very good to us, and I don't think they were much incommoded by the military presence.'

The house party came to an end in 1941. In December, the Fitzwilliams were notified that the Intelligence Corps would be moving to Wentworth for the duration of the war. The entire East Front, where the state rooms were located, was to be taken over: Maud and Billy would have to move into a suite of rooms in the 'Back Front' – the baroque West Front that overlooked the gardens at the back of the house.

Preparing the East Front for the troops' arrival was a mammoth task. It took an army of domestic staff, helped by extra recruits from the village, several weeks to pack up its contents. The Whistlejacket Room, the Van Dyck Room, the State Dining Room and the rest of the galleries and ante-rooms in the State apartments were stripped of their treasures. Chandeliers were bagged; furniture and pictures sheeted or moved; plate, porcelain and other objets d'art packed into crates.

Working around the clock, under the direction of Captain Taylor and Colonel Landon, the comptroller and land agent at Wentworth, the servants formed human chains, criss-crossing the length of the corridors, passing the lighter objects from hand to hand. The bulk of the contents of the State Rooms was stored in the private chapel and in the great subterranean network of cellars and passages; the remainder was moved to Billy and Maud's new apartment in the West Front.

Mouldings, panelling, furnishings and rugs all had to be protected from the wear and tear of the new tenants. In the ante-rooms and drawing rooms, posses of Estate workmen sawed Essex board in situ, crafting it into protective casing carefully calculated to fit snugly against the decorative panelling and around the precious carved stone fireplaces. In the galleries, the servants struggled to roll the handwoven carpets into portable bundles which then had to be heaved downstairs to be stored in the vast space under the Grand Staircase. Damask curtains and tapestries, too ancient to take down without the risk of tearing them, were swathed in canvas covers by the housemaids; in the Marble Salon, a temporary wooden floor was constructed to sheath the priceless marble-inlaid floor.

For those who witnessed it, it was an unnerving sight. Centuries of history were being dismantled and wrapped. Along the corridors, paintings, loosely covered in baize, were stacked in bundles against the walls. Beside them, beneath the niches where they had stood, suits of armour and statuary were laid out, shrouded in cloth, like corpses, on the floor. Everywhere, housemaids hovered over packing crates, carefully wrapping porcelain and silver in felt and old newspaper. 'I wrapped so many beautiful things,' remembered Ethel Jones, a former laundry maid at Wentworth, who was drafted in to help with the packing. 'Ooh, there must have been about twenty-five teapots! Not just any old teapots they weren't. There were porcelain ones in all colours and gold ones with beautiful hand-painted pictures on them. There were one with a painted view of Wentworth House. I expect it came from Rockingham kilns over by Pottery Lane. Family had a lot from there. You had to keep pinching yourself. You couldn't believe you were packing it all up. We all thought world were coming to an end. War were going badly. Germans were bombing us. Family were moving to back front, soldiers taking over. You wondered what things would be like when time came to open up them crates again. One thing I'll never forget was a glass goblet. It had the words "Milton For Ever" inscribed on it. Her Ladyship happened by just as I was wrapping it. She told me not to pack it. "Give it to Jack May," she said. He were her butler. She wanted it in her room where she could see it. We all knew she were worried sick about Lord Milton.'

'The thing that frightened Grannie Mumbo the most was that Peter would be killed,' Lady Barbara Ricardo, Maud's granddaughter, recalled. 'She didn't think he was going to come through the war. It overshadowed everything else. She worried dreadfully. Like every mother did.'

Peter, a reserve officer in the Grenadier Guards, was called up immediately war was declared. He was thirty on New Year's Eve 1940. His first six months of the war were spent training with his regiment at the Guards Depot at Windsor Castle. By the spring of 1941, he was fighting in a Commando unit in the Middle East. 'He had a reputation for being exceptionally brave. All his soldiers adored him,' Lady Barbara remembered. 'It was extraordinary really because as a little boy he was so feeble. Then he turned into this incredibly brave young man. I suppose it was Eton really. It enabled him to escape from the family, to develop his own character. At home he was always being molly-coddled by his parents or his sisters, or being pushed into doing this, that, or the other. The trouble was, he was the only son and heir.'

In the seven years since their marriage, Peter and Obby had produced one child – a daughter, Juliet, born in 1935. 'There were a lot of talk about it in the villages,' Geoffrey Steer, the son of an Elsecar miner, recalled. '"Won't be long now before he'll be having an heir," they'd say. When he left to fight, there were a lot of speculation. "Who's going to take over if Young Lordie's killed?" People said it were Lady Milton's fault there weren't no heir. Called her a silly billy, they did. Every time she got to be expecting, what u'd happen? She'd be going riding, wouldn't she, on't 'orse. Oh, it used to play 'em up. She had lots of miscarriages.'

The village gossips were correct in spreading rumours of miscarriages, but they were unkind to blame Obby for failing to produce an heir. Poor Obby had a most dreadful time. As Lady Barbara recalled, there were complications at Juliet's birth. 'Why they didn't give her a caesarian, heaven knows. Perhaps they didn't in those days. You see, it damaged her insides. She couldn't have any more children after Juliet, that's what my mother said.'

Early in 1943, Peter was recruited by SOE, the Special Operations Executive in charge of top-secret wartime operations. He was one of five officers handpicked to lead a highly dangerous mission in the North Sea. Code-named 'Operation Bridford', its objective was to secure desperately needed supplies of a small but essential aircraft part: tiny ball-bearings obtainable only in Sweden.

Three years earlier, the supply line had been cut when the Germans occupied Norway, gaining control of the Skagerrak, the narrow sea channel leading to Sweden's ports. Unless the German blockade could be broken, Britain's aircraft-assembly lines were at risk. A memo circulated by the Ministry of Aircraft Production at the end of 1942 spelt out in simple terms what a delivery of 100 tons of the ball-bearings would achieve: '100 tons would be sufficient to cover 75 per cent of the airframe work on 1,200 Lancasters and 60 per cent of the airframe work on 1,600 Mosquitos.' Realistically, the Ministry of Aircraft Production calculated, 500 tons of the ball-bearings were needed.

Operation Bridford, devised by Sir George Binney, one of the founders of SOE, was a last-ditch attempt to break the German blockade. Dubbed the 'Scarlet Pimpernel' for his audacity, Binney proposed deploying five high-speed motor gunboats (MGBs), disguised as merchant shipping, to slip undetected – and under the noses of the Germans – through the Skagerrak to a remote inlet along the rocky Swedish coast where secret agents would be waiting to load the ships with a precious cargo of ball-bearings. Speed was of the essence; after a quick turnaround, the heavily laden 'grey ladies', as the boats became known, would steal out of the inlet to run the gauntlet of enemy shipping on the return journey back to their base at Immingham, a small fishing port on the Humber. 'We have our traditions in *Nonsuch*, our aspirations in *Hopewell*, and our light-heartedness in *Gay Viking* and *Gay Corsair*,' Binney wrote as the boats, each powered by three diesel engines, were being fitted up for their mission. 'I have been groping to find a suitable name which would crystallize the steadfastness of our purpose. I think *Master Standfast* will do that.'

Peter, operating under the cover name 'Peter Lawrence' to save him from being singled out in case of capture, was assigned as Chief Officer to the *Hopewell*. 'None of the family knew what Peter was doing. We weren't supposed to know, it was secret,' Barbara recalled. 'We knew he was doing something hush-hush.

If my grandmother had known how dangerous it was, she would have been horrified.'

The Ministry of Transport had accepted responsibility for Operation Bridford on one condition: that the MGBs' twenty-man crews – all volunteers – were fully aware of the level of risk.

It was a round trip of 1,000 miles to the pick-up point on the Skagerrak and back to the grey ladies' base at Immingham. The window of opportunity was small: the boats, armed with machine guns and scuttling charges in case of capture, would sail on moonless winter nights when moderate weather conditions were exceptional in the northern latitudes of the North Sea. Their course lay across channels bristling with enemy shipping – and enemy aircraft. By day, they would use fog banks for concealment. By night, they would run with no lights, moving in diamond formation at an average speed of twenty knots, following the foaming phosphorescent wake of the boat ahead. German patrols on the lookout for blockade runners did not use lights either: the risk of collision was added to the likelihood of detection and perilous seas. With the exception of their speed and their shallow draughts – meaning the boats could glide through minefields with impunity – they were ill-equipped for their mission. They had not been designed to carry heavy loads; their powerful engines, early experiments in jet-engine technology, were notoriously unreliable. Above all, they had not been built to endure the notorious storm-force conditions that could whip up on the North Sea.

Binney had mounted the operation once before: 'Cabaret', the code-name given to his previous attempt, had been a disaster. The crew had almost died, not under enemy fire, but from exhaustion and dehydration brought on by severe seasickness. 'Service with the Motor Gunboats,' Binney wrote in a top-secret report on the failure of Operation Cabaret,

> is essentially a young man's occupation owing to the exceptional physical strain and stress in rough weather. Experience with naval crews in Operation Cabaret opened our eyes to the fact that in any long spell of bad weather at sea one must expect at least half of the ship's company

(not excluding junior officers) to be completely 'flaked out', however good their sense of discipline under normal conditions. Fatigue induced sea-sickness – or vice versa – to the point of complete physical collapse.

The corkscrew motion produced by the triple-screw vessels was unlike anything the Royal Navy crews had experienced before. In the depths of winter, the seas in the northern latitudes were short and steep: the grey ladies' ballast was poor – the motion they produced was different from the usual pitch and roll. Long and narrow – 117 feet in length with a ten-foot beam – the boats barely fitted between the troughs: to get into the succeeding trough, they had to leap over each oncoming wave. 'The boats didn't cut through water, they bounced,' one crewman grimly recalled. 'They were like corks,' remembered another, 'the motion was that bad.'

Tougher crews, Binney had concluded, were required for Operation Bridford. Jettisoning the Royal Navy crews, he recruited trawlermen from the docks at Grimsby and Hull. Hardened sailors, they were men who had grown up in the slum districts that fringed the harbours and whose sea legs had been formed in their early teens as 'Deckie Learners' on the fishing fleets that sailed in any weather beyond the coastal reaches of the North Sea. As conditions on board the MGBs proved, even they were not immune to sea-sickness. But they were at least inured to it. 'There were three of us working below deck in the engine room,' Irwin Jones, an able seaman on the *Gay Viking*, remembered. 'The diesel fumes were sickening. You couldn't eat a thing. If I'd been on that boat 100 days I couldn't have ate nought. You couldn't sleep when you were off watch, the motion was that bad. There was only one bloke out of all the boats who wasn't sea sick. When the weather were rough, which it nearly always was, the rest of us were sick most of the way through the trip. You just had to work through it. We had a bucket each and a bottle of fruit juice cordial to take the taste away.'

Depending on the weather, it took a minimum of thirty-six hours to reach the pick-up point on the Skagerrak. 'During many subsequent years at sea I never met crews so completely compatible, especially in such cramped conditions,' one of the crewmen remembered. The living quarters on board the MGBs were primitive. Only the Captain had his own room: the rest of the eighteen-man crew were accommodated in the deckhouse below the bridge, a sparse room built of plywood measuring thirty-six feet by fourteen feet. To keep the weight of the boats to a minimum, it was devoid of comfort or decoration, the crews resting – rather than sleeping – when they were off watch in the rows of hammocks. A portrait of Churchill was one of the few ornaments allowed. It was a far cry from the luxuriousness and spaciousness of Britain's biggest house.

'We were wary of him to begin with,' Able Seaman Jack Baron, who served on board the *Hopewell* with Peter, recalled. 'We knew he was an Earl. You wouldn't have thought anyone in his position would want to do anything like that. But he seemed to take it all in his stride. He came down to our level, he didn't expect us to go up to his.'

'I think he drove himself to do it,' Barbara explained. 'It was probably because so much was put on him as a boy – by his mother, his father, his four sisters expecting him to be frightfully good at everything. He had been so overprotected. It annoyed him. He wanted to escape. Being brave, doing something frightfully dangerous, was a way of escaping, of proving something to himself.'

Operation Bridford began on 26 October 1943. In the gathering gloom of a late autumn afternoon, the flotilla put to sea from Immingham, proceeding down the Humber in diamond formation. Wisps of blue diesel smoke trailed from the 3,000-horsepower engines: braced at low speed, they fired intermittently, like weapons, emitting a sudden, short, explosive sound. Half an hour after leaving the Humber Boom, the boats ran into thick fog, reducing visibility to less than half a cable. Rounding the Bull Light Vessel off Spurn Point, they steered northwards via the inner route for Flamborough Head. There, they executed a wide turn to starboard on to 030 degrees to pass through the cleared channel that would take them through the coastal minefield. Once through, pushing out a broad bow-wave, the boats increased speed to fifteen knots, shaping a north-easterly course for the Skagerrak.

The men who had recruited and trained the ninety-five crewmen – George Binney and his five Chief Officers, one of them Peter Fitzwilliam – stood on the bridges of the boats. 'They didn't stand on the quay and wave us goodbye,' remembered one Able Seaman. 'They came with us.'

At Wentworth, the clocks had stopped in the East Front. Along the miles of passages, in the state apartments, up in the North and South Towers and in 'Bedlam' and 'The Village' – the guest accommodation in the outer reaches of the house – a thousand hands told a different time.

Bracket clocks, carriage clocks, eight-day clocks, mantel clocks, long-case clocks, wall clocks – there were more clocks than there were rooms; a dazzling array of timepieces collected over the centuries. Housed in cases of polished wood, smooth and shiny as chocolate, or fashioned from gold and brass, their dials were carved from ebony and ormolu, or sculpted in painted enamel. Some showed the phases of the moon or Elysian scenes; others bore the sombre hallmarks of the Master Clockmakers of the North: Fletcher Brothers of Barnsley, Stott of Wakefield, Slater of Burslem. There were quarter-chiming clocks that rang carillons and clocks that struck only on the hour, their chime rods and strike hammers set to ring a named sequence of bells. Potsdam, Parsifal, Canterbury, Tennyson and Trinity – for hundreds of years the peal of the four-, five- and six-bell chimes had resonated in the labyrinth of rooms.

Now the Army had silenced them. With the East Wing under occupation, its rooms were out of bounds to the 'clockman', the servant employed by the Fitzwilliams to wind Wentworth's clocks.

Dust sheets covered the furniture that remained in the Van Dyck Room. The Nanking vases, the eighteenth-century ormolu chandelier, the gilt marble-topped console table, inlaid with a lute border, had all been packed away. Grey metal filing cabinets – standard Army issue – stood haphazardly between the officers' desks. The lack of symmetry in their arrangement was in pointed contrast to the perfect classical forms etched on the panelled ceiling above. Pale squares, defined by layers of coal dust that had settled over time, marked the spaces on the walls where the Fitzwilliams' valuable collection of Van Dycks had hung. 'There was a family superstition surrounding one of the Van Dycks,' Lady Barbara Ricardo recalled. 'It was the famous picture of the Earl of Strafford. The saying was that if his portrait was ever moved, the family would lose Wentworth.'

The Fitzwilliams' estates had descended through the female line: 'Black Tom Tyrant', the notorious Thomas Wentworth, 1st Earl of Strafford, was one of their ancestors. Chief adviser, trusted friend and confidant to Charles I, he was beheaded on Tower Hill in May 1641 when the King, under pressure from Parliament and the people, was forced to sign his death warrant. Wentworth was Strafford's home: a fine Tudor mansion had once stood on the site of the Palladian house. The years following his execution had been the family's darkest hour. Parliament, by an Act of Attainder, had confiscated Strafford's honours and estates. It was not until Charles II came to the throne that the attainder was reversed.

In the portrait painted by Van Dyck in 1640, the Earl is shown with his secretary, Sir Philip Mainwaring, months before his impeachment for high treason. 'Whoever names him without thinking of those harsh dark features, ennobled by their expression with more than the majesty of an antique Jupiter,' Thomas Macaulay, the great nineteenth-century historian, felt moved to write after seeing the painting:

> of that brow, that eye, that cheek, that lip, wherein, as in a chronicle, are written the events of many stormy and disastrous years, high enterprise accomplished, frightful dangers braved, power unsparingly exercised, suffering unshrinkingly borne; of that fixed look so full of severity, of mournful anxiety, of deep thought, of dauntless resolution, which seems at once to forbode and defy a terrible fate, as it lowers on us from the living canvas of Van Dyck.

The canvas – in defiance of family superstition – was moved in 1941.

Nemesis – when it came – did not come in the form of a German bullet. War was the making of Peter Fitzwilliam. In 1944 he was awarded a Distinguished Service Order for his courage after completing twelve missions on the MGBs. It came instead in the shape of Kathleen 'Kick' Kennedy, the sister of the future President of the United States.

Two dynasties: one ancient, one aspirant. Their meeting – in June 1946 – is not the starting-point, but a compass fix to which to return. The tragic prologue to their story leaps from the pages of Shakespeare: 'Star-crossed lovers', the 'fearful passage of their death-marked love' began before they ever met.

On 25 June 1943, an oppressively humid day, wearing a Red Cross uniform under her raincoat, loaded down with a gas mask, a tin helmet, a thirty-five-pound knapsack, a first-aid kit and a water flask strapped to her waist, Kick Kennedy boarded the *Queen Mary* in New York, bound for England.

30

'Mother, you wouldn't recognize this boat as the same one you made that comfortable luxury cruise on in 1936,' Kick wrote excitedly to Rose Kennedy a few days into her voyage. 'There are eight of us in a cabin and when I say on top of one another I do mean on top of one another! We didn't leave New York until the following day at noon after nearly 18,000 troops had been packed in all over the ship. They are sleeping in the hallways, decks etc. It really is the most pathetic-looking sight in the world to see the way they are living.'

The *Queen Mary* was one of many luxury liners to be commandeered as a US troop carrier in mid-1943. 'Heavy fighting is coming before autumn leaves fall,' Winston Churchill warned the British people at the end of June. Persistent cloud and light rain had hovered over the Atlantic for weeks: under the cover of the propitious weather conditions, wave upon wave of the troop ships – grey misty shapes slipping through a grey mist – stole from ports along America's East Coast carrying their precious cargo: reinforcements of men and materials – the build-up to the Allies' invasion of Europe.

Kick was one of a number of Red Cross volunteers travelling on the *Queen Mary*. The atmosphere on board the ship was tense: 300 officers, 160 Army nurses and 18,000 GIs crammed every inch of floor space. 'The only lounge available to the officers is the one main one and you can imagine how crowded that is at all hours of the day,' Kick wrote. 'And the deck space is about 40 feet long for walking. I pace 400 or 500 times a day trying to eke a mile out of it.'

It had been 'Black May' for the German U-boats: that month, a total of forty-one were destroyed in the Atlantic as a result of developments in sonar and radar technology and the breaking of the German Navy's Engima code. But still, as Kick recorded, the danger was great: 'About a half-hour after each sharp swerve we are informed that this good ship has just missed a sub. There's another one. It was probably about nine miles to starboard.' As the ship zigzagged its way across the Atlantic, when not pacing the decks or standing in a long line with her mess kit waiting for the twice-daily regulation meals, Kick spent her time on her bunk reading or writing home to her family. 'This life on an Army troop transport has been an eye-opener. It seems too unreal and far removed from anything I've ever known that I can't believe I'm a part of it. Sometimes it almost feels like a dream . . . This arrival certainly is going to be very different from the last one.'

Five years earlier, in 1938, the Kennedy family had docked at Plymouth on a mild overcast day in March amidst a storm of publicity.

Kick, then aged eighteen, wearing, as the newspapers reported, a beaver coat, 'her hat a brown heart-shaped halo with a spotted veil, her eyes blue starry bright', had lined up with her brothers and sisters against the handrail of the 20,000-ton liner *Washington* to pose for photographers. Her father, Joe Kennedy, who had travelled ahead of his family, was there to greet them. 'Now I've got everything,' he announced to the horde of waiting reporters, 'London is going to be just grand.'

Joe Kennedy was America's new Ambassador to Britain. His appointment was highly controversial: it was the first time America had sent an Irish Catholic – and a self-made man – to the Court of St James.

Brash, abrasive and extraordinarily rich, in the 1920s Kennedy had amassed one of America's largest private fortunes. To the disdain of Manhattan's ruling White Anglo-Saxon Protestant families and the old Bostonian Catholic dynasties, his money had been made through a series of speculative ventures. As a movie mogul in Hollywood he had cashed $5 million and produced the first talking picture starring the 'Queen of Hollywood', Gloria Swanson. In 1929, in the weeks leading up to the Wall Street Crash, he netted $15 million driving the bear market, selling his vast share portfolio and making millions more when he reinvested it after the index reached rock bottom. By 1930, when he was forty-two, he was reputedly worth over $100 million.

Kennedy was deeply ambitious. Exploiting his friendship with Jimmy Roosevelt, President Franklin D. Roosevelt's eldest son, he had lobbied relentlessly for the job of Ambassador. When the President was first told by his son that the freckle-faced, red-headed Irishman wanted to represent his country in London, he had laughed so hard 'he almost toppled from his wheelchair'. The idea, as FDR subsequently told Dorothy Schiff, the owner of the *New York Post*, was 'a great joke, the greatest joke in the world'.

The position of Ambassador to Britain – one held by five future US Presidents – had traditionally been reserved for the heads of America's powerful old-moneyed Protestant families. Kennedy, the son of a saloon keeper, had grown up in East Boston on the wrong side of the tracks. Just two generations separated him from the 'coffin ships'. His grandparents had been among the hundreds of thousands who risked their lives crossing the Atlantic in the mid-nineteenth century to escape death from starvation during the Irish Potato Famine.

It was not only Joe's pedigree that had caused the President to rock with laughter: his reputation hardly equipped him for such high office. A notorious philanderer, he had been famously linked with Gloria Swanson; he was also rumoured, as a consequence of his activities in the bootleg whisky trade in the Prohibition years, to have links with crime. Yet Roosevelt owed Kennedy a substantial favour. In the early 1930s, Joe's millions had helped him win the democratic nomination; further donations in 1932 and 1936 had been instrumental to the success of his Presidential campaigns. Mulling over whether to give him the job he so coveted, FDR decided to play his own joke.

Jimmy Roosevelt was with his father when Joe called to discuss the appointment. After ushering him into the Oval Office, the President asked Kennedy to stand opposite him by the fireplace, so that he could 'get a good look at him'. 'Joe,' he said, 'would you mind taking your pants down?' Looking, as Jimmy described, 'silly and embarrassed', Kennedy did as he was asked, his trousers dropping to the floor.

'Joe, just look at your legs,' FDR chided. 'You are just about the most bowlegged man I have ever seen. Don't you know that the Ambassador to the Court of St James's has to go through an induction ceremony in which he wears knee breeches and silk stockings? Can you imagine how you'll look? When photos of our new Ambassador appear all over the world, we'll be a laughing stock. You're just not right for the job, Joe.'

'Mr President,' replied Kennedy, 'if I can get the permission of His Majesty's Government to wear a cutaway coat and striped pants to the ceremony, would you agree to appoint me?'

'Well, Joe, you know how the British are about tradition. There's no way you are going to get permission, and I must name a new Ambassador soon.'

'Will you give me two weeks?'

Joe left, leaving the President chuckling. He had already decided to give him the job. He wanted Kennedy out of the way. Over the years, their relationship had been competitive and mistrustful. Mooted as a challenger to Roosevelt, Kennedy had frequently criticized the President in public. Privately, as he confided to his Secretary to the Treasury, Roosevelt regarded him as a 'very dangerous man'. Banishing him to the plum position at the Court of St James seemed a smart way of getting rid of him. He also hoped, in making such a maverick appointment, that Kennedy, with his reputation for straight-talking, would offer a clear perspective on the increasingly threatening European situation: as FDR knew, previous US Ambassadors to London – resolute Anglophiles drawn from America's grand Protestant dynasties – had displayed a tendency to turn native.

Quite how unconventional Joe Kennedy was became apparent on his first day in London, when he railed against the refined interior of the US Embassy. 'I have a beautiful blue silk room and all I need to make it perfect is a Mother Hubbard dress and a wreath to make me Queen of the May. If a fairy didn't design this room, I never saw one in my life,' Kennedy wrote to Jimmy

Roosevelt. 'I have just made my first trip around through the building. Not only was the designer a fairy, but he was probably the most inefficient architect I have ever seen.'

From the moment he arrived in London, America's new Ambassador courted the British Press, his lavish entertaining and unconventional style supplying the newspapers with yards of lively copy. Characterized as the gum-chewing envoy with 'lots of go', Kennedy was hailed as 'One of the most dynamic men in the present-day life of the United States'. 'To the London crowd', the *Star* reported, he embodies 'the sparkling vitality of a continent'. After he referred to the Queen as a 'cute trick', it made front-page headlines; so did his breach of royal etiquette at a ball at Buckingham Palace when, striding directly up to her, he had asked her to dance without waiting to be invited to do so by her equerry. Guests invited to dinner at the Ambassador's residence overlooking Hyde Park at 14 Princes Gate, a palatial six-storey building staffed by twenty-six servants, were treated to the latest Hollywood film after their meal; when the King and Queen dined, they were shown an uncut version of *Goodbye Mr Chips*.

But it was the Ambassador's nine children – the boys with their American crewcuts and handsome faces, the girls similarly wholesome-looking – the whole Kennedy magic – that most enthralled the British Press. Joe Kennedy was as ambitious for his children – his 'nine hostages to fortune', as he once called them – as he was for himself. 'You watched these people go through their lives and just had a feeling that they existed outside the laws of nature, that there was no other group so handsome, so engaged,' Charles Spalding, a family friend, recalled of a weekend spent at Hyannis Port, the Kennedys' summer home, in the late 1930s. 'There was endless talk – the Ambassador at the head of the table laying out the prevailing wisdom, but everyone else weighing in with their opinions and taking part. It was a scene of endless competition, people drawing each other out and pushing each other to greater lengths. It was as simple as this: the Kennedys had a feeling of being heightened and it rubbed off on the people who came into contact with them. They were a unit.'

Fleet Street followed the young Kennedys' every move: six-year-old Teddy's attempt to take a photograph upside down at the Changing of the Guard outside St James's Palace; thirteen-year-old Bobby's awkward efforts to engage Princess Elizabeth in conversation at a tea party at Buckingham Palace. Judging from the Kennedys' giddy letters home to their friends, they were evidently as enthralled with their new life in Britain as the British public seemed to be with them. 'Met the King this morning at Court Levee,' wrote Jack Kennedy to his friend Lem Billings: 'It takes place in the morning and you wear tails. The King stands and you go up and bow. Met Queen Mary and was at tea with Princess Elizabeth, with whom I made a great deal of time. Thursday night I'm going to Court in my new silk breeches which are cut to my crotch tightly and in which I look mighty attractive.'

Seventeen-year-old Eunice was similarly entranced by her presentation at Court: 'As I entered the Palace more excitement and joy seized me than ever before in my life,' she wrote in her diary.

During the first moment of waiting, I was breathlessly excited; then a strong rich voice called MISS KENNEDY and I started to walk alone toward their Majesties. I glanced upward and wondered if ever I would reach the throne thirty feet away; but somehow, I did. As I made my curtsey . . . I realized that at this moment I was the center of interest of this King and Queen and all the pompous ceremony that England holds so sacred. Shortly after midnight, I left the Palace for home, happy in the realization that I had achieved the aim of every young girl – that of being presented at the Court of St James – the world's greatest empire – 'The Empire upon which the sun never sets'.

But of all the Kennedy children, it was Kick who drew the most attention.

In 1938, in her first season as a debutante, she dazzled English society as few American women ever had. Catapulted into the limelight – and into the highest strata of the pre-war social whirl – by her father's position, she was presented at Court two months after arriving in London. In advance of her debut, *Queen*, the leading society magazine, devoted a one-page spread to her, bearing the headline 'America's Most Important Debutante'. At the coming-out ball that followed Kick's presentation, the Ambassador spared no expense. Eighty guests were entertained to dinner at Princes Gate, a further 300 joining them for the dance afterwards. London's most fashionable jazz band, the Ambrose Band, was hired for the evening to play in the ballroom, filled with clouds of purple and pink flowers.

Kick danced every dance, her partners including the Duke of Kent, Prince Leopold and Viscount Newport. At eighteen, she was not conventionally beautiful. She had mousy-brown hair, her face was a little too square and her figure slightly plump. The catch-all expression 'handsome' was how she was described. It was her personality that captivated the Press and her contemporaries. 'When she came into a room,' her friend Dinah Bridge, Lady Astor's niece, said, 'everybody seemed to lighten up. She made everyone feel terribly happy and gay.' 'She was just "Darling Kick",' recalled Janie Compton, Kick's closest friend from her debutante days. 'I adored her. She was absolutely enchanting. A heavenly person. She was very genuine, very kind and very funny.' Kick's letters home to her friends in America about life in London were comic and ironic, traits largely absent in those of her brothers and sisters. Of her own presentation at Court she wrote to Jack's friend Lem Billings, 'Wish you could be here for it. I so often think of you when I meet a guy who thinks he's absolutely the tops and is just a big ham . . . Very few of them take any kidding at all.' In another letter to Billings, written from Cliveden, the Astors' country seat, she wrote breezily, 'Very chummy and much gaiety. Dukes running around like mad freshmen.'

Kick was her father's daughter: like the Ambassador, she was tough and unconventional – sides to her character which impressed her English contemporaries in the course of one grand country house weekend. Soon after arriving in England, she was invited to stay at Hatfield House, the home of the Marquess of Salisbury and the Cecil family. In the late 1930s, the vast Jacobean mansion was still run in high Edwardian style, requiring a 100-strong staff.

Veronica Fraser, the daughter of Lord Lovat, was one of a dozen young people in the house party. At the start of the weekend, Kick, she remembered, was regarded as an interloper. As an Irish-American Catholic, she was a social upstart in her fellow guests' eyes, and some of them took a dim view of having an 'outsider' foisted in their midst. The boys decided to play a joke on her; in a peculiarly aristocratic version of bullying, they stole all her left shoes and hid them in Hatfield's centuries-old maze. For the entire weekend Kick was forced to hobble around on a mismatched pair of right-feet shoes. 'Why are you limping, Kick?' the other girls, entering into the boys' conspiracy, were primed to ask. 'Oh,' she replied when it came to Veronica's turn, 'Robert broke my leg before dinner.' What a great sport, Veronica thought. She was also charmed by Kick's disarmingly frank ignorance of the social etiquette at a grand country house weekend. At least ten times on her first day, she nudged Veronica or caught her eye, mouthing 'OK, so what do I do now?'

Veronica, like many of her contemporaries, was bowled over by Kick's informality. Small things made a deep impression – like the way, after a game of tennis, she would slip off her shoes in front of strangers in the state rooms of some stately home. To her generation, Kick's lack of inhibition, in contrast to the strict social conventions they had been taught to observe, was a breath of fresh air. Swiftly, she became hugely popular. In the mornings, she and her brothers would ride out together along Rotten Row in Hyde Park; there were dances and dinners every night. She was invited to all the grandest house parties, staying with the Dukes of Devonshire and Marlborough at Chatsworth and Blenheim Palace, as well as with the Astors and the Cecils at Cliveden and Hatfield House.

In September 1939, the party came to an end.

Days after the Nazis invaded Poland, Joe Kennedy, fearful for the safety of his family – and to Kick's frustration – insisted she and her mother and sisters should return to the States. 'I can't get excited about landing but I suppose it will come when we sight that Statue of Liberty,' she wrote to her father on 18 September from on board the US liner *Washington*. 'It can't be eighteen months since we were on this boat going in the other direction. It all seems like a beautiful dream. Thanks a lot Daddy for giving me one of the greatest experiences anyone could have had. I know it will have a great effect on everything I do from herein.'

'All my ducks are swans,' Joe once said of his children, but Kick was 'especially special'. She had grown up participating with Jack and Joe Junior in the spirited conversations that took place over meals in the Kennedy household, the other children sitting with their governess on a small table of their own. 'Those three – Joe Junior, Jack and Kick – were like a family within the family,' a friend of the Kennedys recalled. 'They were the pick of the litter, the ones the old man thought would write the story of the next generation.'

'So-o-o what's the sto-o-ry?' was one of Kick's catchphrases. Months after her return to England in the summer of 1943, she would become the story.

A story that her devoted father could never have imagined – or wanted to see written.

'Today it is windy and wet and we really are getting near England. I really am becoming quite excited at the thought,' Kick wrote on 27 June 1943 as the *Queen Mary* drew close to land.

The seagulls picked the ship up first, followed by a large flying boat which circled, then darted away to report its arrival. Kick stood on deck among the thousands of soldiers lining the rails. Relieved the journey was over, they chatted excitedly, reporting every low-hanging cloud as landfall. The ship turned and swerved constantly. Its lines of approach were narrower now, the threat from German U-boats greater. The waters close to England were the most dangerous of all. Four Spitfires roared out of the haze shrouding the horizon. Buzzing above the ship, they flew so close she heard the whistle of their wings.

The *Queen Mary* was due to dock at Glasgow. From there Kick planned to catch an early-morning troop train to London with the other Red Cross recruits. She had deliberately told none of her friends that she was coming. Staring out across the horizon, hoping to catch her first sight of land, her excitement was tinged with trepidation. It had been nearly four years. During her absence she had felt desperately left out. In Washington, she had transformed her flat into a shrine to her pre-war life, covering the walls with photographs of her English friends, as one American ruefully remarked, 'a living room of Lords and Ladies'. Everyone she had known before the war had joined up; the men were fighting overseas or stationed at training camps around Britain, her girlfriends working in armaments factories or at secret Government establishments like Bletchley Park. Kick had longed to be part of it, but her father had forbidden her to leave America. Desperate to get back to England, in the second year of the war she had even persuaded her brother Jack to intercede on her behalf: 'Kick is very keen to go over,' he wrote to his father, 'and I wouldn't think the anti-American feeling would hurt her like it might us – due to her being a girl – especially as it would show that we hadn't merely left England when it got unpleasant.'

The Ambassador had been the chief cause of the 'anti-American feeling' – more accurately, the anti-Kennedy feeling. The tide of the family's popularity had turned. Vilified in the British Press, branded 'Jittery Joe' and 'Run Rabbit Run', his fierce opposition to America's intervention in the war and his defeatist pronouncements on Britain's ability to win it had caused him to be loathed. 'Mr Kennedy is a very foul specimen of double crosser and defeatist,' a Foreign Office official reported in a memo initialled by Lord Halifax, the Foreign Secretary. 'He thinks of nothing but his own pocket. I hope this war will at least see the elimination of his type.' In 1939, after the Nazis conquered Poland in eighteen days, Kennedy had announced that England did not stand a 'Chinaman's chance'. His views remained unchanged as the war progressed: 'The British have had it. They can't stop the Germans and the best thing for them is to learn to live with them,' he told his aide as the Battle of Britain blazed. Hounded out of London by Winston Churchill, in November 1940 the Ambassador had been forced to resign.

From the outset of the war, Kick had taken the opposite stance to her father, publicly advocating America's intervention long before Pearl Harbor. A passionate Anglophile, she ended her letters to her friends with popular patriotic catchphrases – 'There'll always be an England' and 'The English lose the battles but they win the wars'. Yet, having got to England at last, Kick was nervous that she might find herself a social pariah. Not having shared or suffered the hardships of war, bearing the stigma of her father's anti-British pronouncements, she feared her old friends might shun her.

Britain, in the throes of war, was a very different country to the one she had left behind. At the mouth of the Clyde, the roofless houses, the burnt-out buildings, the piles of rubble where the bombs had fallen, were clearly visible from the *Queen Mary*. The GIs crowding the decks were aghast at their first sight of war: they had seen pictures of it, they had read about it, but this was real. The ship dropped anchor at the centre of the harbour; on the quay opposite, the tiny figures of a band of pipers swung into view. Dressed in kilts, they paraded up and down playing martial music – an official greeting party sent to pipe the American troops into the war. Scores of lighters, flat-bottomed boats designed to carry the soldiers to shore, hugged the sides of the *Queen Mary*; it would take as long to offload the 18,000 men as it had to pack them on to the ship. Waiting her turn to get on to the lighters, standing for what seemed like interminable hours alongside the GIs with their heavy packs and rifles at their shoulders, other anxieties troubled Kick.

One, particularly, had preoccupied her during her last months in Washington. In her absence, many of her closest English friends had become engaged or married: Sissy Lloyd-Thomas and David Ormsby-Gore; Janie Kenyon-Slaney and Colonel Peter Lindsay; Debo Mitford and Andrew Cavendish. Kick was twenty-three years old. In a letter to Janie, after hearing the news of the engagements, she had confided: 'Sometimes I feel that I am never going to take that on. No one I have ever met made me completely forget myself and one cannot get married with that attitude.' Her inability to fall in love upset her deeply, as John White, who wanted to marry her, recalled. A few months before leaving Washington, Kick, on the verge of tears, had said to him, 'Listen, the thing about me you ought to know is that I'm like Jack – incapable of deep affection.'

It was not from want of admirers. 'I think she probably had more sex appeal than any girl I've ever met in my life,' recalled Tom Egerton years later when he was in his early seventies. 'She wasn't especially pretty, but she just had this appeal.' Kick's scrapbooks from her debutante days are full of love letters and messages from would-be suitors. 'Darling Kick, when – oh when', reads one; 'You'll always mean everything to me', another. She had had many offers of marriage; before the war, William Douglas-Home, to whom Kick was 'the merriest girl you ever met', had proposed to her at dawn by a fountain at Hever Castle. The next morning, she appeared to have forgotten all about it and asked him, so he remembered, to drive her to some other beau. In 1938, Peter Grace, the American shipping heir, had crossed the Atlantic to claim her. On knocking at the door of 14 Princes Gate he was told by the butler that she had gone to the races. He went straight back to Southampton and caught the boat home. 'We were close,' he later recalled,

> I had taken her out every night in New York, but I don't blame her. She was a young girl, extremely attractive around all these dukes and princes. She was getting around in the highest circles in England. To some people if you get in with all the highfalutin people in London, that sweeps you away. I sort of figured she was caught up on that glamour, and you can't fight that.

Yet the dukes and princes had not captured Kick's heart either. It was as if she was playing a game with them. In the months before her departure for England, she had shown Betty Coxe, her flatmate, letters that she had received from her various English admirers. Which did Betty think was the most appealing, she had asked. After playing the same game with her brother Jack, she had been teasingly cautioned: 'I would advise strongly against any voyages to England to marry any Englishman. For I have come to the reluctant conclusion that it has come time to write the obituary of the British Empire.'

Within days of arriving in London, any doubts Kick had that she might not be welcome had been dispelled.

> Yesterday Lord Beaverbrook rang up and asked me down for the week-end. I am going to dine with him next week even though he said, 'this admirer is the combined age of all your other admirers'. Lady Astor also rang and asked me to come to Cliveden. She said Jakie [Astor] had been invited to stay with the Duchess of Kent but refused until he found out whether or not I was coming to Cliveden.

As soon as word got out that she was in town, the invitations flooded in. 'Everyone has been more than kind – it's been sort of overwhelming,' she wrote to Jack a month after her arrival.

> In our country one would take such hospitality for granted more or less but coming from the English it's quite unexpected and very, very comforting. I feel that my devotion to the British over a period of years has not been without foundation and I feel this is a second home more than ever. No one with the exception of Mr Aurean [sic] Bevan, MP for Wales has mentioned a thing about Pops which fact has quite amazed me . . . Of course a lot of it I can put down to British reserve which feel that some things are better left unsaid but mostly I blame it on their ability to make friends which last all their lives. They are slow about it at first but once made then it's lasting – wholly and completely.

In London, blitzed and battered as it was by war, the social scene was swinging. 'You had to go out. Life had to go on,' remembered Kick's friend Lady Virginia Ford. 'You had to behave in what to a later generation would have seemed an uncaring manner. But dear heavens if you didn't do that you would have gone mad.' At the most glamorous venues, big bands played through the night until dawn, the evenings following a set pattern. For those up in

London on leave, the first priority was to discover who was in town. Women working at factories or at Government establishments were given one day off in every eight; officers in the forces, stationed in Britain at training camps and airfields, were entitled to forty-eight hours' leave a fortnight. With so many people scattered, as Sally Norton, the daughter of Lord Grantley, recalled, Kick's set depended on a 'bush telegraph', run by Mr Gibbs, the hall porter at Claridges. 'Ah, Miss Norton,' Gibbs would say. 'Lord Hartington is in London. Miss Kenyon-Slaney is staying here. Lord Grantley is over at the Ritz, and here is his room number.' If the 'Mr Gibbs' system failed, everyone knew to congregate at the Ritz Bar at eight for drinks. The taxi service 'Rely On Us', which continued to operate throughout the blackout, would ferry them around town – to dinner at the Mirabelle before going on to the Café de Paris to dance. At two or three in the morning, they would move on to the fashionable Four Hundred Club, where they would stay until it was time to catch the milk train back to camp or to work.

Kick was lucky to be based in London. The American Red Cross had assigned her to an exclusive officers-only club in Hans Crescent in Knightsbridge where her job was to boost the morale of the GIs – as she described '5½ days of jitter-bugging, gin rummy, ping-pong, bridge and just being an American girl among 1,500 doughboys a long way from home'. The London posting meant that Kick could go out most nights, her admirers queuing up to escort her.

On her first Saturday night in London, it was Billy, Marquess of Hartington, who took her out.

Of all Kick's suitors, in every respect but one, Billy was the most eligible. The eldest son of the Duke of Devonshire, his family owned over 180,000 acres of land in Britain and Ireland, bringing in revenues of more than a quarter of a million pounds a year. In addition to their main seat at Chatsworth, they owned Hardwick Hall in Derbyshire, Bolton Abbey in Yorkshire, Compton Place at Eastbourne and Lismore Castle in Ireland. They had several townhouses in London, including Chiswick House on the River

Thames. 'Chiswick?' Billy's grandmother had famously questioned. 'Oh, we sometimes used it for breakfast.'

Kick had met Billy, who had been mooted as a husband for Princess Elizabeth, at a Royal Garden Party at Buckingham Palace in the summer of 1938. Like Kick, he was nice-looking – as opposed to good-looking. Almost six feet four inches tall, he had a slight self-conscious stoop; his hair was dark, his face pale and elfin, its most striking feature his dark 'Labrador' eyes. Aged twenty at the time, he had fallen in love with Kick. 'I remember going to a dance and sitting next to Billy,' recalled the Countess of Sutherland, 'and he spent the whole dinner telling me how wonderful Kathleen [Kick] was.' As Fiona Gore, the Countess of Arran, remembered, 'here was this lively American girl who through some odd circumstance had become the toast of the town, and she was paying all this attention to Billy. It gave him such confidence. She swept him right off his oh so steady feet.'

Five years after they first met at Buckingham Palace, Billy was still in love with Kick. Unable to forget her, in the months before she returned to England, he had broken off his engagement to Sally Norton. Within a month of Kick's arrival in London, he invited her to stay at Compton Place. 'I have just returned from a day and a half spent in the country with Billy at Eastbourne,' Kick wrote to her brother Jack at the end of July.

> It's right on the East Coast and has been blitzed quite badly but the family continues to go there during the summer months. For 24 hours I forgot all about the war. It's the most lovely spot and all the fruit which one never gets in London at your disposal. Peaches sell for $1.50 apiece over here and I returned to London clutching a dozen under my arm. Billy is just the same, a bit older, a bit more ducal but we get on as well as ever. It is queer as he is so unlike anyone I have ever known at home or any place really . . . It's all rather difficult as he is very, very fond of me and as long as I am about he'll never marry. However much he loved me I can easily understand his position. It's really too bad because I'm sure I would be a most efficient Duchess of Devonshire in the post-war world and as I'd have a castle in Ireland, one in Scotland, one in Yorkshire

and one in Sussex, I could keep my old nautical brothers in their old age. But that's the way it goes. Everyone in London is buzzing with rumours and no matter what happens we've given them something to talk about.

Yet beneath the bravura, Kick's letter to Jack hinted at feelings of hurt and rejection – that Billy's love for her, however strong, was constrained by his 'position'. 'I can't really understand why I like Englishmen so much,' she continued, 'as they treat one in quite an off-hand manner and aren't really as nice to their women as Americans but I suppose it's just that sort of treatment that women really like. That's your technique isn't it?'

'I think Kick had a thing about Billy right from the beginning,' her close friend Janie Compton recalled. In May 1940, when he was serving as an officer in the Coldstream Guards, after Kick received news that the British Expeditionary Force had been defeated in France, she wrote anxiously to her father:

At the moment it looks as if the Germans will be in England before you receive this letter. In fact from the reports here they are just about taking over Claridges now. I still keep telling everyone 'the British lose the battles but they win the wars'. I have received some rather gloomy letters from Janie and Billy. Billy's letter was written from the Maginot Line. Daddy, I must know exactly what has happened to them all. Is Billy all right?

In society circles, Billy and Kick's engagement had been predicted almost from the moment they first met. The gossips blamed Kick for the fact that it had not happened; her string of unrequited suitors was well known. 'Stop all this foolishness,' Lady Astor had implored her in the spring of 1942, 'and come right over and marry Billy.' But as Kick knew, contrary to the gossip, she and Billy had not been lovers before the war. Their relationship had been a non-starter. Billy was unobtainable: he had not asked her to marry him, and, as she believed after returning from her weekend at Compton Place, he never would.

The truth was, as Billy confided to a friend, he regarded his love for Kick as a 'Romeo and Juliet thing'. It was unthinkable that he should marry a Catholic. To do so would be to betray centuries of family history and tradition.

The Devonshires' fortune and reputation had been founded on their opposition to Catholicism. In the 1530s, at the time of the dissolution of the monasteries, Sir William Cavendish, a Crown Commissioner appointed by Henry VIII to seize Catholic assets, had been rewarded for his loyalty with grants of land from the spoils of confiscation and a position at Court. His rapid advancement had enabled him to win the hand of Bess of Hardwick, a wealthy Derbyshire heiress whose legacy included the valuable Hardwick and Chatsworth estates. In the Glorious Revolution, Protestant intriguing further consolidated the family's wealth and prestige; in 1694, Sir William's descendant was honoured with a dukedom after backing the right horse in the contest between the Protestant William of Orange and the Catholic James II. By the close of the nineteenth century, the Devonshires had become as virulently anti-Irish as they were anti-Catholic. In 1882, Billy's great-uncle, Lord Frederick Cavendish, Chief Secretary to Ireland, was sensationally murdered in Phoenix Park in Dublin by 'The Invincibles', an Irish Nationalist terrorist organization. Four years later, his grandfather, the 8th Duke, kept the Whig Party out of power when he founded the breakaway Liberal Unionist Party in opposition to Gladstone's policy of Home Rule for Ireland.

Kick was an Irish-American Catholic, the daughter of a man who publicly celebrated Irish nationalism. Of lesser importance, but significant, was her social pedigree. If Billy succeeded his father, he would become the 11th Duke of Devonshire. Seven out of ten of his predecessors had married the daughter of a Duke, a Marquess or an Earl. Of the three exceptions, the 8th married the daughter of a German Count and the 6th Duke had died unmarried; only one, the 3rd Duke, had married a commoner – and that was way back in 1718. His wife, Catherine Hoskins, was an heiress from Surrey. The one thing Kick had in her favour was that she was an heiress too. In the 1920s, Joe Kennedy had set up a trust for his nine children; by the mid-1940s, they were reputedly worth $10 million each.

Yet all the money in the world could not count against the weight of history, embodied in the prejudices of Billy's father, Edward, the 10th Duke of Devonshire. 'The one thing he has always dreaded,' Kick admitted to her family, 'is that one of his sons should marry an RC.' A rotund, shabby figure, he was described by his younger son Andrew Cavendish as 'the worst-dressed, the most unostentatious, and least ducal figure'. Sir Henry 'Chips' Channon, the diarist, concurred: 'He was a frustrated man, hated being a Duke and was really a bit bored by all his possessions and palaces.' Field sports and the countryside were Edward's great passions. One of his favourite pastimes was to sit for hours, a grocer's apron tied around his waist, making salmon lures from feathers he had collected from the hats of his titled guests. The Duke's dislike of 'Papists' was legendary. It was said that he had contemplated moving the master bedroom in his London town-house to avoid seeing the spire of Westminster Cathedral. 'I think it's fair to say that my father was a bigoted Protestant,' Andrew Cavendish recalled. 'My father and mother both felt very strongly that Catholics proselytized and that our family had a long tradition opposed to Catholicism.'

It was a widespread prejudice among the Protestant English aristocracy. The deep schism dividing the two faiths stemmed from the forging of power and identity and the defence of ownership over hundreds of years. The 10th Duke believed, along with the majority of Protestants of his generation and class, that all Catholics were bent on plotting the recatholicization of England. It was a view that had some foundation: in the Britain of the 1940s, Catholic children grew up praying for the conversion of England, well versed in 'Faith of Our Fathers', a martial hymn to the English martyrs. In the Duke's world the allegiances of the Reformation, the Civil War and the Glorious Revolution still resonated. Catholicism, so he believed, posed nothing less than a threat to the state: the strongest proof of a popish plot was the Catholic Church's stipulation that the Protestant party in a mixed-faith marriage should sign an agreement to raise their offspring as Catholics: if they refused, the Church would not sanctify the union. The Duke was horrified by his eldest son's infatuation with Kick: if Billy were to marry her, it would be tantamount to defeat in the battle his family had so successfully waged against Catholicism for centuries.

At great personal cost, motivated by a sense of duty, Billy had resolved to honour his father's – and his family's – beliefs. In the summer of 1943, his position remained unchanged: he loved Kick as passionately as he had done before the war, but he would never ask her to marry him. 'The religious difficulties seemed insurmountable': knowing that he 'would never be happy or be much good without her', as he would later write to her mother, he felt 'that if she could find someone else she could really be happy with, it would be much better & more satisfactory for her'.

But within months, Billy would change his mind.

31

William John Robert Cavendish, Marquess of Hartington, eldest son of the 10th Duke of Devonshire, was being heckled. The political meeting at the school hall in Darley Dale, an isolated hamlet on the banks of the River Derwent in Derbyshire, was packed.

'Do you think a boy like this can represent us?' one of the hecklers yelled.

'Young man, you ought to be in the front line, not standing there talking politics,' a woman shouted.

Billy Hartington, speaking from the stage, struggled to make himself heard. 'I've been in the Army five years and have seen action overseas,' he responded. 'I hope to take my place in the front line shortly.'

His answer was barely audible, drowned out by laughter and shouts of abuse, hurled from around the hall.

'What can you, the son of a Duke, do for the working man?' one man demanded.

'Did you ever do a day's work?' shouted another.

'Well,' Billy stuttered, 'I've been in the Army for five years . . .'

The rest of his sentence was lost.

It was January 1944. Billy had resigned his commission in the Coldstream Guards to stand for Parliament in West Derbyshire. 'The by-election was a grave error of judgement on my father's part,' admitted his brother, Andrew Cavendish. 'My family treated it like a rotten borough. I suspect my brother was pushed into it.' 'He should never have come back. He should have stayed with his regiment,' Lady Maureen Fellowes, a close friend of the Devonshires, remembered bitterly. 'He was just too nice. He would never have said, "Go to hell, Father." He didn't want to hurt anyone.'

The Cavendish family had held the seat for almost 200 years. In 1938, Billy's father had supported his uncle, Henry Hunlocke, as the Tory candidate. The old Duke saw it as a means of keeping it warm for his eldest son. Early in 1942, when Hunlocke resigned from Parliament, the Duke insisted that Billy leave his regiment and return to West Derbyshire to fight the seat.

Billy's victory was meant to be a fait accompli. Yet both the Press and the Devonshires had underestimated the tenacity of his socialist opponent, Charles White. They had also misjudged the mood of the electorate after four long years of war. The hecklers crowding the school hall at Darley Dale were White's men. They – and their candidate – viewed the contest as a personal vendetta. White's father, the one man to have wrested the seat from the Cavendish family in the previous two centuries, had been beaten by Billy's uncle in 1938. Focusing his campaign on the injustices of Britain's class system, White presented himself as a champion of the people – the cobbler's son fighting the heir to the Dukedom from the 'Palace on the Peak'.

White began the campaign by casting doubt on Billy's courage and patriotism, accusing him of having used his aristocratic connections to dodge the war in order to contest the seat. Speaking at a political meeting, he told the audience, 'Lord Hartington will have to explain to the parents and relatives of serving men and women in West Derbyshire how he can more or less please himself so far as military service is concerned while men and women in the ranks must comply with the rigid military requirements and discipline.' Sniping at the Devonshires' historic stranglehold over the constituency, he continued: 'Boys and girls are sacrificing their lives to kill dictatorship on the Continent: political dictatorship must not be allowed to develop here.'

'He looks absolutely repulsive. He hates the Cavendishes like poison,' was Kick's verdict on Charles White. During the three-week campaign, she did not leave Billy's side. In spite of the hopelessness of a permanent future together, in the six months since her return to England, she and Billy had become inseparable. 'She fell in love with him,' said her close friend Janie Compton, 'it was as simple as that.'

Alarmed that Kick's Catholicism might rebound on Billy's

electoral prospects, the Duke, who regarded her as nothing less than an 'evil influence', had ruled that she must travel incognito. 'News of me wouldn't add any votes,' she wrote home to her family, 'so I was known as Rosemary Tong, the village girl. Wasn't allowed to open my mouth, although I did go canvassing for votes one afternoon with Billy's sister.' Whenever and wherever Billy spoke, Kick was at the back of the crowd, gauging the audience's reaction. The class bitterness shocked her: 'It really was something to see,' she told her family. 'He was asked every sort of question from the Beveridge plan right on down to "Why isn't the park at Chatsworth plowed up?" "Why didn't your father pay more death duties?" "What do you know about being poor?"'

As the days wore on, the viciousness of the campaign intensified. Touring the villages and remote hamlets in the largely rural constituency, Billy was ridiculed wherever he went, his privileged position a constant target.

'In the interests of the national salvage campaign, may I ask how it is that, when everybody's railings and gates have been taken away, the big gates at Chatsworth are still standing?' one man challenged Billy.

'They were made in 1690 and are considered works of national importance,' he replied. 'If we are asked to have them melted down, we'll do so right away.'

Behind the scenes, White disseminated rumours that Billy's politics were linked to Oswald Mosley's. Billy's brother, Andrew Cavendish, had recently married Debo Mitford, whose sister, Diana, was the wife of the British fascist. 'Are you in favour of Mosley being at large?' White's supporters were primed to ask. 'I am not my brother's keeper,' Billy was forced to reply defensively. 'My sister-in-law and my brother – who is at the moment in action in Italy – don't hold with Mosley. They loathe him.' Even Billy's ability to milk a cow became a campaign issue. 'Can you milk a cow?' White asked him at one meeting. 'Yes,' he replied, his frustration evident, 'I can milk a cow, and I can also spread muck. Some of my opponents seem rather good at that too.'

White did not confine his campaign to lambasting the Devonshires' wealth and privilege: he also appealed to the electorate's hopes for the post-war world. His nine-point manifesto included 'common ownership of the great industrial and natural resources of the country' and rapid demobilization and civil retraining programmes for members of the armed forces. Most popular of all was the Beveridge Plan, Labour's blueprint to build a welfare state to combat 'Want, Disease, Ignorance, Squalor and Idleness' – the sins of the 'Wicked Thirties'.

By comparison, Billy's campaign was timidly lacklustre. Aimed at preserving the status quo, his slogan was, 'A vote for Hartington is a vote for Churchill'.

In a misguided attempt to bolster Billy's vote, Churchill, the Prime Minister, wrote him an open letter midway through the campaign. Its sentiments, harking back as they did to a feudal past, played straight into the hands of his opponent.

My dear Hartington
I see that they are attacking you because your family have been identified for about 300 years with the Parliamentary representation of West Derbyshire. It ought, on the contrary, to be a matter of pride to the constituency to have such long traditions of constancy and fidelity through so many changing scenes and circumstances.

Moreover, it is an historical fact that your family and the people of West Derby have acted together on every great occasion in this long period of our history on the side of the people's rights and progress.

It was so in the revolution of 1688, which finally established the system of Constitutional Monarchy under which we have enjoyed so many blessings. It was so at the passage of the great Reform Bill of 1832, which laid the foundations of the modern electorate. It was so in the repeal of the Corn Laws in 1846, and in the extension of the franchise in 1884.

Once again it is the old cause of freedom and progress that is being fought for, though this time not only among the hills of West Derbyshire, but in the devastating world war.

As the campaign drew to a close, Billy could see that he was likely to lose. Confiding in Kick, he predicted a huge swing to

Labour. 'It's all very upsetting,' Kick wrote to her family, 'they know just what the working people want to hear and they give it to them. There is no doubt about it, there is a terrific swing to the left. People want to hear about how much money they are going to get out of the Beveridge Plan, not how much money the Tory government is spending on the war.'

On polling day, a large crowd gathered outside the Counting Station at Matlock Town Hall. The result – a massive swing to the Socialists, as Billy had predicted – astonished Britain. Charles White won by 5,000 votes, almost the same majority Billy's uncle had achieved in 1938. His victory was hailed by the left-wing Press: 'It is a blunt intimation that the country wants to see NOW, in the Government's reconstruction policies, a clearer promise of justice and happiness for the common man,' ran the *Daily Herald*'s leader: 'A world in which men's minds will be directed to the future rather than to the past: to the prospects of their children, rather than to the accomplishments of their landlords' ancestors.'

It was a very public humiliation for Billy. Day after day during the campaign he had been forced to stand before his countrymen defending himself against charges of cowardice and upholding his family name. He had failed. Conceding defeat, his overriding desire to put the record straight on the issue that had hurt him the most was evident at the start of his speech: 'It has been a fierce fight,' he began. 'Now I am going out to fight for you at the Front.'

'It just leaves a bad taste,' Kick wrote home a few days later from Chatsworth, where she and Billy had retreated to spend one last week together before he returned to his regiment. 'His father was most disappointed and kept saying: "I don't know what the people want." Billy just said, "I do, they don't want the Cavendishes." I think it shook his father a bit to hear it from Billy.'

The by-election was a breaking point for Billy. The days spent on the hustings had convinced him that Britain would be a very different place when the war was over. Socialism, he believed, with its swingeing attack on the privileges and power of the aristocracy, its radical agenda of high taxation and nationalization and its nascent proposals for a welfare system that would transfer the obligation of care in the community from the family to the State, threatened to undermine everything the Dukes of Devonshire stood for. As he told Kick, he even doubted whether the family would be able to live at Chatsworth after the war. What was the point, Billy agonized alone, in defending the values and the traditions of a potentially redundant aristocratic dynasty by sacrificing his love for Kick?

A week after the count at Matlock, Kick celebrated her twenty-fourth birthday at Chatsworth. The Duke, sensing that his son was about to do 'the one thing', as Kick described, 'he had always dreaded', made a point with his present. 'Received a lovely old leather book from the Duke for my birthday,' she noted. 'The Duchess said she had nothing to do with it, and when I opened it up I knew why. It was the Book of Common Prayer of the Church of England.'

'I think something will have to be decided one way or another before we both go nuts,' Kick wrote to her parents on 4 March 1944. 'Somehow I can't make myself see that the Lord in Heaven (not the one in question) would make things so difficult.'

Billy had asked Kick to marry him. But he had imposed one condition: that his sons should be raised as Protestants.

Naively, Kick assumed the Vatican would grant her special dispensation to marry. Until the late 1920s, the English Catholic Church had allowed the sons of a mixed-faith marriage to be brought up as Protestants providing the daughters were raised as Catholics. The moment Billy proposed, she wrote to her father asking him to use his connections in the Catholic Church to establish whether the recently revoked law could be applied to her case. Obtaining permission to marry Billy, so she thought, was surely a formality. The Kennedys had become America's first Catholic family: at the invitation of President Roosevelt they had represented the United States at the Papal Inauguration in 1939. They had even been granted the rare privilege of a private audience with Pope Pius XII afterwards. Kick was stunned when her mother reported back: 'I do not seem to think Dad can do anything,' she wrote. 'He feels terribly sympathetic and so do I and I only wish we could offer some suggestions.'

Rose Kennedy's letter threw Kick into turmoil. If, as Billy demanded, she refused to raise their children as Catholics, the Catholic Church would not recognize their marriage. The consequences were dire: not only would she be excommunicated, unable to receive Holy Communion or to make an act of confession, but, in marrying without the blessing of her Church, she would be committing fornication, a sin of 'grave matter'. To deliberately and wilfully turn away from God to commit a sin of 'grave matter' was, according to the teachings of St Paul, a mortal sin. By marrying Billy she would be severed from God's sanctifying grace, condemned to eternal damnation. It left her with a brutal choice: either she gave up Billy, or, if she married him, she would have to face exile from the Catholic Church.

'She was deeply, deeply religious,' Janie Compton recalled, 'it was a fundamental part of her nature.' It was an aspect of her character that sometimes disconcerted her friends. Ursula Wyndham Quinn remembered sharing a room with her at a country house weekend early in 1944. At bedtime, after they had chatted for a while, Kick knelt down and prayed. What struck Ursula as so peculiar was that she prayed for some fifteen minutes. The next morning, the moment she got up, she prayed again and then went off to Mass. Religious issues peppered her conversation. John White, another of her close friends, jotted down the gist of their religious debates in his diary. 'Kick calls to me [*sic*] all birth control is murder,' he wrote. 'I say her position is just Catholic Church technique for helping keep membership.' Later, he recalled her naivety about sex: steeped in the dogma of the Catholic Church, she would refer to it coyly, in the rare moments they discussed it, as 'the thing the priest says not to do'.

Kick's dilemma was made worse by her mother's rigid lack of empathy or understanding. To Rose, the thought that any daughter of hers would risk exile from the Catholic Church for the sake of the man she loved was unimaginable. Billy's intransigence, his refusal to allow Kick to raise their children as Catholics, to her mind represented an intractable obstacle: 'When both people have been handed something all their lives, how ironic it is that they cannot have what they want most,' she wrote.

I wonder if the next generation will feel that it is worth sacrificing a life's happiness for all the old family traditions. So much wealth, titles etc seem to be disappearing. But I understand perfectly the terrific responsibilities and the disappointment of it all. It is Lent now and I am praying morning, noon and night, so do not be exhausting yourself and running your little legs off going to Church, as your first duty is towards your job . . . We had a letter from someone in Boston whose third cousin watched you go to Communion frequently, so the news has been carried across the waters . . .

Billy's mother, the Duchess of Devonshire, was far more sympathetic. She recognized that her eldest son loved Kick and could not bear the thought of him being unhappy. She also understood how wretched Kick felt, realizing that the last thing she wanted to do was to turn Billy down. In an effort to find a solution, the Duchess invited Kick to meet the Reverend Edward Keble Talbot, Chaplain to King George VI. In a letter to her parents, marked confidential, Kick wrote an account of their meeting at Churchdale, the Devonshires' estate in Derbyshire:

The Duchess with my full knowledge, asked a very great friend of hers, Father Ted Talbot, to come and stay to talk to me . . . Her idea was for him to explain what the Cavendish family stood for in the English Church. He also took a great deal of trouble to explain to me the fundamental differences between the Anglican and Roman Churches. Of course I explained that something one had been brought up to believe in and which was largely responsible for the character and personality of an individual is a very difficult thing for which to find a substitute. Further, I explained that I had been blessed with so many of this world's goods that it seemed rather cheap and weak to give in at the first real crisis in my life. Of course both the Duchess and Father Talbot don't for a minute want me to give up something. They just hoped that I might find the same thing in the Anglican version of Catholicism.

By the end of her stay at Churchdale, Kick, as she told her parents, had made her choice. 'When I left Churchdale on Tuesday, yesterday, I felt most discouraged and rather sad. I want to do the right thing so badly and yet I hope I'm not giving up the most important thing in my life.' Billy would not capitulate on the question of the religious upbringing of a future son and heir: forced to choose between Billy and God, Kick had chosen God. 'Poor Billy is very, very sad,' her letter continued,

> but he sees his duty must come first. He is a fanatic on this subject and I suppose just such a spirit is what has made England great despite the fact that Englishmen are considered so weak-looking etc. If he did give in to me his father has told him he would not be cut off, in fact nothing would happen. They, meaning Mother and Father, would just make the best of it. That makes things even more difficult.

It was the Duchess who captured the heartbreak of Kick's stay at Churchdale. Maintaining an emotional distance from her own parents, Kick enclosed an extract from the letter Billy's mother had written to her a few days after she left. 'I am no good at saying things,' the Duchess confided,

> so I am writing to say how you are always in my thoughts and how I feel for you alone here without your mother and father when you are going through so much and have had such overwhelmingly difficult things to decide about. It is desperately hard that you should have all this great unhappiness with the second front always at the back of one's mind. I know how lonely you must feel and almost forsaken but we must trust in God that things will come out for the best in the end. I do hope you know how much we love you and if there is even the smallest thing we can do to help you have only to say – and always please come and see me at any time if you feel like it and come and stay. There is always a bed for you – you have only to telephone.

Kick ended her letter to her parents by thanking them: 'You two have been wonderful and a great strength. I'm sure Mother's prayers are helping all the time.'

By mid-March, a month after Billy's defeat at the by-election, the combined weight of the two families had apparently been brought to bear. Both parents believed the marriage was off, that neither Kick nor Billy was prepared to compromise their religious beliefs. But in the coming weeks, as the two of them spent time alone together in London, the truth was they could not bear to let each other go.

Their meetings were brief – snatched when Billy was able to get leave from his regiment. The Second Front – the Allied Forces' invasion of Europe – was expected at any moment. Frantically, Kick and Billy sought a way around their impasse. Billy came up with one solution, a compromise founded on his belief that, when the war was over, aristocratic titles would have no currency. If, he promised Kick, any future social upheaval were to change Britain's class system, he would allow her to raise their children as Catholics. But in the event that a dukedom continued to confer the traditional pre-eminence, their children would be brought up as Protestants. Yet whatever their private pact, according to the teachings of the Catholic Church, if Kick went ahead and married Billy, she would still be committing a mortal sin. She was unwilling to stake her State of Grace in the eyes of God on the future – and nebulous – state of Britain.

At the end of March 1944, turning to the Church for guidance, Kick arranged a meeting with Bishop Matthew, the Auxiliary Bishop of Westminster. It was a final attempt on her part to see if she could obtain some sort of dispensation to marry. She went to the meeting with a heavy heart, believing her mission to be impossible. But what the Bishop told her was what she longed to hear. A dispensation was out of the question: as the Bishop explained, it would place the Church in a very difficult position. Instead, he advised Kick that it would be better to go ahead and marry on the basis that dispensation would be given at some point in the future. 'Of course he wouldn't guarantee that anything could be done,' she wrote to her family afterwards. 'I am certainly not going to count on everything being made OK – I shall only hope for it.' For the first time, she hinted that she was considering changing her mind. 'If I do marry Billy within the next two months, please be quite sure that I am doing it with the full knowledge of what I'm doing and that I'm quite happy about it and feel quite sure that I am doing the right thing.' Crucially, the Bishop had reassured her on the one point she was most anxious about. Contrary to the views of the other senior Churchman who had been consulted, Bishop Matthew advised Kick that if she were to marry Billy she would not be committing a mortal sin. According to his interpretation of canon law, she was not wilfully turning away from God. 'As my Bishop said,' she triumphantly informed her parents, '"No one can say that you are committing a sin because a sin is done from a selfish motive. What you are doing is done entirely from a non-selfish motive."'

In the last week of April, after spending three days in Yorkshire with Billy, Kick finally agreed to marry him on his terms. The moment she said yes, it was left to Billy to compose his first – and difficult – letter to the formidable Rose Kennedy. Suspecting that Rose regarded him as the devil incarnate for having caused her daughter's fall from grace, somehow he had to find the words to explain himself to his future mother-in-law.

Dear Mrs Kennedy

I feel so ashamed at not having written to you before and I hope you won't think too harshly of me for my bad manners. The situation has changed so much from day to day, and I'm afraid I've kept on putting off writing to you until we could reach a decision one way or the other.

I have loved Kick for a long time, but I did try so hard to face the fact that the religious difficulties seemed insurmountable, and I tried to make up my mind that I should have to make do with second best. I felt too that if she could find someone else she could really be happy with, it would be much better & more satisfactory for her.

But after Christmas I realized that I couldn't bear to let her go without ever asking her if we couldn't find a way out and I knew that the time before I should have to go and fight was getting short.

I could not believe, either, that God could really intend two loving people, both of whom wanted to do the right thing, and both of whom were Christians, to miss the opportunity of being happy, and perhaps even useful, together because of the religious squabbles of His human servants several hundred years ago.

I do feel extremely strongly about the religion of my children both from a personal and from a national point of view, otherwise I should never have asked Kick to make such sacrifices in agreeing to their being brought up Anglican.

I know that I should only be justified in allowing my children to be brought up Roman Catholic, if I believed it to be desirable for England to become a Roman Catholic country. Therefore, believing in the National Church of England, as I do very strongly, and having so many advantages, and all the responsibilities that they entail, I am convinced that I should be setting a very bad example if I gave in, and that nothing would justify my doing so.

I do feel terribly keenly the sacrifices I'm asking Kick to make, but I can't see that she will be doing anything that is wrong in the eyes of God. My first worry has been to decide whether she could really be happy with me, having made these sacrifices. Obviously if I felt she could not, and if I felt that she would live with a sense of guilt, I should not be justified in asking her to marry me. But I do think in my heart that she is so holy and good that God will continue to help her and that she can be happy, and I know that selfish though it sounds, I should never be happy or be much good without her.

I will try with all my power to make her happy, and I shall never be able to express my gratitude to you and to Mr Kennedy for your understanding and goodness in giving your consent.

Please excuse this dopey and after reading over, pompous letter, I think we both feel a bit punch drunk after the emotional battering of the last few months.

I shall never be able to get over my amazing good fortune in being allowed to have Kick as my wife; it still seems incredibly wonderful.

Please try not to think too harshly of me for what must seem to you a tyrannical attitude. I promise that both Kick and I have only done what we really believed in our hearts to be right.

Thousands of miles away, across the Atlantic, far from consenting to the marriage, Rose and Joe Kennedy were appalled. Rose was in hospital in Boston for a minor operation when she received the telegram announcing the wedding would take place in seven days' time. On a sheet of paper headed 'Personal Reminiscences Private', she wrote of feeling 'disturbed, horrified – heartbroken'. Joe was equally shocked. 'Joe phoned me, said he hadn't slept . . . Talked for a minute of our responsibility in allowing her to drift into this dilemma, then decided we should think of a practical way to extricate her. I said I would think it out and then call him later.'

The Kennedys, an American dynasty in the making, were as mindful of setting a bad example as the Devonshires: their political ambitions turned on the Irish Catholic vote. 'Everyone pointed to our family with pride as well-behaved, level-headed and deeply religious,' Rose noted. 'What a blow to family prestige.' Resolving to do their utmost to stop the ceremony from going ahead, she and Joe sent a telegram to Kick: 'Heartbroken – think – feel you have been wrongly influenced. Sending Archie Spell's friend to talk to you. Anything done for Our Lord will be rewarded hundredfold.'

'Archie Spell' was Archbishop Spellman, the Archbishop of New York. Under instructions from Rose and Joe, drawing on his connections in the Catholic Church in London, Spellman dispatched various clergymen to persuade Kick to change her mind. In the first week of May, a flurry of coded telegrams flew to and fro across the Atlantic as Spellman's stooges reported back. 'EFFORT IN VAIN', Archbishop Godfrey, the Holy See's Chargé d'Affaires to the Polish Government in exile and the first apostolic delegate to Britain since the Reformation, cabled to Spellman after visiting Kick. 'MOTHER COULD TRY AGAIN WITH ALL HER POWER. AM CONVINCED THIS ONLY CHANCE.'

Kick was deeply upset by both her parents' and the rest of her family's reaction. None of her brothers and sisters back home had offered their congratulations. Jack Kennedy expressed their view in a letter to his friend Lem Billings. Drily offering his verdict on the marriage, he wrote: 'As sister Eunice from the depth of her righteous Catholic wrath so truly said: "It's a horrible thing – but it will be nice visiting after the war, so we might as well face it."' There was only one member of the family Kick could count on: her eldest brother Joe, stationed in England in the West Country with the US airforce.

Throughout that week Kick spoke to Joe daily. 'Whenever she heard from you she would call me and ask me what I thought,' he later wrote to his parents. 'I did the best I could to help her through. She was under a terrific strain all the time, and as the various wires came in she became more and more upset.' Out of loyalty to Kick and against his parents' wishes, Joe stoically defended the couple. 'Billy is crazy about Kick,' he told them, 'and I know they are very much in love. Everyone talks about it. I am much more favourably impressed with him than I was the last time I was over here. I think he really has something on the ball, and he couldn't be nicer. I think he is ideal for Kick.'

By now nothing was going to convince Kick to change her mind. On the day before she married Billy, she sent one last telegram to her father: 'RELIGION EVERYTHING TO US BOTH WILL ALWAYS LIVE ACCORDING TO CATHOLIC TEACHING PRAYING THAT TIME WILL HEAL ALL WOUNDS YOUR SUPPORT IN THIS AS IN EVERYTHING ELSE MEANS SO MUCH PLEASE BESEECH MOTHER NOT TO WORRY AM VERY HAPPY AND QUITE CONVINCED HAVE TAKEN THE RIGHT STEP.'

She received no reply. Rose was inconsolable. It had not occurred to her that her own implacable stubbornness was a trait shared by her daughter. Kick's piety, her craving for approval, had led Rose to believe that she would succumb to matriarchal pressure. To the last, she clung to this belief: on the day of the wedding, still bent on stopping it, she instructed Archbishop Spellman to send a telegram to Archbishop Godfrey in London: 'WILL YOU KINDLY CALL ON KK EXPLAINING THAT HER MOTHER IS GREATLY DISTRESSED NEWS OF CONTEMPLATED ACTION AND IF POSSIBLE PERSUADE HER TO POSTPONE THIS STEP.'

The bouquet of pink camellias Kick clutched in her hand as she ran up the steps past the hordes of waiting pressmen to be married was the only remnant of a grand society wedding. The flowers, grown in the Camellia House at Chatsworth, had been sent down by train that morning. The Duchesses of Devonshire of centuries past had worn tiaras and jewel-encrusted long silk gowns at their weddings; Kick was wearing a knee-length pink crêpe dress and a hat of blue and pink ostrich feathers, set off by a salmon-coloured taffeta veil. The dress had been made the night before by a friend, the material purchased with ration coupons – some contributed by the local milkman. To complete her outfit, Kick had borrowed a gold mesh bag and a large diamond brooch. She was not about to walk down an aisle in the private chapel of some stately home: the venue for the wedding was Chelsea Town Hall, a municipal-grey public building on London's busy King's Road. It was all over in ten minutes. Billy's best man, Charles Granby, the heir to the Duke of Rutland, who had never been to a civic ceremony before – commonly the scandalous and tawdry resort of divorcees – was shocked by the brevity and austerity of it all.

For many of the guests – especially the bride and groom's relations – the day was to be endured rather than enjoyed. Kick was escorted by her brother Joe, the only member of the Kennedy family to attend the wedding. As the two of them dashed up the steps to the Register Office, dodging the flashbulbs of the world's press, Joe, as Kick wrote, was 'quite conscious after seeing his face plastered all over the papers that he was "finished in Boston"'. Since the announcement of the marriage two days earlier, the Press on both sides of the Atlantic had had a field day. 'Parnell's ghost must be smiling sardonically,' crowed the *London News*. 'It was the Lord Hartington of the eighties who headed the Liberal-Unionist revolt that wrecked Gladstone's Home Rule Bill . . . Now a Hartington is to marry a Catholic Irish-American who comes from one of the great Home Rule Families of Boston.' Over in America, as the *Boston Traveller* caustically observed, Kick's marriage would 'bring her into a family prominent in the defence and spread of Protestantism throughout the British realm'.

The Devonshire family, putting on a brave face, turned out in force. The Duke and Duchess were there, as were Billy's grandmothers – the Marchioness of Salisbury and the Dowager Duchess of Devonshire – and his two sisters, Lady Anne and Lady Elizabeth Cavendish. Anne was mortified at having to wear stockings that were laddered and torn, but with the wartime restrictions she had no other pair. Meeting the Duchess for the first time, Joe liked her enormously; the Duke he described as 'a shy old bird . . . as jittery as an old duck'. Ushered into a drab room, brightened only by vases of pink carnations, Joe and the Duke witnessed the marriage. The ring Billy placed on Kick's finger was inscribed with the words 'I love you more than anything in the world.' Afterwards, the wedding party posed for photographs on the steps of the Town Hall. 'It seemed better than have the photographers take them anyway and have them turn in awful ones,' Joe told his parents. 'I saw no point in looking extremely grim throughout so I looked as if I enjoyed it.' As the group posed for the Press, crowds of Red Cross girls and American GIs, Kick's compatriots from her volunteer work, muscled into the frame. 'The result,' she noted later, 'is that the Marquess and Marchioness are surrounded by the strangest-looking group of wedding guests that has ever, ever been.'

The reception was held at the Devonshires' townhouse in Eaton Square. 'The chef at Claridges supplied an enormous chocolate wedding cake and the Dukie-Wookie supplied the champagne,' Kick wrote in a separate letter to her mother. 'We sent out telegrams the day before, thinking and hoping many would not come but over 150 showed up.' The guests were an eclectic bunch; along with the GIs and Red Cross girls from the club in Hans Crescent, Kick had invited the hall porters. Mingling with the Devonshire family and a handful of society grandees, 'a few of the GIs,' as Kick recalled, 'became rather tiddly on the champagne, carrying on long conversations with Lady Cunard who looked more terrifying than ever.' At one point during the reception, one of the soldiers accosted Billy: 'Listen, you God damn limey,' he told him, 'you've got the best damn girl that America could produce.' Kick was irrepressible, as she later confessed, 'I enjoyed every minute of it and I shouldn't have thought I was very well married without it.'

Two days after the wedding, for the benefit of his parents, Joe composed his own, more measured account of the day. As the Kennedy heir he was mindful of the family's position in the whole affair. 'As far as publicity was concerned over here, I think we got off pretty well,' he wrote. 'Only one paper had much of a discussion about it . . . I suppose Boston went wild.' Hoping to reassure Rose and Joe and bolster their spirits, he confided, 'Somehow I think things will work out OK. It doesn't look so now, but I am sure something will happen . . . As far as Kick's soul is concerned, I wish I had half her chance of seeing the pearly gates. As far as what people will say, the hell with them. I think we can all take it. It will be hardest on Mother, and I do know how you feel, Mother, but I do think it will be all right . . .'

Kick heard nothing from Rose and Joe on the day of the wedding.

That morning, Rose left New York for a retreat in Virginia. At the airport, swamped by reporters, she issued a terse statement. The family, she said, had been unable to communicate with Kick, much as they would have liked to, due to wartime cable restrictions. She herself, she added, was 'physically unfit to discuss the wedding with Kick or anyone'.

The following day, Kick read her mother's statement in the newspapers. Aware of its fallacy, knowing the number of cables that had been sent to and fro across the Atlantic in the course of the previous week, she immediately called Joe. He responded by sending a one-line telegram to their father: 'THE POWER OF SILENCE IS GREAT.' Kennedy senior relented; breaking the silence, he sent a cable back by return. While there is no record of its content, Kick was immensely relieved, evident in the telegram she composed in reply: 'MOST DISTRESSED ABOUT MOTHER PLEASE TELL HER NOT TO WORRY YOUR CABLE MADE MY HAPPIEST DAY WIRE NEWS COMPTON PLACE EASTBOURNE SUSSEX HAVE AMERICAN PAPERS BEEN BAD ALL LOVE KICK.'

It would be two months before Rose could bring herself to speak to her daughter.

*

'Dearest family,' Kick wrote on 18 May, twelve days after her wedding, 'I have now become a camp follower. Am living in a small hotel near to where Billy is stationed. It is very comfortable and we have the prize suite. I wouldn't compare it to Daddy's set-up at the Waldorf Towers, but as I often said it takes all sorts of experience to make life worthwhile . . .' Writing five days later, she told them, 'I am feeling better now than I have since I left America. This is the first really good rest I have had for a year. Have put on some weight and am getting plenty of sleep. MARRIED LIFE AGREES WITH ME!'

After a five-day honeymoon at Compton Place, the Devonshires' seaside home at Eastbourne, Kick and Billy had moved into the Swan Hotel at Alton in Hampshire, a modest half-timbered building in the village. Preparations were in full swing for the Normandy landings; Billy's regiment, the Coldstream Guards, was due to take part in the invasion. It was simply a question of when.

While Billy spent his days training with his regiment at the military camp outside the village, Kick explored the countryside on a bicycle and delighted in the comedy of manners that unfurled at the Swan during their stay.

[It] gets funnier and funnier every day. Little did we know what we were in for when we arrived in this town. There never has been a funnier assortment of people in one spot than in this hotel. The little bellboy, a native of Dublin, informed me that his name was Kennedy and we might be related. Every time Billy or I stick our noses out of our room – there he [is] waiting to march in front of us, flinging open doors and saying 'This way, Marquess' at the top of his lungs. Last night we went to call on the Chef, as he had put us up such a delicious picnic on the Sunday. The Chef told me a long sad story about how he almost came to work for us in the Embassy days. He said one of the secretaries had gotten the letters mixed up so he never came. The food here is exceptionally good and much better than any London restaurant. Last night he christened the dessert after Billy by calling it 'croûte Cavendish'. I must say it was most disgusting but we had to grin, eat and bear it.

There is another old retired Army man here who has had his house taken over by the Americans so he lives here. He collects prints and happened to have one of the 3rd Duke of Devonshire. He has already given it to us as a wedding present.

D-Day, the anticipated invasion of Europe, finally came on 6 June. Wave upon wave of British and American troops were to follow the battalions that had landed on the beaches of north-west France. On 17 June the Coldstream Guards received orders to leave for the Front.

It had been 'the most perfect month', Billy wrote later that evening. 'How beastly it is to be ending things . . . This love seems to cause nothing but goodbye. I think that that is the worst part of it, worse even than fighting.'

Kick missed Billy dreadfully in the weeks after he left for France. Returning to London, feeling lonely and isolated, she was also profoundly disturbed by her mother's silence. Since her wedding day, she had done all she could to win Rose back. She had sent messages of love to her via her father and her brothers and sisters and written her numerous letters – all of which her mother had ignored.

Rose was incapable of seeing beyond Kick's apostasy. The idea that a daughter of hers was living in sin was unbearable, her horror validated by the reaction the marriage had provoked among leading Catholics. In the weeks following the wedding, she had received many letters offering nuptial condolences. 'May the Blessed Mother give her the necessary grace to see the error of her ways before many weeks have passed,' Father Hugh O'Donnell, an influential Catholic priest, had written. Across the Atlantic, the reaction was equally strong. At Chatsworth, the Devonshires were inundated with letters from irate Catholics accusing Kick of having sold her soul for a title. Writing to his wife with the zealotry of a convert, Evelyn Waugh had remarked, 'Kick Kennedy's apostasy is a sad thing. It is Second Front nerves that has driven her to this grave sin and I am sorry for the girl.'

On 6 July Kick sat down to compose yet another letter to her mother. It merely repeated thoughts and sentiments she had expressed in others she had written to Rose since her wedding – letters her mother had failed to answer. In the same way Rose could not bring herself to see beyond Kick's apostasy, Kick refused to recognize her mother for the rigid, overbearing and emotionally frigid woman that she was. On the contrary, Kick absolutely adored her. As Kick's abject letter reveals, her happiness depended on her mother's approval.

Darling Mother
This letter is just meant for you. It's a birthday letter – Hope it arrives by July 23rd.

By now I hope you are happy about my marriage, I suppose I really always expected to marry Billy. Some day – some how.

However you and Daddy know that I never would do anything against your will. You two have been so wonderful to me as well as to every member of the family. The older I get and the more I see makes me realize this and a lot of other things. First, that you are the most unselfish woman in the world. Any house where we have all been has been difficult to run and you have always put us before any of your own desires or pleasures. We all have happy personalities and get along with people far easier than most people – this is due to the happy atmosphere which has always surrounded us.

When I see some homes I marvel at you more and more.

Certain qualities I have – people admire. They are all traits that you have instilled in me.

In the matter of my marriage – I knew you would be upset, but I felt sure you would see the ultimate good. I knew you would never forbid anything if you felt it meant my happiness. It must have been hard for you to resign yourself to the idea of my doing something quite against all your principles – I repeat, the one thing I don't want you ever to think is that my religious or moral education has ever been lacking. You have done more than enough to show me the gateway to Heaven. Please God I can do half as well for the little Cavendishes.

I miss you so much and long to see you. We have so much to talk about. There wasn't anyone to really take your place at the time of the wedding and it seemed so odd that at the time, the moment, the period of one's life which one has looked forward to for so long, the dearest person in the world wasn't there –

Please have a wonderful birthday. Think of me and always remember that if I spend the rest of my life trying to repay you for everything it will be very little. All love to you, from Kick

Seven weeks after the wedding Rose finally contacted her daughter. Her letter was in part duplicitous; privately, in conversations with Archbishop Spellman, she was still contriving to have the marriage annulled. 'Here it is the fourth of July again, and another summer is almost half over,' she wrote to Kick.

We are all looking forward now to having Joe home and we only wish you and Billy were going to be along too . . .

. . . I really didn't expect that you would be married until after the invasion or at least until I knew more definitely of your plans. However, that is all over now, Dear Kathleen, and as long as you love Billy so dearly, you may be sure that we will receive him with open arms . . .

Joe Junior never did come home. On 12 August, the reality of war was brought home to the Kennedy family when Joe was killed after his plane, a Liberator bomber, exploded on a secret mission over the North Sea. Kick was devastated. Joe was her favourite brother, her 'pillar of strength', the one member of the family to have supported her through the months of anguish over Billy. 'When he felt that I had made up my mind he stood by me,' she later wrote. 'In every way he was the perfect brother doing, according to his own lights, the best for his sister with the hope that in the end it would be the best for the family.' The evening she heard of Joe's death, she spoke to his great friend Mark Soden. 'I'm so sorry I broke down tonight,' she wrote after the phone call. 'I still can't believe it. It's hard to write. I don't feel sorry for Joe – just for you and everyone that knew him 'cause no matter how he yelled, argued, etc, he was the best guy in the world.'

On 16 August, Kick flew home to America to grieve with her family.

32

'I've got a telegram here,' Joe Kennedy said to Eunice, his twenty-two-year-old daughter.

'Is it about Billy?' she asked.

'Yes, he's been killed.'

Billy Hartington was killed in action on 10 September 1944. It was three months after he had left his new wife to rejoin his regiment in France. They had spent just five weeks together.

The telegram reporting Billy's death was delivered to Joe Kennedy's suite at the Waldorf Hotel in Manhattan. Kick, still in deep mourning for her brother Joe, who had died barely four weeks earlier, was eight blocks away, shopping at Bonwit & Teller, the department store, where she had arranged to meet her younger sister, Eunice, for lunch. Under Joe's instructions, Eunice went in search of her, finding her on the second floor.

'Before we go I think we ought to go back and talk to Daddy,' she said.

'Something's happened?' said Kick, searching her sister's face for an answer.

'Why don't you go talk to Daddy?'

Eunice did not tell Kick what had happened on the walk back to the Waldorf. When they got there, Joe was waiting for them at the door to his suite. Ushering Kick in, he closed the door. After he had told her Billy was dead, she remained alone in the room. She did not emerge until later that evening when the family gathered for dinner, her eyes red and swollen from crying. The meal was tense. Neither Billy's death nor his name was mentioned.

The following morning, Patsy White, Kick's closest friend, flew up to New York from Washington, to be with her. After she had met Joe Kennedy at the Waldorf, a driver took her over to the Plaza where Rose and Kick were staying with the rest of the family. The room she was shown into was in a state of upheaval. Rose, Kick and the other Kennedy girls were sitting there with clothes strewn all around them. Kick was deathly pale: 'A great cloud of misery was hanging over everything,' Patsy recalled. When she finally got to be alone with her friend, Patsy asked her what she had been doing since she had heard the news. 'Mostly going to Mass,' Kick murmured, barely looking at her. 'Mother keeps saying, "God doesn't send us a cross heavier than we can bear." Again and again she keeps saying it.'

That evening, Joe Kennedy took them all out to a French restaurant on Park Avenue. During dinner he suggested getting tickets for a show on Broadway and seemed surprised when no one jumped at his offer. As the meal went on, Patsy was unnerved by the way Kick was expected to behave as if nothing had happened. But then she remembered that Kick had once told her that Kennedys were brought up not to cry. For the next two days the charade continued. The two friends were hardly given a chance to be alone. In the whirl of frenetic activity laid on by the other Kennedys, Patsy remembers Kick's silent grief. She often caught her staring uncomprehendingly at a photo of Billy in uniform that she always kept at her side. There was to be no future, no children. Later, talking about Billy, Kick told her, 'The amazing thing was that Billy loved me so much. I felt needed, I felt I could make him happy.'

A few days later, Kick was comforted by a letter she received from Billy's mother, the Duchess of Devonshire, its warmth a startling contrast to the chilliness she had experienced from her own mother. 'My Darling Kick,' the Duchess wrote,

> I want you never, never to forget what complete happiness you gave him. All your life you must think that you brought complete happiness to one person. He wrote that to me when he went to the front. I want you to know this for I know what conscientious struggle you went through before you married Billy, but I know that it will be a source of infinite consolation to you now that you decided as you did. All your life I shall love you – not only for yourself but that you gave such perfect happiness to my son whom I loved above anything in the world. May

you be given strength to carry you through these truly terrible months. My heart breaks when I think of how much you have gone through in your young life.

Slowly, the details of Billy's death emerged.

In the weeks before he died, his battalion had been engaged in heavy fighting in Northern France. They were exhilarating times: the Germans were in retreat. In early September, the battalion crossed the Somme River, pushing east towards Brussels. Billy's unit was one of the first to liberate the city: as the German retreat was driven on, victory seemed within grasp. Thousands of locals from the towns and villages turned out to cheer the Allies on, festooning the soldiers' tanks and armoured vehicles with garlands of flowers. Writing to Kick shortly before his death, Billy admitted to feeling 'so unworthy of it all living as I have in reasonable safety and comfort during these years . . . I have a permanent lump in my throat and I long for you to be here as it is an experience which few can have and which I would love to share with you.'

But on 8 September, at Beverlo, fifty miles east of Brussels, the battalion encountered a setback: the Germans, heavily entrenched, were no longer in retreat. In the battle to capture the village, Billy lost a quarter of his men. A fellow officer and pre-war friend of the Devonshires was fighting alongside him:

During the attack on Beverlo I saw him walk across to one of his sections as calmly as if he had been in the garden at Compton Place. That same morning he had been standing on the back of one of our tanks directing the fire on to the German tanks and was largely responsible for their destruction. All the time, under fire. Many of our guardsmen asked who was the officer from the 5th Battalion, for it was impossible not to be inspired by his presence.

Billy cut a distinctive – and dangerously visible – figure on the battlefield. As an officer he was not required to wear regulation uniform. In place of khaki he wore a white riding mac and brightly coloured trousers. He rarely wore a helmet.

The morning after the attack on Beverlo, Billy's company set out to capture the nearby town of Heppen. It was held by elite troops from the German SS divisions. With his batman at his side, Billy walked ahead of the company, carrying a pair of wirecutters. 'Come on, you fellows, buck up,' he said as he led his men forward.

Later that afternoon, a farmer and his son returned to their farm on the swampy ground at the edge of the town, the scene of some of the fiercest fighting. 'The English losses were very heavy: six tanks were left behind on the battlefield,' Frans Magelschots recalled. 'We finally found eleven English and thirty German corpses. The whole battlefield looked horrible.' In the farmhouse itself, they came across more than a dozen bodies. Five lay outside the front door. 'Two bodies were lying next to one another, a German and English soldier having strangled each other to death. Some had bayonets in their bodies, some even spades. It had been a hand-to-hand battle, eye to eye.' By the back door of the house, Frans and his father found two more bodies: one was unlike any of the others. Wearing a white mackintosh and bright trousers, it was unblemished except for one small bullet hole through the heart.

Billy was buried in Belgium alongside the men from his company who also died that day. On 20 September, ten days after his death, Kick flew back to England for the memorial service at Chatsworth. Lord Halifax, the British Ambassador to the United States, arranged for her to fly back on a military transport plane. Her fellow passengers were Sir Charles Portal, the Chief of the British Air Staff, and Field Marshal Alan Brooke, the Chief of the Imperial General Staff, who were returning from America following urgent discussions with the US administration on the progress of the war.

The flight was top secret, expected to leave at some point in the middle of the night. Waiting for the all-clear to cross the Atlantic, Kick wrote the following entry in her diary:

So ends the story of Billy and Kick !!!
Yesterday the final word came. I can't believe that the one thing that I

felt might happen should have happened – Billy is dead – killed in action in France Sept 10th. Life is so cruel – I am on my way to England, Writing is impossible.

A few days later, struggling to come to terms with his death, Kick confided her misery to her family. 'I just feel terribly, terribly sad,' she wrote.

I know that Daddy said I had a lot of problems that might never have been worked out and that perhaps later in life I might have been very unhappy. That's all quite true, but it doesn't fill the gap that I now feel in my life. Before it had its purpose, I knew what it would be. Now I feel like a small cork that is tossing around. I know that there are hundreds like me, and lots more unfortunate, but it doesn't heal the wound. The nice Bishop, who was so helpful before I was married, wrote the following: 'Having borne you both so much in mind I am very anxious that you should begin again swiftly and easily the use of the Sacraments and the full practice of your faith. I have always been convinced that the reason why you took the line you did about the marriage was because you wanted your husband to be happy in what might prove the last portion of a short life.' Isn't that nice? I am going to see him this Tuesday and he is going to say a Mass for Billy and Joe at which I shall receive Communion. I hope that makes Mother as happy as it makes me.

It was Kick's first Holy Communion since her marriage. According to the teachings of St Paul, her mortal sin was absolved with Billy's death. Providing she confessed her sin, she was entitled to participate in the Sacraments.

Rose Kennedy was overjoyed at her acceptance back into the Catholic faith. Writing to Kick at Chatsworth, she told her,

I have been thinking about you day and night ever since you left and praying for you and loving you more and more . . . I have been to Mass for Billy frequently, in fact, I am on my way now (7.15 a.m.). After I heard you talk about him and I began to hear about his likes and dislikes, his ideas and ideals, I realized what a wonderful man he was and what happiness would have been yours had God willed that you spend your life with him. A first love – a young love – is so wonderful, my dear Kathleen, but, my dearest daughter, I feel we must dry our tears as best we can and bow our heads to God's wisdom and goodness. We must place our hand in His and trust Him.

But in the depths of her soul, Kick could not place her 'hand in His and trust Him'. Although, in her rudderless state, she craved her parents' – and the Church's – approval, her faith had been profoundly shaken. During the weeks she stayed at Chatsworth, she was unable to sleep in a room alone. Kick asked Billy's sister, Elizabeth Cavendish, to share her bedroom. 'I never met anyone so desperately unhappy,' Elizabeth remembered. 'Her mother had tried to convince her that she had committed a sin in this marriage, so in addition to losing her husband, she worried about having lost her soul.' It was her faith she doubted: while the Catholic Church had welcomed her back, Kick found it difficult to come to terms with the irony that her sin could only be absolved through the death of her husband. 'Well, I guess God has taken care of the matter in His own way, hasn't He?' she remarked bitterly to a friend.

Unable to share her spiritual doubts with her family and suffering the grief of bereavement, Kick sank into a deep depression.

Six weeks before he died, Billy had written her a letter from France:

I have been spending a lovely hour on the ground and thinking in a nice vague sleepy way about you & what a lot I've got to look forward to if I come through this all right. I feel I may talk about it for the moment as I'm not in danger so I'll just say that if anything should happen to me I shall be wanting you to try and isolate our life together, to face its finish, and to start a new one as soon as you feel you can. I hope that you will marry again, quite soon – someone good & nice.

In the autumn of 1944 Kick could not imagine that anyone would ever replace him. 'If Eunice, Pat & Jean marry nice guys for fifty years they'll be lucky if they have five weeks like I did,' she told her parents. 'Tell Jack not to get married for a long time. I'll keep house for him.'

But, as Peter Fitzwilliam spun Kick around the dance floor a little over eighteen months later, at a ball at the Dorchester Hotel, it was love at first sight.

33

He could only watch from a distance. He did not want to see the impending devastation close up. On a cold, blustery day in April 1946, two months before Peter Fitzwilliam and Kick Kennedy first met, a column of lorries and heavy plant machinery trundled across the Park at Wentworth, their massive tyres and thick caterpillar tracks scoring long gashes in the wet grass. Peter stood at an upper window in the house. Beneath him, on the lawn in front of the entrance to the Pillared Hall, stretched a line of Nissen huts. Built by the army to accommodate the Intelligence Corps troops, they now housed squatters – homeless refugees from the bombing raids that had devastated Sheffield.

Peter had come through the war, but Wentworth House and its surrounding Estate had not. In the Marble Salon, wooden boards still covered the precious marble-inlaid floor, and in the padlocked chapel and behind barred doors in the cellar rooms below the house the hundreds of crates containing the Fitzwilliams' collection of porcelain and silver and other priceless bibelots, carefully packed by their servants, were still stored. Stacked against them, swathed in dust sheets and green felt, was the family's collection of Old Masters and innumerable bundles of lesser paintings that had been removed from their frames. Peter doubted whether the pictures or the contents of the crates would ever assume their former positions in the state rooms in the house.

'Operation Moonshine' was the code-name given to the last of the SOE Motor Gunboat runs. Peter had completed seven missions to win his Distinguished Service Order. In the critical months of preparation for the invasion of Europe, Britain's special ball-bearing needs had been largely met by the little ships: 347 tons of essential aircraft parts were smuggled out of Sweden along the Skaggerak sea channel, bristling with German patrol boats. Miraculously, just two of the 'grey ladies' had been lost and only one crew member killed. 'Moonshine' had ended in the summer of 1945. Since leaving the Motor Gunboats, Peter had been fighting the newly elected Labour Government to save Wentworth House from destruction.

He had lost the first round. Along the roads that ran around the perimeter of the Park, detachments of German POWs had removed gates and fence posts to allow the convoy of lorries and machinery in. It had already left a hideous trail. In the immediate vicinity of Wentworth, thousands of acres of the Fitzwilliams' farm- and woodland had been torn up and tree-lined avenues, buildings and roads obliterated. The church in the village, built by Peter's great-grandfather, had lost the top of its spire, blasted to oblivion by the ongoing mining operations. A raw expanse of white rock was all that was left of the surrounding countryside. Stripped bare to the limestone, craters, tens of feet deep, and mountainous ridges of rubble were the only features in the lunar landscape.

Now, the army of contractors, sent by Manny Shinwell, the Minister of Fuel and Power, threatened to destroy Wentworth House. Ninety-eight acres of woodland in the Park were to be quarried for coal. Next on the contractors' list were the beautiful formal gardens. The coal, the Minister had decreed, was to be mined right up to the back door of the house.

'It is all just too utterly heart breaking,' Maud Fitzwilliam confided to her friend Lucia, Viscountess Galway.

> I adore every stick and stone of the beloved place . . . the destruction that is going on with that awful open-cast coal is appalling – it really is cruel.
>
> . . . Poor Peter is heartbroken over it, and they now threaten to come right through and destroy the terrace and the gardens right up to the house, which will be left like a desert island in the midst of mess and utterly treeless for the next hundred years . . . am going there next week to pack up some things I left there – as nothing will be safe; though Peter says it is so devastating to see he couldn't bear my seeing it, but I feel I must.

Six months earlier, in September 1945, the Labour Government, under the wartime Emergency Powers still in force, had stamped a requisition order on the Park and the formal gardens behind the house. The land straddled the point where the Barnsley Seam, famous for its top-quality 'Yorkshire Hards', came to within yards of the surface. It was fuel the country desperately needed. War had created a shortage of manpower in the coal industry, jeopardizing supplies. In the winter of 1946, 40,000 Bevin Boys – young men conscripted during the war to the coalfields – were employed in Britain's 1,600 collieries, but still they could not produce enough. To feed the demand for coal, the Park and gardens at Wentworth – together with the 2,000 acres of the Fitzwilliams' estate already being mined – were scheduled to become the biggest open-cast mining site in Britain. The coal was worked from the surface, with mechanical excavators used to dig down to the seam, seventy feet below the ground. This way, the Government reasoned, it could be mined quickly and cheaply without the need to employ large numbers of men.

On the day the quarrying in the Park began, Arthur Eaglestone, the miner who had worked at New Stubbin colliery before the war, was among a small group of men gathered on the footpath that ran alongside the contractor's site. 'The Germans have landed after all,' one of them remarked. They had come to watch what Peter could not bear to observe at close hand. Standing in the shadow of the great oaks planted in commemoration of victory at the Battle of Blenheim, they looked on in horror as the cranes and excavators swung into action, their claws gouging into the soil, exposing great tracts of limestone below. 'Daffodil bulbs were uprooted by the thousand,' Eaglestone wrote afterwards, 'and hundreds of trees wrenched from the earth and flung to one side, strewn white and fatally wounded.' As he witnessed the devastation, Eaglestone recalled a meeting at Wentworth House half a century earlier when a delegation of miners and their wives had crossed the Park from Rawmarsh to plead with the 6th Earl to be allowed to return to work after weeks on strike. 'He lectured them on the folly of agitators,' Eaglestone remembered, 'and the virtue of work. They thanked him – one can imagine with what bitter resignation – and straggling home again across the Park, a woman who was in the company gave birth to a child. And now the children of that child were taking over.'

It was Peter's inheritance that was being ripped up. Writing to Lucia, Viscountess Galway, Maud admitted one blessing: 'Am thankful my beloved Billy is not able to see it – or anyway to be beyond minding.'

Midway through the war, in February 1943, Billy Fitzwilliam had died at Wentworth from cancer at the age of seventy. Speaking at his funeral, the Bishop of Sheffield had praised the Earl's relationship with his thousands of employees: 'It would be a sad day for this country,' he told the congregation, 'if there were lost that association of inheritance with responsibility, and of wealth with social service, which was the tradition of stewardship that the late Earl received and has quietly and conscientiously maintained.'

The Bishop's remarks were hopelessly out of kilter with the sentiments of the British electorate. Two years after Billy died, in July 1945 – in the first General Election in a decade – a Labour Government was elected with a landslide majority and a mandate for radical reform. 'After the long storm of war, we saw the sunrise,' Hugh Dalton, the new Chancellor of the Exchequer, wrote. 'No one wanted to return to the Britain of the 30s. They wanted to go forward, and were confident that they could do so.'

By laying the foundations of a Welfare State, Labour had pledged to build a new Britain – to eradicate the 'five giant evils' Beveridge had identified in his 1943 report: Want, Squalor, Disease, Ignorance and Unemployment. For the first time, old age pensions and unemployment, sickness, widows and maternity benefits were to be available for all.

Class politics and the memory of the hardship of the 1930s underpinned the Labour victory: the notion of a clean break with a dark past. In its manifesto, *Let Us Face the Future*, Labour had vowed to end the hegemony of 'the privileged rich', the 'Czars of Big Business', 'the hard-faced men and their political friends' who had prospered in the inter-war depression, the controllers of 'the banks, the mines, the big industries' in whose hands 'the concentration of too much economic power' had led to 'great economic blizzards' and mass poverty. The nationalization of Britain's key industries – coal, gas, electricity, the railways, iron and steel – was Labour's second talisman. The transfer of the country's great industries to public ownership would secure greater productivity and efficiency, the profits to be ploughed into nourishing a fairer society.

The consequences of the Labour victory were catastrophic for Peter in almost every respect. Virtually overnight, the Government's proposals for social reform – paid for partly by high taxation of the super-rich – and their plans to nationalize the coal industry had decimated the putative value of his father's legacy.

Billy Fitzwilliam had left almost £2 million in his will; £60 million at today's values, it was substantially less than the £2.8 million his grandfather, the 6th Earl, had bequeathed, but the true extent of Billy's wealth was masked by the transfer of the family's historic coal holdings into a limited company for tax avoidance purposes in 1933. With the nationalization of the collieries, the massive coal revenues which had sustained Wentworth House, and on which the family's fortune had been built, were set to go. There was to be no income from the open-cast mining operations either. The land had been requisitioned under the regulations of the Defence Act, introduced at the start of the war. Under the Emergency Powers they conferred, the Government could compulsorily seize any piece of land or property in Britain to do with it as it pleased. Compensation was payable solely for loss of rent: no compensation was awarded for 'any diminution or depreciation in value ascribable only to loss of pleasure or amenity', nor was the owner entitled to a share in the profits from the commercial exploitation of the land.

The nationalization of coal had also rendered Peter, now the 8th Earl Fitzwilliam, more or less redundant. Historically, the power and status of the Earls Fitzwilliam in their neighbourhood had been based on their ownership of coal via the huge numbers of men they employed. Without it, the obligations of 'inheritance with responsibility, and of wealth with social service' that the Bishop of Sheffield had spoken of at his father's funeral no longer applied. Propelled by a huge mandate from the country, the Labour Government – to use the words of the 6th and 7th Earls – had severed 'the ties that bound'.

Of all the major transfers of ownership, coal was the most romantic in Labour mythology, the industry where the excesses of capitalism had left 'blood on the coal'. The miners had waited a quarter of a century for Britain's pits to be nationalized: it was way back in 1919 when the interim report of the Sankey inquiry, the Royal Commission set up by Prime Minister David Lloyd George to investigate the coal industry, had concluded that 'even upon the evidence already given, the present system of ownership and working in the coal industry stands condemned and some other system must be substituted for it, either nationalization or a method of unification by national purchase and/or by joint control.' Within weeks of the 1945 General Election, the Coal Nationalization Bill was among the first of Labour's radical legislative proposals to be introduced to Parliament.

After the hard, desperate years of the 1930s, power was at last in the miners' hands and they seized it. Almost a tenth of the Parliamentary Labour Party were miners' representatives – newly elected MPs who had worked underground, or in the industry's affiliated unions. Many of them chose the passage of the Bill through the House of Commons as the moment to make their maiden speeches. And the moment for revenge. As the Bill went through its second and third readings, one by one they stood up to vent their bitterness at the coal owners' historic stranglehold over the industry.

'I was hewing in a Durham colliery as recently as June last year and my experience embraces almost every activity in and around a mine,' Charles Grey, MP for Durham, began. 'For years, they [the coal owners] have treated the miner abominably. Low wages, long hours, miserable compensation, bad conditions, wretched death benefits and virtual slavery were the lot of the miner.'

Speaking of his own experience, he said: 'I have had the distressing and demoralizing effect of working for 6 shillings, sixpence ha'penny a day, and taking wages into a home which could not produce the minimum of necessities for a decent standard of existence. I recognized years ago that I was enmeshed in a vicious system designed for profit, in which the whole human element was subordinated to production for profit.' Frank Fairhurst, MP for Oldham, had spoken before him. 'I was born in the year of the 1892 strike. My father was a miner, and my four brothers were miners, so I know something of what it is to live in a mining home in a mining village,' he told the House. 'The history of coal mining is one of the blackest in existence and is a terrible indictment of the system under which we, in this country, have lived. It is saturated with the blood, sweat and toil of the miners, and the drawn and pinched faces of women of past generations are imprinted on the industry.' Recent history – the collective experience of Britain's million miners in the bleak inter-war years – drew the most fire from the new intake of MPs: their abandonment by successive Governments, the 1926 coal strike, but above all else, the failure of the Sankey inquiry. 'Instead of honouring the findings of the Commission,' Fairhurst exclaimed angrily, 'at the request of the coal owners, the Government of that time washed their hands of it and gave back control to 1,400 owners and 4,000 mineral royalty owners. There began a period of mismanagement, conflict and strife, with the resulting poverty, misery, depressed areas and depressed communities almost unparalleled.' The time had come for the coal owners to atone for the misery they had inflicted: 'Never again will the present mine owners have a chance to work the mines,' Fairhurst vowed. 'They will never be forgiven for what happened after 1926.' Pointing at the Tory benches opposite, he accused them of being 'poor nebulous-minded troglodytes and Rip Van Winkles'. So 'vicious, concentrated and channellized' had their 'ideology on profits, privilege and power become', he continued, 'they cannot appreciate the fact their world is dying: and if the future is to live, then die it must.'

The Government met with little resistance from the Opposition.

There was no sympathy for the coal owners. In the last years of the war, Britain's coalmines had been under state control: the consensus was that the nationalization of the collieries was long overdue. The Tories' chief concern was to ensure that the coal owners were properly compensated for the loss of their pits. On the Labour benches, the far left argued that the mines should be confiscated, with no compensation at all paid to the coal owners. 'One would think, from the compensation they are expecting, that they had been guardian angels,' one former miner said bitterly in the debate. 'When I was taking home 30 shillings a week, I had quite another name than angels for them. I thought they wanted horns. I am not concerned about how much compensation they are to get. I think in terms of confiscation, and the less the owners get, the better I shall like it.'

This was the backdrop against which Peter was fighting to save Wentworth House. The Coal Nationalization Act was making its way through Parliament between January and May 1946: for months the fate of the house hung in the balance. Manny Shinwell, the senior Government official who had served the requisition order, was responsible for steering the legislation through the House of Commons. Shinwell was one of the 'wild men of the Clyde', a left-wing group of Glasgow Labour MPs returned in the General Election of 1922. President of the Maritime Workers' Union – a 'stormy petrel of trade unionism', as a fellow socialist described him – Shinwell had been imprisoned for sedition in the George Square riots of January 1919. Born in 1884, the son of Jewish immigrants, he had grown up in a two-room flat in a tenement block in Glasgow, 'a grim and squalid-looking building', he later wrote, 'on the banks of the Clyde'.

As a newly appointed Minister, Shinwell toed the Cabinet line during the passage of the Bill, concurring that the coal owners should be compensated for the loss of their pits, but his hatred of the 'old brigade', the men who had run the 'foolish, callous, profit-hunting system' which, as he believed, had operated in British industry before the war, was well known. In 1944, he had published a political pamphlet entitled *When the Men Come Home* in which he set out his vision of a post-war Britain: The 'old brigade are busy', he wrote.

> They talk blandly of the necessity of returning to the pre-war economic set-up of this country, of the sanctity of the rights of private enterprise. All the old-time balderdash which since the beginning of Britain's industrial power has been trotted out to support an unequal, wasteful and poverty-ridden social order is with us again. Are you going to be simple enough to swallow it? I hope not . . . We must plan in the interests of the community as a whole, stamping out with ruthless severity any attempt on the part of the 'interests' – landed, financial, industrial and the rest – to defeat the common will.

A supporter of the abolishment of hereditary titles, Shinwell, without naming him, had identified Peter Fitzwilliam as an example of the excesses of the 'old brigade'. Midway through the war, Peter had made the headlines when he paid the highest recorded price for a horse at the Newmarket sales. 'Surely you are not so dull,' Shinwell appealed to his readers, 'that you cannot appreciate that whatever misery you may have endured, everything is as it should be in a country where at the recent yearling sales at Newmarket a filly was sold for 8,000 guineas. This sum represents about forty years' wages of what is commonly regarded as a well-paid workman. Need anything more be said?'

Peter was convinced that Manny Shinwell's decision to mine the gardens and Park at Wentworth was vindictive. 'It was the most ghastly period,' remembered Joy Powlett-Smith, a cousin of Peter's by marriage, who was living in Wentworth village in 1946. 'It was the time of the rise of the Socialist Party. They were as red as hell and they were only down the road at Elsecar. There was a big contingent of them there. They didn't mind drinking the Lord's beer every year when he gave his party for all his tenants. It was an awful time. They sent this darn thing – a massive digger. Huge it was, as high as the village church, and they dug and dug. It was politically vicious. The impression we all had was that it was a vicious, spiteful act.'

★

It was the proposal to mine the formal gardens – a site directly behind the baroque West Front – that threatened to blight Wentworth House. The magnificent 300-year-old beech avenue that ran down the Long Terrace, the raised walkway along the western edge of the gardens, the pink shale path, with its dramatic floral rondels, together with ninety-nine acres of immaculately tended lawns, shrubbery and luxuriant herbaceous borders, were scheduled to be uprooted – scars to the landscape that would not heal in Peter's generation. The overburden from the open-cast mining – top soil, mangled plants and pieces of rubble – was to be piled fifty feet high outside the main entrance to the West Front, the top of the mound directly level with Peter's bedroom window and the guest rooms in the private apartments at the back of the house. Next to the tip, space was to be allocated for repair shops and machinery parks, as well as canteens and offices for the site workers.

Half a mile away, in Wentworth village, the locals had been living next to the noise and devastation wrought by the contractor's excavator – a ninety-foot walking crane, called a Monaghan – for more than two years. Bert May lived in Church Drive, the lane that ran alongside the field where the first open-cast operations had begun. 'Every time it scraped the floor it picked six tons up. The engine inside of that machine was as big as a submarine engine. It came right up to our railings, he could have put his bucket in our garden. It wasn't towed, it could walk. It moved on steel plates. First time I saw it coming down the road towards me, it frightened me to death. It was like a dinosaur. He used to work all through the night – thump, thump, thump, thump. You could hear the bucket clanging as it swung round. If we got to sleep before he had his break at midnight, it were all right – otherwise it were awful, you barely slept. There were these powerful lights up on the gib. You could see the glare of them for miles. Then there was the dust. The muck he blew were awful. Great clouds of it everywhere day and night.'

Shinwell's requisition order had come as a bolt from the blue. In the last years of the war, Peter had willingly sacrificed his Estate to the country's need for coal. Between 1943 and 1945, more than a million tons had been mined from the fields outside the boundaries of the Park. Months before the end of the war, Major Lloyd George, Shinwell's predecessor at the Ministry of Fuel and Power, had given Peter a guarantee that the Park and formal gardens would not be mined. Shinwell's order was in breach of his promise: 'An undertaking was given that further workings would not be contemplated except in *a really desperate emergency*. It is considered that this was never meant to apply to any other than a war emergency,' Peter and his land agent, Colonel Landon, complained vociferously to the new Minister in September 1945.

Shinwell claimed the coal under the Park and gardens at Wentworth was needed to keep Britain's trains running. Arguing his case at a Cabinet meeting held at Downing Street on 24 January 1946, he said:

> The total quantity of coal I desire to work on the Wentworth Estate is 371,000 tons, of which 220,000 tons is the good-quality Barnsley coal which is urgently required for the railways . . . The Barnsley coal I desire to work is equivalent to nearly three-quarters of a week's requirements for the British railways. I have already reported the precarious position of railway stocks, and the losses suffered during the Christmas and New Year holidays have worsened it.

But, as Peter had argued in his letter to Shinwell, the Minister's reasoning was illogical: 'Coal cannot now be obtained in any quantity to relieve the necessity of what remains of the present winter. The coal position may be greatly improved before next winter, and if these workings were in the meantime carried out, it might well be found that the destruction had been wrought to no real purpose.'

Acting on his instinct that Shinwell's requisition order was motivated by spite, Peter commissioned a group of mining engineers and geologists from the Department of Fuel Technology at Sheffield University to investigate the feasibility of the Minister's proposal.

The team's findings revealed that Shinwell's plan to mine the garden site at Wentworth was deeply flawed. The coal, in the words of the experts from Sheffield, was 'not worth the getting'. Far from being the 'exceptionally good-quality coal . . . the fine South Yorkshire Hards suitable for firing locomotive boilers' that Shinwell alleged, the geologists assessed after inspecting the site that it was 'very poor stuff . . . reduced to very poor boiler slack by its nearness to the surface'. They also took issue with the Minister's claim that the blasting operations would not damage the foundations of Wentworth House:

At the working place nearest the mansion (100 yards) the hard rock is forty-eight feet thick, at another place nearby fifty-three feet thick. At a point close to the area to be worked there is seventy-seven feet of rock. The proposed method of working is to bore down into the rock and blast it with a heavy charge. The rock is disrupted by a series of heavy earthquake shocks. It cannot sanely be held that any building will escape damage when its foundations are submitted to such shocks.

The team levelled further criticism at Shinwell's boast that an 'effective restoration programme' would be launched to restore the land after the mining operations had finished. '"Effective restoration" forsooth,' William Batley, a member of the team, wrote angrily to the Secretary of the Georgian Group, a society dedicated to the preservation of historic buildings. 'What a cock-eyed yarn. These Ministers of State must think we are a lot of simpletons – spinning us the tale. It is just bunkum, sheer bunk.' The verdict of the Sheffield experts was damning: the proposed operations at the garden site did not in their view 'justify the spoliation and destruction'.

Technically, Peter was powerless to stop Shinwell. The Defence Act brooked no opposition. He was philosophical about the nationalization of the mines and the end of his family's association with coal, recognizing the necessity of the legislation, but the needless destruction of Wentworth House was a different matter. It was a question of principle: he was not prepared to give up the Fitzwilliams' centuries-old tenure at the house without a fight.

★

To the Government's amazement, the Yorkshire miners and the Labour-controlled local authorities were on Peter's side.

'It is sacrilege. Against all common sense,' Joe Hall, President of the Yorkshire branch of the National Union of Mineworkers, told the Press in April 1946. 'The miners in this area will go to almost any length rather than see Wentworth House destroyed. To many mining communities it is sacred ground. I have known the spot since boyhood and some of my happiest hours have been spent there. The Park at Wentworth is an oasis in an industrial desert. It has taken at least a century to produce these lovely grounds and gardens. Yorkshire people cannot stand by and see it all devastated in a few weeks.'

It was a landscape the Fitzwilliams had shared with their miners and the local communities. The woodlands and fields, the three ornamental lakes that cascaded down to the pit villages of Rawmarsh and Greaseborough, belonged in the collective memory. 'You could go anywhere in the Park, you weren't restricted at all,' May Bailey remembered. 'We used to go every Sunday and also in't summer when't nights were nice. All the villages used to go. We used to shout, "Are you goin't Park? Oh ay, we'll see you then. We're going round Lily Pond first." In winter, we'd skate on them ponds. There were three of them, lakes they were. We'd have a pit lamp, there were no torches in them days. When I was older, I went courting by them. You could go anywhere. You could walk right up't Wentworth House. You couldn't go in mind, but you could stand right in front of't. You were never stopped.'

For generations of miners, the Park at Wentworth was elemental in the life cycle of the pit villages. It was the venue for agricultural shows, flower competitions and the June garden fête, annual rituals attended by thousands of miners and their families. It was the place where the Fitzwilliams' family landmarks – the weddings, christenings and comings of age – had been magnificently and collectively celebrated, and where a constant round of sports had been played out: games of cricket, football matches, pit pony races

34. Pyrotechnic portraits of Billy and Maud, Earl and Countess Fitzwilliam, at the party to celebrate the christening of their son Peter, February 1911

35. The pony drivers from Billy's collieries at Elsecar and New Stubbin playing polo on the lawn in front of Wentworth House during the General Strike, 1926

36. Peter, Lord Milton, aged four, is introduced to a member of the househol staff at Wentworth

37. Peter, and his mother, Maud, at a garden party held in the grounds of Wentworth House to raise funds for the families of local soldiers fighting in the First World War

38. Peter, aged two on his first hunter

39. Debutante Lady Barbara Ricardo (née Montagu-Stuart-Wortley), with her grandmother, Maud, Countess Fitzwilliam (*right*), and her mother, Elfrida, Countess of Wharncliffe (*left*), following her presentation at Court, 1938

40. Maud, Countess Fitzwilliam, and Peter, taken shortly after his twenty-first birthday

41. Peter and Olive 'Obby' Fitzwilliam at their wedding in Dublin Cathedral, April 19

42. Billy relaxes on the Riviera, 1938

43. Peter in 1944

44. The Kennedy family at Buckingham Palace, *c*. 1938

5. Kathleen 'Kick' Kennedy with her brother Jack

46. Kick and Billy, Marquess of Hartington, flanked by the Duchess of Devonshire and Joe Kennedy Jnr, at their wedding at Chelsea Register Office, May 1944

47. Vesting Day, 1 January 1947, the day the National Coal Board took control of Britain's 1,647 mines

48. The wreckage of the plane in which Pe and Kick were killed in May 1948

49. Students of the Lady Mabel College of Physical Education are coached in badmin in the Marble Salon at Wentworth. The priceless stone-inlaid floor has been covered protective flooring

50. Eric, 9th Earl Fitzwilliam

51. Tom, later 10th Earl Fitzwilliam

52. Mourners at the 9th Earl Fitzwilliam's funeral in April 1952. Leading the procession (*right to left*) are Tom Fitzwilliam, his brother Toby, Lady Juliet Fitzwilliam (Peter's daughter), and her mother, 'Obby', Countess Fitzwilliam. Lady Mabel Smith follows behind

53. The desecration of the landscape around Wentworth House after the open-cast mining

and tugs o' war, all fiercely contested between the competing local villages and collieries. The Park had been the stage for events that had connected Wentworth and its community to the wider world: King George V's visit in 1912 and the commemoration parades for local men killed in action in the Great War. And it had been a much-needed point of focus during the hard months of the 1926 coal strike when the Fitzwilliams had fed the miners' children in the marquees. Outraged at the 'frontal attack', the 'acts of vandalism' and 'ravaging', in the winter of 1946 hundreds wrote letters of protest to the Minister of Fuel and Power.

Shinwell was unmoved. Speciously dismissing their letters as 'half a dozen postcards, all in the same handwriting', he accused Peter of 'intrigue', refusing to believe that the volume of local protest was based on genuine feeling. Adamant that the Earl had used the last remnants of his feudal powers to whip up a false storm, in an internal memo to his Cabinet colleagues Shinwell wrote, 'claims made as to the enjoyment of the estate by the people are exaggerated. I have no intention of sacrificing the national interest to a nobleman's palace and pleasure grounds, the sanctity of which is no longer respected to the same extent as heretofore.'

He was wrong. Incensed at the Minister's high-handedness – particularly his refusal to meet a deputation of miners to discuss the issue – Joe Hall, President of the Yorkshire branch of the National Union of Mineworkers, resorted to the Press. 'Whatever might be our view of the Gentry of this country, they certainly do not sacrifice natural beauty to easy profits,' he told them on 6 April. 'The Labour Government supposedly stands for the preservation of rural beauty. It is amazing to me that they persist in this scheme at Wentworth. Only a complete disregard of the beauties of the English countryside could prompt sheer vandalism of this description. I have almost got to the point of asking for a forty-eight-hour stoppage of work in this coalfield to put an end to this terrible sacrilege.'

Two days later Hall sent a letter to Clement Attlee, the Prime Minister:

My purpose in writing to you is to vigorously protest against a scheme which is about to be operated at Wentworth, near Rotherham . . . As one who has been an auditor for the National Labour Party for twenty years, and who fought for you to get the Trades Union Movement affiliated to the Party I make this personal appeal to you to do all in your power to prevent what can only be described as vandalism.

Wentworth is the beauty spot of the Rotherham and Barnsley districts, the garden and spacious grounds having been enjoyed by our mining folk for very many years . . .

I sincerely hope you will, as my political leader in our first Labour Government in power, leave no stone unturned to save this pleasure resort.

A worried Private Secretary passed Hall's letter to the Prime Minister, attaching an anxious memo:

Prime Minister, I should not have troubled you with the private protest against the proposal to extend open-cast coal mining to the gardens at Wentworth House, but you should see the letter which has now come in from Mr Hall, the President of the National Union of Mineworkers (Yorkshire area) . . . I have seen reports in the Press that the miners may strike for 48 hours if the present proposals are adhered to and though Mr Hall says nothing of this kind, and the Press reports may be incorrect, I should have thought the Minister [Shinwell] might find it necessary to reconsider the position if the miners persist in their opposition to the scheme.

'Yes', Attlee wrote at the bottom of the memo.

Conservation groups, the media and the local authorities in the neighbourhood of Wentworth joined the miners in the chorus of protest. 'Nobody can possibly guarantee that this blasting will do no damage when it is carried out so close to the house,' Lord Rosse, representing the National Trust, wrote to Captain Noel-Baker, a Conservative MP, urging him to put pressure on the Government in the House of Commons. 'The best one can say is that it is a gamble which may come off, but to gamble with a building of real historic and national importance such as Wentworth is nothing short of criminal. There is still time to have this stopped or at least to have the programme modified so as to lessen the danger.' Other public bodies took up the crusade: 'It is a thoroughly unnecessary piece of vandalism,' the Secretary of the Council for the Protection of Rural England wrote to an official at the Royal Institute of British Architects. 'For the sake of a few hundred thousand tons of bad coal this priceless estate will be mined and lost irretrievably. It is a scandal if the PM and the Cabinet do not overrule Mr Shinwell.' The *Economist* was equally critical: the coal, it claimed, would be 'quickly produced and as quickly consumed, leaving the land ruined and useless for perhaps half a century and the coal problem just where it was before'.

Until the Government had wind of the South Yorkshire miners' threat to strike, the volume of protest had fallen on deaf ears. Seizing his chance, Peter, who was in daily contact with Joe Hall, telephoned Downing Street to request a meeting with the Prime Minister. He wanted to show Attlee the plans that he, together with his miners at Elsecar colliery, had come up with for an alternative means of mining the coal. Drift mining – sinking shallow, walk-in tunnels beneath the land around Wentworth House – was the method they proposed. In this way, they argued, the site would yield a greater tonnage of coal, of a better quality, and at less cost. Crucially, the coal could be won without destroying a 'single tree or shrub', or running the risk of destroying the 'mansion' itself. Hall had endorsed the proposal: 'I am confident,' he assured the Prime Minister, 'that within six months a greater quantity of cleaner coal could be won more economically without the least disturbance of the ground.'

'I suppose I must see him,' Attlee scrawled across the note his Private Secretary had sent him to advise him of Peter's request. Even two years earlier, Peter's wealth, his social position, and his connections in Churchill's Coalition Government had enabled him to prevent the Park and gardens at Wentworth from being mined. Now, in the changed post-war world, he was barely able to secure an audience with the PM.

The minutes of the Cabinet meeting held on the morning of 15 April 1946 – the day Peter and Attlee were due to meet – show that before Peter even had the opportunity to present his drift-mining plan, the Prime Minister had rejected it out of hand. Marked 'Secret' – a standard procedure for minutes relating to Cabinet meetings – they summarize the discussion:

> THE PRIME MINISTER said that some local agitation had developed against the Government's decision to extend the working of open-cast coal in Wentworth Park; and the owner, Earl Fitzwilliam, was calling on him later in the day to discuss the matter. He was likely to ask whether this coal could not be secured by underground mining [drift mining]. Would this be possible?

Shinwell, as requested by Attlee, had 'reconsidered the position'. But he had not changed his view. The Fitzwilliam Estate was to be the source 'First of all, of coal. Secondly, of more coal.' The Cabinet, according to the minutes of the meeting, was swayed by the Minister's arguments:

> THE MINISTER OF FUEL AND POWER said that underground working would not be appropriate on this site. It would take two years to get the coal which could be obtained in eight months by open-cast working, and underground miners would be needed: these were not available locally, and one of the main objects of open-cast working was to supplement the output of the underground labour force. The local agitation against this project had been worked up by a comparatively small number of people and did not, in his view, correctly reflect public opinion in the district . . . It would be a sign of weakness on the Government's part to abandon or modify the scheme now that the contracts had been let and work was about to begin.

Shinwell's victory served notice on the raison d'être of Wentworth – the way of life that had been lived there for centuries. A grand house party could hardly be held on an industrial site, nor the hunt meet on a lawn that, as one local observed, would 'resemble the fields of Passchendaele'. Among the miners, it left a bitter taste. Like Peter, they believed the desecration of Wentworth was an act of class hatred. 'Shinwell's reaction was, let him have it,' Charles Booth recalled. 'I was a trainee engineer at Elsecar at the time. I was one of the men who'd worked on the scheme to sink the drift mine. The Government wouldn't hear of it. They had to desecrate the gardens. So desecrate them they did.' The miners at the Fitzwilliams' New Stubbin pit, as Ralph Boreham recalled, were of a similar view. 'There were some at that time – the functionaries in the Labour Party, Communist types – as were saying, "Why should he [Earl Fitzwilliam] have all that and we've got nothing?" Idiots they were, powerful idiots. It were awful, I didn't like it. I've never felt that way about nobody. Most of the men round here felt the same as me. That Estate were a beautiful place. We loved to see it as it were. We didn't want to see it wrecked. Nationalization of the pits, that were different, mind. Time had come for that. It were right. But not the destruction of Wentworth House. There was some destruction. It all crumbled after that. It were spite, we reckoned. Simple as that.'

Maud Fitzwilliam was at Wentworth when the bulldozers turned up. 'The brutes of contractors rushed in, two days before they were to start,' she wrote to Lucia, Viscountess Galway,

> mowing down shrubs, trees and specimen Rhododendrons of every kind, to say nothing of miles of every sort and kind of daffodils – things we had collected for years and the overburden is to be put 50 feet high in the gardens up to the gallery window. It is absolute vandalism, as the coal could have been got far better from below . . . they just would not listen – 10 feet of the spire of the church has already gone, and I should think the house is bound to crack. It is utterly heartbreaking.

At the eleventh hour, Peter decided he would rather give the house away than see it destroyed. Days after his meeting with the Prime Minister, he approached the National Trust to offer Wentworth to the nation. Some weeks later, James Lees-Milne and Lord Rosse, the National Trust's representatives, travelled up from London to inspect the house and grounds. James Lees-Milne was both stunned and shocked by what he saw:

'It is certainly the most enormous private house I have ever beheld,' he noted in his diary.

I could not find my way about the interior and never once knew in what direction I was looking from a window. Strange to think that up until 1939 one man lived in the whole of it. All the contents are put away or stacked in heaps in a few rooms, the pictures taken out of their frames. The dirt is appalling. Everything is pitch black and the boles of the trees like thunder. To my surprise, the Park is not being worked for surface coal systematically, but in square patches here and there. One of these patches is the walled garden. Right up to the very wall of the Vanbrugh front every tree and shrub has been uprooted . . . Where the surface has been worked is waste chaos and, as Michael [Lord Rosse] said, far worse than anything he saw of French battlefields after D-Day. I was surprised too by the very high quality of the pre-Adam rooms and ceilings of Wentworth; by the amount of seventeenth-century work surviving; by the beautiful old wallpapers; and by the vast scale of the layout of the Park, with ornamental temples sometimes one-and-a-half miles or more away.

The National Trust was nervous of taking on a building which, potentially, faced imminent destruction: at Peter's suggestion, it proposed to accept covenants over the Park and gardens to ring-fence the house from further mining operations. If these were in place, the negotiations for its transfer to the nation could proceed. But the last-minute rescue plan was quashed by the Government after the Ministry of Town and Country Planning intervened. Responding to a letter from one of the Trust's officials seeking clarification as to whether, if the covenants were accepted, the open-cast mining would stop, a civil servant, on behalf of his Minister, warned the National Trust off. 'It would be a great mistake for the Trust in this, or indeed, in any other case of threatened property where the owner still maintains a substantial interest, to accept covenants in the middle of a controversy as a means of protecting in effect, the owner, against what purports to be a public interest.' Refusing to credit Peter's decision to offer Wentworth to the nation at face value, the civil servant dismissed it as his 'latest intrigue', accusing him of 'merely trying to preserve his own sovereignty and privacy against the public at large'. Cautioning the National Trust against accepting the covenants, he concluded, 'A Covenant to preserve a thing of beauty that no one but the owner and his friends can see is not much public benefit.' Once again, the Government, against the body of evidence, had persisted in Shinwell's view that 'claims made as to the enjoyment of the estate by the people' were 'exaggerated'.

Not wishing to 'embarrass' the Government by protesting against its decision, having failed to secure a guarantee that no further open-cast mining would be carried out, the National Trust's Historic Buildings Committee voted to put the negotiations over the future of Wentworth House on hold.

The Whitehall vendetta continued; shortly after the National Trust rejected Peter's offer, the Government served a second requisition order: this time, on the house itself. The Ministry of Health, so Peter was informed, proposed to take over the 'greater part of Wentworth House for the housing of homeless industrial families'. The Park and formal gardens had been desecrated: the 'seventeenth-century work', 'the beautiful old wallpapers', the 'high-quality' mouldings and ceilings that James Lees-Milne had so admired, were unlikely to withstand such an assault from within.

It was Billy Fitzwilliam's redoubtable sister, Lady Mabel Smith, who saved Wentworth House from the 'industrial families'. Yet had Billy still been alive, he would rather have surrendered his home to the homeless than allow his sister to interfere in its fate.

'Mabel was taboo at Wentworth when we were growing up. Absolutely taboo,' Joyce Smith recalled of her aunt. 'She was a rabid socialist. She didn't get on with her brother at all. They hardly ever saw each other. She was horrified by Uncle Billy's lifestyle at Wentworth. "He had so much and everyone else had so little" – that was her line. She was a bit of a crank about it, really. She had all these ideas about the equality of man. Uncle Billy would have run a mile rather than talk to her.'

Mabel, who was seventy-seven in 1947, had lived near Wentworth all her life. She was married to Joyce's uncle, Colonel Mackenzie Smith, and her home was at Barnes Hall in Eccleshall, a suburb of Sheffield. 'It was frightfully austere,' Joy Powlett-Smith, Joyce's sister-in-law, remembered of a visit to the house in 1946. 'It was a big place – about fourteen bedrooms, I'd say. Very exposed, up on the edge of the moors. It was horribly draughty. Mabel was very keen on "fresh air". There were no coal fires, only portable gas fires. No carpets, just mats on the wooden floors, which were stained black. There was no electricity, only candlelight or gaslight. There was very little furniture: a few chairs, but hard, uncomfortable ones. The curtains, I remember, barely covered the length of the shutters. They were woven from untreated wool.'

Mabel was two years older than Billy. Part of their childhood had been spent at Hoober Hall, a house on the Fitzwilliam Estate a half a mile or so from Wentworth. It was here, when she was in her early teens, that Mabel's social conscience was awakened. 'I was very close to her,' Joyce recalled. 'She once told me what made her become a socialist. Every year, when she was a child, her mother gave a party for the village children from the schools near Hoober Hall. All the village children came. Well, of course they did, the Fitzwilliams owned and ran all the schools in those days. The children were invited for sports and Aunt Mabel and her brother and her sisters ran in these races. There was one village girl who was the same age as Mabel – she was twelve or thirteen – and they were great friends. One or other of them always won the race. One year this girl didn't turn up and Mabel said, "Where's Janie?" "Oh," they said, "she's left school now and gone into service. She won't be coming any more." Mabel was horrified to think that there she was being taught at home by her governess, and this, her little contemporary, had had to go into service. From that moment on, she told me, she made up her mind that she was going to get education for them all.'

A well-known and much-loved figure in the district, Mabel had been true to her promise. She had devoted her life to improving education in the pit villages in the West Riding, first as a local councillor, and then as a leading member of the board of the Workers' Education Authority.

Early in 1947, after receiving the Ministry of Health's requisition order, Peter asked his aunt for help. Despite – or possibly because of – his father's antipathy they had always got on well. 'The funny thing was,' Joyce remembered, 'Peter adored Mabel. She used to have these Christmas parties at Barnes Hall for all the cousins. I suppose Uncle Billy let him go because otherwise he would have felt left out, though I expect he thought he'd been contaminated when he came back!'

Mabel suggested turning Wentworth House into a school. In 1947, using her connections in the West Riding Education Authority, she persuaded the County Council to take it on a fifty-year, full-repairing lease. The Fitzwilliams were to be allowed to retain their private apartments in the West Front. Thanks to Lady Mabel, the house was to be converted into a training college for female PE teachers.

West Riding County Council signed the lease in September 1947. During the negotiations, the councillors made one stipulation: that Wentworth House should be renamed after Lady Mabel. It was to be called the Lady Mabel College of Physical Education. 'It was a wonderful irony that the only Fitzwilliam to survive in the name of the place was Mabel,' Joyce chuckled, 'the person who had been so taboo in my Uncle Billy's time. I was terribly pleased. I felt she'd come into her own. She'd been the only member of the family to have been of real public value.'

It was a huge relief to Peter. A specialist women-only teacher training college was a more palatable option than having the house overrun by scores of homeless families, and the County Council had guaranteed to pay its running costs and to repair any structural damage. Far from brooding over the loss of Wentworth and the coal inheritance he had grown up to expect, during the course of 1947, Peter threw himself into a variety of new business schemes.

He expanded his Stud Farm at Malton, the Fitzwilliams' estate near York, and was hoping to secure the Coca-Cola franchise for the North of England. He was also negotiating with the Ministry of Food and Agriculture to import groundnuts from Africa. He hoped to convince the Ministry that, with the strict rationing in force, groundnuts, high in calories and protein, offered a nutritious supplement to the meagre post-war diet.

As James Lees-Milne, the National Trust official, was leaving Wentworth House, he was introduced to Obby Fitzwilliam, Peter's wife. 'Lady Fitzwilliam in a pair of slacks, rather dumpy and awkward, came downstairs for a word just before we left,' he noted in his diary. 'I fancy she is not very sensitive to the tragedy of it all.'

It was not that Obby was insensitive to the tragedy of Wentworth; a greater personal tragedy was unfolding. The war had imposed separate lives on Peter and Obby, placing a further strain on their heirless marriage. While Peter was serving with SOE, Obby had worked in a factory near Slough making parts for fighter aeroplanes. By the close of 1947, their marriage had fallen apart. 'I think my mother was philosophical about my father's temporary amours, realizing that (presumably until Kick Kennedy) they were not important,' Juliet, their daughter recalled. 'No other man really mattered to her, that I do know.'

Among the skeleton staff that remained at Wentworth, the rumours spread. 'There were a lot of talk up at the house. They all talked. They said he was going to have a divorce.'

34

A thunderstorm, the worst for as long as anyone could remember, was raging over the Ardèche, a mountainous region some fifty miles north of Avignon in southern France. It was late afternoon on 13 May 1948. Paul Petit, a farmer, would normally have been out on the slopes with his animals, but the violence of the storm was so great that he was resigned to staying at home. His farmhouse, a crumbling medieval building constructed from red stone, was situated a few hundred yards below the peak of Le Coran. He lived alone: in the rugged, desolate country, aside from his brother and his father, there were no other neighbours for miles around.

Gale-force winds, and hailstones the size of a two-pound coin, had battered the house for some hours. At about 5.30 p.m., Paul thought he heard the high-pitched scream of racing engines. Rushing outside, he watched in horror as a light aircraft shot out of the cloud base and disintegrated in mid-air, the pieces of the plane spiralling into a ravine on the mountainside opposite.

In the driving rain, running as fast as he could, Paul set off along the slippery stone trail that snaked its way to his father's house to fetch help.

It took the two men three-quarters of an hour to find the wreckage. They struggled through the undergrowth, up the steep, heavily wooded slope where Paul had seen the plane crash, with torrents of water, running down from the mountain above, making the climb harder. They came across the starboard engine first: located near the bottom of the slope, it was twisted beyond recognition. Eighty yards further up, they found the petrol tank; 100 yards above it, the fuselage of the plane, resting on a narrow ridge. The starboard wing was missing, the cockpit flattened from top to bottom: the passenger compartment had been torn open by the rocks when it hit the ground.

It was immediately clear to Paul and his father when they prised open the door to the fuselage that the four people inside the plane were dead. The pilot and co-pilot were crumpled against the instrument controls in the cockpit, their earphones still on. The two passengers were in the rear of the plane. Peter Fitzwilliam lay beneath his upturned seat. He was badly disfigured. On his left side, the lower half of his body was completely crushed.

Kick's was the only body Paul and his father were able to drag clear of the wreckage. The right side of her face was torn by a long gash: her jaw, pelvis and both her legs had been pulverized in the crash.

'Chance Invite Sends Kennedy Girl to Her Death'.

Within hours, news of the accident was flashed around the world. But exactly why Peter and Kick were in the plane together – and the reason for their journey – was covered up: the Devonshires, the Kennedys and the Fitzwilliams closed ranks to conceal the circumstances that had led to their deaths.

Peter and Kick had been together for almost two years when they were killed. Yet unlike her relationship with Billy Hartington, the ebbs and flows of the affair are not charted in the voluminous collections of Kennedy letters. The public archives divulge no poignant testaments to their love: in fact there is no official record of the affair ever having taken place at all. The burning of the Fitzwilliams' correspondence in the bonfires at Wentworth soon after their deaths ensured that none of their letters have been preserved. Not a single member of the Kennedy family ever spoke of the affair – or even acknowledged it. The Devonshires and the Fitzwilliams waited almost forty years before they broke their silence.

After the accident happened – as with the subsequent Kennedy tragedies that were to follow Kick's death – numerous conspiracy theories were spawned. These were circulated in private and seldom publicly aired. Some said the couple were on their way to Rome to obtain special dispensation from the Pope to marry. Evelyn Waugh believed they were killed eloping; Lady Astor circulated the ridiculous rumour that the accident was engineered by Vatican agents to prevent another sacrilegious union.

There is nothing mysterious about why the plane crashed. The French air accident investigator's report is conclusive, leaving no room for conspiracy or conjecture. Nor is there any mystery surrounding its destination: the privately chartered plane was en route to Cannes airport in the South of France. But the real mystery is why Peter and Kick were flying at all when one of the worst storms in years was forecast for the Rhône Valley. In 1948, only a handful of people knew the answer. Close friends and confidants of the couple blamed their families.

In part, the absence of letters on the Kennedy side is explained by the fact that Kick kept her affair with Peter secret from all but one member of her family until the very last. It was Jack Kennedy in whom she confided. The autumn before her death, staying at Lismore, the Devonshires' estate in Ireland, during a quiet chat together on the banks of the Blackwater River, she whispered to her brother, 'I've found my Rhett Butler at last.'

The affair seemed madness from the start.

35

It began with a dance. Peter and Kick met for the first time on the night of 12 June 1946 at a ball at the Dorchester Hotel, London's most glamorous venue in the heart of Mayfair.

The Season, the first since 1939, was in full swing. Despite the tribulations of rationing and the piles of rubble that still littered the streets, grim reminders of wartime suffering, the capital was celebrating. The theatres in the West End had reopened; Latin American dancing – the rumba and the mambo – was all the rage. In the salons and ballrooms of Mayfair and Belgravia, evening gowns, tiaras and white tie and tails were beginning to return, in place of the usual drab sea of uniforms.

The ball at the Dorchester was a fundraising event for the widows and dependants of Commando soldiers killed and seriously injured in the war. It was a glittering occasion, and the leading lights of London society turned out in force; even the future Queen Elizabeth was there.

Kick was chairing the Ball Committee and had helped to organize the dance. That night, she wore a pink taffeta ballgown and a pair of aquamarine and diamond clips. Eighteen months after Billy's death, the greyness of bereavement had lifted. The previous year had been an introspective one: immersing herself in her voluntary work for the American Red Cross, she had also spent a number of months in retreat at a nunnery in Kendal in Cumbria.

The start of the 1946 Season marked her reappearance on the social scene. To her delight, she found herself as popular as she had been before the war. Aged twenty-six, she had lost none of her allure: at a party a few weeks before the Dorchester ball, an eighteen-year-old debutante was overheard to remark, 'It's absolutely maddening, Kick's taking all my dance partners.'

'What do you expect?' her friend replied. 'You're just a deb. She's an attractive American widow.'

Peter – a highly decorated war hero – was one of the star guests at the ball. Before joining SOE in 1942, he had fought with the Commandos in the Middle East. It was inevitable that he would be introduced to Kick, the Chairwoman of the Committee.

Inviting her to dance, he spun her round the ballroom. 'It was overnight and it was the real thing,' Charlotte Harris, a close friend of Kick's, remembered many years later. 'One got the impression that she'd discovered something she didn't really plan to experience in life.'

John White, her old friend from Washington, was overwhelmed by the force of her passion. 'As she talked of Fitzwilliam, the man sounded like the hero of *Out of Africa*, a professional Englishman, a devastatingly charming rogue,' he later recalled. 'Rarely in life do you see someone so bubbling over with love, everything that love should be, every bit of it. Poor old Billy Hartington. But again he probably would have been blown away if she had felt that way about him. Very few people could stand that much love, the sheer blast of emotion.'

From the outset, Peter and Kick's affair ran a tumultuous course, scandalizing and dividing London society. In their exclusive close-knit world, few secrets remained secret for very long. Though the couple were discreet, confining their meetings to late-night trysts at Kick's house in Westminster or at the homes of close friends, word soon got out. People were shocked, not simply because a titled Catholic war widow was having an affair with a Protestant married man, but because Peter was regarded as the antithesis of her late husband – kind, gentle, moral Billy.

Among Kick's friends, Peter's reputation had gone before him. An habitué of Whites Club in St James's, he was known to belong to a hard-drinking, hard-gambling clique of wealthy philanderers. In austerity-shrouded Britain, their excesses were especially frowned upon. Games of baccarat for stakes of £10,000 were not unusual. Peter's personal betting and racing losses were rumoured to amount to more than £20,000: the equivalent today of some £500,000.

Kick's world was very different. In the months leading up to the ball at the Dorchester, she had acquired a new set of friends. A true Anglophile, she had chosen to base herself in London, rather than in America, and had bought a small Georgian townhouse in Smith Square, a stone's throw from the Houses of Parliament. Here, in the spring of 1946, she hosted a series of small and intimate literary and political salons for some of the leading figures of the day: Winston Churchill, Anthony Eden, George Bernard Shaw and Evelyn Waugh were regular guests.

Waugh was horrified when Kick confided her new love. He had known Peter in the Army when they were stationed together at a Commando training camp near Glasgow. As Waugh recorded in his diary, one girl, following a row at a party in the Officers' Mess, called Peter and his friends – who included Randolph Churchill, the Prime Minister's son, and Lord Stavordale, the heir to the Earl of Ilchester – 'dandies' and 'scum'. Noting the girl's remarks, Waugh was almost as censorious: 'The smart set,' he wrote, 'drink a very great deal, play cards for high figures, dine nightly in Glasgow, and telephone to their trainers endlessly.' Later, he confessed to finding 'the indolence and ignorance of the officers . . . remarkable'. But, as a Catholic convert, it was the religious implications of Kick's liaison with Peter that so upset Waugh. 'If you want to commit adultery or fornication & can't resist, do it, but realize what you are doing, and don't give the final insult of apostasy,' he admonished her.

Kick's Protestant friends were equally opposed to the affair. Janie Compton, her great friend in London before the war, found it particularly upsetting. To begin with, she did not understand it at all: 'Peter and Kick were absolutely different personality types with absolutely different friends. She was totally different to him. She had intellectual friends. His world wasn't a bit like that. He belonged to a set where you gambled terrifically and drank a lot. He was terribly naughty – frightfully – with loads of girlfriends. And that was just not Kick. Not a bit Kick. As time went by, I got the impression that he must have been a very good lover. It was the only way to explain it. It's awful, but it can have such a major impact.'

Peter's friends at Whites were similarly perplexed. What could he possibly see in her, they speculated, clustered in a haze of cigar smoke in the club's comfortable leather armchairs. Though she was reputedly charming, Kick's devout Catholicism and unremarkable looks hardly matched up to their vision of the perfect mistress.

Besides the gambling set at Whites, Peter's social circle included the forerunners of the 'jet set': an exclusive clique of predominantly English and European super-rich. In the winter, they went fox-hunting and horse-racing, flying to race courses and hunting fields in France, Ireland and England; in the summer, they villa-hopped, charting private planes to visit each other at a series of invariably beautiful homes dotted around the Mediterranean.

Theirs was a dazzling crowd, the money they lavished on entertainment a lure to Hollywood film stars, fashion models and raffish figures from the beau monde such as Edith Piaf and Truman Capote.

Peter's closest friend – and a leading light in the set – was Prince Aly Khan. Six months younger than Peter, he was the son of the Aga Khan, the billionaire leader of an estimated 15 million Ismaili Muslims in Asia and Africa. Stories of the Aga Khan's wealth were legion; on his fiftieth birthday, his followers gave him his weight in gold – 220 pounds – and on his seventieth, when he had grown even fatter, in platinum. Double-decker buses in London sported advertisements for a brand of chocolate that bore the slogan 'Rich and Dark like the Aga Khan'. In Manhattan, the colour of Prince Aly's skin was an object of similar fascination: Diana Vreeland, writing in the mid-1940s, noted that it was 'exactly the colour of a gardenia. A gardenia isn't quite white. It's got a little cream in it.'

'They called me a bloody nigger,' Prince Aly once said of his upper-class English contemporaries, 'and I paid them out by winning all their women.' Suave and good-looking, the owner of six houses and a suite at the Ritz, the Prince was an international playboy and lothario known for his extravagant gestures. When he married the actress Rita Hayworth in 1949, he filled the swimming pool at his house on the Riviera with 200 gallons of eau-de-cologne for the wedding reception.

The close friendship between Peter and the Prince sprang from their common interests and similar temperaments. In the years immediately after the war, both their marriages were failing; in 1947, Aly, married to Joan Yarde-Buller, the former wife of Joel Guinness, had numerous affairs, including one with Pamela Churchill, who had recently separated from Winston's son, Randolph. Like Peter, Aly's passions were horses and women. Michael Wishart, the English artist, remembered staying at Château de l'Horizon, Aly's gleaming white Moorish-style villa on the Riviera. Here the Prince held court 'resplendent as a basking shark, surrounded by a claque of pretty girls wearing the lower halves of bikinis'; Aly wore, as Wishart described, a pair of swimming trunks 'with the would-be tantalizing admonition "not to be opened until Christmas" embroidered down the fly'. Aly's reputation as a demon lover was legendary. 'I only think of the woman's pleasure when I am in love,' was one of his maxims. He was famed for practising a lovemaking technique called 'Imsak', an ancient Arabic art taught to him by an Egyptian doctor that reputedly enabled him to delay orgasm for hours.

Peter and Aly shared other attributes. Aly had also had a 'good war', serving in the French Foreign Legion and in British and American intelligence units. Brave and reckless, both men were known for the restlessness that drove their high-octane lifestyle. 'I once left Aly at four in the morning at Deauville,' remembered Jean Fayard, the Prix Goncourt-winning author. 'When I got back to his house late that same day, he had ridden a horse in the morning, played tennis, flown to England to watch one of his horses, flown back, and then we played bridge until three the next morning.' While Jean and the other guests went to bed, Aly, as Fayard recalled, got in his car and drove along the Grande Corniche to the Casino at Monte Carlo, finally returning at seven to snatch two hours' sleep before beginning a new day.

It was to this decadent world that Peter whisked Kick: throughout 1947, their weekends were spent at Château de l'Horizon, and in private boxes at glamorous racing venues in France and England. 'I never imagined it would last,' remembered Janie Compton. 'I was convinced Peter could never make Kick happy.' As the months passed, and the affair showed no signs of cooling off, Janie did not hide her disapproval from Kick. 'You don't know him. You don't know him,' she would reply.

There was a side to Peter's character that only his close friends knew. 'Peter had all the charm in the world – to a rather dangerous extent, really,' Harry Sporberg, his business partner and former SOE colleague, recalled. Peter's accounts show that, although his gambling debts were huge, he was also extremely generous. In 1947, he stood as personal guarantor to four of his friends' bank overdrafts: the total sum amounted to almost £38,000 – almost £1 million in today's money. As Kick confided to her brother Jack, Peter made her laugh: she had found a man who knew how to play, who swept her along with him and with whom she could have fun after the sadness and sacrifices of the war.

'Peter was mad about Kick, absolutely mad about her. Oh yes!' his niece, Lady Barbara Ricardo, recalled. 'I know exactly why people thought it would never last because he did have masses of girlfriends, so you can understand them thinking that. But he was crazy about Kick. All his life he never seemed to do the obvious thing – go for a conventional upper-class English girl. He was never attracted to the sort of girls people expected him to be attracted to. Girls I suppose from his world. I think his mother was so determined for him, wanting so much for him, always trying to choose the right girl for him before he married. And I think that was probably one of the reasons why he was always trying to escape. Kick was an escape. She also had the double attraction – because of the whole Catholic thing – of being seemingly unobtainable.'

The Fitzwilliams were as virulently anti-Catholic as the Devonshires. 'I remember inviting a girl up to stay for the weekend,' recalled Ian Bond, Peter's cousin. 'On the Saturday evening she asked my mother where the nearest Catholic church was for Mass.

The next morning she'd gone. My mother had sent her home: she wouldn't have a Catholic in the house.' In the winter of 1947, fearing that Peter would seek to obtain a divorce from Obby, Billy Fitzwilliam's trustees voiced their disapproval. 'My father was against the whole thing,' remembered Peter Diggle, the son of Colonel Heathcote Diggle. 'It wasn't just the Catholic issue. He belonged to the old school. Divorce was regarded as a let-down. It was difficult to get divorced. It was a laborious process, even then. The advisers felt it would bring the family into disrepute.'

Maud Fitzwilliam sided with the family trustees. 'My grandmother disapproved of divorce,' Juliet, Peter's daughter, recalled. 'I believe she had heard a rumour that Kick might not be able to have children. If so, this would have horrified her.' But nothing – and no one – could ever drive a wedge between Maud and her son. Ultimately, as Barbara remembered, 'It was how it had always been: what he wanted, she wanted.'

At Christmas, in 1947, Kick told her friends she was going to marry Peter. For the most part, they were against the marriage. 'I liked Peter very much, he was so charming, but if they had married there would have been a reaction,' Andrew Cavendish, Billy's younger brother, recalled. Janie Compton had not changed her view: 'I think there would have been problems and I don't think she would have been happy with him.' David and Sissy Ormsby-Gore were even more disapproving. Devout Catholics, they reminded Kick of what it would mean to marry outside the Church again. David thought Peter the utter antithesis of everything she had been taught to value in terms of public service and sacrifice: surely, he urged, she would feel out of place in Peter's world and come to find it irritating.

Kick would not listen to any of them. Early in February 1948, she caught a boat to America to break the news to her parents. In New York, she told Charlotte Harris of her plans. 'My reaction,' Charlotte remembered, 'was having done just about the worst thing she could have by marrying Billy, Holy Good Night, now look what she's done! Billy I think was a very conscious decision. But not Fitzwilliam. It was passion. It was hysterical. It was all "I gotta do, I gotta go". If she couldn't marry him, she was ready to run off with him. She just wasn't concerned about the consequences.'

Despite her bravado, Kick was nervous. Peter had told her emphatically that he would not convert to Catholicism, nor would he allow his children to be raised as Catholics. She was in the same position as she had been before she married Billy, only this time it was worse. Facing excommunication once again, she was aware that marriage to a Protestant divorcee would involve the Kennedy family in their first major public scandal. While she would never be named as the third party in Peter's divorce suit – a sordid encounter with some unknown woman in a hotel room would be cited in the papers instead – inevitably, the details of her role would be bound to leak out.

On 19 February, Kick joined the Kennedy family at Hyannis Port, their holiday home in Palm Beach, for the traditional winter break. She put off telling Rose and Joe about Peter for as long as she possibly could. Week after week, in the endless round of games and parties, she talked about anything and everything else. Jack had kept her secret well: neither Rose nor Joe had any idea of the affair.

By mid-April, Kick had been in America for two months and still she had failed to confront her parents. The week before she sailed to England – on 22 April – there was just one opportunity left. After visiting friends on the East Coast, she was due to spend her last weekend with Rose and Joe at a party at the Greenbrier Hotel in White Sulphur Springs to celebrate its reopening after four years of service as a wartime army hospital. Jack Kennedy, by now a young Congressman, and Kick's sisters Jean and Eunice were also going to be there.

The weekend party had been trumpeted as the society event of the season. The Greenbrier, owned by Robert Young, a family friend of the Kennedys, was America's premier spa hotel, an elegant 600-room mansion built in the ante-bellum style, set in acres of parkland, framed by spectacular beech forests. It had an illustrious history. Before the war it had been favoured by Hollywood celebrities, European royalty and America's first families: the Vanderbilts, the Roosevelts, the Duke and Duchess of Windsor, and Bing Crosby were among the regular guests.

Some weeks before the party, to his surprise, Kick had invited Jackie Pierrepont to accompany her for the weekend. An old childhood friend, Jackie, who came from a grand Episcopalian family, had shocked society by converting to Catholicism during the war. On the journey to White Sulphur Springs – travelling in one of fourteen private railroad cars laid on by the party organizers to ferry the 300 guests – it soon became evident to Jackie why Kick had asked him: she was badly in need of moral support. As the train wound its way up the East Coast, he noticed that she seemed preoccupied. Suddenly, she brought their small talk to a close.

'I want to do something that is going to make everybody very mad at me,' she said, looking hard at Jackie.

'You're going to leave the Church?' Jackie guessed.

'No, I'm very much in love with this married man.'

Swearing him to secrecy, she confided the whole story. It was almost as if she was rehearsing the conversation she was about to have with her family. She assured Jackie that she was not breaking up a marriage, that in fact it was a disaster already. They debated her decision to tell her parents for the rest of the journey; though Kick knew her father would be furious, she felt confident of being able to handle him: it was her mother's reaction, the idea of hurting her all over again, that she dreaded the most.

The weekend was crowded with activities: golf on the championship links, swimming in the hotel's glamorous first-floor art deco pool, dancing till dawn in the pink ballroom, festooned with balloons. In the afternoons, as the local paper reported, tea was served by 'Negroes dressed as slaves'. Kick had hardly been discreet about her affair; to her discomfort, she found herself the subject of whispered attention. 'We all knew Jean's sister was carrying on with someone,' Margaret Hutchinson recalled, 'and that gave us a lot of scandal to talk about. We all felt that what we called a holy runaround was going on.'

Kick kept delaying the moment she told her parents, finally confronting them on the last night of the weekend. Neither Rose nor Joe kept a record of the discussion, nor were there, understandably, any other witnesses present. But, as Jackie Pierrepont remembered, the next morning, on the train journey up north, Kick remained visibly shaken.

Rose, apparently, had been livid. Forbidding Kick to marry Peter, Rose warned her that, if she went ahead with the wedding, she would be disinherited and – most wounding of all – she would never be seen or spoken to again.

On Kick's arrival in Washington the afternoon after the confrontation, it was Patsy White – the friend who had comforted her after Billy had been killed – to whom she turned. Banishment by Rose meant banishment from the Kennedy clan – from the ritualistic summer and winter gatherings at Hyannis Port. Of all people, Patsy knew how much Kick's family meant to her. 'She never wanted to be separated from her family, even if she were living in England. I never heard Kick criticize her father or mother or brothers or sisters. She was completely happy with them, being a Kennedy, happy with all of them.' The last thing she wanted, as Patsy recalled, was to be 'sent off into perpetual exile'.

Her identity as a Kennedy lay at the very core of Kick's personality. Two months after Billy's death, writing to Lem Billings, she believed it gave her the strength to overcome her grief. 'One thing you can be sure of,' she wrote, 'life holds no fears for someone who has faced love, marriage and death before the age of 25. It's hard to face the future, without someone who you thought would always be there to help and guide and for whom you'd sacrificed a lot. Luckily I am a Kennedy. I have a very strong feeling that that makes a big difference about how to take things . . . I know that we've all got the ability to not be got down.'

The thought of being severed from her family was unbearable to Kick. It also seemed implausible. Though deeply distressed by her mother's threat, she had no reason to believe that Rose really meant to carry it out. She had, after all, eventually forgiven Kick for marrying Billy. Even during the two months when she had been estranged from her mother, she had still been in touch with the rest of her family. Her father had been the crucial link. If he could be won over, Kick reasoned, he might eventually persuade Rose to forgive her, as he had done when she married Billy.

Kick was due to sail back to England – and to Peter – on 22 April. During her last days in Washington, the indications were that Joe would come round to her marriage. Since the row at the Greenbrier, far from forbidding Kick to marry Peter, Joe had called her to tell her about a ruse he had thought up. As Kick told Patsy, he planned to convince the Church authorities that Peter had never been baptized, thereby invalidating his marriage to Obby. Rather than obtaining a divorce, Joe suggested, the marriage could be annulled, leaving Peter and Kick free to marry. It was a ludicrous idea, as Kick knew. Peter's christening in 1911 had been attended by tens of thousands from the pit villages around Wentworth and widely covered in the British Press. Yet while she and Patsy shared a laugh at Joe's expense, giggling at his naivety over the time-honoured practices of the English aristocracy, Kick was profoundly touched by his support.

Throughout her eighteen-month affair with Peter, Kick had suffered none of the doctrinal debates over her religion, both with others and within herself, that had tormented her before she married Billy. She was not about to suffer them now. After the showdown with Rose, Eunice had telephoned Bishop Fulton Sheen to arrange an appointment for Kick to meet him in New York. The Bishop was one of the most charismatic and persuasive in America and Eunice hoped that he would be able to persuade her to change her mind. For her sister's sake, Kick had agreed to see him. But, as Patsy discovered on 20 April, the night before Kick left Washington, she could not go through the charade.

The meeting was scheduled for first thing the following morning. Unable to sleep, Kick came into Patsy's room and lay down beside her.

'I just don't want to do it, I just don't want to do it,' she kept repeating. 'What good can it do? I'm not going to change my mind about Peter. It's just more pressure. What would you do?'

'I'd call Bishop Sheen and cancel the appointment,' Patsy replied.

'You're right,' Kick said. 'It's my life. There's no point going through catechism all over again. I'm going back to England to do whatever I have to do to be with Peter.'

It was two o'clock in the morning. Then and there, she picked up the phone and rang the Presbytery to cancel the appointment.

It had been over two months since she had last seen Peter. Before they fell asleep, she told Patsy excitedly about the Whitsun weekend they had planned in three weeks' time – their first alone together at a villa in the South of France.

Kick sailed from New York on the *Queen Elizabeth*. Oblivious to the full extent of her mother's wrath, she was in high spirits before she left. Tom Schriber, Joe Jr's old friend, had lunch with her at the 21 Club in Manhattan: 'She looked radiant,' he recalled, 'really alive. She was revved up, ready to go. She had written off her mother but not the old man. She said, "I'd like to get Dad's consent. He matters. But I'm getting married whether he consents or not."'

Within a matter of days, Kick would find herself wavering, cowering before her mother's abuse.

'You are a twenty-eight-year-old married woman and a British resident,' Ilona Solymossy, Kick's housekeeper, reasoned with her. 'How could your mother possibly stop you from marrying?'

Rose had pursued Kick across the Atlantic. In early May, days after Kick arrived back in London, her mother turned up on the doorstep of her house in Smith Square. More than thirty years later, Lynne McTaggart, Kick's biographer, tracked down Ilona Solymossy, the only person to witness what happened during the four ugly days of Rose's stay.

Relentlessly – day and night, according to Ilona – Rose bullied Kick. Hounding her around the house, unmoved by her daughter's tears, Rose insisted that she should end her relationship with Peter, call off any marriage plans and return immediately to America. Repeatedly, Rose reminded her daughter of God's view of divorce. Kick wept helplessly. In all her life, Ilona said, she had never seen an adult cower before a parent as Kick did before her mother.

Rose did not – as she had intended – take Kick with her when she left. But she did leave her, as Ilona remembered, with the feeling that she might not be able to go through with the marriage without the support of at least one parent. She was also left in no doubt that her mother would carry out her threat to banish her from the family; terrified that Rose would turn her brothers and sisters against her for good, Kick rang her father.

The weekend she and Peter planned to fly to the South of France for their Whitsun break, Joe was due to be in Paris on business. Perhaps they could meet, Kick thought. If her father would not give his formal consent to their marriage, he might at least give it his blessing.

When Kick came into the room after finishing the call, Ilona had never seen her looking so ecstatic. Joe had agreed to her suggestion: she and Peter were to meet him for lunch at the Ritz Hotel in Paris on Saturday 15 May.

Kick then made a second call, to her friend Janie Compton. 'The meeting was absolutely vital to her,' Janie recalled. 'She telephoned to ask me if I would go with them. So much depended on it. She wanted moral support from me. I knew Joe quite well from the time when he was Ambassador – when Kick and I first became friends. I think she thought Joe wouldn't like Peter, wouldn't see the point of him at all. Joe was so ANTI what he called "you bloody aristocrats".'

Janie, recently married to Max Aitken, Lord Beaverbrook's son, was unable to go. Resigned to the fact that they would be going alone, Peter and Kick spent a couple of days together at Wentworth before leaving for France. Jean Oliver, who worked in the post office in the village, was up at the house one afternoon during their brief visit. 'I'd gone up to the house to see my friend. She was the chef's daughter. We were sitting outside the kitchen door chatting, and Peter and Lady Hartington walked past. They looked so happy and carefree. Peter wanted to show her the family mausoleum. We watched them set off across the Park and I remember she was wearing an immaculate pair of beautiful white shoes. There was all that coal dust and muck around from the open-cast mining! They'd be ruined, I thought!'

Peter and Kick left Wentworth on Wednesday 12 May – the evening before they were due to fly to France. On the drive south to London, they called in on Tom Fitzwilliam at Milton Hall, a few miles outside Peterborough. Mindful that his cousin might be sensitive about welcoming Kick, as he opened the door Peter said to him:

'Look, I've got Kick outside. May I bring her in?'

'For God's sake do,' Tom said. Over dinner, Peter told Tom what they were about to do. 'We're going off to try to persuade old Kennedy to agree to our getting married.' With a laugh, he added, 'If he objects, I'll go to see the Pope and offer to build him a church.'

36

They were late. The ten-seater private jet Peter had hired to fly the two of them to the South of France was due to take off from Croydon Airport at 10.30, and Kick was still packing. Waiting for her at the house in Smith Square, Peter teased her about her voluminous luggage: they were only going away for a long weekend but her two large suitcases contained enough clothes for several weeks. Besides the surfeit of outfits, she had also packed her Devonshire jewels and an assortment of expensive lingerie – a blue silk negligee, lace-embroidered camisoles and a selection of black lace *jarretelles*. For the four-day trip, they were taking 187 pounds of baggage – most of it Kick's.

They left the house in a hurry. Ilona Solymossy was there to wave them off.

'Wish me luck,' Kick yelled as their car pulled away.

'Should I cross my fingers?' the housekeeper replied.

'Yes, both hands!'

'I will even cross my feet!' Ilona shouted, laughing.

By the time they got to Croydon Airport they were half an hour behind schedule. The De Havilland Dove was waiting for them on the tarmac. Peter had hired the plane from Skyways of London, an exclusive Mayfair-based charter firm. It had cost him £81.* He had chosen the same model as the one owned by his great friend Prince Aly Khan. Skyways had also provided a pilot. Aged thirty-four, Captain Peter Townshend was highly experienced: in the course of his career, he had clocked up almost 3,000 hours in the air, 550 of them as Chief Pilot in an RAF Bomber Squadron during the war.

The route to the Riviera was one Townshend had already flown

*Approximately £2,000 at today's values.

eleven times that year. The flight plan was routine: Paris by noon, with a short stopover for refuelling, and then on down to Cannes, with an anticipated arrival time of around 3.30 p.m.

It was 12.45 – forty-five minutes later than Townshend had anticipated – when the Dove, after its delayed departure from Croydon, landed at Le Bourget, the stylish art deco airport favoured by the international jet set, nine miles to the north of Paris. Peter and Kick got off to stretch their legs while the plane refuelled. As they headed into the terminal, Peter, on a whim, decided to telephone his Parisian friends: would they like to join them for an impromptu lunch in the centre of Paris? Telling Townshend they would be gone for just forty minutes, Peter and Kick caught a taxi to the Champs-Elysées – a twenty-minute drive away.

At 1.30 they had not returned. Townshend, waiting on the apron at Le Bourget, was becoming increasingly anxious. That morning, he had checked the meteorological reports: bad weather was forecast over the Rhône Valley, directly en route to Cannes. Climbing down from the Dove, he crossed the tarmac to the control tower to get an update on the weather.

He was given a chart that had been made up at nine that morning: a violent thunderstorm, with abnormally heavy rainfall, was expected over the Rhône Valley at around five o'clock. The flight south would take three hours: if they were to avoid the storm, they would have to leave immediately. To compound his anxiety, the meteorologist told him that the latest update from weather stations in the south suggested that conditions over the Rhône Valley, and to the south-east of the Massif Central, were worsening.

'The pilot,' the meteorologist reported later, 'did not take notes. He went off, came back and seemed visibly worried about the delay caused by his passengers who had not yet returned. "I'm going to be late," he told us, speaking in French, "and it is very boring."'

At two o'clock – the Dove's revised departure time – there was still no sign of Peter and Kick. Townshend, in communication with air traffic control at Le Bourget, altered the take-off slot to 14.20 – almost two hours later than his original flight plan. At 14.20 he altered it again to 15.00; and again, at 15.00, to 15.30. Minutes after he had moved it forward for the fourth time, the couple, accompanied by their lunch guests who had come to the airport to see them off, finally returned. Townshend was furious. Forty minutes had turned into two and a half hours. The delay, he informed them coolly, meant they would be flying over the Rhône Valley at precisely the time a violent thunderstorm was predicted. All commercial flights had been cancelled: although there were no rules governing private aircraft flying in bad weather conditions, the meteorological office at Le Bourget had advised him not to fly. In his view, it was too much of a risk: he intended to cancel the flight.

Annoyed, Peter began to argue with him. What was a little rain, he said. He was not afraid of turbulence: he had crossed the North Sea in storm-force winds in a small motor torpedo boat. Nothing, surely, could be worse than that. Besides, if they did not fly that afternoon, they would have to call off the trip. It was Thursday: they had to be back in Paris by Saturday morning for the meeting with Joe Kennedy at the Ritz. There was no point postponing the flight until the following morning for the sake of spending less than twenty-four hours in Cannes. Changing tack, Peter then exerted all his charm.

'Why did Peter have to be so ruddy stupid!' his niece, Barbara Ricardo, remembered bitterly more than fifty years after his death. 'It was so stupid. So utterly stupid to go and fly when they'd been told there was a storm and that it wasn't safe. If only he'd been more sensible. You see, he was so spoilt by my grandmother. As a child he always got whatever he wanted. He wanted to go, therefore he must. The pilot was an absolute idiot. Peter must have offered a huge amount of money to get the man to fly. That's my opinion. The pilot should have been more firm and said, if you want to go and get killed, go and kill yourself. But I'm not going to get killed.'

Townshend – whether bribed or persuaded by Peter's charm –

gave in: at twenty minutes past three, firing the plane's engines, he taxied to Runway 5 for take-off.

From a report compiled by the Bureau d'Enquêtes et d'Analyses – the French air accident investigation unit – based on the Dove's onboard radio and navigation logs retrieved from the wreckage of the plane, it is possible to piece together the details of the flight.

After take-off, climbing to 1,500 feet over Fontainebleau, the Dove headed south-east for Auxerre. At 16.17, flying at 150 knots at a cruising altitude of 9,500 feet, Arthur Freeman, the co-pilot and radio operator, noted 'Loire ahead' in the navigation log. For the next forty minutes, aside from a small deviation north to avoid turbulence generated by heavy cloud, Townshend stuck to his flight plan. At 16.50, Arthur Freeman asked Lyon air traffic control for a weather forecast for Cannes, where the plane was due to land at 18.30. Ten minutes later, Freeman entered 'Rhône ahead' in the navigation log. At 17.02, as the aircraft approached the Rhône Valley, Lyon radioed the forecast back.

Crucially, as the air accident investigators noted, Freeman had not inquired about the weather conditions immediately ahead.

It was Lyon's last radio contact with the Dove. It is also the moment when Freeman's navigation log stops. Flying at 10,000 feet, the plane had entered the fringes of the storm in the region of Vienne, a little north of the Ardèche mountains. 'In all likelihood electrical discharge in the atmosphere generated by the thunderstorm rendered radio transmission impossible,' the accident investigators reported. 'Also,' they concluded grimly, 'the attempt to control the aircraft in the turbulence prevented the crew from undertaking any other activity.'

For the next twenty-eight minutes, violent updrafts bounced the Dove thousands of feet through the air. According to the inhabitants of the Vienne, who were lashed by torrential rain, hail and forked lightning, the storm was of quite exceptional strength.

At 17.03, one minute after its last contact with the Dove, Lyon's air traffic control also lost contact with a DC 3 flying on the same flight path through the region. A thirty-two-seater, the DC 3 was a bigger plane: later, the co-pilot reported that visibility was zero and the turbulence so intense that both he and the Captain had had to wrestle with the controls to keep the plane level. Fortunately for the crew of the DC 3, they had hit the cumulus nimbus at an altitude of 2,500 feet and were able to descend out of the cloud to make an emergency landing at Valence airport, not far from where the Dove crashed.

No such option existed for Townshend. He had flown into the storm at an altitude of 10,000 feet – the point where the turbulence is generally at its greatest – and the conditions were even more extreme than those encountered by the crew of the DC 3. Extraordinarily, as the accident investigators noted – incredulous at his insouciance – Townshend had made no attempt to find an entry above or beneath the cloud base, the standard procedure when confronted by threatening cumulus nimbus.

'Even modern 747s would not fly wittingly into a thunderstorm at an altitude of ten thousand feet,' a commercial pilot explained. 'Thunderstorms are known to be one of the most formidable hazards in flight. That's why today's planes are equipped with systems to warn of their approach. You either climb above the storm zone or you descend below it. You don't fly through it.'

What Townshend did not know as he grappled with the leaden controls to keep the Dove on course was that the gale-force south-east winds were dragging the plane into the eye of the storm above the Ardèche mountains. Given its ferocity, it is probable that atmospheric static knocked out the electrically powered artificial horizon gyro – a device that measured the plane's position in relation to the horizon. Flying blind in thick cloud, the dials of the instruments on the Dove's dashboard – notoriously difficult to read at the best of times – spinning uselessly in front of him, Townshend became disoriented. He had no way of knowing where he was, or whether he was flying up or down. He may also have suffered hypostasis – a blackout caused by a lack of oxygen. At 10,000 feet, he was already at the upper limit of flying without breathing apparatus. The updrafts in a storm of the intensity of the one over the Rhône Valley that afternoon were capable of sucking a plane thousands of feet upwards, above the oxygen threshold.

Whether as the result of damage caused by the extreme turbulence or a lapse of consciousness, at around 17.30 Townshend lost control of the Dove.

For the last minute or so of the flight, everyone on board must have known the plane was about to crash. Both Townshend and Freeman stuffed handkerchiefs into their mouths – a standard military procedure to avoid biting through the tongue in a crash landing. Hurtling towards the earth in a steep dive, the massive vibration and the whine from the over-revving engines indicating the plane was out of control, the Dove shot out of the cloud base 1,000 feet above the mountains. Confronted by a ridge directly ahead, in a last desperate attempt to pull out of the dive, Townshend yanked the controls sharply towards him. It was too much for the Dove: the massive g-force broke the plane in mid-air, the right wing cracking first, causing one engine to tear loose, then the other. The fuselage followed its own trajectory: landing vertically, it was embedded in rock on the ridge when Paul Petit and his father discovered it.

All four passengers, the autopsy concluded, had been killed on impact.

It was a two-and-a-half-hour climb up the mountain from St Bauzile, the nearest village, to the site of the crash. Some hours after Paul Petit and his father had found the plane, the Mayor of St Bauzile, accompanied by the Petits, several gendarmes and a local journalist, struggled up the stony path leading to the summit of Le Coran to examine the wreckage. Later, Peter and Kick's bodies, carried on makeshift stretchers, were laid on the back of Petit's ox cart and hauled down the mountain to the Mairie at St Bauzile.

To begin with, there was some confusion over the identity of the passengers. The police had found a passport in the woman's handbag: an American passport bearing the name 'Lady Hartington'. Joe Kennedy was staying at the Georges V hotel in Paris when he was woken in the early hours of the morning by a call from a reporter asking him to confirm reports that Kick – rather than

Billy's brother's wife, Debo Cavendish, also called Lady Hartington – was dead. As Joe left the hotel later that morning to travel by train to the Ardèche, he told reporters he hoped there had been a mistake over his daughter's identity. But he knew it was Kick. Among Joe's personal papers there is a note written on Georges V headed paper. 'Written by me,' it says, '½ hour after notified of Kick's death':

> No one who ever knew her didn't feel that life was much better that minute. And ~~probably~~ we know so little about the next world that we must think that they wanted just such a wonderful girl for themselves. We must not feel sorry for her but for ourselves.

At Wentworth, within hours of the crash, the Estate swung into action. Harry Sporberg, Peter's business partner, took charge, sending Peter's racing trainer to France to identify his body. Before plans could be made for the funeral five days later, a number of sensitive matters had to be dealt with first. Rowena Sykes, a nineteen-year-old maid at the house, was at home in Jump, a pit village a few miles from Wentworth, when she received a message the morning after Peter was killed. 'It was Whitsuntide and I'd got the weekend off. Next door to where I lived there was a hairdresser. She had a telephone. It was the only one in the village, nobody had telephones in them days. A neighbour came round and said there was a call for me. It was Mrs Lloyd, the housekeeper. "Would I go back to the house straight away," she said. All the maids were called back. There were seven of us. £1 12 shillings and sixpence a month we got. We had to go up to Lord Fitzwilliam's bedroom and strip it. Move the pillows, open the windows, change the sheets, everything. He'd been in there with the Kennedy girl a few days before. They wanted her scent got rid of because Lady Fitzwilliam [Obby] was on her way up from London to Wentworth for the funeral. Then we had to go and clear out the Chapel. There was all this furniture, and pictures and what have you in there. It had all gone in when the soldiers took over the house. It had never come out, it was still there. They wanted to put Peter's coffin in the Chapel – to lay it in state before they buried him in the Church.'

It was left to Joe Kennedy to deal with the formalities of Kick's death. On the evening of Friday 14 May, after identifying her body, he phoned home to Hyannis Port where the rest of the family had gathered. Unsurprisingly, he said nothing about her disfiguring wounds. He told the family how 'beautiful' she looked. She had been found on her back 'asleep' with her shoes gone. Wasn't that just like Kick, who always went barefoot?

Joe alone was confronted by the gruesome – and uncomfortable – details of Kick's death. Soon after identifying her body, the police handed over her personal effects. As well as a family photo album and a string of rosary beads, they included a vaginal douche. The daughter of America's most prominent Catholic family, and the widow of a man once mooted as a husband for England's future Queen, had died on her way to an illicit weekend with a married man.

Hours after the plane crashed, the Devonshires, the Fitzwilliams and the Kennedys closed ranks. They used both Ilona Solymossy – Kick's housekeeper – and Peter Fitzwilliam's secretary as conduits to channel an acceptable version of the story to the Press. 'Chance Invite Sends Kennedy Girl to Her Death', read the headline in the *New York Daily News*, a newspaper owned by Joseph Patterson, an associate of Joe Kennedy's. The paper was the first to 'break' the story of the 'circumstances' leading to the couple's death. Quoting Peter's secretary, Kick was described as an 'old friend of both Lady and Lord Fitzwilliam's'. 'Lady Hartington', the paper reported, had 'casually encountered Lord Fitzwilliam' at the Ritz Hotel in London. On discovering that she was unable to secure a train or plane ticket to visit her father in the South of France, the paper continued, Lord Fitzwilliam offered her a seat on the plane he had chartered to visit 'racehorse breeders' on the French Riviera. 'Lady Hartington,' so the paper alleged, 'had been delighted with the offer of a lift.' The inconsistency of the facts – that Joe Kennedy had been in Paris, rather than the South of France – did not trouble the *New York Daily News*. Nor did the fact that the French Riviera was not known for its racehorse breeding.

In Britain, a virtual news blackout was imposed. Of the four tabloids with the highest circulations, only one, the left-wing *Daily Mirror*, printed the story. On the Friday, the morning after the accident, the *Daily Mail*, the *Daily Express* and the *Daily Herald* had all carried reports in their Stop Press columns that a British light aircraft had crashed, the identities of the passengers as yet unknown. Yet in the days that followed, there was no further news – no reports even that Kick and Peter had been killed. High up in the organization of each of the newspapers, someone had clearly decreed that the story be pulled.

Joe had Kick's body transported up to Paris where it lay at the Catholic church of St Philippe du Roule, watched over by a nun from the Order of the Sisters of Hope. For four days, Kick's final resting place remained undecided. Responding to inquiries from the Press, Joe, dazed, answered, 'I have no plans. No plans.'

It was finally agreed that Kick would be buried at Chatsworth, the Devonshires' home in Derbyshire. The Kennedys left the arrangements for the funeral to the Duchess of Devonshire. They did not even choose her epitaph. 'Joy she gave, Joy she has found' were the words the Duchess chose to be carved on the headstone above her grave.

Yet, for all Joe Kennedy's faults, Kick had been right to place her faith in him. Four months later, writing to the Duchess of Devonshire, on whom he had lent heavily in the days after Kick's death, Joe was still paralysed by grief. 'Dearest Moucher,' he wrote:

> It probably isn't news to you to know that I thought about you a great deal since I came back to America. I think that the only thing that helped me retain my sanity was your understanding manner in the whole sad affair. I would like to be able to tell you that I am very much better, but I just can't.
>
> I can't seem to get out of my mind that there is no possibility of

seeing Kick next winter and that there are no more weeks and months to be made gay by her presence. I realize that people say, 'You have many other children, you can't be too depressed by Kick's death,' and I think that, to all intents and purposes, no one knows that I am depressed. In fact, I have never acknowledged it even to Rose who, by the way, is ten thousand per cent better than I am. Her terrifically strong faith has been a great help to her, along with her very strong will and determination not to give way . . .

I know I tried to tell you, while I was in London, how grateful I am to Edward and you for your whole attitude in those dark days. I don't know whether I made myself very clear or not, but it will do no harm to repeat again that I will never forget it and I will always be deeply grateful to you and your family . . .

Joe was the only member of the Kennedy family present at Kick's funeral. Neither her mother, Rose, nor her brothers and sisters were there. For Rose, as Lem Billings, a close friend of the family's recalled, 'that airplane crash was God pointing his finger at Kick and saying NO!' Days before the funeral, Rose had arranged for a memorial Mass card to be sent out. The prayer printed on it was a plea for plenary indulgence, applicable to souls in purgatory. One of Kick's friends tore it up in a rage. Those who had loved and now mourned Kick could not forgive Rose. 'Somerset Maugham [the celebrated British novelist] came to stay with us out in Tanganyika some years after Peter died,' Barbara, Peter's niece, remembered. 'And he told us that Kick's mother had put a curse on her daughter. She'd put a curse on her own daughter, that's what her friends believed.'

Rose lied about Kick's death until the day she died. In her autobiography, *Time to Remember*, she wrote that Kick and a 'few friends' were returning from a holiday on the Riviera en route to meeting Joe in Paris when the plane crashed. There were no public foundations set up in Kick's name or privately published commemorative books, as there were after Joe, Jack and Bobby died. Kick's brothers and sisters knew not to talk about her in their mother's presence: even her brothers imposed their own vows of silence. Independently, Jack and Bobby visited Ilona Solymossy in the months after her death. On leaving the housekeeper, their parting words were the same: 'We will not mention her again.' In 1951, when Bobby Kennedy's eldest daughter was born, he wanted to name her Kathleen Hartington Kennedy: the family had one stipulation – that she never be referred to as 'Kick'.

On 20 May 1948 Joe Kennedy stood in the sheltered graveyard behind Edensor Church at Chatsworth and watched Kick's coffin being lowered into the earth. He had lost his eldest and favourite son, Joe: now his favourite daughter was being laid to rest in the grounds of a famously anti-Catholic family in a foreign country from which, a decade earlier, he had been asked to leave. 'I can still see the stricken face of old Joe Kennedy,' Alistair Forbes recalled nearly thirty years later, 'as he stood alone, unloved and despised, behind the coffin of his eldest daughter amid the hundreds of British friends who had adored her and now mourned her.'

At Wentworth, Peter's funeral had taken place the previous day.

37

The gypsies came before dawn, scattering flowers along the road leading to the church where Peter was to be buried. In his father's day, an avenue of splendid lime trees, carefully pollarded by the Estate labourers, had lined Church Drive, but now, on one side, just three of the trees were left. The others had been uprooted by the excavators that had wrecked the fields beyond. The denuded landscape, the mounds and craters of naked limestone, stretched away to the south as far as the eye could see. The flowers stood out against the brilliant white of the road. The original grass track had long since been covered by thousands of pieces of limestone debris from the fields nearby.

At three o'clock, the hour given by the Estate officials as the likely time when Peter's coffin, mounted on a bier pulled by eight of the Fitzwilliams' employees, would leave Wentworth House, there was no sign of the gypsies. They had scattered the flowers and gone – a Romany custom to honour the souls of those who had been kind to them.

The funeral was private: the first private funeral in the history of the Earls Fitzwilliam. The orchestrated public mourning performed at Peter's great-grandfather's funeral in 1902, and at those of previous Earls before him, belonged to the past. Overnight, after vesting day – 1 January 1947 – the day Britain's collieries were transferred to public ownership, the numbers employed by the family had fallen from thousands to hundreds. A skeleton staff of just eleven servants remained on duty at the house: with the acreage subsumed by the open-cast mining operations, even the Estate departments were being slowly run down.

Yet still, on the morning of 20 May 1948, thousands came from the villages around Wentworth. 'He were a grand lad,' May Bailey, the former scullery maid at the house, recalled. 'He were popular.

Everyone liked him, they wanted to see him off.' But tragedy, as some admitted, and the macabre symbol of the Fitzwilliams' and Wentworth's catastrophic unravelling, also drew the crowds. 'Ay,' said one man from the village, 'they said they'd brought him home, but I doubt there was much left of him in that coffin. They told his mother he had died asleep, that his body had been thrown out of the plane and was barely touched. I heard different: they said he was in pieces, and not many pieces at that.'

Along Church Drive, the crowd started forming at two o'clock. At the top of the road, by the green door that led into the gardens of Wentworth House, they came to pile wreaths of flowers on to the waiting farm carts. An hour later, heads were bared when the green door opened for the coffin, draped in a Union Jack, drawn by the Fitzwilliams' eight employees.

Maud, Obby and her thirteen-year-old daughter, Juliet, led the procession that followed the bier as it was hauled the mile from the house. Maud was bowed by grief; a crêpe funeral veil shrouded her face. 'I don't think she ever got over it,' Lady Barbara Ricardo, her granddaughter, remembered. 'She absolutely doted on Peter. He was more important to her than anything else. The extraordinary thing was later in life, when she was much older – I suppose she must have been in her seventies – my mother went up to see her one Christmas and my grandmother showed her a photograph of Peter. She said to Mummy, "Elfie darling, do tell me, who is the man in the photograph? I often look at it and I can't work out who this handsome young man is. Who is he?" Mummy said, "Darling, it's your son." She said, "Darling, I don't have a son." My mother said, "Mummy, you did have a son. He's gone now." Somehow or other, the kindness of the good Lord – or who, I don't know – enabled her to forget. Misery and fate and everything else had caused her to lose that part of her memory.'

The farm carts, loaded with the wreaths of flowers, joined the procession, separating the three women from the other mourners. A decrepit figure in his mid-sixties, wearing an unusually tall black silk top hat – a sartorial relic from the Victorian age – walked at the head of the long line that followed behind the carts. His mourning suit was ill-fitting: the trousers were too short, inelegantly hitched around his waist, and the tail coat too long. The very sight of him, his position in the bleak procession, told a sorry story: Eric, Peter's successor – the new and 9th Earl Fitzwilliam – was the last of the 6th Earl's male descendants left.

Peter's great-grandfather had been Earl for almost half a century. In the mid-1800s, he had produced eight sons; by any reckoning, it was a firm guarantee of his family's title. But just two of his sons had produced sons themselves: William, Lord Milton, the father of Billy, the 7th Earl, and William Charles Fitzwilliam, Eric's father. Genes, rather than untimely deaths in colonial wars or the twentieth century's two World Wars, were to blame. Four of the 6th Earl's sons had died childless before they reached fifty: aside from Billy and Eric, the others had produced eight daughters. With Peter's death, the Fitzwilliam title was in danger of becoming extinct.

Eric drew cold stares from the villagers as he shuffled past. 'No one wanted him. No one liked him. He weren't someone you could respect. "Him," they'd say, nodding at 't big house. Then they'd tip their hand. "Him as 'ud like a drink."'

Eric's minder, Harold Brown, paid for by a Fitzwilliam family trust, hovered behind the new Earl. A solitary and eccentric bachelor, for much of his life Eric had been a hopeless alcoholic. In his youth, his wild excesses of drinking and extravagance had led his father to declare him bankrupt. Now approaching his seventies, he was mysteriously proud of his family nickname, 'Bottle by Bottle' – a name he sometimes used when introducing himself to strangers.

All hope that Wentworth House and the Estate could pull through this dark period in its history had gone. 'When Peter got killed, that were it then,' Geoff Steer, a miner's son who was at the funeral, recalled. 'Wentworth House died with him.'

The village church was packed; there was standing room only at the back. The congregation was half-way through the 23rd Psalm when hundreds of miners, still wearing their working clothes, their faces blackened by coal dust and grime, came hurrying up the path. The day shift at New Stubbin and Elsecar, the Fitzwilliams' former pits, had just ended. Under the new management, they had not been allowed to leave the shift any earlier. Crowding into the back of the church, the men spilled out among the gravestones outside.

These were the sons and grandsons of the miners who had led the 6th Earl's funeral cortège in 1902. In four decades, the Fitzwilliam family and Wentworth House had been all but destroyed.

It was the turn of the miners and their families next.

The titanic battle between capital and labour that rumbled through Britain's coalfields in the twentieth century, sweeping up Wentworth, was not over. By the mid 1990s, fifty years after the nationalization of the coal industry, of the seventy pits in the South Yorkshire coalfield that in 1900 had employed 115,000 miners, only four remained, employing a workforce of under 2,500 men. By the close of the century, Wentworth, and the pit villages for miles around, had been devastated by blight: criss-crossed by more motorways per square mile than in any other part of the country, they were roads to nowhere, funded by the Government and Europe in a futile attempt to generate employment in a region afflicted by the highest numbers of unemployed in Britain.

For all the saints, who from their labours rest,
Who Thee by faith before the world confessed,
Thy name O Jesus be forever blessed
Alleluia, Alleluia . . .

Vaughan Williams's hymn was the last to be sung at Peter's funeral. Midway through the singing, the voices of the congregation, and those of the hundreds of miners standing among the gravestones outside, were drowned by the roar of the engines from two approaching Lancaster Bombers, flying at a few hundred feet.

Swooping low over the church with the missing spire, the pilots performed an aerial salute, dipping the planes' wings in tribute to a brave man.

Epilogue

Six months after Peter was killed, Wentworth House was taken over by the Lady Mabel College of Physical Education.

The grand Marble Salon, where in 1912 the celebrated prima ballerina Anna Pavlova had danced for the King, became the college gymnasium, filled with climbing ropes, vaulting horses and balancing beams. The other once magnificent state rooms suffered a similar fate. The Whistlejacket Room, with Stubbs's famous portrait of the racehorse still in situ, was converted into a dance studio; the gilded Ante-Room, where Peter and the vicarage children had learnt to waltz, was designated a Junior Common Room for the first intake of forty students.

The trainee sports mistresses slept and dressed in dormitories in Bedlam, the wing along the East Front where the bedrooms for the Fitzwilliams' bachelor guests had traditionally been. 'We were absolutely in awe of the place. It was so vast, it was overpowering,' a former student recalled. An air of disorder and decay, as another remembered, pervaded the grandeur. 'We had to kill the rats with our hockey sticks. At night it sounded like thunder above. You could hear them running through. It was so loud it would wake you up.' In the daytime, the sheep that grazed on the front lawn would wander into the house. 'They would get into Bedlam and drink the water out of the toilets in the bathrooms that had been installed at the end of the wing. We used to have to shoo them down the corridor with a broom. Whenever we went out to play lacrosse, the games mistress would shout "Charge", to disperse them, but they still kept coming into the house.'

'Bottle by Bottle', the dissolute 9th Earl Fitzwilliam, posed a further hazard. 'He used to roam the house with his Jack Russell terriers. One was called Peril. You could hear him coming: "Peril! Peril! Come on, Peril!" Sometimes he'd stagger into our classes, or turn up in the middle of our dinner. He'd be absolutely cut. Somehow, the Principal managed to usher him out; it wasn't the sort of thing she wanted her girls to see.'

Eric was living at the back of the house in the apartment that Billy and Maud had occupied during the war. The suite of forty rooms resembled an Aladdin's Cave, crammed with paintings, fine pieces of furniture, porcelain and silver – the precious family heirlooms that had once filled the other 325 rooms in the house. A few months after Peter's death, there had been a massive clearout. Five hundred items, a mere fraction of the contents of the house, had been auctioned in one of the first of the great country house sales. The unwanted furniture had raised £55,000, almost £1 million at today's values. With the arrival of the Lady Mabel College, space was the issue, not money. The family was still immensely rich. Their estate boasted tens of thousands of acres of land in Yorkshire and Ireland and a number of houses in Mayfair; the compensation due for the nationalization of their coal interests had been fixed at several millions.

Wentworth House had not been structurally damaged by the open-cast mining operations, despite the Sheffield geologists' predictions. But aesthetically, it was ruined. Anyone walking along the majestic fifty-yard Picture Gallery in Eric's apartment, past the Titians, Van Dycks and paintings by Guido and Raphael, would see the slag heaps that had desecrated the gardens outside, framed in the window at its far end.

Eric spent most of his day in a sitting room overlooking the industrial site. 'He would do nothing but drink all day,' Godfrey Broadhead, a forester on the Estate, recalled. 'Sometimes the Earl would ask me to go out into the Park to see what I could find. I'd come back with feathers and birds' eggs, and bits and pieces that I'd picked up from the ground. He liked that.' A staff of seven servants had been kept on to look after him: as one housemaid recalled, they dreaded going into the room. 'I never saw him sober. He used to drink whisky and smoke Pasha cigarettes around the clock. You can imagine going into his room. It was horrible.'

The 9th Earl's alcoholism was steadily killing him. As Eric's health disintegrated, two brothers, Tom and Toby, were contesting which of them should succeed him. The time bomb their mother, Evie, had set under the noble house of Fitzwilliam in 1914 was about to explode.

The final act in the Fitzwilliam drama was played out at the Royal Courts of Justice in central London in the winter of 1951. The case between the two brothers was heard before a judge in the Chancery Division. It was left to him to resolve a mystery that for more than half a century the family had kept secret, hoping it would never come to light. Was Toby, the elder son of George and Evie Fitzwilliam, legitimate, or had they married after he was born? It was a question none of the family's surviving members could conclusively answer, least of all Toby himself.

The Fitzwilliams were in danger of being undone by their obsession with secrecy and their inclination to destroy their own records. Evie and George were dead and there was no marriage certificate: mere scraps of evidence had survived from the late nineteenth century when the marriage was supposed to have taken place.

Peter's sudden death, and the absence of male heirs in the main branch of the family, had forced the case. Eric, the 9th Earl, was the last of the 6th Earl's male descendants; there being no living male descendants of the 7th and 8th Earls Fitzwilliam, it was necessary to go back to George, the third son of the 5th Earl, to find an heir. The 5th Earl had died in 1857; Tom and Toby were his great-grandsons, the last of the male heirs left.

It was not simply the devolution of the family's title and great fortune that was at stake; the future of the Earldom depended on the outcome of the case. Toby, who was sixty-three, had a son and a grandson to carry on the title. Tom, who was forty-seven, had never married. For almost twenty years Tom had been in love with the wife of the heir to the Duke of Norfolk by whom he had an illegitimate daughter and with whom he was still very much involved. It was doubtful whether he would ever produce a son: unless Toby won the case, the centuries-old Earldom would die with Tom.

It was, as the judge was keen to stress, a 'friendly contest'. Eighteen months before the court hearing began, the two brothers had exchanged letters. 'I would like you to know that I am really delighted you are clearing this matter up now & once and for all,' Tom wrote to Toby. 'If the case should go in your favour (or for that matter in mine) I would like you to know that my affection & feelings for you will not be altered in the very smallest degree.' Toby, the elder sibling, was less sanguine. Riddled with self-doubt, and 'very unhappy', he expressed his 'utmost dislike for the whole thing'. 'I feel very deeply being the person responsible for bringing all these family skeletons into the limelight,' he confessed to his brother.

The moral character and motives of George and Evie Fitzwilliam – and particularly their mother, Evie – lay at the heart of the case. The brothers' relationship with their parents had determined both their lives. Ultimately, Tom had supplanted his brother in his parents' affections after Toby, the elder by sixteen years, was cast out. It was Tom who had inherited the family's spectacular Elizabethan mansion, Milton Hall, and the gracious lifestyle of a gentleman farmer. Toby, cut off in his father's will, had been forced to work, earning a living as Secretary to the British Field Sports Society. 'So far as I am concerned I have no faith in the case whatsoever,' he wrote to Tom.

> Nor from my own point of view have I much concern about which way it goes. Many years ago I realized nothing would be coming my way so I have faced nothing on expectations. For nearly twenty years I have had a marvellous job which has made me more happy than I can say. What more does a man want? . . . I should be the happiest man on earth if it wasn't for this b----y case.

For Toby, the case involved raking over a past he had vowed to forget. Both his parents, so he believed, had betrayed his love. He was convinced his mother had destroyed the papers proving his legitimacy out of spite.

In June 1920, shortly before undergoing a serious operation,

Evie Fitzwilliam had written a letter to her husband, George, to be handed to him in the event of her death. 'My darling one,' she began.

> You and I have loved one another as no other man and wife ever did. I have always played the game with you and you have been goodness and straightness itself. For all this I am grateful . . . I hate leaving you and Tom as I love you both so much and you have both loved and honoured me. God help you to bear my loss. Keep straight for Tom's sake. Let him look to us *both* as two of his best friends.

In what she believed to be her last words to her family, Evie had excised Toby. She could not have been a worse friend to her elder son. At the time of writing, they had been estranged for six years. She had not seen or spoken to him since the day in November 1914 when he had been given special leave by his Commanding Officer to go to Milton Hall before leaving for France to fight on the Western Front. Toby's marriage to Beryl Morgan had been the cause of their falling out. Evie never forgave him for marrying 'the granddaughter of a draper'. She had even refused to meet her grandchildren.

The rift had been a source of lasting unhappiness to Toby. Until the day Evie died, in March 1925 – five years after the operation she thought would kill her – he had tried to make it up with his mother. Ten years after their last meeting, he had almost succeeded. 'The prospect of seeing you again is too splendid,' he wrote excitedly in January 1924, after she had issued an invitation for him to come and stay for the weekend. 'I must keep all I've got to tell you till we meet. I do hope you are strong and well now. I heard how ill you had been for a long time. As for me, you'll find me thinner than ever and going bald very fast. The result I think of an obstreperous family.'

Toby had assumed that Beryl and their two children, Rosemary and Richard, were also invited for the weekend. He was wrong. Ten years after the event, his mother's anger over his marriage had not subsided. She wrote back by return: 'I want you to quite understand that we do not intend to have anything whatsoever to do with your wife and her family, nor do we wish them discussed. Now having got the unpleasant part of my letter over I wish to say that if you agree to this *you* will always be welcome here.' Toby was devastated. Writing to his father, he said, 'I can hardly tell you how much I was looking forward to seeing everyone this weekend . . . I believe I know what your opinion would be of any man, most of all your son, if he accepted such a condition and have therefore most reluctantly written to Mother refusing. I cannot tell you what a grief and disappointment it is to me and can only hope that some day things will come right.'

They never did – despite it being a wish his father shared. Ten months later, Evie became seriously ill. 'I don't know how things will turn out, but there is no doubt it is touch and go,' George wrote to Toby. 'My only regret for the moment, if anything should happen to her, is the thought that you and she never came together again and made friends – anyhow, forgive her for my sake.' Four days later, Toby received a call from his father to tell him that Evie, who was fifty-eight, was dying. Rushing up to Milton immediately, he arrived too late.

But it was what he perceived as his father's betrayal that had caused Toby the most distress. Although their relationship had been volatile, they had remained on more or less friendly terms throughout the years that he had been estranged from his mother. After Evie died, they had grown closer; Toby and his family frequently stayed with George at Milton. As the elder son, Toby had expected to inherit the Hall and the estate. But when George's will was read out after his death in 1935, he had left everything to Tom.

'I had been treated by my father as his eldest son all my life, and I imagined that Milton was being left to me and it was a very great shock,' Toby later recalled. 'I have never once grumbled or felt any umbrage about not being left Milton or any money at all, but I had the most frightful feeling that my father deceived me all his life. It was the biggest shock I had had, I was really – we were good friends and to wake up never having been told anything just knocked me out.'

Toby believed that his father had cut him out of his will to honour his mother's last wishes. His inheritance was the price Evie had demanded he pay for his marriage to Beryl. In 1914, in a series of vituperative letters, she had sworn that if the marriage went ahead Toby's life 'would be ruined for ever' and that he would 'estrange himself for ever'.

Toby had never doubted his legitimacy, though he had come to realize that he might have difficulty proving it. He had been raised as George and Evie's eldest son and heir and neither of his parents had ever told him that he was illegitimate. On the contrary, in the rare moments that the subject was discussed, they had both assured him that he had been born in wedlock. As late as 1930, five years after his mother's death, George had reiterated to Toby that he regarded him as his legitimate son and heir.

It was only after Toby married Beryl that Evie began to spread rumours behind his back that he was illegitimate. Up until then, she had gone out of her way to stress to friends, and to members of the Fitzwilliam family, that he had been born after she and George married.

If, in 1914 or soon after, Evie had destroyed the papers that proved his legitimacy, as Toby believed she had, she could not have known that, decades later, the future of the Earldom would be at stake. Her motive in destroying the papers – if she had done so – was to prevent Toby from inheriting the Milton estate.

Given the strength of Evie's feelings against Beryl, Toby had no doubt that she was capable of such a vengeful act. Indeed, there was evidence to suggest that she had contemplated it in 1909, when Toby had fallen in love with an actress whom he had wanted to marry. In the years before the First World War, marriage to an actress was still regarded as scandalous. Though Evie herself had once been on the stage, she forbade the union. Toby, like his great-uncle Milton before him, was banished to Canada. A close family friend, Mary Fullerton, was at Milton the morning he left in disgrace:

I went to Peterborough station and saw Toby off to Canada. The actress and her mother were at the Station Hotel and Toby, who had been very unwilling to go to Canada, had a word with them on the steps of the hotel before he left on the train. I returned to Milton and found Evelyn Fitzwilliam in a peculiar mood. She was furious with Toby over his attachment to this girl. Up to this time I had never heard any suggestion that Toby was not legitimate and he was generally regarded and treated as if he was legitimate and George Fitzwilliam's heir. Evelyn Fitzwilliam then said she had the papers proving Toby's legitimacy, but that she was now going to destroy them. She mentioned that she had been married in Scotland. I was amazed to hear any doubts about Toby's legitimacy, and I implored her not to do anything hastily. I pointed out that Toby was going to Canada to start a new life, and begged her to forget the past and let him start again. I left with the impression that she would not do anything hastily. I cannot remember that I ever went to Milton again. There was no doubt in my mind that after this incident I was out of favour because I had taken Toby's side and acted as I did. Evelyn Fitzwilliam was very strong-minded. George Fitzwilliam was a weak character as far as she was concerned, and she absolutely ruled the roost.

It is possible that documents proving Toby's legitimacy had once existed. This impression was directly confirmed by his aunt, George's sister Alice. She remembered a conversation with Evie, in the library at Milton, which took place before the First World War – and before Evie and Toby had fallen out. 'My sister-in-law . . . I can see her now standing with her back to the library window,' Alice remembered. 'She said: "Are you one of the people who think that Toby was born before we married?" I said: "I am afraid I am because we have always been told so," and she said at once: "Well, it is not true." George came in from the other room and said: "No, and I have got the papers."'

'The papers' he was referring to were the documents relating to their wedding in Scotland in the autumn of 1886, some eighteen months before Toby was born. In 1930, five years before he died, George made a recorded statement, sworn in front of a Commissioner of Oaths. It proved only that George was under the impression he might have been married in advance of his first son's birth. 'When travelling in Scotland in the year 1886,' he said,

'I went through a form of marriage with my late wife, Daisy Evelyn Fitzwilliam, which we believed to be valid.'

Had George given the Commissioner of Oaths a selective version of events in his statement, or was he telling the truth? For Toby to be proved legitimate it was necessary for the court to establish that the Scottish marriage had actually taken place.

Fifty years earlier, when Billy Fitzwilliam's uncles and aunts had accused him of being an impostor – a changeling who had no right to succeed to the Earldom – the family had pulled back from the brink of going to court. In February 1951, in their second inheritance dispute of the century, and facing their demise, they had no choice.

At the outset, the case, with its mountain of supporting documents – thousands of pages of depositions, sworn affidavits, and for the most part unilluminating bills and correspondence – threatened to become the most expensive in British legal history: a real-life rival to Dickens's Jarndyce v Jarndyce. Rumour, gossip and a lack of hard facts were the defining features of Fitzwilliam v Fitzwilliam – as they had been when Billy's right to succeed had been disputed within the confines of the family.

The two brothers were represented by England's most distinguished silks. Toby's leading barrister was Sir David Maxwell-Fyfe, who had been Britain's Assistant Chief Prosecutor at the Nazi war-crime trials at Nuremberg. Maxwell-Fyfe's challenge was to convince the judge, Mr Justice Pilcher, that, on the balance of probabilities, George and Evie had been married in Scotland, and that it was a valid marriage under Scottish Law. Tom's legal team contested that the marriage had never taken place at all.

The couple had met in the spring of 1886, when George, an Army officer, was twenty-two years old, and Evie, then twenty, was an actress. The lawyers were hard-pressed to produce all but the barest of sketches of their relationship. George, who spent a good deal of time at drinking clubs and music halls in London's West End, had apparently been introduced to Evie at the Gaiety Theatre, where she was appearing in the chorus of a sentimental musical called *Little Jack Shepherd* under her stage name, Eva Raines.

George, of medium height with a shock of fair hair, heir to the 23,000-acre estate at Milton, was both handsome and supremely eligible. The judge, from the little he could gather, said he pictured him as a 'simple, straight-forward and affectionate young man'. Considerably less was known of the young Evie. As the search for records to confirm her identity revealed, it seems she was not the daughter of a respectable country doctor, as she claimed. But whoever she was, her charms were not in doubt: 'She was the most lovely woman I have ever seen,' Alice Williams Wynn, George's sister, remembered. That George was swept off his feet by Evie was not in dispute.

In September 1886, Evie accepted an engagement to play a minor role in a touring musical comedy called *The Beggar Student*. It was scheduled to open in Glasgow at the Grand Theatre on 20 September 1886. At some point during the Scottish tour, the alleged marriage was supposed to have taken place.

'One could almost smell the lavender and hear the whispering of the silk beneath the crinoline,' one newspaper reporter commented of the elderly women in their eighties and nineties who took the stand. In the absence of official records, or witnesses to the marriage – in short, any evidence relating to the venue, the precise date, or the form the ceremony had taken – the lawyers were largely reliant on their testimony. The women had known the couple in the late 1880s and 1890s. Forced to cast their minds back over sixty years, they told the court the little they knew.

Had George merely accompanied Evie to Scotland and lived with her in what the judge referred to as 'a state of concubinage', or had they married while they were there? Brandishing an ear trumpet, the eighty-three-year-old Kate Rickards was a key witness. The daughter of Evie's former landlady in London, she had gone on the tour as a companion to the actress. Unhappily for Toby, Mrs Rickards was unable to provide details of the wedding: in the course of her eight-hour appearance in the witness box, she was not even able to confirm the couple had married. Picking over the fragments of her memory, the barristers, struggling to make themselves heard, barked their questions.

'Can you tell us on what terms of affection they were to each other?'

'Very, very great affection,' she replied. 'They were very, very devoted to one another.'

Seizing on her recollection of the journey to Glasgow, they quizzed her over the only reference George and Evie had made to marriage.

'We went up by train. Going over the border they chaffed me and said I must be very careful because we were going into Scotland and I might find myself married whether I wanted to or not.'

In the 1880s, Scotland was a notorious destination for eloping couples. The butt of music-hall jokes, it was known as a place where marriages could be contracted quickly and informally. Yet despite having teased Kate on the train, George and Evie did not tell her of their own plans to marry. In any event, Kate, it transpired, was firmly under the impression they were already married. Arriving in Glasgow, the trio had rented a small flat on Sauchiehall Street. 'We had two bedrooms and a sitting room. They had one bedroom and I had the other. They lived there as Mr and Mrs Fitzwilliam, as man and wife, and so naturally I thought they were married.'

If, as George's evasive statement to the Commissioner of Oaths intimated, he and Evie had married in Scotland, they had had every reason to keep their wedding secret from Kate. It seems they had deceived her mother. In 1886, Kate was a naïve eighteen-year-old; as she confessed, her mother would never have allowed her to go to Scotland with an unmarried man and woman.

It turned out, so Toby's lawyers submitted, that George and Evie had in fact been married twice. However, the circumstances of their English wedding were as mysterious as the one in Scotland. Once again, Kate Rickards had been there. But, for the second time, George and Evie had chosen to keep her in the dark.

In the winter of 1888, two years after the alleged Scottish marriage, Kate was living with the couple at their flat at 88 New Bond Street in London, where they were known to servants, tradesmen and friends as Mr and Mrs Fitzwilliam. One morning, Evie woke

Kate early. It was New Year's Eve – 31 December 1888 – a little over six months after Toby had been born. 'She [Evie] came in one morning and asked if I would be a witness. She did not say what it was for or anything. I went to St George's Hanover Square, and it was a very dark, clammy, foggy morning and there was no one in the church at all so far as I could see, and they went through a ceremony. It seemed not a bit like a wedding. I did not think it was a wedding and it did not dawn on me that it was.'

Kate Rickards was cross-examined by Mr Milner Holland, the King's Counsel representing Tom. 'When you left New Bond Street, are you telling His Lordship you did not know where you were going to?'

'No.'

'You did not know which way you were going to turn after you got out of the door?'

'I did not know where they were going, I did not know it was a church they were going to; they did not mention anything about a marriage.'

'You see, Mrs Rickards,' Milner Holland continued, 'I must press you about this; here was your closest girlfriend and a man you considered to be her husband with whom you had been living for a long time but without, according to you, without a word of explanation suddenly asking you to put on your hat and come out on a cold December morning and go to church; and then what happened?'

'Well, we simply went into the church and they had the ceremony. I did not think anything about it, I mean I simply did as I was asked.'

'You knew what the ceremony was?'

'Did not dawn on me that it was a marriage service, I do not know why.'

'And do you mean to say when you got inside they did not tell you what they had got you there for?'

'No, I understood before that I was supposed to witness their signatures and I simply waited. You see, there was not a soul in the church except this pew opener.'

'Did you not put a few pertinent questions to Evie afterwards?'

'No, it was not mentioned and we never talked about it.'

Toby's lawyers reasoned that George and Evie had every reason to keep their wedding secret. In the 1880s it was regarded as a disgraceful and shocking thing for a young man of good family to marry an actress. In the Guards regiments, the rules were plain. If an officer married an actress, he had to resign his commission.

But why then a second wedding in London? George, in numerous statements to his solicitor, had claimed that he and Evie had married at Hanover Square because they were told the Scottish marriage was invalid. 'Your Lordship ought to accept George's own account,' Toby's barrister, Sir David Maxwell-Fyfe, urged the judge, 'that they were married in Scotland and somebody threw doubts on it . . . Your Lordship knows how wiseacres always haunt London clubs full of information of that kind, and in some way they accepted that and thought they should get married again.'

Unluckily for George, news of the Hanover Square wedding leaked out, forcing him to resign his commission in the Blues. The pew opener at St George's, a Dickensian figure by the name of Sargeant and the only other witness to the marriage besides Kate Rickards and the Vicar, was the servant of an old Fitzwilliam retainer. Via Sargeant, word reached the senior branch of the family. It was the 6th Earl's view of the alleged wedding in Scotland and his reaction to Toby's birth that finally enabled the judge to decide the case.

William, Earl Fitzwilliam, who was George's uncle, and who had been appointed guardian to George and his two sisters after the death of their father, was firmly convinced that Toby was illegitimate. It was not until two and a half years after Toby was born that George's guardian heard of the baby's existence. Writing to George in the winter of 1891, the Earl expressed his grave displeasure:

I have just heard that you propose taking a little boy to Milton. I know nothing about the poor little fellow, but I should not be doing right if I did not point out to you the disastrous effects of taking him there. The evil effects of such an example would be very great, and would mar your future influence for good in the neighbourhood, and later on the consequences would fall very heavily on both you and your sisters. If you take that little boy to Milton, you permanently close the door to your sisters, whether they were actually there at the moment or not. Your sisters suffer now, and must continue to suffer, much on your account; do not add to it more than you can help.

The 6th Earl's letters to his nephew were among the very few contemporaneous pieces of evidence. 'It is perfectly clear, indeed it is not in dispute,' Mr Justice Pilcher told the court in his Judgment, given on the twentieth day of the hearing, 'that the opinion which the Sixth Earl formed when he first heard of Toby's existence, namely that he was illegitimate, never altered until the date of his death in 1902.'

Mr Justice Pilcher ruled against Toby. Tom's side had convinced him that the Scottish wedding had never taken place. George and Evie had lied: their claims to have been married in Scotland, both in their conversations with friends and with members of the family and in the various sworn declarations and statements made to their lawyers, were a 'put-up job', a 'stage performance', 'a bluff' by 'theatrical people' who were 'theatrically-minded'. In the damning words of Tom's barrister, 'They knew full well that there had never been any ceremony in Scotland and that these remarks were made to keep up appearances knowing that they were always and had been untrue.'

Evie Fitzwilliam, the judge concluded, could not possibly have destroyed the papers proving Toby's legitimacy: none had ever existed for her to destroy.

Toby never commented on the outcome of the case. But there was at least some consolation. Throughout his life, his predicament had struck a chord with his cousin Billy, the 7th Earl Fitzwilliam. It is possible the question mark over Toby's legitimacy reminded Billy of his own troubles in the 1890s when the family had accused him of being an impostor. In the early 1930s, he made an unusual provision in his will: should the younger brother, Tom Fitzwilliam, ever succeed to the Earldom, he stipulated that Toby should receive an annual allowance of £8,000 from his estate. It was an act of remarkable generosity on Billy's part. An income of £8,000 a year was more than enough to live on comfortably: in the early 1950s, it was equivalent to almost £170,000 today.

The dry, precise language of Mr Justice Pilcher's sixty-page Judgment failed to conceal the family's torrid unravelling. In just five decades, the dynasty had been destroyed by love.

In 1956, four years after he had become the 10th Earl Fitzwilliam, Tom finally married Joyce Fitzalan-Howard, the older woman he had loved for almost half his life and by whom, ironically, in the mid-1930s, he had had an illegitimate daughter. The marriage embroiled the family in yet another scandal. In order to marry Tom, Joyce divorced Viscount Fitzalan of Derwent, her husband of thirty-three years' standing and the heir to the Duke of Norfolk, the head of England's premier Catholic family. Tom and Joyce's marriage signalled the end of the Fitzwilliam line: in 1956, Joyce, aged fifty-eight, was too old to produce an heir.

Tom lived until 1979. Although he retained the suite of forty rooms at Wentworth House, he chose to live at Milton Hall, visiting Wentworth for just three weeks in every year for the grouse-shooting season and the St Leger at Doncaster. A few months before he died, his final act as the 10th and last Earl Fitzwilliam – one commensurate with his predecessors' philanthropy – was to transfer the village of Wentworth into a charitable trust. The future rents from the hundreds of properties were to be ploughed back to improve its amenities and to maintain the standard of housing.

The local authority gave up their lease on Wentworth House in the mid-1980s. After the Lady Mabel College of Physical Education closed in 1979, Sheffield City Polytechnic took over the historic property. But the annual maintenance costs, running into hundreds of thousands of pounds, were prohibitive: the heating bill alone was £1,000 a week.

For the second time in its twentieth-century history, Wentworth House was unmistakably a white elephant. The extraordinary size of it, and its location in what was now one of the most depressed regions in Britain, prevented it from being put to institutional use. It had been built for show, for one purpose only: to be one powerful man's stately home. After the years of occupation by the local authority, Tom Fitzwilliam's trustees balked at the expense of putting it right. In 1988, Lady Elizabeth Anne Hastings, Tom's daughter and beneficiary, put the house up for sale. It had been in the family's possession for more than 250 years. Before that, their ancestors had first built a house on the site in the thirteenth century.

In a twist of historical coincidence, 1988 was also the year that many of the pits in the South Yorkshire coalfield closed down, the culmination of a bitter and bloody clash between the country's miners and Margaret Thatcher's Government. The dispute which precipitated the year-long miners' strike of 1984/5 had begun at Cortonwood colliery, a pit situated on land formerly owned by the Fitzwilliams a few hundred yards from Lion's Lodge, the most northerly of the eight gatehouses that led into Wentworth Park.

In 1989, the house and some thirty acres surrounding it was bought by Wensley Haydon-Baillie. His tenure was short. A flamboyant businessman, the son of a surgeon, he already owned a large country house in the New Forest, and a mansion next to Kensington Palace in London's 'Millionaires' Row'. After making his fortune in banking and engineering, Haydon-Baillie invested in a company called Porton International, founded in the mid-1980s to market drugs developed at the Government's classified biochemical research station at Porton Down. At one point, the company, launched on the promise that it would soon be introducing a cure for the disease herpes, was valued at around £400 million. It failed to live up to City expectations. While it supplied anti-germ-warfare vaccines to US troops in the first Gulf War, the cure for herpes never materialized. By the summer of 1998, Haydon-Baillie admitted to having debts of £16 million. Shortly after, Wentworth House was repossessed by his bankers.

After standing empty for a year, its lawns neglected and the roof in danger of collapse, it was bought by an anonymous bidder for the knockdown price of £1.5 million – cheaper per square yard than a council house in the nearby town of Rotherham.

The mystery that shrouds the twentieth-century history of Wentworth House continues. It is currently owned by Clifford Newbold, a former Londoner in his early seventies, and a reclusive figure about whom little is known. He remains aloof from the village, determined to guard his privacy and to shield Wentworth House from the inquisitive eyes of visitors drawn to its grounds. 'Its closure to the public is a crying shame,' Simon Jenkins wrote in his book *England's Thousand Best Houses*. His view is echoed in the village, where memories of the Fitzwilliams die hard. 'It should be our Chatsworth, our Blenheim,' one man in his eighties remarked.

Today, as a consequence of the 10th Earl Fitzwilliam's legacy, Wentworth village looks much as it would have looked in the family's heyday. It is one of the most timelessly beautiful communities in South Yorkshire. Untarnished by development, the yellow stone cottages, with their green-painted guttering and doors, and white window frames, still bear the Fitzwilliam colours. Yet fittingly for a family whose reticence has veiled their recent history, the true magnificence of the last Earl's legacy can only be seen after dark.

Along the top road north of the village, a narrow country lane leads to Hoober Stand, a pyramid-shaped folly erected by the Fitzwilliams' ancestor, the 1st Marquess of Rockingham, to commemorate the English victory over the Scots at the Battle of Culloden. At night, the view over the surrounding country stretches for miles. To the south, the hills above Sheffield are coloured by a livid orange glare; to the south-west, Rotherham and Rawmarsh blaze, a sodium-lit sprawl; the M1 marches along its western edge. But like totality in a solar eclipse, in the midst of this, one of England's greatest urban conurbations, there is a vast expanse of black. Startling in its size and density, it conceals woodland, fields and parkland. It is the land once encompassed by the nine-mile perimeter wall that encircled Wentworth House.

Notes

PREFACE

p. xvii 'He had left . . .': 'Richest by century', *Sunday Times*, 26 March 2000. £3.3 billion, the contemporary value of £2.8 million, was calculated on the basis of Britain's GDP in 1902.

'In the century to come . . .': ibid.

p. xviii 'the train bored . . .': Roger Dataller (pseud.), *Oxford into Coalfield*, J. M. Dent & Sons, 1934, p. 11.

p. xix 'A feeling of awe . . .': *Sheffield Daily Telegraph*, 26 February 1902.

'The workmen on the various estates . . .': ibid.

INTRODUCTION

p. xxi 'I've never seen him . . .': author's interview with Joan Steele, spring 2004.

p. xxii 'The Fitzwilliams had a secret life': author's interview with Peter Diggle, November 2005.

'My grandmother made me promise . . .': author's interview with Lady Ann Bowlby, March 2004.

'That generation of the family were very proud . . .': author's interview with Ian Bond, April 2006.

CHAPTER ONE

p. 3 'In addition to the main family seat . . .': the will of William, 6th Earl Fitzwilliam, Probate Registry, London.

'Milton looked very tall and good-looking . . .': Charles, Viscount Halifax, to his sister, Emily Meynell Ingram, 25 February

1902, Borthwick Institute for Archives, University of York, A2.267.3.

p. 4 'He had a perfect horror . . .': Fitzwilliam v Fitzwilliam, Royal Courts of Justice, February 1951.

CHAPTER TWO

p. 5 'Gold and green . . .': Wentworth House furniture inventory, 1902. Private Collection.

p. 6 'As late as the 1920s, a boy from Greaseborough . . .': Roger Dataller (pseud.), A *Pitman's Notebook*, Jonathan Cape, 1925.

p. 7 'There was no electric light . . .': conversation with Elfreda, Countess of Wharncliffe, recorded in 1977 by Roy Young.

p. 8 'They did nothing else except lamps . . .': ibid.

p. 9 'Agnes and I were over at Wentworth . . .': Charles, Viscount Halifax, to his sister, Emily Meynell Ingram, 2 March 1902, Hickleton Papers, Borthwick Institute for Archives, University of York, A2.267.3.

'Affairs at Wentworth seem in a most wretched state . . .': Mary Sutton to Edward Wood, 9 March 1902, Hickleton Papers, Borthwick Institute for Archives, University of York, A2.140.

'Agnes tells me the rows . . .': Charles, Viscount Halifax, to his sister, Emily Meynell Ingram, 7 March 1902, ibid., A2.267.3.

p. 10 'I think in my yesterday's note . . .': Kathleen Doyne to her Aunt Berta, 21 February 1902. Private Collection.

'They'd done nothing . . .': conversation with Elfrida, Countess of Wharncliffe, recorded in 1977 by Roy Young.

p. 11 'She made the milk go sour . . .': ibid.

'They wanted to kick him out . . .': ibid.

p. 13 'Tied with a pink silk ribbon . . .': Sheffield Archives, Unlisted Material, Wentworth Woodhouse Muniments, Box 236.

CHAPTER THREE

p. 14 'a spurious child . . .': Thomas Bayliss, King's Bench Division, Royal Courts of Justice, 10 March 1902. Case name: 'Re a Solicitor – Ex parte The Incorporated Law Society'.

'The Home Secretary was required to attend . . .': a custom established after the 'warming pan' incident of 1688, when Mary of Modena, second wife of James II, was accused of smuggling a changeling into the bedchamber as heir to the throne.

p. 15 'Lord Milton, their elder brother . . .': Sheffield Archives, Unlisted Material, Wentworth Woodhouse Muniments, Box 236.

'Billy's birth certificate . . .': ibid.

p. 16 'Certain members of the family . . .': Thomas Bayliss, King's Bench Division, Royal Courts of Justice, 10 March 1902, Case name 'Re a Solicitor – Ex parte The Incorporated Law Society'.

'"Gentlemen", wrote . . .': Dr Millar to Messrs Walters and Co., 9 New Square, Lincoln's Inn, 7 March 1901, Sheffield Archives, Unlisted Material, WWM, Box 236.

p. 17 'Hannah Boyce's statement . . .': ibid.

p. 18 '1872 July 26 – the first cry . . .': ibid.

'Among Billy's documents . . .': letter from Hannah Boyce to Mr Barker, 30 January 1901, ibid.

p. 19 'Dear Lady Countess Fitzwilliam . . .': Hannah Boyce to Maud, Countess Fitzwilliam, 26 February 1913, ibid.

'Lady Fitzwilliam has received the enclosed . . .': Billy to Mr Barker, 9 March 1913, ibid.

'On 10 March 1902 . . .': *Yorkshire Post*, 11 March 1902, 'Earl Fitzwilliam's identity – strange allegations by a solicitor'.

p. 20 'There had been a serious falling-out . . .': ibid.

'In lieu of the questions submitted . . .' Sheffield Archives, Unlisted Material, WWM, Box 236.

p. 21 'You cannot be surprised . . .': *Daily Telegraph*, 11 March 1902.

p. 22 'As vouched for . . .': Fitzwilliam v Fitzwilliam, Royal Courts of Justice, February 1951.

CHAPTER FOUR

p. 23 'One of the hard lessons . . .': letter from Harriet, Countess Fitzwilliam, to her daughter Lady Frances Doyne, 17 January 1877. Private Collection.

p. 24 'My grandfather never spoke about his father . . .': author's interview with Lady Barbara Ricardo, February 2004.

'I couldn't believe there was so little . . .': Michael Shaw Bond, *Way Out West: On the Trail of an Errant Ancestor*, McClelland & Stewart, 2001, p. 12.

'I imagined . . .': ibid.

'Searching through . . .': ibid., p. 14.

p. 25 'Fits are treated as madness . . .': G. Battiscombe, *Shaftesbury*, Constable, 1974, p. 259.

'When Christ healed . . .': G. E. Berrios and Roy Porter, *A History of Clinical Psychiatry*, Athlone, 1995, p. 165.

'In the first century . . .': ibid., p. 166.

p. 26 'Dr Beau, who conducted a study of sixty-seven epileptics . . .': Owsei Temkin, *The Falling Sickness*, The Johns Hopkins Press, 1971, p. 262.

'Even as late as the 1880s . . .': Berrios and Porter, *A History of Clinical Psychiatry*, p. 170.

p. 27 'William may have to . . .': cited in Bond, *Way Out West*, p. 14.

'Please do let me know . . .': ibid., p. 13.

'I see no prospect . . .': ibid., p. 22.

'This Asylum for the Insane . . .': cited in W. Parry Jones, *The Trade in Lunacy*, Routledge and Kegan Paul, 1972, p. 106.

p. 28 'Modelled on grand country houses . . .': Andrew Scull, *The Most Solitary of Afflictions: Madness and Society in Britain 1700–1900*, Yale University Press, 1993, pp. 300–301.

'It is painful . . .': J. Conolly on the 9th Report of Commissioner for Lunacy, 1854, cited in Parry Jones, *The Trade in Lunacy*, p. 180.

'At Ticehurst . . .': Charlotte MacKenzie, *Psychiatry for the Rich*, Routledge, 1992, p. 105.

'In 1857, lifting the veil of secrecy . . .': Crichton Royal Asylum, 18th Annual Report, 1857, quoted in Scull, *The Most Solitary of Afflictions*, p. 298.

p. 29 'They are encountered . . .': ibid.

'I am sorry to say . . .': cited in Bond, *Way Out West*, p. 14.

'William, I am happy . . .': ibid.

'I hope the ups . . .': ibid., p. 21.

p. 30 'Dear Father and Mother . . .': Milton to Lord and Lady Fitzwilliam, April 1872. Private Collection.

'It is almost impossible . . .': *The World*, 5 March 1902.

'silent of hosts . . .': unpublished memoir, cited with the kind permission of David Peake.

'A good many of them were frightened of him . . .': Lady Mabel Smith, Royal Courts of Justice, Fitzwilliam v Fitzwilliam, February 1951.

p. 31 'Maurice fell . . .': cited in McKenzie, *Psychiatry for the Rich*, p. 101.

p. 32 '3 roasted oxen . . .': quoted in Bond, *Way Out West*, p. 28.

p. 33 'I have been thinking . . .': Henry Wentworth-Fitzwilliam to his sister Frances Doyne, July 1860. Private Collection.

p. 34 'There appears some reason . . .': Harriet, Countess Fitzwilliam, to George Wentworth-Fitzwilliam, April 1861, Northampton Archives.

'My son's conduct . . .' Earl Fitzwilliam to Lord Chichester, April 1861, cited in Bond, *Way Out West*, p. 24.

'He wishes you to read . . .': Countess Fitzwilliam to George Fitzwilliam, April 1861, Northampton Archives.

CHAPTER FIVE

p. 36 'With respect to the charge . . .': *The Standard*, 10 May 1862.

'The diamond earrings . . .': ibid., 3 May 1862.

'He offered the broker . . .': ibid.

p. 37 'His lawyers . . .': ibid.

'Sailed at 5 . . .': *Cheadle's Journal of the Trip Across Canada 1862–1863*, Graphic Publishers, Ottawa, 1931, p. 15.

'I am sorry I did not look up . . .': Milton to Henry Wentworth-Fitzwilliam, 20 June 1862. Private Collection.

p. 38 'Weather blowing stormy . . .': *Cheadle's Journal of the Trip Across Canada 1862–1863*, p. 16.

'Turned out towards 11 . . .': ibid.

'About 1 o'clock . . .': ibid., p. 19.

p. 39 'Very cold and raw . . .': ibid., p. 20.

'When starving . . .': Robert Ballantyne, *Hudson Bay Company*, Boston, Phillips, Sampson, 1859.

p. 40 'Their journey . . .': Viscount Milton and W. B. Cheadle, *The North-West Passage by Land*, London, Cassel, Petter and Galpin, 1865.

'He was leaning . . .': ibid., p. 9.

p. 41 'So long as . . .': quoted in Bond, *Way Out West*, p. 224.

CHAPTER SIX

p. 42 'Poor squinny . . .': *The Diary of Lady Frederick Cavendish*, ed. J. Bailey, London, 1927, vol. 2.

'The Fitzwilliams and the Devonshires . . .': David Cannadine, *The Decline and Fall of the British Aristocracy*, Yale University Press, 1990, p. 10.

'In the course of . . .': *The Diary of Lady Frederick Cavendish*, vol. 2, p. 19.

'I am worried . . .': ibid.

p. 43 'It is no light thing . . .': Mary Butler to Lady Frances Doyne, 1 June 1867. Private Collection.

p. 44 'When I knew . . .': Mary Butler to Lady Frances Doyne, 13 June 1867. Private Collection.

'It was very kind of you . . .': ibid.

'Will you thank . . .': ibid.

'You may be certain . . .': Mary Butler to Lady Frances Doyne, 8 July 1867. Private Collection.

p. 45 'Dearest Fanny . . .': Harriet, Countess Fitzwilliam, to Lady Frances Doyne, 5 July 1867. Private Collection.

'I never knew her . . .': conversation with Elfrida, Countess of Wharncliffe, recorded by Roy Young in 1977.

p. 46 'Admitting defeat . . .': Harriet, Countess Fitzwilliam, to Lady Frances Doyne, 9 August 1867. Private Collection.

'The late Lady Milton . . .': statement sworn before the Commissioner of Oaths, 1900, Sheffield Archives, Unlisted Material, Wentworth Woodhouse Muniments, Box 236.

p. 47 'On Tuesday . . .': Harriet, Countess Fitzwilliam, to Lady Frances Doyne, 28 December 1871. Private Collection.

p. 48 'The voyage . . .': Lord Milton to Lord and Lady Fitzwilliam, April 1872. Private Collection.

'25th May . . .': Matilda Kingdon, unpublished diary. Private Collection.

p. 49 'the half-breeds came . . .': ibid.

p. 50 'Re-reading Dr Millar's statement . . .': Sheffield Archives, Unlisted Material, WWM, Box 236.

'My intercourse . . .': ibid.

CHAPTER SEVEN

p. 53 '"Yes," it read . . .': undated. Henry Wentworth-Fitzwilliam papers. Private Collection.

p. 55 'In 1900, they were short of proof . . .': November 1900, 'Lord Milton Supplemental Instructions to Mr Butcher, Walters & Co.' Sheffield Archives, Unlisted Material, Wentworth Woodhouse Muniments, Box 236.

'From a young age . . .': Henry Wentworth-Fitzwilliam to Lady Frances Doyne, July 1860. Private Collection.

'Only those . . .': Laura, Viscountess Milton, to Harriet, Countess Fitzwilliam, n.d. Private Collection.

p. 56 'In a sanctimonious letter . . .': Harriet, Countess Fitzwilliam, to Henry Wentworth-Fitzwilliam, 22 February 1874. Private Collection.

'I fear that dear William . . .': Henry Wentworth-Fitzwilliam to Lady Frances Doyne, 14 January 1877. Private Collection.

'There was little . . .': cited in *Way Out West: The Story of an Errant Ancestor*, McClelland & Stewart, Toronto, 2001, p. 235.

p. 57 'As Michael Bond . . .': ibid.

p. 58 'I asked her to furnish . . .': Mr Barker to Billy, 7th Earl Fitzwilliam, 20 March 1902, Sheffield Archives, Unlisted Material, WWM, Box 236.

'As Billy's solicitor discovered . . .': Mr Ponsonby to Mr Barker, 21 April 1902, ibid.

'Pink bedroom . . .': Furniture Inventory, Sheffield Archives, WWM, T72.

p. 59 'Claim followed counter-claim . . .': see Correspondence Between Parties' Solicitors, Sheffield Archives, WWM, T72.

'4th and 5th housemaid bedroom . . .': Furniture Inventory, Sheffield Archives, WWM, T72.

p. 60 'Dear Charley . . .': Henry Wentworth-Fitzwilliam to Charles Wentworth-Fitzwilliam, 27 March 1902, Sheffield Archives, Unlisted Material, WWM, Box 236.

'The inkstand . . .': Mr Barker to Mr Cowper, 14 January 1903, Sheffield Archives, WWM, T72.

p. 61 'The case set up . . .': ibid.

CHAPTER EIGHT

p. 65 'I don't know who . . .': Roger Dataller (pseud.), *From A Pitman's Notebook*, Jonathan Cape, 1925, p. 200.

p. 66 'As kids we . . .': Jim Bullock, *Bowers Row*, EP Publishing, Wakefield, 1976, p. 183.

'Well, aye, aye . . .': Dataller, *From a Pitman's Notebook*, p. 24.

'The times I liked best . . .': Bullock, *Bowers Row*, p. 30.

p. 67 'I've worked in the pit . . .': testimony of John Saville, 1842, Children's Employment Commission, Appendix Reports and Evidence from Sub-Commissioners, 2 vols., London, 1842.

'I ran away . . .': testimony of Thomas Moorhouse, ibid.

p. 68 'The roads are very wet . . .': testimony of David Swallow, ibid.

'Samuel Scriven saw . . .': cited in Alan Gallop, *Children of the*

Dark: Life and Death Underground in Victoria's England, Sutton, 2003, p. 162.

'In the first decades . . .': A. J. P. Taylor, *English History 1914–1945*, Oxford University Press, 1965, paperback edition, 1992, p. 171.

CHAPTER NINE

p. 70 'They called it . . .': *Christian Budget*, 8 November 1899.

'Writing in a state . . .': ibid.

'Four thousand . . .': J. E. MacFarlane, *The Bag Muck Strike, Denaby Main*, Doncaster Library Service, 1987, p. ix.

'The familiar sounds . . .': Roger Dataller (pseud.), *A Yorkshire Lad*, unpublished memoir.

p. 71 'Putrid and stagnant . . .': testimony of Tom Hibbard, Margaret L. Hibbard, *The Pit Boy from Denaby Main*, unpublished memoir, Doncaster Library.

'A few hours after dawn . . .': *Mexborough and Swinton Times*, 9 January 1903.

'Four companies . . .': ibid.

'Suffering was etched . . .': J. Wilson, *The Story of the Great Struggle, 1902–1903*, Christian Commonwealth Co., London, 1904, pp. 42–3.

p. 72 'The children crackled . . .': *Mexborough and Swinton Times*, 9 January 1903.

'You hadn't much trouble . . .': J. E. MacFarlane, *Denaby Main, A South Yorkshire Village*, Studies in the Yorkshire Coal Industry, Manchester University Press, 1976, p. 123.

'In the months before . . .': MacFarlane, *The Bag Muck Strike*.

p. 74 'The oldest houses . . .': Roger Dataller (pseud.), *Oxford into Coal-face*, J. M. Dent & Sons, 1934, p. 13.

'It's a dirty hole . . .': Phyllis Holcroft, unpublished memoir, 1899.

'People from the other places . . .': MacFarlane Papers, Doncaster Archives.

'The houses cost . . .': ibid.

p. 75 'Each midden . . .': testimony of Tom Hibbard, Margaret L. Hibbard, *The Pit Boy from Denaby Main*, unpublished memoir.

'Epidemics . . .': *Mexborough and Swinton Times*, July 1901.

'The ruin of the children . . .': *Christian Budget*, 8 November 1899.

p. 76 'The entire village . . .': MacFarlane, *Denaby Main, A South Yorkshire Mining Village*, p. 143.

'As one miner . . .': *Christian Budget*, 8 November 1899.

p. 77 'He was quite dead . . .': Roger Dataller (pseud.), *From a Pitman's Notebook*, Jonathan Cape, 1925, p. 84.

p. 78 'Dear Margaret . . .': B. F. and H. Huckham, *Great Pit Disasters: Great Britain, 1700 to the present day*, David and Charles, 1973, p. 29.

p. 79 'In 1903, Denaby and Cadeby . . .': MacFarlane Papers, Doncaster Archives.

'Those days . . .': ibid.

'In the early 1900s . . .': ibid.

'Well, he was dead now . . .': Bullock, *Bowers Row*, p. 219.

p. 80 'The dangerous conditions . . .': John Benson, *British Coalminers in the Nineteenth Century: a Social History*, Gil and Macmillan, 1980, p. 65.

'The roads into the village . . .': *Mexborough and Swinton Times*, 9 January 1903.

'The police . . .': ibid.

p. 81 'Sprigs of Christmas holly . . .': ibid.

'There goes . . .': ibid.

'Their eyes . . .': *Mexborough and Swinton Times*, 16 January 1903.

p. 82 'The expected trouble . . .': *Mexborough and Swinton Times*, 9 January 1903.

'My father moved . . .': MacFarlane Papers, Doncaster Archives.

p. 83 'When I was a boy . . .': *Mexborough and Swinton Times*, 16 January 1903.

'There were two classes of tent . . .': Wilson, *The Story of the Great Struggle, 1902–1903*, p. 34.

'Someone had hoisted . . .': *Mexborough and Swinton Times*, 16 January 1903.

p. 84 'Many seemed to think . . .': Wilson, *The Story of the Great Struggle, 1902–1903*.

'I was returning . . .': ibid, p. 34.

CHAPTER TEN

p. 85 'Thank God it's over . . .': *Daily Mail*, 10 January 1903.

'If we are beaten . . .': *Mexborough and Swinton Times*, 16 January 1903.

'The colliery company . . .': Lord Beveridge, *Power and Influence*, Hodder and Stoughton, 1953, p. 11.

p. 87 'The weekly allowance . . .': *Mexborough and Swinton Times*, 9 January 1903.

'It was a terrifying . . .': MacFarlane Papers, Doncaster Archives.

'It was the custom . . .': Consuelo Vanderbilt Balsan, *The Glitter and the Gold*, Heinemann, 1953, p. 68.

p. 88 'One woman . . .': *Daily Chronicle*, 9 January 1903.

p. 89 'The poor mother . . .': J. Wilson, *The Story of the Great Struggle, 1902–1903*, Christian Commonwealth Co., London, 1904, p. 35.

'Fields of crops . . .': Roger Dataller (pseud.), *From a Pitman's Notebook*, Jonathan Cape, 1925, p. 219.

p. 90 'Fred Smith, a miner . . .': unpublished memoir, printed in the *Ivanhoe Review*, Bulletin of the Archives and Local Studies Section, Central Library, Rotherham, No. 6, Spring 1994.

'Six miles or more . . .': ibid.

p. 91 'Crossing the Worksop Road . . .': ibid.

'There was a ballroom . . .': Brian Masters, *The Dukes*, Blond and Briggs, 1975, p. 195.

'The Duke's annual income . . .': David Cannadine, *The Decline and Fall of the British Aristocracy*, Yale University Press, 1990, p. 710.

'The Duke spent . . .': Masters, *The Dukes*, p. 195.

'Winter or summer . . .': ibid., pp. 194–5.

p. 92 'From here . . .': ibid.

'My father knew . . .': Fred Smith, unpublished memoir.

p. 93 'A blinding snowstorm . . .': *Mexborough and Swinton Times*, 27 February 1903.

p. 95 'Trade Unionism is being . . .': Ramsay MacDonald, Secretary of the Labour Representation Committee, July 1901.

'As the historian . . .': George Dangerfield, *The Strange Death of Liberal England*, Constable, 1936, paperback edition, Peregrine Books, New York, 1980, p. 224.

CHAPTER ELEVEN

p. 96 'It carried . . .': Sir Philip Magnus, *King Edward VII*, John Murray, 1964, p. 273.

'He travelled comfortably . . .': ibid., p. 422.

'He liked his favourite . . .': ibid., p. 275.

'There were 150 ships . . .': *The Times*, 31 July 1909.

'Gathered in the dark . . .': ibid.

p. 97 'At moments . . .': John Grigg, *Lloyd George: The People's Champion 1902–1911*, Eyre Methuen, 1978, p. 203.

'I went down a coalmine . . .': Lloyd George, speech at Limehouse, 30 July 1909, reprinted by *Daily News* in pamphlet.

p. 98 'As she entered . . .': *The Times*, 2 August 1909.

p. 99 'The King thinks . . .': cited in Magnus, *King Edward VII*, p. 430.

'This is a war Budget . . .': Lloyd George in House of Commons, 29 April 1909.

p. 100 'I claim that the tax . . .': Lloyd George, speech at Limehouse, 30 July 1909, reprinted by *Daily News* in pamphlet.

'The ownership of land . . .': Grigg, *Lloyd George: The People's Champion 1902–1911*, p. 207.

p. 101 'On my arrival here . . .': Earl Lloyd George's collection, cited ibid., p. 209.

'The King, of course . . .': ibid.

p. 102 'I am not cut out . . .': David Lloyd George to Megan Lloyd George, 13 September 1911, National Library of Wales.

'*The Times* listed . . .': *The Times*, 4 August 1909.

p. 103 'This was the one . . .': cited in Robert K. Massie, *Nicholas and Alexandra*, Gollancz, 1967, p. 161.

'Ashore and afloat . . .': ibid.

'Lord Rosebery . . .': statement by Lord Rosebery issued on 22 June 1909, cited in Grigg, *Lloyd George: The People's Champion 1902–1911*, p. 198.

'Lord Ridley . . .': press statement by Lord Ridley issued on 3 May 1909, quoted ibid., p. 197.

p. 104 'After an encounter . . .': A. C. Benson, diary, 10 November 1908, Magdalene College, Cambridge, cited in Kenneth Rose, *King George V*, Weidenfeld & Nicolson, 1983, p. 118.

p. 105 'it was generally supposed . . .': George Dangerfield, *The Strange Death of Liberal England*, Constable, 1936, paperback edition, Pedigree Books, New York, 1980, p. 26.

'What a relief . . .': Lord Stamfordham to Lord Curzon, 11 August 1911, Curzon Papers, India Office Library.

'The power of the peerage . . .': Michael Bentley, *Politics without Democracy, 1815–1914*, Fontana, 1984, p. 332.

p. 106 'The signs were ominous . . .': ibid.

CHAPTER TWELVE

p. 109 'That path . . .': author's interview with Geoffrey Steer, August 2005.

p. 110 'Tropical lianas . . .': author's interview with Bert May, October 2004.

p. 111 'It was the . . .': author's interview with Charles Booth, July 2004.

'Thirty-six bedrooms . . .': 7th Earl Fitzwilliam, handwritten note on allocation of rooms for the royal visit. Private Collection.

'Following the death of the 6th Earl . . .': itemized bills, Sheffield Archives, Wentworth Woodhouse Muniments, T72.

p. 112 'The secret of one scent . . .': Housekeeper's Book. Private Collection.

'2 pecks of Damask . . .': ibid.

'Londonderry', 'Rosse' . . .': list of guests staying at Wentworth for the royal visit, Billy, 7th Earl's, list. Private Collection.

'The men had a good long . . .': *Sheffield Daily Telegraph*, 10 July 1912.

p. 113 'The place of honour . . .': ibid.

'At precisely one minute to five o'clock . . .': *Mexborough and Swinton Times*, 13 July 1912.

'I am instructed . . .': *Sheffield Daily Telegraph*, 9 July 1912.

p. 114 'After careful consideration . . .': papers of Herbert Asquith, 1st Earl of Oxford and Asquith, Bodleian Library, University of Oxford, MS 6 fol. 115r.

p. 115 'Men! Comrades! . . .': pamphlet circulated by Tom Mann of Dockers' Union, R. Page Arnot, *The Miners: Years of Struggle*, George Allen & Unwin, 1953, p. 115.

'On 17 August . . .': cited in Harold Nicolson, *King George V: His Life and Reign*, London, 1953, p. 158.

'The difficulty . . .': ibid.

p. 116 'The King . . .': Knollys to Asquith, Roy Jenkins, *Asquith*, Collins, 1964.

p. 117 'On 27 March . . .': Margot Asquith Diaries, 27 March 1912, Bodleian Library, University of Oxford, quoted with kind permission of Mr Christopher Osborn.

p. 118 'He was on his feet . . .': George Dangerfield, *The Strange Death of Liberal England*, Constable, 1936, paperback edition, Pedigree Books, New York, 1980, p. 293.

'Lord Cecil . . .': Page Arnot, *The Miners: Years of Struggle*, p. 111.

p. 119 'I was terribly harassed . . .': Margot Asquith Diaries, Bodleian Library, University of Oxford.

'I was pleased to meet you . . .': cited in R. Smillie, *My Life for Labour*, Mills & Boon, 1924, p. 221.

'I don't see why . . .': ibid., p. 223.

p. 120 'Our men have been . . .': cited in Page Arnot, *The Miners: Years of Struggle*, p. 82.

'He does not work . . .': cited ibid., p. 83.

p. 121 'I urged the importance . . .': Cosmo Gordon Lang, Archbishop of Canterbury, correspondence and papers, Lambeth Palace, London.

p. 122 'The nineteenth century . . .': J. G. Lockhart, *Cosmo Gordon Lang*, Hodder and Stoughton, 1949, p. 239.

p. 123 'Five-minute stops . . .': *Yorkshire Post*, 10 July 1912.

'On the afternoon . . .': *Sheffield Daily Telegraph*, 9 July 1912.

'Na then . . .': cited in Lockhart, *Cosmo Gordon Lang*, p. 217.

'As they did so . . .': author's interview with Bert May, October 2004.

CHAPTER THIRTEEN

p. 124 'An army fights . . .': interview with Elfreda, Countess of Wharncliffe, recorded in 1977 by Roy Young.

'There were six . . .': author's interview with Peter Diggle, April 2004.

p. 125 'A visiting servant . . .': Marchioness of Bath, *Before the Sunset Fades*, Longleat Estate Co., 1951, p. 22.

'One lady's maid . . .': Lady Augusta Fane, cited in F. E. Huggett, *Life Below Stairs*, Robin Clark, 1978, p. 37.

'I always remember . . .': John R. Russell, Duke of Bedford, *A Silver-Plated Spoon*, Cassell, 1959, p. 64.

'After waiting . . .': Consuelo Vanderbilt Balsan, *The Glitter and the Gold*, Heinemann, 1953, p. 82.

p. 126 'The guest list . . .': Billy, 7th Earl Fitzwilliam's handwritten list. Private Collection.

p. 127 'One of them . . .': H. Montgomery Hyde, *The Londonderrys*, Hamish Hamilton, 1979, p. 66.

'She was in love with . . .': Elizabeth, Countess of Fingall, *Seventy Years Young*, Collins, 1937, p. 208.

p. 128 'What a man . . .': Frances, Countess of Warwick, *Afterthoughts*, Cassell, 1931, p. 42.

'Wild rumours . . .': cited in Geoffrey Bennett, *Charlie B*, Peter Dawnay, 1968, p. 166.

'The letter was . . .': cited ibid., p. 165.

p. 129 'Matters have . . .': cited ibid., p. 166.

'Ill-considered . . .': cited ibid., p. 168.

CHAPTER FOURTEEN

p. 132 'Some 500 miners . . .': *Sheffield Daily Telegraph*, 10 July 1912.

p. 134 'His Lordship . . .': Fitzwilliam family scrapbook. Private Collection.

p. 135 'Hundreds of millions . . .': Roger Dataller (pseud.), *From a Pitman's Notebook*, Jonathan Cape, 1925, p. 111.

'We were getting along . . .': interview with Albert Wildman, *Sheffield Daily Telegraph*, 10 July 1912.

'Work I could not . . .': Miners' Federation of Great Britain, Messrs R. Smillie & V. Hartshorn's Report of the Cadeby Colliery Explosion Inquiry, 1912.

p. 136 'When I got to . . .': ibid.

'When I got 200 or 300 yards . . .': ibid.

p. 137 'It was the handymen . . .': author's interview with May Bailey, February 2004.

p. 138 'We went slowly . . .': interview with Albert Wildman, *Sheffield Daily Telegraph*, 10 July 1912.

'As Albert . . .': ibid.

p. 139 'Some three hundred . . .': ibid.

'On a stone . . .': ibid.

p. 140 'We had been working . . .': *Mexborough and Swinton Times*, 13 July 1912.

'For the most part . . .': ibid.

p. 141 'The King and Queen . . .': cited ibid.

p. 142 'For a greater part . . .': *Yorkshire Post*, 10 July 1912.

'It was William Brown's . . .': ibid.

p. 143 'I fear I must . . .': Lord Stamfordham to Viscount Halifax, 29 June 1912, Hickleton Papers, Borthwick Institute for Archives, Charles, 2nd Viscount Halifax Papers.

p. 145 'the ill-fated colliery . . .': *Sheffield Daily Telegraph*, 10 July 1912.

p. 146 'At 6.45 . . .': King George V's diary, Royal Archives, Windsor Castle.

p. 147 'They hadn't got . . .': interview with Elfrida, Countess of Wharncliffe, recorded by Roy Young in 1977.

'Today the deep . . .': Lady Mary Fitzwilliam's diary. Private Collection.

'Their obvious . . .': *Mexborough and Swinton Times*, 13 July 1912.

'Mindful of . . .': Lord Halifax to W. J. Birkbeck, 11 July 1912, Borthwick Institute for Archives, Hickleton Papers, Charles, 2nd Viscount Halifax Papers.

p. 148 'A horrible sight . . .': Coroner, cited in *Mexborough and Swinton Times*, 13 July 1912.

p. 149 'My friends . . .': King George V, cited in *Sheffield Daily Telegraph*, 12 July 1912.

p. 150 'Mr Chambers . . .': Home Office Report, R. A. S. Redmayne, HM Chief Inspector of Mines, *Explosions at the Cadeby Main Colliery*, HMSO, 1913.

p. 151 'All my hopes . . .': J. G. Lockhart, *Cosmo Gordon Lang*, Hodder & Stoughton, 1949, p. 217.

p. 152 'My dear Fitzwilliam . . .': King George V to Billy, 7th Earl Fitzwilliam, 14 July 1912. Private Collection.

'The Queen . . .': Cosmo Gordon Lang, Archbishop of York Papers, Correspondence, Lambeth Palace Archives.

CHAPTER SIXTEEN

p. 155 'Gallantry of . . .': *The Times*, 3 November 1914.

'They would call it Ypres . . .': Lyn Macdonald, *1914*, Michael Joseph, 1987, p. 386.

'At lunchtime . . .': ibid., p. 393.

p. 156 'Whole brigades . . .': ibid., p. 425.

'All leave was prohibited . . .': G. J. C. Wentworth-Fitzwilliam v W. T. G. Wentworth-Fitzwilliam et al., Royal Courts of Justice, February 1951, Day 6, Sheffield Archives, Uncatalogued Material, Wentworth Woodhouse Muniments, Box 345.

p. 157 'I believe . . .': Toby Fitzwilliam to George Fitzwilliam, 20 May 1914, ibid., Box 343.

'You have insulted . . .': George Fitzwilliam to Toby Fitzwilliam, 21 May 1914, ibid.

p. 158 'My dear Father . . .': Toby Fitzwilliam to George Fitzwilliam, 19 May 1914, ibid.

'My dear Mother . . .': Toby Fitzwilliam to Evie Fitzwilliam, 20 May 1914, ibid.

p. 160 'There are some people . . .': G. J. C. Wentworth-Fitzwilliam v W. T. G. Wentworth-Fitzwilliam et al., Royal Courts of Justice, February 1951, Day 6, Sheffield Archives, Uncatalogued Material, WWM, Box 345.

'In his summing up . . .': G. J. C. Wentworth-Fitzwilliam v W. T. G. Wentworth-Fitzwilliam et al., Royal Courts of Justice, February 1951, Day 20, ibid., Box 344.

'I trust letters . . .': Toby Fitzwilliam to Mr Battock, 10 May 1914, ibid., Box 343.

p. 161 'Toby Darling . . .': Evie Fitzwilliam to Toby Fitzwilliam, 23 September 1913, ibid.

'My dear Beryl . . .': Evie Fitzwilliam to Beryl Morgan, 24 September 1913, ibid.

'My father . . .': deposition of Margot Lorne, Johannesburg, October 1950, Sheffield Archives, Uncatalogued Material, WWM, Box 343.

'Beryl Darling . . .': Evie Fitzwilliam to Beryl Morgan 29 September 1913, ibid.

p. 162 'Beryl wasn't extremely pretty . . .': author's interview with Deirdre Newton, November 2005.

'For a time . . .': deposition of Margot Lorne, Johannesburg, October 1950, Sheffield Archives, Uncatalogued Material, WWM, Box 343.

'A pathological occurrence . . .': Sir David Maxwell-Fyfe, G. J. C. Wentworth-Fitzwilliam v W. T. G. Wentworth-Fitzwilliam et al., Royal Courts of Justice, February 1951, Day 1, ibid., Box 345.

'What luck . . .': anon. postcard, postmarked Bristol, 13 October 1913, ibid., Box 343.

p. 163 'My Dear Beryl . . .': Evie Fitzwilliam to Beryl Morgan, 20 October 1913, ibid.

p. 164 'In those days . . .': Frances Warwick, *Afterthoughts*, Cassell and Co., 1931, p. 198.

'A fellow marrying like that . . .': deposition of Lt-Col James Burns-Hartopp, August 1950, Royal Courts of Justice, Sheffield Archives, Uncatalogued Material, WWM, Box 343.

'George hasn't one ounce . . .': Charles Fitzwilliam to George Douglas, 9 February 1889, ibid.

'Just imagine . . .': Warwick, *Afterthoughts*, p. 193.

'My mother's reactions . . .': G. J. C. Wentworth-Fitzwilliam v W. T. G. Wentworth-Fitzwilliam et al., Royal Courts of Justice, February 1951, Day 7, Sheffield Archives, Uncatalogued Material, WWM, Box 345.

p. 165 'Darling, I'm not one bit . . .': Evie Fitzwilliam to Beryl Morgan, 2 November 1913, ibid., p. 343.

'Darling, Do be an Angel . . .': Evie Fitzwilliam to Beryl Morgan, 4 November 1913, ibid.

'My dearest Mum . . .': Beryl Morgan to Evie Fitzwilliam, 8 December 1913, ibid.

p. 166 'I remember . . .': author's interview with Deirdre Newton, November 2005.

'I feel I could never . . .': Toby Fitzwilliam to Mr Battock, 21 April 1914, Sheffield Archives, Uncatalogued Material, WWM, Box 343.

p. 167 'My dear Toby . . .': Evie Fitzwilliam to Toby Fitzwilliam, 26 April 1914, ibid.

'My dear Beryl . . .': Evie Fitzwilliam to Beryl Morgan, 26 April 1914, ibid.

p. 168 'I would write . . .': Toby Fitzwilliam to George Fitzwilliam, 27 April 1914, ibid.

'I do not intend to . . .': George Fitzwilliam to Toby Fitzwilliam, 30 April 1914, ibid.

'Under no circumstances . . .': Evie Fitzwilliam to Toby Fitzwilliam, 3 May 1914, ibid.

p. 169 'She told me . . .': Kate Rickards, G. J. C. Wentworth-Fitzwilliam v W. T. G. Wentworth-Fitzwilliam et al., Royal Courts of Justice, February 1951, Day 4, ibid., Box 345.

p. 170 'Dear Toby . . .': Evie Fitzwilliam to Toby Fitzwilliam, 3 November 1914, ibid., Box 343.

'My feelings were . . .': Toby Fitzwilliam, G. J. C. Wentworth-Fitzwilliam v W. T. G. Wentworth-Fitzwilliam et al., Royal Courts of Justice, February 1951, Day 6, ibid., Box 345.

p. 171 'To Toby's surprise . . .': ibid.

'There was nothing . . .': Toby Fitzwilliam, cross-examined by Sir David Maxwell-Fyfe, G. J. C. Wentworth-Fitzwilliam v W. T. G. Wentworth-Fitzwilliam et al., Royal Courts of Justice, February 1951, Day 6, ibid.

p. 172 'Evie was a woman . . .': deposition of Margot Lorne, Johannesburg, October 1950, ibid., Box 343.

'I went to school . . .': Tom Fitzwilliam, G. J. C. Wentworth-Fitzwilliam v W. T. G. Wentworth-Fitzwilliam et al., Royal Courts of Justice, February 1951, day 12, ibid., Box 344.

'A little time . . .': deposition of Margot Lorne, Johannesburg, October 1950, ibid., Box 343.

CHAPTER SEVENTEEN

p. 177 'Thousands of black-suited . . .': *Rotherham Advertiser*, 31 January 1920.

'Fifty thousand . . .': *Mexborough and Swinton Times*, March 1921.

p. 178 'They did not know . . .': author's interview with Charles Doyne, March 2004.

'Thirty million working days . . .': *Mexborough and Swinton Times*, 3 January 1920.

p. 179 'In the month of January . . .': R. Page Arnot, *The Miners: Years of Struggle*, George Allen & Unwin, 1953, p. 189.

'For the manufacturer . . .': Duff Cooper, *Haig*, Faber and Faber, 1936, p. 404.

'In the five years . . .': Noel Annan, *Our Age*, Weidenfeld & Nicolson, 1990, p. 66.

'It went back . . .': ibid., p. 19.

'I said . . .': cited in Duff Cooper, *Haig*, p. 418.

p. 180 'It is not their duty . . .': cited ibid.

'Chatter about revolution . . .': *Mexborough and Swinton Times*, 6 September 1919.

p. 182 'There is neither shadow . . .': Fitzwilliam family scrapbook. Private collection.

'Nothing . . .': *Mexborough and Swinton Times*, 19 April 1919.

p. 183 'The lecturer said . . .': ibid.

'The association was established . . .': author's interview with Dr Quentin Outram, Senior Lecturer in Economics, Leeds University Business School, September 2005.

'Mowbray and Stourton . . .': list of MOAGB members supplied by Dr Quentin Outram.

CHAPTER EIGHTEEN

p. 185 'At his answer . . .': *The Times*, 9 May 1919.

'Don't you think . . .': ibid.

p. 186 'If this Commission . . .': ibid.

'He was the owner . . .': *The Times*, 8 May 1919.

'I suppose . . .': ibid.

p. 188 '7,000 . . .': F. M. L. Thompson, *English Landed Society*, 1963, p. 27.

'Twenty-nine peers . . .': David Cannadine, *The Decline and Fall of the British Aristocracy*, Yale University Press, 1990, pp. 710–11.

'Less than 5 per cent . . .': Royal Commission, Mining Royalties, 1893.

p. 189 'Robert Smillie . . .': *The Times*, 8 May 1919.

'I want to examine . . .': ibid.

p. 191 'There are houses . . .': cited in R. Page Arnot, *The Miners: Years of Struggle*, George Allen & Unwin, 1953, p. 200.

'The total profits . . .': cited ibid., p. 190.

'Many of the coal owners . . .': cited ibid., p. 193.

'Even upon the evidence . . .': cited ibid., p. 200.

p. 192 'During the Great War . . .': estimate based on the Marquess of Bute's and the Earl of Dunraven's wartime coal income – the former above Billy Fitzwilliam on the list of Britain's wealthiest mineral royalty owners, the latter below him. The source of the list is B. Fine, *The Nationalization of the UK Coal Royalties, 1938: Compensation Payments* (computer file), Colchester, Essex: UK Data Archive (distributor), January 1983. SN:1825.

'They are all decent . . .': *Mexborough and Swinton Times*, 5 July 1919.

p. 193 'If they throw themselves . . .': David Lloyd George, House of Commons debate, March 1919.

'Was it a huge game . . .': Vernon Hartshorn, House of Commons debate, 18 August 1919.

p. 194 'Delegates . . .': decision taken by MFGB Executive Committee, 9 January 1920, cited in Page Arnot, *The Miners: Years of Struggle*, p. 217.

CHAPTER NINETEEN

p. 196 'Three footmen waited . . .': author's interview with Bert May, Jack May's son, June 2004.

'Some minutes later . . .': *Rotherham Advertiser*, 31 January 1920.

'Under the watchful gaze . . .': ibid.

'Walking twenty paces . . .': ibid.

p. 197 'A lone bugler . . .': ibid.

'From the direction . . .': ibid.

'Some of the veterans . . .': *Mexborough and Swinton Times*, January 1919.

p. 198 'At a nod . . .': *Rotherham Advertiser*, 31 January 1920.

'Haig's speech . . .': ibid.

CHAPTER TWENTY

p. 201 'They had moved . . .': author's interview with Armand Smith, June 2004.

p. 202 'in the words . . .': *Chips – The Diaries of Sir Henry Channon*, ed. Robert Rhode James, Weidenfeld & Nicolson, 1967, p. 24.

'We saw it through a gauze . . .': author's interview with Armand Smith, June 2004.

CHAPTER TWENTY-ONE

p. 203 'My grandfather . . .': author's interview with Joyce Smith, April 2004.

'We were very happy . . .': ibid.

'The thing that . . .': ibid.

p. 204 'One morning . . .': ibid.

'It was a child's dream . . .': ibid.

p. 205 'I longed to meet him . . .': ibid.

'If Peter . . .': ibid.

p. 206 'Armand and I . . .': ibid.

'They thought . . .': author's interview with Lady Barbara Ricardo, November 2005.

p. 207 'When the monthly nurse . . .': author's interview with Joyce Smith, April 2004.

'If you call a baby . . .': ibid.

'His birth meant . . .': author's interview with Lady Barbara Ricardo, November 2005.

'Billy spared no expense . . .': Roy Young, *The Big House and the Little Village*, Wentworth Garden Centre, 2000, p. 47.

p. 208 'One showed . . .': *Mexborough and Swinton Times*, 18 February 1911.

'Anything Peter wanted . . .': author's interview with Lady Barbara Ricardo, November 2005.

'He rode out . . .': author's interview with Charles Doyne, June 2004.

p. 209 'We were all mad about . . .': interview with Elfrida, Countess of Wharncliffe, recorded by Roy Young in 1977.

'At the tender age . . .': article by Peter Fitzwilliam, *Hunting*, December 1936.

'In the nursery . . .': author's interview with Joyce Smith, April 2004.

p. 210 'There was . . .': ibid.

'Then, at that sort . . .': cited in *The Country House Remembered*, ed. Merlin Waterson, Routledge & Kegan Paul, 1985, p. 115.

p. 211 'There was quite a party . . .': author's interview with Charles Doyne, June 2004.

'One of the young men . . .': author's interview with Joyce Smith, April 2004.

'They'd had a paper chase . . .': author's interview with Bert May, November 2004.

p. 212 'It was terribly difficult . . .': author's interview with Joyce Smith, April 2004.

'He was very keen . . .': author's interview with Charles Doyne, June 2004.

'He had many girlfriends . . .': author's interview with Lady Barbara Ricardo, March 2004.

'He used to take her . . .': author's interview with Griffie Phillips, September 2004.

'In the 1920s . . .': author's interview with Robert Tottie, former deputy agent at Wentworth, August 2005.

p. 213 'Lordie was a bit of a lad . . .': author's interview with Bert May, November 2004.

'You didn't marry a person . . .': author's interview with Peter Diggle, November 2005.

'My mother . . .': author's interview with Joyce Smith, April 2004.

p. 214 'The fact of my illegitimacy . . .': Fred Smith, 'We asked them for bread,' *Ivanhoe Review*, No. 8, Summer 1995, Archives and Local Studies Section, Rotherham Metropolitan Borough Council.

p. 215 'We thought . . .': author's interview with Joyce Smith, April 2004

p. 216 'It was a lot of rot . . .': author's interview with Gracie Woodcock, June 2004.

'It weren't her face . . .': author's interview with Walt Hammond, July 2005.

p. 217 'The gatekeepers were expected . . .': author's interview with Gordon Hempsey, August 2005.

'He used to haunt . . .': author's interview with Joyce Smith, April 2004.

p. 218 'During the school . . .': testimony of Mrs Bradley, 18 October 1988, Archive, Wentworth Estate Office.

'He is a backward . . .': extract from Admissions Register, Royal School for the Deaf, Derby, Admission No. 766.

p. 219 'According to his . . .': author's interview with Lily Fletcher, February 2006.

'A Statement of Particulars . . .': n.d., Archive, Wentworth Estate Office.

'I was frightened . . .': author's interview with Lily Fletcher, February 2006.

p. 220 'Dear Mother . . .': letter written with Lily Fletcher by Edgar Bower to his dead mother, 16 October 1988, Archive, Wentworth Estate Office.

'When he told me . . .': author's interview with Lily Fletcher, February 2006.

p. 222 'I believed Edgar . . .': ibid.

'The doctor sent . . .': author's interview with Gracie Woodcock, June 2004.

'It was the love . . .': author's interview with Lily Fletcher, February 2004.

p. 223 'When we pulled up . . .': ibid.

'Everybody . . .': letter written with Lily Fletcher by Edgar Bower to his dead mother, 16 October 1988, Archive, Wentworth Estate Office.

p. 224 'We went up . . .': author's interview with Lily Fletcher, February 2006.

'They knew . . .': ibid.

'I moved back home . . .': letter written with Lily Fletcher by

Edgar Bower to his dead mother, 16 October 1988, Archive, Wentworth Estate Office.

p. 225 'Such matters . . .': Guy Canby to Edgar Bower, 5 October 1989, Archive, Wentworth Estate Office.

'Mr Broadhead . . .': memo to Guy Canby, 13 May 1996, Archive, Wentworth Estate Office.

'It's a matter . . .': author's interview with Elizabeth Wilde, February 2006.

p. 226 'He ain't buried . . .': author's interview with Gracie Woodcock, June 2004.

CHAPTER TWENTY-TWO

p. 229 'On the evening . . .': War Office Situation Report No. 1, 3 May 1926, Public Record Office, Kew, WO 30/143.

'Everything I care for . . .': Stanley Baldwin, House of Commons Emergency Debate, 3 May 1926.

'Home Office Directorate . . .': Keith Jeffrey and Peter Hennessy, *States of Emergency*, Routledge & Kegan Paul, 1983, p. 6.

p. 230 'Enemies . . .': Winston Churchill, House of Commons Emergency Debate, 3 May 1926.

'The owners are the provokers . . .': House of Commons Emergency Debate, 3 May 1926.

p. 231 'I do believe . . .': George Lansbury, House of Commons Debate, 25 June 1926.

'In 1919 . . .': Lloyd George at an interview with the leaders of the Triple Alliance, quoted in Jeffrey and Hennessy, *States of Emergency*, p. 7.

p. 232 'It should be impressed . . .': secret telegram from War Office to GOC-in-C, Home Commands, 3 May 1926, Public Record Office, Kew, WO 30/143.

'Commanders in the field . . .': ibid.

'The M.T. Drivers . . .': telegram, 2 May 1926, ibid.

'There are very few light . . .': Stanley Baldwin, House of Commons Emergency Debate, 3 May 1926.

p. 233 'All of Europe . . .': cited in letter from Lady Sybil Middleton to Lady Halifax, 24 May 1926, Hickleton Papers, Borthwick Institute for Archives, University of York A2.280.2.

'Clip-clop . . .': Roger Dataller (pseud.), *From a Pitman's Notebook*, Jonathan Cape, 1925, pp. 126–7.

p. 234 'GEORGE REX . . .': the King's Proclamation, cited in R. Page Arnot, *The Miners: Years of Struggle*, George Allen & Unwin, 1953, p. 421.

p. 235 'If tha' goes out . . .': author's interview with Walt Hammond, August 2005.

'You must . . .': author's interview with Gordon Scott, August 2005.

p. 236 'There was never a major . . .': Roger Dataller (pseud.), *A Yorkshire Lad*, unpublished memoir.

'He was generous . . .': author's interview with Jim McGuinness, August 2005.

'Wages-wise . . .': author's interview with Ralph Boreham, August 2005.

'We knew our place . . .': author's interview with Charles Booth, April 2004.

p. 237 'Bearing each a . . .': Dataller, *A Yorkshire Lad.*

'Here we are . . .': Sir W. Riddell to Lady Dorothy Halifax, 9 May 1926, Hickleton Papers, Borthwick Institute for Archives, University of York, A2.280.2.

'Yesterday 20 tanks . . .': Lady Manners to Lady Dorothy Halifax, 6 May 1926, ibid.

'Its citizens . . .': Sir W. Riddell to Lady Dorothy Halifax, 9 May 1926, ibid .

p. 238 'I don't think . . .': Mabel, Countess Gray, to Lady Dorothy Halifax, 12 May 1926, ibid.

'5th Infantry Brigade . . .': War Office Situation Report, Public Record Office, Kew, WO 30/143.

CHAPTER TWENTY-THREE

p. 239 'Broad Yorkshire . . .': author's interview with Walt Hammond, miner from New Stubbin colliery.

'Twenty-four hours . . .': Roger Dataller (pseud.), *A Yorkshire Lad*, unpublished memoir.

'Caesar had been . . .': Roger Dataller (pseud.), 'From a miner's journal', *Adelphi* magazine, vol. II, No. 2, July 1924.

p. 240 'The horses knew . . .': Jim Bullock, *Bowers Row*, EP Publishing, 1976, p. 195.

'My father . . .': interview with Elfrida, Countess of Wharncliffe, recorded by Roy Young in 1977.

p. 241 'My mother . . .': Bullock, *Bowers Row*, p. 184.

'When I went . . .': ibid.

p. 242 'If the mice . . .': ibid., p. 37.

'There used to be . . .': ibid., p. 215.

'Despite everything . . .': ibid., p. 184.

'There is no night . . .': Dataller, 'From a miner's journal'.

p. 243 'As soon as . . .': Bullock, *Bowers Row*, p. 185.

'He had finished . . .': ibid., p. 179.

p. 244 'When my father . . .': ibid., p. 177.

'I have never . . .': ibid., p. 184.

p. 245 'When I got . . .': ibid., p. 185.

'The ponies were put . . .': ibid., p. 196.

p. 246 'The pony was always . . .': Fred Smith, 'We asked them for bread', *Ivanhoe Review*, Rotherham Archives and Local Studies Section, No. 8, Summer 1995.

'The ponies knew . . .': Bullock, *Bowers Row*, p. 197.

'I could write . . .': ibid., p. 201.

'I know that . . .': Smith, 'We asked them for bread'.

p. 247 'The worst accidents . . .': Bullock, *Bowers Row*, p. 197.

'In 1925 . . .': *Mexborough and Swinton Times*, 26 March 1926.

'You would . . .': Bullock, *Bowers Row*, p. 198.

'Fortunately . . .': ibid., p. 195.

'The older lads . . .': ibid., p. 197.

p. 248 'I remember . . .': Frank Johnson, interviewed by Brian Elliott, *Yorkshire Mining Veterans*, Wharncliffe Books, 2005, p. 85.

'I should not be living . . .': Arthur Clayton, interviewed by Brian Elliott, ibid., p. 21.

'Lord Fitzwilliam's . . .': author's interview with Joyce Smith, April 2004.

p. 249 'There used to be . . .': author's interview with Ralph Boreham, August 2005.

'We'd play cricket . . .': author's interview with Ernest Whitworth, August 2005.

'He said . . .': author's interview with Geoffrey Steer, August 2005.

CHAPTER TWENTY-FOUR

p. 250 'SECRET . . .': Public Records Office, Kew, WO 30/143.

p. 251 'Most people . . .': Lady Bentinck to Lady Halifax, 10 June 1926, Hickleton Papers, Borthwick Institute for Archives, University of York, A2.280.2.

p. 252 'Lord Portarlington . . .': Lady Sybil Middleton to Lady Halifax, 24 May 1926, ibid.

'The Horse Guards . . .': Mabel, Countess Grey, to Lady Halifax, 12 May 1926, ibid.

'Rex is . . .': Lady Sybil Middleton to Lady Halifax, 24 May 1926, ibid.

'I was in despair . . .': Lady Bentinck to Lady Halifax, 10 June 1926, ibid.

p. 253 'Instead of me . . .': Lady Mary Clive, *Brought Up and Brought Out*, Cobden-Sanderson, 1938, p. 162.

'When they . . .': ibid., p. 165.

'It was of course . . .': ibid., p. 163.

'Our triumph . . .': ibid., p. 167.

p. 254 'The washing water . . .': ibid.

'As soon as . . .': Lady Sybil Middleton to Lady Halifax, 24 May

1926, Hickleton Papers, Borthwick Institute for Archives, University of York, A2.280.2.

p. 255 'The shop girls . . .': Lady Mary Clive, *Brought Up and Brought Out*, p. 169.

'As Thomas Jones . . .': Keith Jeffrey and Peter Hennessy, *States of Emergency*, Routledge & Kegan Paul, 1983, p. 122.

p. 256 'A total of 4,000 . . .': A. J. P. Taylor, *English History 1914–1945*, Oxford University Press, paperback edition, 1992, p. 245.

'An MI5 report . . .': Public Records Office, Kew, HO 144/6116.

'The result of the GS . . .': Lord Birkenhead to Lord Irwin, 30 May 1926, cited in John Campbell, *F. E. Smith*, Jonathan Cape, 1983, p. 775.

p. 257 'This coal trouble . . .': Lady Bentinck to Lady Halifax, 10 June 1926, Hickleton Papers, Borthwick Institute for Archives, University of York, A2.280.2.

'Britain's colliers . . .': George Hall, created Viscount Hall in 1946, Emergency House of Commons debate, 3 May 1926.

p. 258 'Writing to . . .': Miss Brodigan to Stanley Baldwin, 19 June 1926, Public Records Office, Kew, CAB 21/296.

'Blaina . . .': report attached to letter above, ibid.

p. 259 'In 1870 . . .': R. Page Arnot, *The Miners: Years of Struggle*, George Allen & Unwin, 1953, p. 526.

p. 260 'By the mid-1920s . . .': ibid., p. 354.

CHAPTER TWENTY-FIVE

p. 262 'I hawe gotta . . .': Roger Dataller (pseud.), *From a Pitman's Notebook*, Jonathan Cape, 1925, pp. 208–9.

p. 263 'The Fitzwilliams were liked . . .': author's interview with May Bailey, June 2004.

'If anyone went without . . .': author's interview with Gracie Woodcock, June 2004.

'I'll slay . . .': *Mexborough and Swinton Times*, 28 May 1926.

'We called her Lady Bountiful . . .': author's interview with Bert May, September 2004.

'When the Vicar . . .': Roy Young, *The Big House and the Little Village*, Wentworth Garden Centre, 2000, p. 137.

p. 264 'All the mothers . . .': author's interview with May Bailey, June 2004.

'Lady Maud . . .': author's interview with Rita King, August 2005.

'The calves' foot . . .': family recipe book. Private Collection.

p. 265 'They had these huge set pots . . .': author's interview with May Bailey, June 2004.

'Acting upon . . .': *The Times*, 13 September 1911.

p. 266 'Most people ran out . . .': Luke Evans, unpublished memoir, Doncaster Library, Local Studies Section.

'It was clog and boot . . .': Ernest Kaye, interviewed by Brian Elliott, *Yorkshire Mining Veterans*, Wharncliffe Books, 2005, p. 55.

'I can remember . . .': Jack Parkin, ibid.

p. 267 'The owners . . .': Lord Londonderry to Winston Churchill, Churchill Papers, Churchill College, Cambridge, Char 18/28.

'It would be possible . . .': Lord Birkenhead to Lord Irwin, 30 May 1926, cited in John Campbell, *F. E. Smith*, Jonathan Cape, 1983, p. 775.

p. 268 'Coal, iron and steel . . .': Quentin Outram, *Class Warriors: The Coalowners, Industrial Relations and the 1926 Mining Lockout: The Struggle for Dignity*, ed. J. McIlroy, A. Campbell and K. Gildart, University of Wales Press, Cardiff, 2004, pp. 107–35.

'With the exception of one . . .': ibid.

p. 269 'Evan Williams . . .': cited in Martin Gilbert, *Winston S. Churchill*, Heinemann, 1976, vol. 5, p. 185.

p. 270 'I spent . . .': Miss Brodigan to Stanley Baldwin, 19 June 1926, Public Records Office, Kew, CAB 21/296.

'You say that . . .': Winston Churchill to Lord Londonderry, 3 November 1926, Churchill Papers, Churchill College, Cambridge, Char 18/28.

p. 271 'It would seem . . .': Churchill to Stanley Baldwin, 10 September 1926, quoted in Gilbert, *Winston S. Churchill*, p. 202.

'I am not happy . . .': telegram from Lord Birkenhead to Winston Churchill, ibid., p. 203.

'The Moscow . . .': ibid., p. 220.

p. 272 'The whole machinery . . .': Stanley Baldwin, Emergency Debate in the House of Commons, 3 May 1926.

'If wages are . . .': ibid.

p. 273 'Well? . . .': Roger Dataller (pseud.), 'From a miner's journal', *Adelphi* magazine, vol. 11, No. 2, July 1924.

p. 274 'Through forces . . .': cited in R. Page Arnot, *The Miners: Years of Struggle*, George Allen & Unwin, 1953, p. 533.

'We never forgot . . .': conversation with Jack Steer, recorded by John Wrigley in 1966.

CHAPTER TWENTY-SIX

p. 275 'Morning Prayers were a chance . . .': author's interview with May Bailey, February 2004.

p. 276 'By golly . . .': author's interview with Bert May, March 2004.

p. 277 'I was a choir boy . . .': author's interview with Charles Booth, February 2006.

'He was a grand fellow . . .': author's interview with Walker Scales, May 2004.

p. 278 'He were a friend . . .': author's interview with Walt Hammond, August 2005.

'We could have . . .': ibid.

'He'd mix around . . .': author's interview with May Bailey, February 2004.

'Everyone used to come . . .': author's interview with Walker Scales, May 2004.

p. 279 'He never went anywhere . . .': author's interview with Peter Diggle, June 2004.

'God lived in't big house . . .': author's interview with Jim McGuinness, July 2004.

'There were a lot of talk . . .': author's interview with Walt Hammond, August 2006.

'There was a boy . . .': author's interview with Bert May, March 2004.

'His Lordship . . .': ibid.

p. 280 'My grandmother . . .': author's interview with David Sylvester, January 2006.

'Lord Milton . . .': ibid.

p. 281 'Ooh, Lord Milton . . .': author's interview with May Bailey, June 2004.

'I started down the mine . . .': author's interview with Jim McGuinness, July 2004.

'She was a notable girl . . .': author's interview with Walker Scales, September 2004.

p. 282 'All the boys in the village . . .': author's interview with May Bailey, June 2004.

CHAPTER TWENTY-SEVEN

p. 286 'Dear Jim . . .': Billy Fitzwilliam to Jim Landon, 8 May 1931. Private Collection.

'It were his father . . .': author's interview with Walt Hammond, August 2005.

p. 287 'Aside from . . .': *The Times*, 10 June 1931.

p. 288 'There are . . .': minutes of Milton Committee Meeting, 10 June 1931. Private Collection.

'Once a year . . .': author's interview with Roy Young, May 2004.

p. 289 'Captain North began . . .': minutes of Milton Committee Meeting, 10 June 1931. Private Collection.

p. 290 'Admiral Hugh Douglas . . .': ibid.

'*Tout passe* . . .': Duke of Portland, *Men, Women and Things*, Faber and Faber, 1937, pp. 1 and 2.

'in the years immediately . . .': David Cannadine, *The Decline and Fall of the British Aristocracy*, Yale University Press, 1990.

p. 291 'A silent revolution . . .': cited ibid., p. 111.

'One, Sudbrooke Holme . . .': cited ibid., p. 119.

'If I close . . .': Frances, Countess of Warwick, *Afterthoughts*, Cassell and Co., 1931, p. 247.

'In 1870 . . .': Cannadine, *The Decline and Fall of the British Aristocracy*, p. 92.

p. 292 'Nearly all these . . .': Duke of Portland, *Men, Women and Things*, p. 2.

p. 293 'Times change . . .': Frances, Countess of Warwick, *Afterthoughts*, p. 246.

'Margaret Sweeny . . .': Margaret, Duchess of Argyll, *Forget Not*, W. H. Allen, 1975, p. 92.

p. 294 'Over Grapefruit Supreme . . .': lunch menu, Milton Committee, 10 June 1931. Private Collection.

'I want to suggest . . .': minutes of meeting, Milton Committee, 10 June 1931. Private Collection.

'Mr Hebden . . .': ibid.

'Alfred Wright . . .': ibid.

CHAPTER TWENTY-EIGHT

p. 297 'The train bore me . . .': George Orwell, *The Road to Wigan Pier*, Victor Gollancz, 1937, paperback edition, Penguin Twentieth-Century Classics, 1989, p. 14.

p. 298 'It is a kind of duty . . .': ibid., p. 14.

'Here are one or two . . .': ibid., p. 49.

'It is in the rooms . . .': ibid., p. 55.

p. 299 'Rent, 9 0 ½d . . .': ibid., p. 85.

p. 300 'You see very few . . .': ibid., p. 89.

'They were rough times . . .': author's interview with Ralph Boreham, August 2005.

p. 301 'Though both my wife . . .': Walter Brierley, 'Frustration and bitterness – a colliery banksman', the *Listener*, 9 August 1933.

p. 302 'Capacity to work . . .': Roger Dataller (pseud.), *A Yorkshire Lad*, unpublished memoir.

'I could give you . . .': Jim Bullock, *Bowers Row*, EP Publishing, 1976, p. 224.

p. 303 'One day . . .': ibid.

p. 304 'I remember . . .': B. L. Coombes, *These Poor Hands*, Victor Gollancz, 1939, p. 215.

'We are sitting . . .': cited in Kenneth Rose, *King George V*, Weidenfeld & Nicolson, 1983, paperback edition, Phoenix Press, 2000, p. 370.

p. 305 'Interrupting his holiday . . .': A. J. P. Taylor, *English History 1914–1945*, Oxford University Press, 1965, paperback edition, 1992, p. 288.

'It was the "Invisibles" . . .': ibid., p. 287.

p. 306 'In the years after . . .': ibid., p. 289.

'It was a time . . .': minutes of Milton Committee Meeting. Private Collection.

p. 307 'It were the last hurrah . . .': author's interview with Walker Scales, June 2004.

p. 308 'You never saw him . . .': author's interview with Charles Booth, May 2004.

'As dusk fell . . .': *Mexborough and Swinton Times*, 2 January 1932.

'Coloured lights . . .': author's interview with Charles Booth, May 2004.

'The freedom of Wentworth . . .': *Sheffield Daily Telegraph*, 1 January 1932.

'Me father and grandfather . . .': author's interview with Ralph Boreham, August 2005.

p. 309 'The setting . . .': *Sheffield Daily Telegraph*, 1 January 1932.

p. 310 'Ay, that party were a treat . . .': author's interview with Ralph Boreham, August 2005.

p. 311 'There were a great gang of us . . .': author's interview with Geoffrey Steer, August 2005.

'As a Trades Union Secretary . . .': *Mexborough and Swinton Times*, 2 January 1932.

p. 312 'At Elsecar . . .': ibid.

'Ever since . . .': ibid.

p. 313 'There are two men . . .': ibid.

'I am overwhelmed . . .': ibid.

'He made a short speech . . .': author's interview with Walt Hammond, August 2005.

p. 314 'As a child . . .': Lynne McTaggart, *Kathleen Kennedy*, Weidenfeld & Nicolson, 1984, p. 210.

'Grandpa didn't want . . .': author's interview with Lady Barbara Ricardo, November 2005.

p. 315 'I was sitting . . .': ibid.

CHAPTER TWENTY-NINE

p. 320 'I was on the bus . . .': author's interview with Charles Booth, February 2006.

p. 321 'Our kitchen door . . .': Alicia Dufton, *Recollections of a Lifetime*, unpublished memoir, Doncaster Library, Local Studies Centre.

'Everything was moving . . .': author's interview with Bert May, June 2004.

p. 322 'A stick of bombs . . .': author's interview with Charles Booth, February 2006.

'The war turned . . .': author's interview with Lady Barbara Ricardo, March 2006.

'The other ranks . . .': Dr Patrick Hewlings, cited in John Martin Robinson, *The Country House at War*, Bodley Head, 1989, p. 138.

'We were very comfortable . . .': ibid.

p. 324 'I wrapped so many . . .': author's interview with Ethel Jones, October 2002.

'The thing that . . .': author's interview with Lady Barbara Ricardo, March 2006.

p. 325 'He had a reputation . . .': ibid.

'There were a lot of talk . . .': author's interview with Geoffrey Steer, August 2005.

'As Lady Barbara . . .': author's interview with Lady Barbara Ricardo, March 2006.

p. 326 '100 tons would be sufficient . . .': cited in Ralph Barker, *The Blockade Busters*, Chatto & Windus, 1976, p. 150.

'We have our traditions . . .': ibid., p. 153.

'None of the family . . .': author's interview with Lady Barbara Ricardo, November 2005.

p. 327 'Service with the Motor Gunboats . . .': Public Records Office, Kew, London, HS 7/191.

p. 328 'The boats didn't cut . . .': cited in Barker, *The Blockade Busters*, p. 187.

'They were like corks . . .': author's interview with Irwin Jones, February 2004.

'There were three of us . . .': ibid.

'During many . . .': cited in Barker, *The Blockade Busters*, p. 159.

p. 329 'We were wary of him . . .': author's interview with Jack Baron, February 2004.

'I think he drove himself . . .': author's interview with Lady Barbara Ricardo, March 2006.

'In the gathering gloom . . .': Barker, *The Blockade Busters*, p. 163.

'Rounding the Bull Light . . .': ibid.

p. 330 'They didn't stand . . .': ibid.

p. 331 'There was a family . . .': author's interview with Lady Barbara Ricardo, March 2006.

CHAPTER THIRTY

p. 333 'Mother . . .': KK, round-robin letter to family, 27 June 1943, cited in Amanda Smith, *Hostage to Fortune: The Letters of Joseph P. Kennedy*, Viking Penguin, 2001, p. 562.

'Heavy fighting . . .': Winston Churchill, speech in London, 30 June 1943.

'The only lounge available . . .': KK, round-robin letter to family, 27 June 1943, cited in Smith, *Hostage to Fortune*, p. 562.

p. 334 'About a half-hour . . .': ibid.

'This life . . .': ibid.

'her hat . . .': *Daily Express*, 16 March 1938.

'Now I've got . . .': ibid.

p. 335 'When the President . . .': James Roosevelt, *My Parents: A Differing View*, Chicago, 1976, p. 208.

'After ushering . . .': ibid., p. 209.

p. 336 'a very dangerous man . . .': *The Presidential Diaries of Henry Morgantheau* (microform), 8 December 1937, Clearwater Publishing Co., New York, 1980.

'I have a beautiful . . .': JPK to James Roosevelt, 3 March 1938, FDR Library/James Roosevelt.

p. 337 'After he referred . . .': E. Wilder Spaulding, *Ambassadors Ordinary and Extraordinary*, Washington, 1961, pp. 218–19.

'You watched . . .': P. Collier and D. Horowitz, *The Kennedys: An American Drama*, Summit Books, 1984, p. 131.

p. 338 'Met the King . . .': JFK to Lem Billings, August 1938, ibid., p. 102.

'As I entered . . .': Eunice Kennedy Shriver, *Recollections*, John F. Kennedy Library, Rose Kennedy Papers, Series 7.10.

p. 339 'Eighty guests . . .': Laurence Leamer, *The Kennedy Women*, Ballantine Books, 1996, p. 257.

'When she came . . .': interview with Dinah Bridge, recorded 1966, JFKL Oral History Program.

'She was just . . .': author's interview with Janie Compton, November 2005.

'Wish you could . . .': cited in David Michaelis, *The Best of Friends*, New York, 1983, p. 160.

'Very chummy . . .': KK to Lem Billings, 29 April 1938, cited in Doris Kearns Goodwin, *The Fitzgeralds and the Kennedys: An American Saga*, Simon and Schuster, 1987, p. 541.

p. 340 'Veronica Fraser . . .': Lynne McTaggart, *Kathleen Kennedy*, Weidenfeld & Nicolson, 1984, p. 33.

'The boys . . .': ibid.

'Small things . . .': ibid.

'I can't get . . .': KK to JPK, 18 September 1939, cited in Smith, *Hostage to Fortune*, p. 381.

p. 341 'All my ducks . . .': cited in Collier and Horowitz, *The Kennedys*, p. 71.

'Those three . . .': ibid.

'Today it is windy . . .': KK, round-robin letter to family, 27 June 1943, cited in Smith, *Hostage to Fortune*, p. 562.

p. 342 'a living room . . .': Torb Macdonald, cited in Leamer, *The Kennedy Women*, p. 329.

'Kick is very . . .': JFK to JPK, spring 1940, cited in Kearns Goodwin, *The Fitzgeralds and the Kennedys*, p. 607.

'Mr Kennedy . . .': cited in Collier and Horowitz, *The Kennedys*, p. 119.

'The British have had it . . .': ibid., author's interview with Harvey Klemmer, p. 122.

p. 343 'In her absence . . .': McTaggart, *Kathleen Kennedy*, p. 91.

'Sometimes I feel . . .': KK to Janie Compton, cited in ibid.

p. 344 'Listen, the thing . . .': Collier and Horowitz, *The Kennedys*, p. 143.

'I think . . .': Tom Egerton, cited in Leamer, *The Kennedy Women*, p. 225.

'Darling Kick . . .': ibid, p. 260.

'before the war . . .': ibid.

'On knocking . . .': ibid, p. 261.

'In the months . . .': Joan and Clay Blair, *The Search for JFK*, Berkeley/Putnam, 1976, p. 128.

'I would advise . . .': JFK to KK, 10 March 1942, cited in Leamer, *The Kennedy Women*, p. 337.

p. 345 'Yesterday . . .': KK, round-robin letter to family, 14 July 1943, cited in Smith, *Hostage to Fortune*, p. 564.

'Everyone has been . . .': KK to JFK, 29 July 1943, ibid., p. 566.

'You had to go out . . .': Lady Virginia Ford, cited in Leamer, *The Kennedy Women*, p. 338.

p. 346 'With so many . . .': cited in McTaggart, *Kathleen Kennedy*, p. 76.

'5½ days . . .': KK to Frank Waldrop, 20 July 1943, cited in Kearns Goodwin, *The Fitzgeralds and the Kennedys*, p. 666.

p. 347 'Chiswick? . . .': cited in McTaggart, *Kathleen Kennedy*, p. 52.

'I remember . . .': Collier and Horowitz, *The Kennedys*, p. 103.

'I have just returned . . .': KK to JFK, 29 July 1943, cited in Smith, *Hostage to Fortune*, p. 566.

p. 348 'I think Kick . . .': author's interview with Janie Compton, November 2005.

'At the moment . . .': KK to JPK, 21 May 1940, cited in Kearns Goodwin, *The Fitzgeralds and the Kennedys*, p. 607.

p. 349 'Romeo and Juliet . . .': Fiona Gore, cited in Collier and Horowitz, *The Kennedys*, p. 104.

p. 350 'The one thing . . .': KK, round-robin letter to family, 18 May 1944, cited in Smith, *Hostage to Fortune*, p. 592.

'the worst-dressed . . .': Andrew Cavendish, cited in Leamer, *The Kennedy Women*, p. 263.

'He was a frustrated . . .': Sir Henry Channon, *Chips: The Diaries of Sir Henry Channon*, 1967, p. 547.

'One of his favourite . . .': cited in Leamer, *The Kennedy Women*, p. 263.

'It was said . . .': cited in McTaggart, *Kathleen Kennedy*, p. 47.

'I think it's fair . . .': Andrew Cavendish, cited in Leamer, *The Kennedy Women*, p. 263.

p. 351 'The religious difficulties . . .': the Marquess of Hartington to RK, 30 April 1944, cited in Smith, *Hostage to Fortune*, p. 584.

CHAPTER THIRTY-ONE

p. 352 'Do you think . . .': *Derbyshire Sunday Express*, 13 February 1944.

'The by-election . . .': Andrew Cavendish, cited in Laurence Leamer, *The Kennedy Women*, Ballantine Books, 1996, p. 359.

'He should never . . .': Lady Maureen Fellowes, ibid.

p. 353 'Lord Hartington . . .': *Derbyshire Times*, February 1944.

'He looks absolutely repulsive . . .': KK, round-robin letter to family, 22 February 1944, cited in Amanda Smith, *Hostage to Fortune: The Letters of Joseph P. Kennedy*, Viking Penguin, 2001, p. 574.

'She fell in love . . .': author's interview with Janie Compton, November 2005.

p. 354 'evil influence . . .': KK, round-robin letter to family, 18 May 1944, cited in Smith, *Hostage to Fortune*, p. 592.

'News of me . . .': KK, round-robin letter to family, 22 February 1944, cited ibid., p. 574.

'It really was . . .': ibid.

'In the interests . . .': *Derbyshire Times*, 11 February 1944.

'Are you in favour . . .': ibid.

'Can you milk a cow . . .': *Evening Standard*, 9 February 1944.

p. 355 'My dear Hartington . . .': published in *Derbyshire Times*, 11 February 1944.

p. 356 'It's all very upsetting . . .': KK, round-robin letter to family, 22 February 1944, cited in Smith, *Hostage to Fortune*, p. 574.

'It has been a fierce . . .': *Sheffield Daily Telegraph*, 15 May 1948.

'It just leaves . . .': KK, round-robin letter to family, 22 February 1944, cited in Smith, *Hostage to Fortune*, p. 574.

p. 357 'Received . . .': ibid.

'I think something . . .': KK to parents, 4 March 1944, cited in Doris Kearns Goodwin, *The Fitzgeralds and the Kennedys: An American Saga*, Simon and Schuster, 1987, p. 675.

'I do not seem . . .': RK to KK, 24 February 1944, cited in Smith, *Hostage to Fortune*, p. 577.

p. 358 'She was deeply . . .': author's interview with Janie Compton, November 2005.

'Ursula Wyndham Quinn . . .': cited in Leamer, *The Kennedy Women*, p. 356.

'Kick calls to me . . .': cited in D. Collier and P. Horowitz, *The Kennedys: An American Drama*, Summit Books, 1984, pp. 142–3.

'The thing the priest . . .': ibid.

p. 359 'When both people . . .': RK to KK, 24 February 1944, cited in Smith, *Hostage to Fortune*, p. 577.

'The Duchess with . . .': KK to parents, 22 March 1944, cited ibid., p. 578.

p. 360 'When I left . . .': ibid.

'I am no good . . .': ibid.

p. 361 'If, he promised . . .': Collier and Horowitz, *The Kennedys*, p. 159.

'Of course . . .': KK, round-robin letter to family, 4 April 1944, cited in Smith, *Hostage to Fortune*, p. 581.

p. 362 'Dear Mrs Kennedy . . .': Marquess of Hartington to RK, 30 April 1944, cited ibid., p. 584.

p. 364 'Personal Reminiscences . . .': cited ibid.

'Everyone pointed . . .': ibid.

'EFFORT IN VAIN . . .': Archbishop William Godfrey to Archbishop Francis Spellman, n.d., cited ibid., p. 586.

'As sister Eunice . . .': JFK to Lem Billings, 19 May 1944, cited in Collier and Horowitz, *The Kennedys*, p. 161.

p. 365 'Whenever she heard . . .': JPK Jr to his parents, 8 May 1944, cited in Smith, *Hostage to Fortune*, p. 587.

'RELIGION EVERYTHING . . .': KK to JPK, 5 May 1944, cited ibid., p. 586.

'WILL YOU KINDLY . . .': Archbishop Francis Spellman to Archbishop William Godfrey, 6 May 1944, cited ibid.

p. 366 'The dress . . .': Lynne McTaggart, *Kathleen Kennedy*, Weidenfeld & Nicolson, 1984, p. 161.

'Charles Granby . . .': ibid.

'quite conscious . . .': KK to RK, 9 May 1944, cited in Smith, *Hostage to Fortune*, p. 589.

'Parnell's ghost . . .': cited in McTaggart, *Kathleen Kennedy*, p. 159.

'Over in America . . .': *Boston Traveller*, 4 May 1944.

p. 367 'Anne was mortified . . .': McTaggart, *Kathleen Kennedy*, p. 161.

'a shy old bird . . .': JPK Jr to his parents, 8 May 1944, cited in Smith, *Hostage to Fortune*, p. 587.

'The ring . . .': Smith, *Hostage to Fortune*, p. 518.

'It seemed better . . .': JPK Jr to his parents, 8 May 1944, cited ibid., p. 587.

'The chef . . .': KK to RK, 9 May 1944, cited ibid., p. 589.

'a few of the GIs . . .': ibid.

'Listen, you God damn . . .': KK, round-robin letter to family, 18 May 1944, cited ibid., p. 592.

'I enjoyed . . .': KK to RK, 9 May 1944, cited ibid., p. 589.

p. 368 'As far as . . .': JPK Jr to his parents, 8 May 1944, cited ibid., p. 587.

'The family . . .': McTaggart, *Kathleen Kennedy*, p. 163.

'THE POWER OF SILENCE . . .': JPK Jr to JPK, 7 May 1944, cited in Smith, *Hostage to Fortune*, p. 587.

'MOST DISTRESSED . . .': KK to JPK, 8 May 1944, cited ibid.

p. 369 'Dearest family . . .': KK, round-robin letter to family, 18 May 1944, cited ibid., p. 594.

'I am feeling better . . .': KK, round-robin letter to family, 23 May 1944.

'[It] gets funnier . . .': ibid.

p. 370 'the most perfect month . . .': KK, diary and scrapbook, 17 May 1944, cited in Kearns Goodwin, *The Fitzgeralds and the Kennedys*, p. 682.

'May the Blessed . . .': cited ibid., p. 679.

'Kick Kennedy's . . .': Evelyn Waugh to Laura Waugh, 12 May 1944, *The Letters of Evelyn Waugh*, ed. Mark Amory, Weidenfeld & Nicolson, 1980.

p. 371 'Darling Mother . . .': KK to RK, 6 July 1944, cited in Smith, *Hostage to Fortune*, p. 597.

p. 372 'Here it is . . .': RK to KK, 30 June 1944, cited ibid., p. 595.

'pillar of strength . . .': *As We Remember Joe*, ed. J. F. Kennedy, University Press, Cambridge, Mass., privately printed, 1945.

'I'm so sorry . . .': cited in McTaggart, *Kathleen Kennedy*, p. 175.

CHAPTER THIRTY-TWO

p. 373 'I've got a telegram . . .': cited in Lynne McTaggart, *Kathleen Kennedy*, Weidenfeld & Nicolson, 1984, p. 185.

'Before we go . . .': ibid.

p. 374 'A great cloud . . .': cited in Laurence Leamer, *The Kennedy Women*, Ballantine Books, 1996, p. 379.

'Mostly going to Mass . . .': cited in McTaggart, *Kathleen Kennedy*, p. 186.

'That evening . . .': Leamer, *The Kennedy Women*, p. 379.

'The amazing thing . . .': Patsy White, cited in D. Collier and P. Horowitz, *The Kennedys*, Summit Books, 1984, p. 171.

'My Darling Kick . . .': the Duchess of Devonshire to KK, 13 September 1944, cited in Amanda Smith, *Hostage to Fortune: The Letters of Joseph P. Kennedy*, Viking Penguin, 2001, p. 600.

p. 375 'so unworthy . . .': Marquess of Hartington to KK, 4 September 1944, cited in Leamer, *The Kennedy Women*, p. 377.

'During the attack . . .': cited in KK, round-robin letter to family, 23 September 1944, cited in Smith, *Hostage to Fortune*, p. 602.

p. 376 'The English losses . . .': Frans Magelschots interviewed by Henriette Claessens-Heuten, cited in Nigel Hamilton, *JFK*, vol. 1, *Reckless Youth*, Random House, 1992, p. 862.

'Two bodies . . .': ibid.

'So ends the story . . .': KK, diary, 20 September 1944, cited in Smith, *Hostage to Fortune*, p. 601.

p. 377 'I just feel terribly . . .': KK, round-robin letter to family, 23 September 1944, cited ibid., p. 602.

'I have been thinking . . .': RK to KK, 25 September 1944, cited ibid.

p. 378 'I never met anyone . . .': cited in Collier and Horowitz, *The Kennedys*, p. 172.

'Well, I guess . . .': ibid., p. 171.

'I have been spending . . .': KK to her parents, 20 September 1944, cited in Smith, *Hostage to Fortune*, p. 601.

'If Eunice . . .': cited ibid.

CHAPTER THIRTY-THREE

p. 380 'In the critical . . .': Ralph Barker, *The Blockade Busters*, Chatto & Windus, 1976, p. 203.

p. 381 'It is all just too . . .': Maud, Countess Fitzwilliam, to Lucia, Viscountess Galway, 2 January and 16 May 1946, Galway Papers, Department of Manuscripts and Special Collections, University of Nottingham.

p. 382 'Daffodil bulbs . . .': Roger Dataller (pseud.), *Northern Review*, Spring 1946.

'He lectured them . . .': Roger Dataller (pseud.), *A Yorkshire Lad*, unpublished memoir.

p. 383 'Writing to Lucia . . .': Maud, Countess Fitzwilliam, to Lucia, Viscountess Galway, 2 January 1946, Galway Papers, Department of Manuscripts and Special Collections, University of Nottingham.

'It would be a sad day . . .': *Sheffield Daily Telegraph*, 19 February 1943.

'After the long storm . . .': Hugh Dalton, *The Fateful Years*, Frederick Muller, 1957, p. 483.

'In its manifesto . . .': David Coates, *The Labour Party and the Struggle for Socialism*, Cambridge University Press, 1975, p. 43.

p. 384 'Compensation was payable . . .': J. M. Robinson, *The Country House at War*, Bodley Head, 1989, p. 14.

p. 385 'Of all the major transfers . . .': Peter Hennessey, *Never Again*, Jonathan Cape, 1992, Vintage paperback edition, 1993, p. 103.

'I was hewing . . .': Charles Grey, 29 January 1946, House of Commons, Parliamentary Debates (Hansard), 5th Series, vol. 418, HMSO, 1946, pp. 749–52.

p. 386 'I was born . . .': Frank Fairhurst, ibid., pp. 739–44.

p. 387 'One would think . . .': Charles Grey, ibid., pp. 749–52.

'foolish, callous . . .': E. Shinwell, MP, *The Britain I Want*, Macdonald & Co., 1943, p. 10.

'In 1944 . . .': E. Shinwell, MP, *When the Men Come Home*, Victor Gollancz, 1944, p. 5.

p. 388 'Surely you are not . . .': ibid., p. 26.

'It was the most ghastly . . .': author's interview with Joy Powlett-Smith, August 2005.

p. 389 'Every time . . .': author's interview with Bert May, June 2004.

p. 390 'An undertaking . . .': Colonel Landon on behalf of Peter, Earl Fitzwilliam, to Minister of Fuel and Power, 11 September 1945, Archives, Council for the Protection of Rural England.

'The total quantity . . .': Cabinet document circulated prior to meeting on 24 June 1946, National Archives, Kew, PREM 8/728.

'Coal cannot . . .': Colonel Landon, on behalf of Peter, Earl Fitzwilliam, to CPRE, Memorandum of Objections, CPRE Archives.

p. 391 'The coal . . .': letter and memorandum from W. Batley, Department of Fuel Technology, Sheffield University, to CPRE, 14 May 1946, ibid.

'At the working place . . .': ibid.

'"Effective restoration" . . .': William Batley, Department of Fuel Technology, Sheffield University, to the Georgian Group, 30 May 1946, CPRE Archives.

'The verdict . . .': letter and memorandum from W. Batley, Department of Fuel Technology, Sheffield University, to CPRE, 14 May 1946, ibid.

p. 392 'It is sacrilege . . .': *Sheffield Daily Telegraph*, 8 April 1946.

'You could go . . .': author's interview with May Bailey, May 2004.

p. 393 'Speciously . . .': *South Yorkshire Times*, 13 April 1946.

'claims made . . .': report of E. Shinwell's comments at Lord President's Committee, 11 January 1946, National Archives, Kew, PREM 8/728.

'Whatever might be . . .': *South Yorkshire Times*, 13 April 1946.

p. 394 'My purpose . . .': J. A. Hall to Clement Attlee, 8 April 1946, National Archives, Kew, PREM 8/728.

'Prime Minister . . .': memorandum from Private Secretary to Prime Minister, 10 April 1946, ibid.

'Nobody can possibly . . .': Lord Rosse to Captain Noel-Baker, 19 May 1946, CPRE Archives.

p. 395 'It is a thoroughly unnecessary . . .': Secretary of CPRE to Mr Spragg at RIBA, 16 April 1946.

'The *Economist* . . .': quoted by Dataller, *Northern Review*, Spring 1946.

p. 396 'THE PRIME MINISTER . . .': minutes of Cabinet meeting on 15 April 1946, National Archives, Kew, PREM 8/728.

'THE MINISTER OF FUEL . . .': ibid.

p. 397 'Shinwell's reaction . . .': author's interview with Charles Booth, April 2006.

'There were some . . .': author's interview with Ralph Boreham, August 2005.

'The brutes . . .': Maud, Countess Fitzwilliam, to Lucia, Viscountess Galway, 22 April 1946, Galway Papers, Department of Manuscripts and Special Collections, University of Nottingham.

p. 398 'It is certainly . . .': James Lees-Milne, *Diaries 1946–1949, Caves of Ice and Midway on the Waves*, John Murray, 1996, p. 44.

'It would be a great . . .': Ministry of Town and Country Planning to National Trust, 9 July 1946, National Archives, Kew, HLG 79/614.

p. 399 'Cautioning . . .': ibid.

'The Ministry of Health . . .': minutes of meeting of National Trust's Historic Buildings Committee, 9 October 1946, National Trust Archives.

'Mabel was taboo . . .': author's interview with Joyce Smith, April 2004.

p. 400 'It was frightfully austere . . .': author's interview with Joy Powlett-Smith, August 2005.

'I was very close to her . . .': author's interview with Joyce Smith, April 2004.

p. 401 'The funny thing was . . .': ibid.

'It was a wonderful . . .': ibid.

p. 402 'Lady Fitzwilliam . . .': Lees-Milne, *Diaries 1946–1949*, p. 4.

'I think my mother . . .': letter to author from Lady Juliet Tadgell.

'There were a lot of talk . . .': author's interview with Ena Bergin, March 2004.

CHAPTER THIRTY-FOUR

p. 403 'A thunderstorm . . .': Final Report on Enquiry into the Accident, 27 October 1948, Bureau d'Enquêtes et d'Analyses (BEA), France.

'It was late afternoon . . .': Lynne McTaggart, *Kathleen Kennedy*, Weidenfeld & Nicolson, 1984, p. 235.

'At about 5.30 p.m. . . .': Final Report on Enquiry into the Accident, 27 October 1948.

'It took the two men . . .': ibid.

'They came across . . .': ibid.

p. 404 'It was immediately clear . . .': ibid.

'The pilot and co-pilot . . .': McTaggart, *Kathleen Kennedy*, p. 236.

'Some said . . .': ibid., pp. 244–5.

p. 405 'I've found my Rhett Butler . . .': cited in Doris Kearns Goodwin, *The Fitzgeralds and the Kennedys*, Simon & Schuster, 1987, p. 733.

CHAPTER THIRTY-FIVE

p. 406 'The ball at the Dorchester . . .': *Daily Express*, 13 June 1946.

'Kick was chairing . . .': *Queen* magazine, June 1946.

'It's absolutely maddening . . .': cited in Lynne McTaggart, *Kathleen Kennedy*, Weidenfeld & Nicolson, 1984, p. 204.

p. 407 'It was overnight . . .': cited in D. Collier and P. Horowitz, *The Kennedys*, Summit Books, 1985, p. 200.

'As she talked . . .': cited in Laurence Leamer, *The Kennedy Women*, Ballantine Books, 1996, p. 400.

'Games of . . .': author's interview with Peter Diggle, November 2005.

p. 408 'one girl . . .': *The Diaries of Evelyn Waugh*, Weidenfeld & Nicolson, 1976, p. 488.

'The smart set . . .': ibid.

'the indolence and ignorance . . .': ibid., p. 491.

'If you want to . . .': cited in McTaggart, *Kathleen Kennedy*, p. 245.

'Peter and Kick . . .': author's interview with Janie Compton, November 2005.

p. 409 'Six months younger . . .': Sally Bedell Smith, *Reflected Glory: The Life of Pamela Churchill Harriman*, Simon & Schuster, 1996, p. 142.

'Stories of the Aga Khan's wealth . . .': Christopher Ogden, *Life of the Party: The Biography of Pamela Digby Churchill Hayward Harriman*, Little Brown, 1994, paperback edition, pp. 196, 198.

'Diana Vreeland . . .': cited in Bedell Smith, *Reflected Glory*, p. 142.

'They called me . . .': Leonard Slater, *Aly: A Biography*, Random House, 1964, p. 50.

p. 410 '. . . resplendent as . . .': Michael Wishart, *High Diver*, Blond & Briggs, 1977, p. 105.

'I only think . . .': cited in Slater, *Aly: A Biography*, p. 4.

'I once left . . .': ibid., p. 123.

p. 411 'I never imagined . . .': author's interview with Janie Compton, November 2005.

'You don't know him . . .': cited in McTaggart, *Kathleen Kennedy*, p. 217.

'Peter had all the charm . . .': cited in Collier and Horowitz, *The Kennedys*, Summit Books, 1984, p. 201.

'the total sum . . .': Probate accounts, Peter, 8th Earl Fitzwilliam, Wentworth Estate Office.

'As Kick confided . . .': Doris Kearns Goodwin, *The Fitzgeralds and the Kennedys*, Simon & Schuster, 1987, p. 733.

'Peter was mad about . . .': author's interview with Lady Barbara Ricardo, November 2005.

'I remember . . .': author's interview with Ian Bond, April 2006.

p. 412 'My father was against . . .': author's interview with Peter Diggle, November 2005.

'My grandmother . . .': letter to the author from Lady Juliet Tadgell.

'It was how . . .': author's interview with Lady Barbara Ricardo, November 2005.

'I liked Peter . . .': cited in Leamer, *The Kennedy Women*, p. 402.

'I think there . . .': ibid.

'David and Sissy . . .': McTaggart, *Kathleen Kennedy*, p. 217.

'My reaction . . .': cited in Collier and Horowitz, *The Kennedys*, p. 203.

p. 414 'Some weeks before . . .': McTaggart, *Kathleen Kennedy*, pp. 222–3.

'I want to do . . .': cited ibid.

'Negroes dressed . . .': ibid., p. 224.

'We all knew . . .': cited in Leamer, *The Kennedy Women*, p. 407.

'But, as Jackie . . .': McTaggart, *Kathleen Kennedy*, p. 224.

p. 415 'She never wanted . . .': cited in Leamer, *The Kennedy Women*, p. 405.

'One thing . . .': KK to Lem Billings, 29 November 1944, cited in Doris Kearns Goodwin, *The Fitzgeralds and the Kennedys*, Simon & Schuster, 1987, p. 697.

p. 416 'As Kick told Patsy . . .': McTaggart, *Kathleen Kennedy*, p. 227.

'I just don't want to . . .': cited in Collier and Horowitz, *The Kennedys*, p. 204.

p. 417 'Before they fell asleep . . .': Leamer, *The Kennedy Women*, p. 406.

'She looked radiant . . .': cited in Collier and Horowitz, *The Kennedys*, p. 204.

'You are a . . .': cited in McTaggart, *Kathleen Kennedy*, p. 228.

'Repeatedly . . .': ibid.

p. 418 'When Kick came . . .': ibid., p. 229.

'The meeting . . .': author's interview with Janie Compton, November 2005.

'Jean Oliver . . .': author's interview with Jean Oliver, August 2005.

p. 419 'Peter said to him . . .': cited in McTaggart, *Kathleen Kennedy*, p. 230.

CHAPTER THIRTY-SIX

p. 420 'The ten-seater . . .': Final Report on Enquiry into the Accident, 27 October 1948, Bureau d'Enquêtes et d'Analyses (BEA) France.

'Waiting for her . . .': Lynne McTaggart, *Kathleen Kennedy*, Weidenfeld & Nicolson, 1984, p. 231.

'For the four-day . . .': Final Report on Enquiry into the Accident, 27 October 1948.

'Ilona Solymossy . . .': McTaggart, *Kathleen Kennedy*, p. 231.

'Peter had hired . . .': Probate accounts, Peter, 8th Earl Fitzwilliam, Wentworth Estate Office.

'Aged thirty-four . . .': Final Report on Enquiry into the Accident, 27 October 1948.

'The route . . .': ibid.

p. 421 'It was 12.45 . . .': ibid.

'As they headed . . .': McTaggart, *Kathleen Kennedy*, p. 232.

'Telling Townshend . . .': ibid.

'At 1.30 . . .': ibid.

'He was given a chart . . .': ibid.

'The pilot . . .': ibid.

p. 422 'At 14.20 . . .': ibid.

'Townshend was furious . . .': ibid., p. 233.

'Annoyed, Peter . . .': ibid.

'Why did Peter . . .': author's interview with Lady Barbara Ricardo, March 2006.

p. 423 'at twenty minutes . . .': Final Report on Enquiry into the Accident, 27 October 1948.

'From a report . . .': ibid. The report forms the basis of the account of the events leading to the air crash, pp. 423–5.

p. 424 'Even modern 747s . . .': author's interview with Captain John Gaudy, May 2006.

p. 425 'Both Townshend and Freeman . . .': McTaggart, *Kathleen Kennedy*, p. 235.

'All four passengers . . .': ibid, p. 238.

'the Mayor of St Bauzile . . .': ibid., p. 236.

'The police . . .': ibid.

p. 426 'Written by me . . .': n.d., Joseph P. Kennedy Papers/Kennedy Family Collection.

'It was Whitsuntide . . .': author's interview with Rowena Sykes, June 2004.

p. 427 'Unsurprisingly . . .': McTaggart, *Kathleen Kennedy*, p. 238.

'As well as . . .': ibid., p. 242.

'Ilona Solymossy . . .': ibid., p. 243.

p. 428 'Joe had . . .': *The Times*, 18 May 1948.

'Responding to . . .': McTaggart, *Kathleen Kennedy*, p. 241.

'Dearest Moucher . . .': JPK to the Duchess of Devonshire, cited in Amanda Smith, *Hostage of Fortune*, Viking/Penguin, 2001, p. 637.

p. 429 'that airplane crash . . .': cited in D. Collier and P. Horowitz, *The Kennedys*, Summit Books, 1984, p. 207.

'Days before . . .': McTaggart, *Kathleen Kennedy*, p. 245.

'Somerset Maugham . . .': author's interview with Lady Barbara Ricardo, November 2005.

'*Time to Remember* . . .': cited in McTaggart, *Kathleen Kennedy*, p. 247.

p. 430 'Independently . . .': ibid., p. 245.

'I can still see . . .': Alistair Forbes, 'Upper classmates', *Times Literary Supplement*, 26 March 1976.

CHAPTER THIRTY-SEVEN

p. 431 'He were a grand lad . . .': author's interview with May Bailey, February 2004.

p. 432 'At the top of the road . . .': *Advertiser*, 22 May 1948.

'I don't think . . .': author's interview with Lady Barbara Ricardo, March 2006.

p. 433 'No one wanted him . . .': author's interview with May Bailey, March 2004.

'Bottle by Bottle . . .': Eric's nickname derived from a popular children's book called *Eric Little by Little.*

'When Peter . . .': author's interview with Geoffrey Steer, August 2005.

EPILOGUE

p. 435 'We were . . .': author's interview with Barbara Lock, May 2004.

'We had to . . .': author's interview with Bridget Crawshaw, May 2004.

'They would . . .': author's interview with June Wightman, May 2004.

'He used to roam . . .': ibid.

p. 436 'He would . . .': author's interview with Godfrey Broadhead, October 2002.

'I never saw . . .': author's interview with Ena Bergin, May 2004.

p. 438 'I would like . . .': Tom Fitzwilliam to Toby Fitzwilliam, 10 June 1949, Sheffield Archives, Unlisted Material, Wentworth Woodhouse Muniments, Box 343.

'Riddled with . . .': Toby Fitzwilliam to Tom Fitzwilliam, 3 June 1949, ibid.

'So far as . . .': ibid.

p. 439 'My darling . . .': Evie Fitzwilliam to George Fitzwilliam, 5 June 1920, ibid.

'The prospect . . .': Toby Fitzwilliam to Evie Fitzwilliam, 26 January 1924, ibid.

'I want . . .': Evie Fitzwilliam to Toby Fitzwilliam, 26 January 1924, ibid.

p. 440 'I can . . .': Toby Fitzwilliam to George Fitzwilliam, 29 January 1924, ibid.

'I don't know . . .': George Fitzwilliam to Toby Fitzwilliam, 21 March 1925, ibid.

'I had been . . .': G. J. C. Wentworth-Fitzwilliam v W. T. G. Wentworth-Fitzwilliam et al., Royal Courts of Justice, February 1951, Day 6, Sheffield Archives, ibid., Box 345.

p. 441 'I went . . .': deposition of Mary Fullerton, ibid., Box 343.

p. 442 'My sister-in-law . . .': testimony of Alice Williams Wynn, Day 5, ibid., Box 345.

'When travelling . . .': deposition of George Fitzwilliam, 1930, ibid., Box 343.

p. 444 'simple, straight-forward . . .': ibid., 19 March, Day 20, ibid., Box 344.

'She was the most . . .': testimony of Alice Williams Wynn, Day 5, ibid., Box 345.

p. 445 'Can you . . .': ibid., Day 4, Box 345.

'We had two . . .': ibid.

p. 446 'She [Evie] . . .': ibid.

'When you left . . .': ibid.

p. 447 'Your Lordship . . .': ibid., Day 18, Box 344.

'I have . . .': 6th Earl Fitzwilliam to George Fitzwilliam, ibid., Box 343.

p. 448 'It is perfectly . . .': ibid., 19 March 1951, Day 20, Box 344.

'George and Evie . . .': ibid., Day 17.

p. 451 'Its closure . . .': Simon Jenkins, *England's Thousand Best Houses*, Penguin, 2003, p. 920.

'It should be . . .': author's interview with Geoffrey Steer, August 2005.

Index